UNDERSTANDING MISCARRIAGES
OF JUSTICE

Understanding Miscarriages of Justice

LAW, THE MEDIA, AND THE INEVITABILITY OF CRISIS

RICHARD NOBLES and DAVID SCHIFF

with a foreword by
Gunther Teubner

OXFORD
UNIVERSITY PRESS

OXFORD
UNIVERSITY PRESS

Great Clarendon Street, Oxford OX2 6DP

Oxford University Press is a department of the University of Oxford.
It furthers the University's objective of excellence in research, scholarship,
and education by publishing worldwide in

Oxford New York

Athens Auckland Bangkok Bogotá Buenos Aires Calcutta
Cape Town Chennai Dar es Salaam Delhi Florence Hong Kong Istanbul
Karachi Kuala Lumpur Madrid Melbourne Mexico City Mumbai
Nairobi Paris São Paulo Singapore Taipei Tokyo Toronto Warsaw
with associated companies in Berlin Ibadan

Oxford is a registered trade mark of Oxford University Press
in the UK and in certain other countries

Published in the United States
by Oxford University Press Inc., New York

British Library Cataloguing in Publication Data

Data available

Library of Congress Cataloging in Publication Data
Nobles, Richard.
Understanding miscarriages of justice: law, the media, and the inevitability of crisis/
Richard Nobles and David Schiff.
p. cm.
Includes bibliographical references and index.
1. Crimes and the press—Great Britain. 2. Mass media and criminal justice—Great
Britain. 3. Law reform—Great Britain. I. Schiff, David, senior lecturer in law. II. Title.
[KD7879.N63 2000]
345.41—dc21 99–087786
ISBN 0–19–829893–5

1 3 5 7 9 10 8 6 4 2

Typeset in Sabon by
Cambrian Typesetters, Frimley, Surrey
Printed in Great Britain
on acid-free paper by
Biddles Ltd., Guildford and King's Lynn

General Editor's Introduction

In this monograph Richard Nobles and David Schiff have woven together the results of a re-investigation of the history of responses to miscarriages of justice with an original re-conceptualization of the nature of the problems. They examine, for example, the implications of the law's expressed commitment to values such as truth and due process, and its effect on the perspectives of the Court of Appeal. They focus particularly on the impact of the media, in enquiring into selected individual cases and then bringing pressure to bear, and explore its effect on the development of the law and legal institutions. The result is to question the prospects for the liberal agenda for reform, and to offer a challenging analysis of one of the deepest and most intractable problems of criminal justice.

Andrew Ashworth

Foreword

A COLLISION OF DISCOURSES

This book changes our understanding of miscarriage of justice. The problem is no longer simply how to design rational reform of the judicial process but how to cope with an inevitable 'clash of cultures'. The clash is between the reality constructs of the law and those of the mass media. Traditionally, miscarriage of justice has been seen as a divergence between external reality and its reconstruction in the courtroom. Wrongful convictions occur when the criminal trial ends with a narrative that does not correspond to what really happened in the outside world. Whenever these divergences become intolerably frequent, judicial institutions must be reformed so as to reduce the amount of legal/judicial error. Nobles and Schiff contest the naive realism of such a view and identify instead colliding reality constructions as the central problem of miscarriage of justice. Due to their different institutional logic, mass media and the law inevitably construct out of the same chain of events divergent reality constructs. It is the informational authority of the mass media that makes miscarriage of justice into a typical and recurring problem for modern society. Without the mass media, miscarriage of justice would be a matter for the conflicting world perceptions of individuals and groups, which have no great potential to compete with the epistemic authority of the courts. *Roma locuta, causa finita.* With the mass media's vivid interest in crime and punishment and their relentless reconstruction of relevant facts, the courts' fact-finding monopoly is fundamentally contested. While this happens in all phases of a criminal process, the contest becomes particularly dramatic when after a criminal conviction the mass media continue their investigation and discover, according to their criteria of truth, a miscarriage of justice. But there is no set of common criteria that would allow for the design of rational procedures to end the contest. There is no forum, no procedure, and no set of criteria that would make possible a common search for truth.

Why should divergences between criminal law convictions and the results of investigative journalism be an inevitable clash of cultures? Nobles and Schiff identify law's commitment to two values, truth and fairness, as the main source of a systematic misunderstanding between law and media. While the media are comparatively free in choosing their sources of information and procedures of verification, criminal law is bound by principles of due process, which inevitably involves the reconstruction of facts in the courtroom. Rules concerning the burden of proof are the most prominent example that demonstrates why legal facts necessarily differ from facts of

life and from journalistic information. Nobles and Schiff analyse in detail
how particularly in the setting of the Court of Appeal a reversal of the
burden of proof takes place which limits the unconstrained reconsideration
of factual circumstances even more. And they show that law is faced with
a tragic choice situation that does not allow it to admit frankly that truth is
partially sacrificed in the name of fairness and both in the name of cost
calculation. Law needs to conceal that choice and does so by adopting the
rhetoric of an infinite search for truth and fairness. In addition, they
demonstrate how law's double commitment influences not only the perception of facts in criminal cases but also the perception of miscarriage of
justice itself. The mass media misread systematically legal decisions on
miscarriage of justice. While for lawyers wrongful conviction requires nothing more than a correction of a procedural flaw with agnosticism as to
innocence and guilt, the media interpret the same decision as proof of innocence.

However, it is not only law's idiosyncrasies that are responsible for the
conflict. The mass media's world perception is not innocent either; it works
under similar but different constraints. While this is often criticized as inter-
est-driven manipulation, a more sober assessment becomes possible if the
mass media are seen as a social system of their own with idiosyncratic reality constructions. The self-reproduction of the mass media is driven by the
binary code information/non-information and not by the true/false code of
the scientific community, not to speak of the legal/illegal code of the law.
Their selectivity in mapping the world is as drastic and reductive as that of
legal reality constructs. In the relation between truth, newsworthiness, and
cost, they face a similar tragic choice situation to that of the law. Most
important for the different perceptions of miscarriage of justice is their
divergence of recursivity, i.e. the constitution of a theme via recursive operations. At first sight, law and the media seem to have a 'criminal event' as
their common theme. At closer scrutiny this dissolves into the difference
between a 'journalistic story' and a 'legal case'. They differ not only in their
threshold of thematization and criteria of normative and factual relevance,
but particularly in their conditions of termination. Saturation of public
opinion versus *res judicata*—this is the core conflict of miscarriage of
justice. While the media are free to reopen their stories at any moment when
public interest reawakens, the law under the imperative of prohibition of
denial of justice is constrained to close a case definitively and to limit its
reconsideration to exceptional situations. And this is the point where the
media become parasitic on law's constraints. The conflict between *res judicata* and newly emerging facts is a guarantee of journalistic news. The
media exploit law's immobility as a public scandal.

What about chances for reform? Will changes in legal doctrine, procedure, or personnel be capable of reducing miscarriages of justice? Nobles and
Schiff are highly sceptical about 'liberal' reforms, which are designed to

soften the reluctant attitude of conservative lawyers to reopen cases and develop more adequate procedures and concepts for an accurate reassessment of legal facts. They doubt equally that lawyers will be able to 'educate' the public so that the mass media begin to share the legal understanding of miscarriage of justice. Due to the different institutional logics of law and media, Nobles and Schiff argue, fact finding in the courts cannot be adapted to investigative journalism and vice versa. Miscarriage of justice will continue to mean something fundamentally different to the media than it means to the law. And they predict that recent political attempts to prescribe new doctrinal concepts, new decision-making bodies, and new procedures that are intended to soften law's tough stance will have only minimal impact. Thus, despite all attempts to reduce miscarriages of justice, the issue will reappear again and again in the future as an irreconcilable conflict.

This scepticism is well-founded if one abandons a somewhat naive—'rationalist' as Nobles and Schiff call it—reform perspective and faces the inevitable clash of cultures, the epistemic war between lawyers and journalists. They predict that the mass media will discover again and again new instances of miscarriage of justice, in spite of any well-intended reform of the criminal law, and will produce again and again crises of the legal system. But, they argue that such crises are only a perception of the media, the legal system will not be put into a real crisis; its self-reproduction requires a strict insistence on the exceptional status of reopening closed cases. Does this not then presuppose a balance of power between the clashing cultures, a kind of Cold War that at best will end in more or less peaceful coexistence with recurrent outbursts of crises? Are there not some imbalances in the conflictual relations between the media and the law? Indeed, some arguments point to the direction of a victory, a partial victory at least. My personal view is that the media will make territorial gains and the law will have to give in. While it is true that both social systems produce idiosyncratic constructions of the outside world that have equal claim to adequacy, the mass media are in a somewhat better position when the constructs differ from each other.

The authority of the legal system is uncontested when it comes to the question of the validity of rules. The validity of legal facts, however, is only secondary, only instrumental for arriving at legal decisions. In contrast, the mass media are the central source of information in society. Of course, many social systems produce factual information, but it is the unique role of the mass media to produce the background knowledge for all other social systems including the law. And its very specialization in information gives the media an advantage over law, whose fact finding is constrained by too many side considerations, *res judicata* most prominently among them. This relative superiority becomes overwhelming in those frequent situations when law attempts to insist on the finality of its fact construction against a coalition of the mass media and the sciences. It is not only a matter of social acceptance and contemporary conventions that science counts as the ultimate arbiter on questions of factual knowledge but a matter of institutionalized division of labour. Although scientific facts are no less cognitive constructs than legal facts, both determined by a set of historically evolved procedures, when it comes to a collision of discourses, science will win on facts. And if the media claim miscarriage of justice and are able to present scientific evidence, the law is in an untenable position. A third argument for the relative superiority of the mass media has to do with the schemata of human action produced. The schemata of the media are closer to individual perception than the schemata of the law. The schema of *homo juridicus*, the rule-obeying reasonable person, that reduces personhood to a bundle of rights and obligations is less attractive, less plausible, and less credible than the schema of *homo media(lis)*, the more or less well-informed, boundedly rational, morally responsible, and emotionally active actor whom the mass media produce as their dominant social construct.

These arguments make it likely that the law in the end will have to give in on the question of *res judicata*. Of course, it cannot give up the finality of its decisions. The autopoiesis of law would be threatened if it followed science and the media on the path to unlimited re-examination of old cases. But maintenance of autopoiesis should not be confused with maintenance of structures. If the conditions for reopening cases and their procedures are clearly circumscribed, the principle of *res judicata* can be drastically restricted without threatening the self-reproduction of law. Indeed, changes in personnel, doctrine, and procedure seem necessary. More 'liberal' personnel would recognize plural reality constructions and the need for the law to accept competing constructs as of equal value, and to experiment with a combination of peaceful coexistence and accommodation where necessary. Legal doctrine would need a new concept of *res judicata* that would allow for more frequent revisions of past decisions but at the same time develop clear criteria for the precarious relation between revision and finality. And more flexibility in procedures would be needed, with an element of lay participation to bring legal perceptions of reality closer to common-sense perceptions.

As Nobles and Schiff demonstrate convincingly, the problem is more than the need for finality within the legal process. There is more scope for the law's adaptation to the time horizon of the mass media and the sciences than lawyers are willing to admit. And a higher tolerance of a frequent reconsideration of legally determined facts is not the end of the rule of law. However, beware of structural corruption! Corruption is not only a matter of the politicization of law or its commercialization. Law in its adaptation to the media should not lose its commitment to—as Nobles and Schiff call it—fairness, individual rights, and due process. This commitment frequently requires a legal reconstruction of facts different from scientific and journalistic accounts. While law could be liberal in its adaptation to the time horizon of the media, here is the point where law should resist giving in to the specific selectivity of the mass media. Any reform should keep in mind the need to design new institutions in such a way that they do not follow the mass media's logic of selecting only high profile cases for reconsideration. Treating equal cases equally—the core normative principle of law—would require that the new review agencies actively inquire into cases of possible miscarriage where the convicted are not supported by networks of friends, politicians, and the mass media.

Gunther Teubner
Frankfurt

Preface

This book grew out of our various writings on the subject of miscarriages of justice: commentary in newspapers, articles in journals, and a report submitted to the Royal Commission on Criminal Justice. It explores a paradox. In a society in which justice is uncertain and contested, and in which the processes of criminal justice are subjected to sustained criticism for their failure to achieve claimed standards of justice, how can we talk meaningfully about miscarriages of justice? There is a lot of *noise* about miscarriages. We attempt to understand what this noise is all about. The structure of the book, and the theory that informs it, is set out in Chapter 1.

Over the years a number of our former students have acted as our research assistants: Mark Pallis, Stephen Requena, Nicola Shaldon, Gretchen Tanguay, and Annecoos Wiersema. We thank them here, particularly Nicola, whose research into the history of the Court of Appeal first identified the patterns that inform much of our work. We are grateful to our LSE colleagues for reading and commenting on draft chapters of the book: Nicola Lacey, Kate Malleson, Jill Peay, and Robert Reiner. We have appreciated the support given to us by Andrew Ashworth, the general editor of this series, both in his encouragement to complete the task, and in his detailed comments on its content. We are grateful for help provided by OUP, particularly our commissioning editor, John Louth, assistant editor, Michael Belson, and copy-editor, Nigel Hope. We are especially indebted to Gunther Teubner for reading the book in a number of its earlier versions, and agreeing to write a foreword to it. Alongside these named individuals, we must also thank the anonymous persons at the Economic and Social Research Council who approved our application for the award that funded the research into the reassessment of scientific evidence on appeal, set out in Chapter 5.

We thank the publishers of our previous writings on miscarriages, for allowing us to draw on and revise our earlier works: Academic Press, Blackwell Publishers, and Edward Elgar Publishing. The full citation to these works is given in the footnote to this preface.[1]

This book reflects the world, as we knew it on 23 July 1999.

R.N. and D.S.
LSE, London

[1] 'The Inevitability of Crisis in Criminal Appeals', *International Journal of the Sociology of Law*, 21 (1993), 1–21; 'Optimism Writ Large: A Critique of the Runciman Commission on Criminal Justice', in M. McConville and L. Bridges (eds.), *Criminal Justice in Crisis* (Aldershot: Edward Elgar, 1994), ch. 4; 'Miscarriages of Justice: A Systems Approach', *Modern Law Review*, 58 (1995), 299–320; 'Criminal Appeal Act 1995: The Semantics of Jurisdiction', *Modern Law Review*, 59 (1996), 573–81; 'The Never Ending Story: Disguising Tragic Choices in Criminal Justice', *Modern Law Review*, 60 (1997), 293–304.

Contents

1

Introduction

A. RETHINKING MISCARRIAGES OF JUSTICE AND CRIMINAL APPEALS

This book has arisen out of our research into the history of miscarriages of justice and of attempts to adopt effective measures to remedy these from early in the nineteenth century to the present. In this history we were struck by the pattern of repeated crisis and reform, and by the part played in such crises by the media. Underlying most reforms of criminal justice and the writings and arguments supporting them are what we identify as the rationalist tradition. This tradition views the history of criminal justice as evolving through a process of enlightened reform, moving criminal justice ever closer, however slowly, to justice without miscarriage. A different perception and assumption inform our approach: that the processes and conditions, which generate undisputed miscarriages of justice and grave concerns about them, cannot be defused by rational reforms. The same processes which lead to miscarriages of justice, and reforms, also set the conditions for further crisis and reform; *plus ça change, plus c'est la meme chose.*[1] Our question is: why should this be so?

Two strands of theory have informed our research, autopoietic systems theory and Calabresi and Bobbitt's classic work *Tragic Choices*. The contribution of autopoietic systems theory to our analysis of criminal justice lies in its focus on the impossibility of making the same communications in different systems, and the lessons which this has for legal reforms based on what, in outward form only, is a common communication in the media, politics, and law: miscarriage of justice. There may be a minimum similarity or congruence in the meaning of miscarriage of justice which allows high profile criminal cases to be utilized within disparate discourses; but there is no one conception of miscarriage of justice that consistently operates between the discourses of these different groups.[2] And, even within the distinct groups, within their systems of communication, it is often difficult to formulate one coherent conception of miscarriage of justice. We believe

---

[1] 'The more things change, the more they stay the same'. This statement is originally attributed to Alphonse Kerr, the nineteenth-century novelist and journalist.

[2] Nor is there a metalanguage of miscarriage of justice 'out there' to which all the various meanings approximate.

that the different conceptions of miscarriage of justice and the relationships between them are worth examining in their own right. To us, they indicate important relationships both within the legal system, and between the legal system and its environment.

To enable us to study the phenomena of discourse on miscarriage of justice, we have relied on autopoietic systems theory; in particular the theory of autopoiesis as developed by Luhmann and Teubner.[3] We have found their approach useful as a 'heuristic device',[4] as 'explaining structural patterns',[5] which has allowed us to locate the problematic of miscarriage of justice for the legal system, and in particular, the difficulties faced by the legal system if its discourse on criminal justice is expected to function as something separate from, and different from, other systems such as politics, or the media. This book is not an attempt to show that autopoietic systems theory is *the* way to understand social life, but in our research we observed mistranslation, and autopoietic systems theory assisted us better than alternatives (hegemony or interest theories) to talk about this. Also, our observations using autopoietic systems theory are compatible with and not contradicted by other analyses of the media.[6] We have come to believe that autopoietic systems theory can inform the praxis of those who engage in criticizing the legal system. We are not here seeking to develop the theory as such, but rather to use what insights it can offer to attempts at reforming criminal justice.[7]

In what follows, we have applied autopoietic systems theory as strictly as it was useful, and possible, so to do. We have also attempted to apply insights from autopoietic theory to matters which are not of central concern to the theory itself. In particular, we discuss factors that affect the authority of law, rather than the autopoietic focus on system maintenance. Autopoietic theory would regard the system of law as continuing for as long as legal communications, using the code legal/illegal, continue. Such a minimal concept of system maintenance is not an important issue to those seeking to reform criminal justice. The ability of the legal system to maintain its authority against other systems involves such non-autopoietic questions as finality and workability. The matters that we identify as creating problems

---

[3] For introductions, see M. King, 'The Truth about Autopoiesis', *Journal of Law and Society*, 20/2 (1993), 218–36; M. King and A. Schutz, 'The Ambitious Modesty of Niklas Luhmann', *Journal of Law and Society*, 21/3 (1994), 261–87. At the end of this article the authors include 'A Selection of Luhmann's Works in English'. For a more critical introduction, see W. T. Murphy, 'Systems of Systems: Some Issues in the Relationship between Law and Autopoiesis', *Law and Critique*, 5/2 [1994], 241–64. For a critique, see A. Beck, 'Is Law an Autopoietic System?', *Oxford Journal of Legal Studies*, 14 (1994), 401–18.

[4] G. Teubner, 'Introduction to Autopoietic Law', in id. (ed.), *Autopoietic Law: A New Approach to Law and Society* (Berlin, 1988), 2. See also G. Teubner, 'How the Law Thinks: Towards a Constructivist Epistemology of Law', *Law and Society Review*, 23 (1989), 727–57.

[5] G. Teubner, *Law as an Autopoietic System* (Oxford, 1993), 49. See also N. Luhmann, 'Closure and Openness: On Reality in the World of Law', in Teubner (ed.), n. 4 above, 335–48, esp. 337–41.   [6] See Ch. 4.   [7] See Ch. 6.

of finality and workability (rules of evidence and procedure) are relegated by autopoietic theory to the status of conditioning programmes for the application of law's binary code: legal/illegal.[8] By using the approach of autopoietic systems theory we have been led to examine how miscarriage of justice is constructed within different systems and the difficulties that the legal system faces in sustaining its construction in the face of alternative constructions within other systems. The general problem of retaining a *legal* construction of miscarriage of justice is, we argue, crucial to Law's authority. We focus in particular on the devices used by the Court of Appeal (Criminal Division) to maintain the legal system's integrity.[9] We also examine how miscarriage of justice is constructed within the media, and how this may build into episodic perceptions that criminal justice is in crisis.[10] And we attempt to construct an account of what happens when the legal system tries to utilize or is challenged by another system's discourse or method.[11]

According to Calabresi and Bobbitt in *Tragic Choices*: 'it is the values accepted by a society as fundamental that mark some choices as tragic.'[12] They consider how society allocates the right to life through the different mechanisms used to allocate high risks of death: markets, professional judgements, and lottery. Each method fails to respect the value afforded to life, but the failures of each method are different: the market values it in money terms; professionals reveal their social prejudices; lotteries are fair but arbitrary. There can be no stability in the choice of methods. To preserve the fundamental value of life one must disguise its inevitable sacrifice by repeatedly changing the method of allocating death.[13] The authors claim that setting up an institution for the distribution of life-giving resources represents an implicit acceptance that the value of life is not priceless. Where the value is fundamental, this institution is not stable. Reforms will repeatedly occur, designed to obscure that implicit acceptance, so as to continue to present life as priceless. Coleman and Holohan criticize the celebration of fundamental values in a world of scarce resources as 'mere sentiment', which is unhelpful to public policy.[14] An alternative interpretation of the dilemma created by scarce resources and fundamental values, and one which underlies Calabresi and Bobbitt's book and our use of it, is that practices generally considered unhelpful to rational public policy (dishonesty,

---

[8] See the following writings by N. Luhmann: 'Law as a Social System', *Northwestern University Law Review*, 83 (1989), 136–50; 'The Coding of the Legal System', in G. Teubner and A. Febbrajo (eds.), *State, Law, and Economy as Autopoietic Systems: Regulation and Autonomy in a New Perspective* (Milan, 1992), 145–85; 'The Unity of the Legal System', in Teubner (ed.), n. 4 above, 12–35.   [9] See Ch. 3.   [10] See Ch. 4.

[11] See Ch. 5.

[12] G. Calabresi and P. Bobbitt, *Tragic Choices* (New York, 1978), 17.

[13] There are many problems with this analysis, not least of which are the authors' failure to identify how particular values come to be considered fundamental. Does this status depend on consensus, is it hegemonic, etc.? And thus, how are society and social values constructed? See M. Elliott, 'The Frontiersmen', *Modern Law Review*, 44 (1981), 345–52.

[14] See their review of *Tragic Choices* in *California Law Review*, 67 (1979), 1379–93.

inconsistency, hypocrisy, and ignorance) may be needed if values are to retain their rhetorical status as fundamental.

A parallel with criminal justice can be suggested; it is that the values of truth (a correct verdict) and fairness (due process and rights), with justice as an implied amalgam of the two, are priceless.[15] They cannot be reduced to a market equation. Nor can they be reduced to each other—allocating punishment through a lottery might be fair, but it would not be accepted as true, or just. The resources available for any society's criminal justice processes are limited. Societies have other things to do with them. So, within criminal trials truth is traded off against fairness, and both against considerations of cost. This trade-off is constantly disguised so that, for example, traditional mechanisms can be presented as if, by being fair, they are also contributing to the pursuit of truth. Economies can be argued to have only marginal effects on the fairness or accuracy of trials in general. But, one cannot deny the possibility, in an individual case, that truth will be achieved in an unfair manner, or sacrificed to fairness, or that both will be sacrificed to cost. A necessary consequence of an inevitably flawed system is presented as an undesired outcome. Calabresi and Bobbitt describe such possibilities as being: 'necessary, [and] unavoidable, rather than chosen . . . to convert what is tragically chosen into what is merely a fatal misfortune'.[16] The mechanisms of allocation Calabresi and Bobbitt discuss, or more importantly, the constant changes in those mechanisms, represent both a means of responding to what is perceived as unintended, and a way of disguising what is really a deliberate tragic choice.

The history of criminal appeals can be re-examined as a response to problems of tragic choice: the conflict and allocation of fundamental values within criminal justice. A process of appeal allows inevitable outcomes (miscarriages of justice) to be seen as mistakes, and rectified. But the difficulty facing those who must treat the inevitable as mistakes is how to respond without undoing the deliberate choices represented by the method of trial.[17] A trial process can be viewed as a first-order determination which trades off, at a centralized level, the fundamental values of truth and fairness against each other, and sacrifices both for reasons of cost. The Court of Appeal operates as a second-order mechanism for disguising the trade-off that has occurred at the first-order. When the Court of Appeal functions

---

[15] See Ch. 2.

[16] See n. 12 above, 21. For further exposition, see the review of *Tragic Choices* by G. Tullock, 'Avoiding Difficult Decisions', *New York University Law Review*, 54 (1979), 267–79.

[17] Much of Calabresi and Bobbitt's analysis revolves around the relationship between first-order determinations about how much of a scarce good will be produced or valued within 'the limits set by natural scarcity', namely the creation of systems and values to which society is committed, and second-order determinations which allocate and distribute those goods and values. It is in the relationship between first-order and second-order determinations, made separately, that the sacrifice of goods and values is disguised, obscuring 'the fact of tragic scarcity and—while the illusion exists—evading the tragic choice' (see n. 12 above, 19–20).

well, the trade-off made at the first-order is relatively stable. When the Court of Appeal functions less effectively, the trade-off made at the first-order is the subject of public awareness, and criticism (resulting in what is often referred to as a crisis of confidence in the criminal justice system). All we are doing through utilizing *Tragic Choices* analysis is recognizing the Court of Appeal's need to avoid the obvious sacrifice of the fundamental values of truth and fairness. *Tragic Choices* analysis draws attention to the fact that devices which can be described as mechanisms for achieving a system's values, can also be described as mechanisms to disguise and displace the inevitable sacrifice of those values.

B. A NOTE ON OUR USE OF THEORY

Those who are familiar with autopoietic systems theory and *Tragic Choices* may be surprised at the claim that this book is informed by both. *Tragic Choices* deals with the methods by which societies avoid publicly trading off values that they regard as fundamental. The idea of a society generating a consensus on fundamental values is, at first sight, alien to a systems theory that locates values within different systems of communication, and denies the existence of identical values within all systems. But autopoietic systems theory does not deny the presence of consensus; it simply gives a more complicated explanation of what constitutes a consensus.[18] When journalists seek to translate their understanding of legal processes into news, and lawyers attempt to turn journalists' stories into evidence or arguments for reform, we have a situation which is both consensus, and a multiplicity of understandings and misunderstandings.

Our use of autopoietic systems theory is not motivated by an acceptance that law must be seen as a system of communication, closed to any direct experience of its environment, which it can only be aware of as 'noise'.[19] We understand the concerns of those who argue that the theory has the potential to obscure or neglect the openness of law to politics, media and general social communication. We also accept that the focus on law as circulating self-referential communications fails to address the different interpretations placed upon such communications by the persons (judges, lawyers, and academics) who inhabit the law. However, the theory is peculiarly apposite to our study. First, our study of miscarriages of justice focuses on their existence as communications. Our concern is to use a theory that informs our understanding of legal and non-legal communications, not to claim that all law is simply communications, or even that it is

[18] The use of autopoietic systems theory answers some of the sociological criticisms of *Tragic Choices* analysis, see p. 3 above.
[19] See P. Kennealy, 'Talking About Autopoiesis—Order from Noise?', in Teubner (ed.), n. 4 above, 349–68.

always best understood when considered as communications. Secondly, our use of the theory does not depend upon our ability to show that law is completely closed to any direct experience of its environment. It is sufficient for our purposes that it is those aspects of law which tend towards closure (self-reference, self-description and self-organization) that constitute the difference between the understandings of miscarriage of justice that are shared by lawyers, and those which dominate in the media. And even in this limited use of the theory, we do not claim that systematic reflexivity of communication in different systems is the whole story of why miscarriages of justice are understood differently in different areas of social life. Instead of crudely asserting that *the law* is this, or thinks that, we have used history, philosophy and non-systems theory sociology to analyse the meaning and operation of appeals and miscarriages of justice, and to some extent convictions, in our society. But we have found that the operation of law, viewed as a system which communicates the *facts* of its own operations to itself and other systems of communication, does exhibit the features and problems identified by autopoietic systems theory. In this area of social life, we feel that the theory passes the test put forward by one of its strongest proponents: 'whether the theory provides a convincing way of understanding some of the complexities of modern societies and the relationships of people to those societies.'[20]

According to Luhmann, a defining feature of an autopoietic system is that it should contain and constitute a 'representation of society within society'.[21] King, in a particularly clear restatement of the theory,[22] asserts that different social systems are distinguished from each other by the meanings each gives to relationships and events in the social world. And those differences are not simply the outcome of different interests, classes or ideologies. Because systems use different coding and different procedures for validating reality, they systematically produce different meanings and understandings of social events. Thus science,[23] law, and media[24] will produce different communications about the same events. And their different meanings cannot be transmitted directly. This leads to situations in which the differences of meaning given to an event by the actors within a system may be less important than the differences attributed to that event by the actors in different systems. There are occasions when studying the differences between the communications of systems may be more informative than studying the differences within a system.

Those who are prepared to accept that law is an autopoietic system, which constructs its world legally in terms of its own procedures, conditioning programmes, and, ultimately, the binary code legal/illegal, may still

---

[20] King, 'The Truth about Autopoiesis', n. 3 above, 222.
[21] N. Luhmann, 'The Representation of Society within Society', *Current Sociology*, 35/2 (1987), 101–8.   [22] 'The Truth about Autopoiesis', n. 3 above.
[23] See Ch. 5.   [24] See Ch. 4.

balk at treating the media as a similar system. What is the binary code of the media: news/not news, interesting/uninteresting, newsworthy/mundane? And can the enormous variety of material communicated in print (let alone by television, radio, computer, film, and video) be usefully described and analysed as a single system? There are a number of replies to such an objection. First, it is not our aim to prove that the media, or any section of it, constitutes a fully autopoietic system with clearly defined boundaries. To talk of the media usefully as a system, one does not have to accept that it achieves the degree of systematic closure that justifies the label autopoietic. We prefer to accept that the extent to which a system is closed and therefore has boundaries is a matter of degree. The procedures by which the media produces its communications about reality (editors, authorities, bulletins, articles, etc.) make its communications systematically different from the rest of what can be claimed to be general social communication. It also exhibits a considerable degree of self-reference: events are not news until the media recognize them as such. Articles refer to *the public* as if it were a fact that could be experienced, and known. There may be readers who cannot accept that the media is even partially closed to other systems, and thus can be differentiated from general social communication, and those who reject the concept of a partially closed system. Even to those readers our analysis of the relationship between the media (essentially the broadsheets) and the legal system in Chapter 4 should be informative, even if the media is taken as an example of undifferentiated social communication.

Another system boundary that may trouble those who study criminal justice is the question of whether criminal justice is a system, or merely an area where different systems (for example science, economy, media, and law) make their respective communications. Is the legal system simply one of the systems of communication in this area? And if so, what is the role of persons who appear to belong to more than one system: legally trained journalists; lawyers who specialize in public relations; policemen who know the law? Our tentative answer is to suggest that there are insights to be gained from treating criminal justice as the site of various systems of communication. While there are many who prefer to define criminal justice in terms of institutional structures, and to analyse the behaviour and discourse of its actors in terms of their various interests and perspectives, we feel that it is valuable to understand these actors as participants in different systems of communication. Much of conventional writing on criminal justice supports the idea that it is not a single system, but a site of different systems. For example, policemen are said to *bend the law*. While one can usefully investigate the institutional reasons why they should do this, one can also investigate the implications and complications that arise from policemen having to communicate within different systems of communication. As we might well recognize in our everyday experience of social life, some interactions are not explained by conflicting interests, but by the fact that the actors are *not speaking the same language*. Translating between different languages is never direct. Words within each language exist only in their relationship to other words in that language. On this basis, and within this area, a translator is not someone who simply explains one part of criminal justice to another. Rather, like the person who speaks two languages, she is able to reconstruct the communications of one system into the communications of the other. And as all translators will tell you, some things are easier to translate than other things, and for some aspects of a language there is simply no translation. There are also examples of persons who think they are speaking the same language, when using the same words, who do not find out that they are not communicating until difficulties of co-ordination arise that can be usefully, in autopoietic terms, be called *perturbations*. From this perspective, identifying the different systems of communication operating within criminal justice, and identifying areas where there is what, in non-autopoietic terms, is called miscommunication is useful. One does not have to identify all the conditions of existence of such miscommunication (interests, etc.) in order to identify some of the patterns and consequences. Autopoiesis is never the whole story.

To be consistent in our approach to criminal justice we have wherever possible avoided speaking of the criminal justice *system*, and in keeping with our description of it as a site, referred to criminal justice, criminal justice process, criminal justice practices, criminal justice procedures, etc. However, in Chapter 4 we use the phrase 'criminal justice system' regularly. This is necessary because the chapter describes newspaper reporting on miscarriages, and the phrase 'criminal justice system' is very common in such reporting, as are the phrases trial system, adversary system, appeal system, judicial system, etc. We never mean to imply that, in autopoietic terms, there is such a system, or that such a phrase should be used without considerable care.

C. A CAVEAT ON FINALITY

Much of the material dealt with in this book overlaps with a more traditional analysis of the criminal justice process in terms of the issue of finality. There is widespread recognition of the rather obvious fact that resources are limited and that the pursuit of values such as truth and rights has to stop somewhere. One cannot hear all criminal cases again and again and again. The scarcity of resources affects every stage in the criminal justice process from the reporting and investigation of crime to the hearing of appeals. However, the issue of finality is peculiar to discussions of trial and appeal. The traditional literature acknowledges that while any trial verdict could be unfair or incorrect, one cannot deal with this possibility by an endless increase in the resources given to every trial, or having unlimited retrials. A line has to be drawn somewhere.

Whilst we do not disagree with this analysis, we feel that there is much more that can usefully be explored. A discussion of finality in these terms assumes that values such as rights and truth are rationally balanced against considerations of cost in some kind of zero sum game. Truth and rights stop at a border established by cost. This analysis, although true on one level, ignores the manner in which truth and rights, at a rhetorical level, continue to occupy territory that has already been sacrificed to cost. Truth and rights do not have a clear border with issues of cost. They are used rhetorically in a manner that far outstrips existing practices. Thus, at a rhetorical level, rather than having a clear boundary with issues of cost, they disguise that boundary.

Another difference between our analysis, and the traditional, rational discussion of finality, is that we take the existence of finality, and the problems that this causes for the legal system, and the other systems within criminal justice, extremely seriously. It is the focus of our book. Finality is not simply necessary because resources are scarce. Without finality there can be no stability in the relationship between the legal system and the other systems within criminal justice. Finality is necessary for the processes and procedures of criminal justice to have boundaries, to have a stable existence. A trial verdict is a moment at which all the inadequacies and imperfections of the pre-trial and trial processes are legitimized. Despite these inadequacies and imperfections, the defendant has been found guilty or not guilty. Unless trial verdicts can routinely produce final verdicts, the trial has no boundaries. There can be no stable process of trial. In turn there can be no official (legal) boundaries to pre-trial procedures. Thus, the issue of finality is not captured by the observation that trial has to stop somewhere. Rather, trial verdicts are inextricably linked to the ability of criminal justice to justify its own boundaries, and produce routine outcomes. The issue of finality is bound up with the ability of the legal system to lend its authority to the routine practices that constitute criminal justice. To the extent that criminal justice relies on legal authority, it can have no stable existence, without finality.

The creation of the Court of Criminal Appeal at the beginning of the twentieth century was a reaction to the perception that there was a developing problem with providing finality at the trial court level. Setting up a Court of Criminal Appeal displaces that potential problem from the trial court to the appellate court. But the issue has not changed. Unless the appellate court routinely endorses the products of the trial court (upholding convictions and deterring appeals) the routine procedures of criminal justice, as legitimized in *normal* trial verdicts, cannot be maintained. The need for the Court of Appeal to maintain the finality of convictions is also its responsibility for upholding the authority of the legal system. A statement that there must be finality, while true, fails to address the complexity and dynamics of this responsibility.

D. THE STRUCTURE OF THE BOOK

The thesis that we have set out in this Introduction has informed the chapters of this book. In Chapter 2, entitled 'Problematizing Miscarriage of Justice', we consider the apparent paradox that miscarriages of justice raise widespread concerns despite the difficulties of formulating, let alone achieving, a state of affairs that would be universally accepted to constitute justice. Our analysis develops the *Tragic Choices* thesis. Despite evidence that miscarriage of justice (in the sense of untrue verdicts of guilt) must be a normal and expected consequence of imperfect arrangements for investigations, prosecutions and trials, they are nevertheless understood as exceptional and unacceptable (cannot be knowingly tolerated) events. And despite the difficulties of presenting a consistent account of the rights and due processes represented by criminal justice, and the further difficulties of believing that the everyday practices of criminal justice (law in action) fully express any such account, fairness as a value is celebrated by its practitioners. As with truth, criminal justice simultaneously fails to achieve fairness, celebrates fairness, and uses fairness to construct miscarriages of justice as occasional and exceptional events.

In Chapter 3 we put this analysis into a historical setting. If miscarriage of justice is a tragic choice situation, we might expect to find that the changes in institutional arrangements that occur in response to recognized miscarriages of justice do not represent solutions in a rational sense. Rather, these changes are an armoury of techniques to disguise the unavoidability of miscarriages of justice. We provide evidence that the inescapability of miscarriages was acknowledged by legal practitioners, most notably the judiciary, from early in the nineteenth century. And changes in institutional arrangements that were debated and discarded for their inability to remedy miscarriage earlier this century are later adopted as solutions, and fail to be such for many of the reasons given for their earlier rejection. This chapter also provides evidence of the vital role played by the press in the history of institutional arrangements for remedying miscarriages of justice. It was the press that created pressure for the creation of a Criminal Court of Appeal that, despite the judiciary's awareness of the impossibility of such a Court satisfying press demands, proved irresistible. The chapter also demonstrates the crucial importance to the judiciary of its relationship of deference to the jury. This is the principal device adopted by the judiciary to justify its extreme reluctance to entertain appeals based solely on questions of fact, i.e. appeals against the truth of a jury's verdict. Our history demonstrates the difficulties facing those who seek to overcome this reluctance, as neither institutional reforms, nor changes in the legislative mandate of the Court, serve to achieve this.

In Chapter 4 we undertake a study of media reporting during the recent crisis of confidence in criminal justice associated with the high profile miscarriage cases that came to the Court of Appeal in the late 1980s and early 1990s. This study seeks to develop two aspects of the thesis. First, having argued that the media have a dominant understanding of miscarriage that prioritizes truth over due process, we provide a synopsis of media reports from the ten-year period 1987–96 to demonstrate this. Secondly, the synopsis provides a case study of the nature of the periodic crises of confidence that develop in the press in response to miscarriages of justice. During this period the media provide the site for the sense of tragic choice (the sacrifice of fundamental values) by taking justice seriously, in order to write of its failure. We use the selected materials, and writings taken from media studies, to illustrate how the media construct certain cases as threats to public confidence in criminal justice. These crises represent a very different relationship between the media and the legal system from the routine reporting of convictions as news. In this routine relationship convictions and acquittals are misread as statements of the truth of a person's guilt or innocence. High profile miscarriages of justice present a threat to this routine misreading of convictions, leading to widespread media reporting around a theme of crisis of confidence. We seek to demonstrate the self-referential basis for the media's construction of this theme, and the difficulties that the media face in sustaining it.

In Chapter 5 we examine changes in the current processes and institutions of criminal justice that are expected to restore public confidence in the safety of convictions: the increased use of scientific evidence, and the new Criminal Cases Review Commission. In the case of scientific evidence, we seek to show how its increased use at trial may actually exacerbate the difficulties faced by the Court of Appeal in seeking to demonstrate that miscarriages of justice are exceptional and unintended, rather than widespread and routine. In particular, the Court's deference to the verdict of the jury (the principal device used by the Court to justify its reluctance to embrace an open-ended system of reinvestigation and rehearing) comes under particular strain in appeals involving a reassessment of scientific evidence on appeal. The chapter opens with a short history of the Court of Appeal's treatment of these kind of appeals, showing that the same deference to the jury is used as with other cases of new or reassessed evidence. We then explore the special difficulties faced by the Court in presenting its deference to the jury as rational. In the last section on scientific evidence we use two of the recent high profile cases (Birmingham Six and Maguire Seven) as case studies, in order to demonstrate the manner in which the Court approaches science in an appeal. These case studies reveal a methodology that opens the Court to widespread criticism in the press and the scientific community. The second part of this chapter, dealing with the universally welcomed Criminal Cases Review Commission, builds upon some of the materials introduced in Chapter 3. The history of the Court of Appeal is in part a history of the relationship between the practices of the Court and the Home Office. This new body was introduced in order to overcome the constitutional problem of asking an executive body to respond to claims that a judicial body had failed in its duty to provide justice. While we accept that there are constitutional difficulties in asking the Home Office to investigate miscarriages of justice, our analysis of the Court's reluctance to entertain appeals leads us to doubt that the new body will be able to sustain a reputation for efficient rectification of miscarriages.

In Chapter 6 we provide an overall statement of a thesis that, we believe, is justified by the material presented in the previous chapters. This takes the form of a debate with what we have identified as the *rationalist* tradition. This tradition understands criminal justice as an expression of basic values. Reform proposals are claims for criminal justice more closely and consistently to approximate to these values. The evolution of criminal justice is seen as a process guided by rational argument. It is a response to calls for more accurate verdicts and fairer procedures. Our position, informed by *Tragic Choices* analysis and autopoietic systems theory, is quite different. Both at trial, and in appeals, the rhetoric of justice refers to ideas of truth and fairness that exceed what the legal system can really hope to deliver. This, especially in the media, creates problems for Law's authority. The inability of Law to live up to the rhetoric of justice represents Law's tragic choice. The role of the Court of Appeal, and the history of its reform, can be understood as a response to the unavoidability of that tragic choice. Law gains legitimacy, and authority, from its claim to provide verdicts that embody the values of fairness and truth. The Court of Appeal has a crucial responsibility for upholding the legal system's authority, and preserving the stability of its practices and procedures. As such, it can neither insist that current procedures represent a complete commitment to Law's rhetorical values, nor publicly abandon those values to the extent that they are not represented in its routine practices.

While *Tragic Choices* analysis points to the difficulties of understanding criminal justice as the progressive achievement of rational reform, our analysis of the media points to the particular difficulties of achieving reforms that increase suspects' rights. The dominant media understanding of miscarriage is in terms of truth rather than rights. As such, a rational process of reform, or at least one likely to receive media support, is inclined to react to high profile miscarriages of justice by reducing suspects' rights in the pursuit of more accurate verdicts.

2

Problematizing miscarriage of justice

Danny McNamee, Paddy Nicholls, Sheila Bowler, Bridgewater Four, M25 Three, Taylor sisters, Cardiff Three, Darvell brothers, Judith Ward, Stefan Kiszko, Tottenham Three, Maguire Seven, Birmingham Six, Guildford Four, Luke Dougherty, the Maxwell Confait case, the Luton post office murder case, the Angus Sibbet murder case, PC Luckhurst, James Hanratty, Derek Bentley, Timothy Evans, Devlin and Burns . . .

A. INTRODUCTION

Just as in the first half of the twentieth century and in the latter half of the nineteenth century, the second half of the twentieth century has witnessed a number of very high profile alleged or acknowledged miscarriages of justice. Such miscarriages have spawned films, plays, television and radio programmes, books, newspaper and magazine articles, Royal Commissions and other official inquiries, Court of Appeal judgments, Parliamentary debates, legal articles and, of course, numerous T-shirts and graffiti.[1] It would be conservative and somewhat unfashionable (and, as we hope to demonstrate, quite incoherent) to claim that the purely legal meaning of a miscarriage of justice, the legal precedent it creates, captures its social meaning and significance. Indeed, despite the concern expressed by legal academics over miscarriage of justice cases, few create legal precedents. And even those appeal cases that do provide legal precedents are often heavily edited when reported and the precedents they create are formulated in particularly open-ended language, such as the phrase 'lurking doubt'. Whereas precedents are rarely created from these cases, they tend to open and close leaving nothing that can be relied on for future cases, a great deal

[1] The graffiti daubed widely on public walls, bridges, and buildings in the East End of London 'George Davis is innocent' in 1974–6 nearly achieved the status of a catch phrase worthy of inclusion in books of quotations. The campaign, of which this graffiti was a part, contributed to George Davis's sentence being remitted in 1976 allowing immediate release from his twenty-year prison sentence for robbery. The conviction was mainly the result of identification by five police officers. However, within one year of his release he was found guilty of another serious crime and was back in prison.

of comment about them occurs outside the confines of courts. There are exceptions, but the relevance of the precedents they create is often problematic for the legal system.[2] But if we move beyond the narrow concentration on legal precedents, then what else can usefully be said about miscarriages of justice, and how is such legal and *non-legal* material to be included and considered? A more open form of academic writing is offered by the tradition of arguing for reform. Miscarriages of justice provide a focus to claims for improvements to the criminal justice process. They offer a strong source of moral outrage in a multicultural and predominantly secular society that lacks moral certainty. There is an element of heresy about claiming that miscarriages of justice are acceptable which is absent from disrespect to other 'lesser values', such as God(s). Contrast current reactions to Lord Denning's statement made in his judgment in the Court of Appeal in 1980 dismissing the civil actions by the Birmingham Six for injuries for assault by the West Midlands police: 'It is really an attempt to set aside the convictions on a side wind. It is a scandal that should not be allowed to continue' with the arguments upholding as fundamental Salman Rushdie's freedom of speech.[3] Those who seek improvements that protect the factually innocent, and those seeking rights for individuals and suspect communities,[4] harness undisputed miscarriages of justice to arguments for reform. Journalism feeds into their work. It identifies cases, establishing them as high profile and undisputed examples of miscarriage of justice. Reformers, including politicians, seek to draw lessons from these undisputed miscarriage of justice cases—what needs to change to prevent them from arising again. Although all these groups seem to know with certainty when a miscarriage of justice has occurred, what exactly is it?

A miscarriage of justice can be defined in many different ways and nearly in whatever way one wishes. At its widest, and most tautological, a miscarriage of justice is simply a failure to achieve justice. Like good, all intelligent beings can understand that justice is to be pursued and evil and injustice to be avoided, but this begs the question of their content.[5] Attempts to introduce content into justice, however well reasoned, raise the issues of relativism, subjectivism, and ideology, which make giving justice a clear and universal meaning highly problematic. For example, it is against the claim made by John Rawls of the lack of reasoning involved in the construction of 'self-evident' principles, or those usually called 'naturalism', as bases for a theory of justice, that he sees the justification for his own

---

[2]   We intend to show why this is the case during the course of this book.

[3]   Examples of these arguments can be found in L. Appignanesi and S. Maitland (eds.), *The Rushdie File* (London, 1989). Lord Denning's position is clarified and criticized by T. McGurk, 'When Television is "a Court of Last Resort" ', *The Listener*, 25 Feb. 88, 9–10.

[4]   These are linked but, as we hope to show, not synonymous concerns.

[5]   Even attempts to reverse these meanings, akin to the use of the term 'wicked' to mean 'excellent', still maintain the sense of opposition.

well-reasoned account of justice.[6] However, even Rawls's well-reasoned account has been criticized in these terms, and even criticized by those who are basically committed to it as a 'statement of liberalism'.[7] If there is no straightforward way to give justice a universal meaning, how can miscarriage of justice be given one?[8]

If we move from philosophical questions to sociological ones, miscarriage of justice is a term which links real events in history, and focuses attention on the processes, institutions, and practices through which these events occurred. As such, whilst justice is an abstract, relative, and, some would claim, ultimately subjective concept, miscarriage of justice can be rooted in something far more concrete. The term miscarriage of justice has a referent in the *real* world. Miscarriage of justice at the level of events takes the form of a list, similar to that set out at the beginning of this chapter. Individuals may wish to add further names, or include examples from other jurisdictions. Indeed all jurisdictions seem to offer their lists of classic, high profile miscarriages, which appear often to have long-standing and severe repercussions for the society in question.[9] But a list which failed to include any of the above names would lose an important referent and, with it, the ability to make important connections with and criticisms of the processes and practices of English criminal justice.

To move beyond a list of names begs the question: what does the list represent? In order to consider this question, we will not offer a definition of miscarriage of justice as such. Although there may be nothing to prevent others from doing so, we believe that the attempted definitions that have been offered have serious shortcomings, especially in the context of the sociological questions that we intend to consider. Let us take an example. A definition of miscarriage of justice may be widened to include whatever those individuals believe is less than justice: unjust laws, inhuman punishments, or failure to prosecute those who abuse the rights

---

[6] J. Rawls, *A Theory of Justice* (Oxford, 1972), 'Concluding Remarks on Justification', 577–87.

[7] See, e.g., B. Barry, *The Liberal Theory of Justice: A Critical Examination of the Principal Doctrines of A Theory of Justice by John Rawls* (Oxford, 1973), especially chs. 1, 13, 14, and 16.

[8] This argument applies even though it might appear easier to know what is a miscarriage than what is justice, just as it appears easier to demonstrate injustice than justice; see Edmond Cahn's argument in *The Sense of Injustice* (Bloomington, 1949), 11–27.

[9] A notable example is the wrongful conviction of Alfred Dreyfus in France for treason in 1894, Zola's famous letter 'J'Accuse . . .!', and the implications for French politics even today. In the United States there are many extraordinary examples, such as the continuing controversy about the conviction, then successful appeal and death before retrial, of Jack Ruby, who apparently shot and killed Lee Harvey Oswald, who in turn had apparently shot and killed President John F. Kennedy. Other countries have similar memorable controversies, such as Sweden, with the continuing saga about the murder of Prime Minister Olof Palme in 1986 and the trial, appeal, and retrial of the main suspect; France, with the implications of the Omar Raddad miscarriage; Australia, with the long saga following the disappearance of baby Azaria Chamberlain, etc.

of others.[10] But such a definition has moved away from the circumstances in which this term is principally used by lawyers, politicians and the media, and also tends to lose contact with the list of generally recognized cases. If the case of the Guildford Four is simply one example of all the injustices in this world, or even all the injustices in the English legal system, why does it have any particular social significance? We will dispense with the vagaries of individual definitions. Rather, our starting point is with those who attempt to seek a meaning for miscarriage of justice, but do so by linking that meaning to the events that are generally recognized as examples of this phenomenon. We will be focusing on communities (lawyers, media, and politicians) and their use of language in connection with definite social practices and historical events.

B. A CONCEPTION OF MISCARRIAGE OF JUSTICE

The general conception of miscarriage of justice, which is shared by the diverse communities of lawyers, media, politicians and in general social communication, is not injustice *per se*, but wrongful conviction. In adopting this conception we believe that our approach is consistent with the epistemology underlying Ronald Dworkin's recent jurisprudence. In the context of giving meaning to the word *law*, Dworkin asks how we can avoid the problem of the 'semantic sting' whereby people only talk about the same things if they accept the same definitions, and simply talk past each other where they do not? Dworkin sought to avoid the semantic sting, in relation to his general account of the meaning of the word law. He did so by asserting that, rather than a concept of law, there is indeed an initial agreement or conception about what it means to identify something as law: that one is seeking the closest relationship between our actual social practices of coercion and their justification.[11] Similarly, we are here concerned with the actual practices occasioning miscarriages of justice and the dominant justifications for holding that such miscarriages have occurred.

What could be wrong about the convictions represented in our list given at the beginning of this chapter? Actually, two principal things: that the people who have been convicted of offences did not in fact commit those offences, or that their convictions were flawed because some part of the process that produced those convictions did not operate as it should. For

---

[10] See, e.g., C. Walker, 'Introduction', in C. Walker and K. Starmer (eds.), *Justice in Error* (London, 1993), ch. 1, particularly 4–6. In 'Miscarriages of Justice in Principle and Practice', in C. Walker and K. Starmer (eds.), *Miscarriages of Justice: A Review of Justice in Error* (London, 1999), ch. 2, particularly 33–8, Walker develops his earlier definition considerably, making it much more extensive.

[11] See *Law's Empire* (London, 1986), 45–6, 90–6, and S. Guest, *Ronald Dworkin* (Edinburgh, 1992), 34–7.

the purposes of this book, we will call the first a concern with truth and the latter a concern with due process. The latter concern is also intimately related with and sometimes referred to as a concern with the suspect's rights. In general we prefer to talk of due process rather than rights, as breach of a suspect's rights has connotations of choice. Due process may be constructed without this element of choice, by affording the suspect procedures that cannot be waived.[12] This mixture of elements is well captured by the following quotation from the Introduction to the Report of the Royal Commission on Criminal Justice, a report written for an audience of politicians, lawyers, the press, and the public:

It may be argued that however practical our recommendations, and however cogent the reasoning behind them, there is a potential conflict between the interests of justice on the one hand and the requirement of fair and reasonable treatment for everyone involved, suspects and defendants included, on the other. We do not seek to maintain that the two are, or will ever be, reconcilable throughout the system in the eyes of all the parties involved in it. But we do believe that the fairer the treatment which all the parties receive at the hands of the system the more likely it is that the jury's verdict, or where appropriate the subsequent decision of the Court of Appeal, will be correct. As will become apparent from our recommendations, there are issues on which a balance has to be struck. But we are satisfied that when taken as a whole our recommendations serve the interests of justice without diminishing the individual's right to fair and reasonable treatment, and that if they are implemented they will do much to restore that public confidence in the system on which its successful operation so much depends.[13]

As this paragraph shows, the Royal Commission's most important concern is the pursuit of truth in terms of the justice of *correct* decisions. Fairness is welcomed to the extent that it contributes to the pursuit of truth, but must occasionally be balanced where the two conflict. The pivot for that balance is concern with public confidence. Without public confidence measures which might at first glance seem to increase the efficiency of criminal justice, such as increased police investigation powers and the admissibility of all available evidence, can actually reduce efficiency through a decline in the public's willingness to report crimes, be witnesses at trials, and, as jurors, to convict defendants.[14] However, the notion of balance adopted by the Royal Commission has been severely criticized.[15] The arguments we

---

[12] Others take the view that it is 'incorrect to conceive of process theory and the rights perspective as ontologically equivalent, although they can certainly be regarded as compatible' (R. Henham, 'Human Rights, Due Process and Sentencing', *British Journal of Criminology*, 38/4 (1998), 603).

[13] The Royal Commission on Criminal Justice, the *Runciman Report*, Cm 2263 (London, 1993), para. 27.

[14] See our analysis of this paragraph in the context of the Report as a whole: 'Optimism Writ Large: A Critique of the Runciman Commission on Criminal Justice', in M. McConville and L. Bridges (eds.), *Criminal Justice in Crisis* (Aldershot, 1994), ch. 4.

[15] See A. Ashworth, *The Criminal Process: An Evaluative Study* (New York, 1998), 30–2, for a succinct statement of this criticism.

present in this book are not only dependent on such criticism of the use of the notion of balance, but on the impossibility of that very idea. Bentham expressed this theme most clearly in decrying the fallacious notion of 'balance of powers': 'The fact is, that whenever on this occasion the word balance is employed, the sentence is mere nonsense.' He went on to say:

Preeminently indeterminate, indistinct, and confused, on every occasion, is the language in which, to the purpose in question, application is made to this image of a balance; and on every occasion, when thus steadily looked into, it will be found to be neither better nor worse than so much nonsense. Nothing can it serve for the justification of: nothing can it serve for the explanation of.[16]

Aside from the difficulties of balancing values against each other, the evidence and arguments provided by radicals and sceptics provide a considerable challenge to anyone seeking to claim that the processes and practices of criminal justice are an expression of, or approximation to, fundamental values. How can one believe that criminal justice is about truth, or due process, when it is so obviously about power, expediency, control, class, the aggressive policing of suspect communities, the impossibility of objectivity, and has little, if anything, to do with justice, or any other values which might claim to lie beneath that epithet?

Let us start with the strengths of the sceptic's position. What are the difficulties of understanding a conviction as a statement that the defendant has committed a particular crime or, even if we cannot be certain about the truth of the defendant's guilt, that the conviction is justified by the moral values inherent in the processes which produced it? Once we have explored the strength of the sceptic's position, we can move on to consider a seeming paradox. How can a system which actually operates at such a great remove from absolutes such as truth, due process, and justice generate periodic concentrated concern with wrongful convictions? For an important part of understanding the social phenomena of miscarriages of justice is to enquire into the miracle of their occurrence.

C. Truth as a Value in Criminal Justice

At a philosophical level the statement that the difficulties of getting at the truth are staggering is a truism.[17] The ability to prove the existence of any

---

16   J. Bentham, *The Book of Fallacies* (London, 1824), 249 and 251.

17   We believe that it is not contentious to make such a sweeping statement. However, we do not mean it to be taken as a damning criticism of the search for truth, or as a post-modern statement of disillusionment with it. Rather, we accept Fernandez-Armesto's defence of the universal search for truth as implicit in all philosophies and traditions. 'Whenever we get an intimation of truth—whether we feel it, listen for it, sense it or think it out for ourselves—we should expect it to talk to us and we should be able to try, if we like, to express it for others' (*Truth: A History and a Guide for the Perplexed* (London, 1997), 229).

current facts, even through the most rigorous scientific methods, is problematic. When such enquiry relates to past events, when it is historical, a
further layer of complication arises. Can we reproduce or reconstruct what
occurred? When one uses methods and processes that are not scientific, the
difficulty of reaching something that can be represented as *the truth* multi-
plies. For a non-scientific system like law, the problems of attempting to
present its findings of fact as the truth are almost overwhelming, and then
magnified when applied to its appeal procedures. Indeed, attempts at
understanding the criminal trial as a scientific process that operates to seek
out the truth are clearly flawed theoretically, epistemologically, and practically.[18] Let us consider briefly the processes of evidence-gathering and trial.

The principal process used by the English courts to determine the truth
at trial is the adversary process. This process is justified mainly by tradition
and only to a limited extent by arguments that it is necessarily the best
means of capturing the truth. Such arguments are rarely put forward in
academic treatises,[19] although numbers of legal judgments make this claim.
In academic treatises the more usual understanding is that the adversary
process is justified by its practical benefits and its fairness rather than by its
unequivocal pursuit of truth. The adversary process has its antecedents in
what are now seen as irrational processes: trial by ordeal and trial by battle
or combat. Both of those methods of trial contained the beginnings of
reliance on others to support or represent one or both of the parties, in the
form of either a deputy (trial by ordeal) or a champion (trial by combat for
writs of right). But, ultimately both relied heavily on the intervention of
spiritual forces to achieve justice. In trial by ordeal and combat justice and
truth share a common bond, supported by a set of common Christian
values. The processes of trial will produce justice because, with the aid of
the divine authorities, truth will triumph over deceit and good over evil.
However without the aid of divine authorities, reliance on the adversary
process to draw out the truth has many limitations.

The modern adversary process has had to be understood, and reformed,

---

[18] See, e.g., S. Shute, J. Gardner, and J. Horder, 'Introduction: The Logic of Criminal Law',
in eid., *Action and Value in Criminal Law* (Oxford, 1993), 1–20; J. Jackson, 'Two Methods
of Proof in Criminal Procedure', *Modern Law Review*, 51 (1988), 549–68; J. Jackson, 'Law's
Truth, Lay Truth and Lawyer's Truth: The Representation of Evidence in Adversary Trials',
Law and Critique, 3/1 [1992], 29–49; R. Smith, 'Forensic Pathology, Scientific Expertise, and
the Criminal Law', in R. Smith and B. Wynne (eds.), *Expert Evidence: Interpreting Science in
the Law* (London, 1989), 56–92; W. L. Bennett and M. Feldman, *Reconstructing Reality in the
Courtroom: Justice and Judgment in American Culture* (New Brunswick, 1981), ch. 7,
'Towards a Theory of the Criminal Trial'; P. Rock, *The Social World of an English Crown
Court* (Oxford, 1993).

[19] E. E. Sward finds examples of such arguments, but mainly refers to examples of the
opposite argument, in 'Values, Ideology, and the Evolution of the Adversary System', *Indiana
Law Journal*, 64 (1989), 301–55. Lord Devlin gives the clearest statement of the argument that
the adversary process is the best means of capturing the truth. See his book, *The Judge*
(Oxford, 1979), ch. 3, 'The Judge in the Adversary System', particularly at p. 61 when he
quotes Denning LJ in *Jones v National Coal Board* [1957] 2 Q.B. 55, 63.

through a secular logic. The trial had to change from an opportunity for divine intervention to a mechanism for the assessment of evidence. In this task, in the common law system, the role of the jury is crucial, although in their earliest forms jurors played an inquisitorial, fact-finding role, rather than a role as impartial umpires as demanded by the adversarial model.[20] Jurors were, in some respects until well into the nineteenth century, qualified to undertake the role of fact-finding because they were expected to have specific, local knowledge. It was their prior knowledge rather than the evidence adduced in court that was expected to determine the jury's assessment.[21] Although this aspect of the jury's role has changed, since the jury is now expected to be impartial and not have any prior knowledge, other links to the irrational origins of the adversary process remain. In particular, what the jury actually does:

It is the oracle deprived of the right of being ambiguous. The jury was in its origin as oracular as the ordeal: neither was conceived in reason: the verdict, no more than the result of the ordeal, was open to rational criticism. This immunity has been largely retained and is still an essential characteristic of the system.[22]

The modern jury is expected to identify the truth, and capture it in one or two words: guilty, or not guilty. On rare occasions the jury may be asked to give other one- or two-word answers to other complex questions. The lack of any reasons for its decisions facilitates the jury's irrational role as a party who can be expected to reach a verdict without the benefit of forensic training. And the manner in which it routinely reaches its decisions further confirms its irrational role. Its members are not encouraged to ask questions, facilities for note-taking have only recently been provided, and it is sent into the jury room without a copy of the transcript. In the context of fraud trials the Roskill Committee felt that the jury was ill equipped to hear complicated technical evidence.[23] We cannot presently know how well the jury functions (the Runciman Royal Commission called for changes to the law of contempt to allow research). However, given the host of reasons why the jury can be expected to act irrationally, it may be appropriate to view the jury more as an impartial arbiter of the reasonableness of the prosecution's case rather than as a forensic tool for truth. Indeed, from this latter perspective, there may be, in our culture and tradition, no obviously better alternative. By contrast, if we expect the jury to act as an accurate forensic tool, able to understand the logic of each aspect of both counsel's arguments and evidence, the need for reform seems obvious. (Looking ahead to

[20] See W. R. Cornish, *The Jury* (London, 1968), 9–12.

[21] See S. Enright and J. Morton, *Taking Liberties: The Criminal Jury in the 1990's* (London, 1990), ch. 1, 'Origins'.

[22] P. Devlin, *Trial by Jury* (London, 1956), 14.

[23] *Roskill Committee Report*, Departmental Committee on Fraud Trials (London, 1986), 142.

Chapter 6, one needs to ask whether those who defend the jury on the basis of its role as impartial protection against unreasonable prosecutions are prepared to accept its *perverse* convictions?)

The key idea in the modern adversary process is that testing evidence through examination and cross-examination, of prosecution witnesses, one's own witnesses, and even oneself,[24] will verify that evidence, and such verification is likely to afford the truth. This key idea relies on advocacy, which is recognized to be the art of persuasion in court.[25] On issues of fact 'cross-examination is the essence of adversarial confrontation', a complex process surrounded by rules of evidence and professional ethics, at which some advocates excel much more than others.[26] This key idea lies behind evidence adduced in court (from those most closely involved rather than third parties or forms of hearsay evidence, and consequently the considerable reliance placed on oral evidence) and even, to some extent, evidence produced prior to trial.

Modern social and psychological knowledge presents tremendous obstacles to faith in the ability of these legal procedures to capture truth. There is what can be called the challenge of fact scepticism. Is the truth out there to be reproduced through legal processes; what truth; isn't truth relative to individuals and communities; isn't there more than one truth; can the court unpack events so as to tease out the truth? Remember that the court does not only deal with the truth of past events (did this suspect do this action?) but also the truth about intentions (did this suspect do this action with the necessary and often particular intention?). Let us take a controversial example. Large proportions of defended rape cases involve a conflict of evidence as to whether or not the victim consented, for the purposes of the rule about consent. Whereas one cannot discount the possibility (or probability) that both parties will not tell the *absolute* truth, perhaps the underlying problem is that there is, simply, no absolute truth. There are two sets of constructed truths, the differences between them reflecting the differences between different interpretations of the same events, more or less plausible interpretations of signals, and more or less plausible interpretations of expectations, which expectations have changing cultural undertones. As stated in the *Heilbron Report*: '10. Whether it is criminal depends on complex considerations, since the mental states of both parties and the influence of each upon the other as well as their physical interaction have to be considered and are sometimes difficult to interpret—all the more so since normally the act takes place in private.' In addition, as the Report makes clear in relation to

---

[24] Not until the Criminal Evidence Act 1898 was the defendant, at common law, competent to testify as a witness, and even now is not a compellable witness at the behest of the prosecution.

[25] On such an art much common sense and informed advice is available. See D. Napley, *The Technique of Persuasion* (London, 1970).

[26] M. Stone, *Cross-Examination in Criminal Trials* (London, 1995), xi.

rape trials, there are other issues and values involved such as protecting the rights and sensitivities of victims, which may impose additional problems for the court and its ability to construct the truth.[27]

To the problems of interpretation we must add (though the two are not independent) those of recollection. Identification evidence has been shown to be unreliable,[28] hence the development of the rules regarding corroboration and the specific instructions that the judge must give to the jury, although not in any particular form of words.[29] Then there are the implications of evidence obtained under conditions of coercion. As a matter of law, evidence of confessions or admissions is admissible in court subject to certain conditions determining whether they are voluntary and/or reliable.[30] However, some research supports the argument that all evidence obtained while in custody, and particularly confession evidence, is inherently unreliable.[31] The implication being, as with identification evidence, the need for a rule requiring evidence of corroboration,[32] but no such rule has been enacted. Confession evidence is under greater and greater attack and the difficulties of formulating a legal code to determine the reliability of confessions has been consistently illustrated.[33] Some of those who confess are expected to be weak-minded or suggestible,[34] rather than guilty.

What we know about human testimony makes reliance on it highly problematic. The dynamics of giving evidence in the adversary process do not accord with current knowledge about the likelihood that an account of the truth will emerge. It has been known for a long time that once we have committed ourselves to a particular view, a particular recollection of events,

[27]   Report of the Advisory Group on the Law of Rape, Cmnd. 6352 (London, 1975).

[28]   See the Report of the Departmental Committee on Evidence of Identification in Criminal Cases, the *Devlin Report*, HC 338 (London, 1976), in which the miscarriages relating to Luke Dougherty and Laszlo Virag substantially resulting from false identifications are fully recounted.

[29]   The *Turnbull* guidelines [1976] 3 All ER 549. For a summary of the main problems with identification evidence, see J. D. Heydon and M. Ockelton, *Evidence: Cases and Materials* (London, 1996), 83–92.

[30]   See P. Mirfield's analysis of the common law rules and sections 76 and 78 Police and Criminal Evidence Act 1984 in *Silence, Confessions and Improperly Obtained Evidence* (Oxford, 1997), chs. 4–7.

[31]   See G. Gudjonsson, *The Psychology of Interrogation, Confessions and Testimony* (Chichester, 1992).

[32]   See M. McConville, *Corroboration and Confessions: The Impact of a Rule Requiring that no Conviction can be Sustained on the Basis of Confession Evidence Alone*, Royal Commission on Criminal Justice Research Study No. 13 (London, 1993).

[33]   For example, see M. Inman's severe attack on the proposals of the Royal Commission on Criminal Procedure 1981 on this, which proposals are the basis of the current law: 'The Admissibility of Confessions', *Criminal Law Review* [1981], 469–82.

[34]   See G. Gudjonsson, 'Psychological Vulnerability: Suspects at Risk', in D. Morgan and G. Stephensen (eds.), *Suspicion and Silence: The Right to Silence in Criminal Investigations* (London, 1994), ch. 6. See also the Court of Appeal judgments in the Cardiff Three case, *Paris, Abdullahi and Miller* (1993) 97 Cr. App. R 99, *Lee* [1984] 1 All ER 1080, and *MacKenzie* (1993) 96 Cr. App. R 98.

the more we are questioned the more likely we are to retain that view or recollection and to be more certain in doing so.

F. C. Bartlett in his classic experiments on 'Remembering', shows that this is a general psychological phenomenon. He shows that people tend to become more confident in their descriptions of what they have seen over time and repetition; and secondly, that witness confidence may be an inverse guide to accuracy ... Unfortunately, the legal process reinforces this psychological tendency. One way in which it does this is by its very repetitiousness.[35]

The persuasive task of the advocate becomes the task of allowing the witness to confirm his or her view or recollection, letting such confirmation become as rigid as possible, and then showing some chink in it in order to discredit it as a whole. It can be argued that the process of adversarial questioning makes evidence, which is dependent on witness recall, less rather than more certain to represent the truth.

It is obvious that some of the rules of the criminal justice process do not enhance the search for truth. Its tolerance of plea bargaining and its reliance on the guilty plea undermine truth.[36] There is no doubt that the practices associated with plea and charge bargaining are common and may involve numbers of defendants pleading guilty to offences of which in fact they are not guilty. In their nature these practices, which are essential to the efficient operation of many of the elements of criminal justice,[37] are antithetical to truth. They operate as procedures of negotiation and provide techniques for the achievement of valued outcomes. Truth is also sacrificed in the negotiation of evidence that occurs before and during the trial process. Each side may in negotiation with the other side, or independently, exclude from their production of evidence some potentially relevant material. The magistrate or jury's adjudication in the end is never 'the whole truth and nothing but the truth'. It is a version of the truth according to some of the witnesses (the best witnesses in the eyes of the parties' lawyers) in response to the tactical priorities adopted for their questioning by the lawyers involved. As McEwan puts it: 'There seems to be a large measure of agreement that

[35] R. Brandon and C. Davies, *Wrongful Imprisonment: Mistaken Convictions and their Consequences* (London, 1973), 36. See also S. Lloyd-Bostock, *Law in Practice* (London, 1988), ch. 1 'The Accuracy of Witnesses', and D. S. Greer, 'Anything but the Truth? The Reliability of Testimony in Criminal Trials', *British Journal of Criminology*, 11 (1971), 131–54.

[36] See the study by J. Baldwin and M. McConville, *Negotiated Justice: Pressures to Plead Guilty* (London, 1977). The Royal Commission (n. 13 above, ch. 7, para. 43) were unable to ascertain the extent of plea and charge bargaining. They gave an equivocal interpretation to the evidence on this from M. Zander and P. Henderson, *The Crown Court Study*, Royal Commission on Criminal Justice Research Study No. 19 (London, 1993).

[37] See J. Baldwin and M. McConville, *Courts, Prosecution and Conviction* (Oxford, 1981), ch. 7, 'The Importance of Confession Evidence', and D. J. McBarnet, *Conviction: Law, the State and the Construction of Justice* (London, 1981), ch. 4 'Pleading Guilty'.

lawyers are there to present highly selective versions of the case.'[38] In this process of negotiation there is a patent inequality in the resources available to each side preparing for the trial. The defence is very reliant on the prosecution to provide it with relevant evidence.

Sociological studies of the criminal justice process have consistently demonstrated the gap between the actual practices, the empirical reality of actions and activities associated with criminal justice, and the rules which are meant to condition those practices. McConville, Sanders, and Leng's classic study *The Case for the Prosecution*[39] gives an explanation for the gap between the rules and practices within criminal justice as integral and structural. As Maguire and Norris describe that study:

These authors argue that much of what is called 'malpractice' is the result not simply of cultural pressures to 'perform', nor of occasional over-enthusiasm by basically honest but frustrated police officers, but is an *integral and routine* part of the investigative process as it has developed in England and Wales. The police, they argue, occupy a position within the adversarial system of justice in which lip-service may be paid to the notion of investigators being engaged in an open-minded 'search for the truth', but bounded by principles of 'due process', but in which their true function is to pursue the goal of 'crime control' above all else. Priority is given to the need (convicting offenders) above the means (compliance with procedural rules), the reality being not a search for truth but a process of 'case construction' in which, once a clear suspect has been identified, the objective of the inquiry becomes the one-sided collection (and sometimes 'manufacture') of evidence to support the police version of what happened. Thus, virtually the sole aim of interviews becomes the extraction of a confession, 'ploys' are used to deny suspects legal advice, witnesses are manipulated into producing statements which precisely support the police account, and contrary evidence is often disregarded and concealed from the defence.[40]

Indeed recent high profile miscarriage cases are full of allegations of police perjury and brutality (Birmingham Six and Guildford Four), non-disclosure of relevant evidence (Judith Ward and Stefan Kiszko), extraction of false confessions (Darvell Brothers, the Maxwell Confait case), and witness manipulation (Bridgewater Four and the Luton post office murder case). Even those who take a less integral and more individual view of malpractice recognize the inevitable gap: 'the high-profile miscarriages of justice were in the main the result of human factors, such as police officers who fabricated evidence, scientists who made mistakes or suppressed evidence. No system is, or could ever be, fully proof against human error or human wickedness.'[41]

---

[38] J. McEwan, *Evidence and the Adversarial Process: The Modern Law* (Oxford, 1998), 11.

[39] M. McConville, A. Sanders, and R. Leng, *The Case for the Prosecution* (London, 1991).

[40] 'Police Investigations: Practice and Malpractice', in S. Field and P. Thomas (eds.), *Justice and Efficiency? The Royal Commission on Criminal Justice* (Oxford, 1994), 74.

[41] M. Zander, 'What is Going On', *New Law Journal*, 143 (1993), 1507–8.

With criminal justice's tangential relation to truth the likelihood of the practices of criminal appeal being resolutely aimed toward truth is not great. This could only occur if the appeal process was wholeheartedly a complete (and completely open) retrial, if it ignored both the terms in which evidence had been produced at trial and the verdict that had been achieved on the basis of that evidence. However, the Court of Appeal (Criminal Division) has never seen itself as a court of retrial (in most regards),[42] but rather as a court of review. It sees its primary responsibility as determining whether the conviction of the appellant concerned was and remains safe. Whether it was safe depends on a current assessment of the earlier practices of the trial court. Whether it remains safe depends on the potential impact of new or fresh evidence. A reassessment of the original trial prioritizes truth only to the extent that truth is prioritized within the routine practices of trials in general. The Court of Appeal's approach will not be informed by literature which casts doubt on the efficacy of trial procedures (or at least not routinely) for that would put trials and pre-trial procedures on trial. Reassessments involving new evidence raise similar problems. They require the Court to consider whether such evidence casts doubt on the accuracy of the verdict. To avoid passing judgment on the effectiveness of trial in general, the Court has to fit such evidence into its understanding of a *normal* trial. Given the perceived (and sometimes celebrated) irrationality of the jury's role, this may involve the court in a somewhat surreal exercise. It may be described as follows: assuming that the jury understood the evidence put to it, and accepted such of the prosecution's evidence as would justify a conviction, how does this new evidence relate to the *facts* imputed to the *mind* of the jury? This exercise offers a limited agenda and, in practice, imposes a significant burden on an appellant. In addition, a sceptical attitude to the truth of evidence does not necessarily assist appellants. A sceptical attitude towards the ability of the Court of Appeal through its processes (oral evidence, cross-examination, etc.) to reach the truth, will hinder the ability of appellants to prove either their innocence, or that their convictions were based on untrue evidence. New evidence, treated sceptically, will fail to undo the jury's *facts*. So, as one might expect, and as we will show in Chapter 3, the Court of Appeal has found it difficult to accept that, in many instances, the burden on appellants has been satisfied.

D DUE PROCESS AS A VALUE IN CRIMINAL JUSTICE

Fact scepticism challenges the ability of criminal justice to obtain truth, both on the basis of the system's rules of procedure, and on the gap between those rules and actual practices. If one attempts to present the rules of criminal

---

[42] We deal with this more fully in Ch. 3.

justice as an embodiment of due process, the same literature on gaps between rules and practices will serve to undermine this alternative claim.[43] However, as with the above discussion of truth, even if we concentrate on the rules, and assume that these are followed, the connection between these rules and a persuasive theory of due process is difficult to establish. The sceptic's critique can be classified as value scepticism.

At the most tautological level, processes are due because they are laid down in the rules. They are because they are. Historical enquiries may reveal that they are the result of pragmatism, or tradition. The latter has little rational appeal, though it may operate quite well in practice. The consequence of an irrational commitment to traditional trial practices has recently been described in the following terms:

> The fact that from these foundations springs an eccentric Gothic edifice composed of extraordinary rules, presumptions, exceptions and confusion has its own charm. The seductive appeal of this structure in itself breeds a sentimental attachment, so that one might feel that preservation of the traditional form of trial, with all its historic characteristics, is indeed worthwhile to protect our heritage, just as we conserve ancient monuments.[44]

The traditional nature of the English criminal trial cannot be doubted: 'The mere form of a criminal trial is surely the most ancient relic in any modern legal system.'[45] Thus, for example, pointing out that in some form or other the right to jury trial has existed since 1166 might help to make a popular case for its continued existence. But rational defence of due processes seeks to root them in standards such as fairness to the accused, or human rights. At a rhetorical level one can agree on the need for criminal justice to reflect the values of due process: one can talk generally of the need for a fair trial, or fair and equal treatment of accused persons. All things being equal, who is going to wish for unfair trials? But agreement on the desirability of such abstract principles does not lead to agreement on their exact ingredients in practice (or their trade-off with truth).

In trying to present English criminal justice as an embodiment (actual or imminent) of values, one is inevitably handicapped by the parochial nature of its procedures. Any process which has a long historical tradition has elements of procedure, even some considered essential by the participants, which have not been copied by other jurisdictions that we would hesitate to call unfair, etc. Again, jury trial provides an excellent example of this. Lawyers, practising and academic, have celebrated the right to jury trial in

---

[43] The nature and implications of the gap between law in the books and law in action in the criminal justice process is the subject of considerable debate. McBarnet's thesis, n. 37 above, especially ch. 8, has been strongly criticized by McConville, Sanders, and Leng, n. 39 above, 174–81. The arguments we present here do not require us to enter into those debates; however, we describe McBarnet's thesis in more detail in section B of Ch. 6.

[44] McEwan, n. 38 above, 32.

[45] S. F. C. Milsom, *Historical Foundations of the Common Law* (London, 1981), 413.

the most extreme terms. Consider the following reactions to the recommendation in 1993 in the Report of the Royal Commission on Criminal Justice that the right to opt for jury trial should be curtailed.[46]

The concept of jury trial is worth nothing unless it is supported by an inalienable right to be tried by a jury. (Sean Enright *New Law Journal* (1993), 1024)
Once you start tinkering with that, you are tinkering with a fundamental freedom. (Richard Ferguson QC, *The Times*, 7 July 1993)
The choice to opt for a jury trial is an essential safeguard against miscarriages of justice. (John Rowe QC, *The Times*, 7 July 1993)
... in cases where the CPS [Crown Prosecution Service] does not agree to trial by jury, the magistrates would have the power to decide. This would be madness. (Lord Williams of Mostyn QC, *The Times*, 7 July 1993)
There are delays and inefficiencies at present, but the way to deal with them is to improve the mechanics, not to erode a fundamental civil liberty. (Lord Williams of Mostyn QC, *The Times*, 7 July 1993)

How does one square these claims, that the present but threatened[47] right of individuals in the English criminal process to opt for trial by jury is fundamental to justice, with the absence of this right in the Scottish legal system or those of most European jurisdictions?

Comparative analysis offers the hope of discovering universal principles which underpin otherwise parochial procedures. Underlying the English legal system is, as we have argued, the adversary process. But this has to be squared with jurisdictions that cannot, with their own historical origins, be defined in these terms. Dividing Western legal systems into adversarial and inquisitorial offers two models of justice. Is one superior? Or are they separate but equal? Or can they mix, and if so, what, in either of them, is essential? And if one concentrates solely on the adversarial nature of English criminal justice, what aspects of English procedure are necessarily adversarial: pre-trial, trial, appeals? And, is the adversary process rooted in the right to conduct one's own case, or the right to cross-examination? Whilst the former indicates a need to avoid judicial comment on the manner in which an accused has conducted his case, including the use of his right not to testify, the latter points to restrictions on, for example, the admissibility of hearsay evidence.

The adversary process is not a value in and of itself but, to the extent that it does not represent a mechanism to obtain truth, can be defended in terms of its contribution to fairness. Such fairness includes access to legal assistance and restraints on police powers, which can then be presented as an attempt to redress the imbalance between the powers of the state and those of the individual. But while the imbalance of power may be obvious, the

---

[46] See n. 13 above ch. 6, para. 13. The examples given below are taken from G. Maher, 'Reforming the Criminal Process: A Scottish Perspective', in McConville and Bridges (eds.), n. 14 above, ch. 6, 64.
[47] The present Government's intention is to implement this change.

appropriate point at which to respond to it is not. Completely removing the imbalance of power (giving the individual as much power as the state) is impossible. Does this indicate that current practices are correct, that more should be done, or that the whole attempt to redress imbalance is hopeless?

Another value in due process, which could be offered as a justification for the current adversary process, is the concept of participation. Defendants' rights to representation, to have counsel conduct cross-examination of witnesses, to know the charges against them, and to have full disclosure of the evidence in the possession of the prosecution, can be seen as rights to participate in the proceedings. Such rights enable defendants to participate in the conduct of their own defences and thus to be agents in the process and not simply objects. Through these processes, justice may not be individual, but it is individualized. Such a concept of due process provides some logical limits to what is defensible. Secret charges, trial *in absentia*, or the complete absence of legal representation present situations in which one can say that the individual has no ability to participate in the proceedings which construct his or her guilt.[48] But what of situations in which participation is possible, but not as full as one might have liked? What should be the links between the trial, where one might expect to participate, and interrogation, where one is an object of enquiry?

If the value which underlies due process is taken to be that of autonomy, then one can attempt to justify those aspects of pre-trial criminal procedure which have little to do with participation, such as police powers of stop and search. These can be seen as reflecting rights of privacy: the minimization of state inference so as to achieve consistency with personal autonomy. But what, if this is the underlying basis for due process, is the appropriate compromise between personal autonomy and the need to carry out investigations and prosecutions? Can one claim that the value underlying English criminal justice is autonomy, and still justify keeping citizens in custody for the purposes of questioning for up to seven days without charge?[49]

Some of the problems of teasing universal values out of the current practices of English criminal justice can be avoided by moving to a human rights perspective. A human rights-based theory of due process may be independent of fairness, or complementary to it. Human rights arguments may be used to justify prohibitions on torturing suspects, even when torture produces reliable evidence. This is not such an inappropriate example, since only in the modern era has torture as a means of obtaining evidence disappeared in the Western world. Historically the use of torture, particularly in

---

[48] And in the extreme one arrives at the nightmare situation of not knowing or understanding one's predicament, represented so powerfully by Franz Kafka in *The Trial*, first published in 1925 and first translated into English in 1937.

[49] Hence the conflict between the arrest provisions of the Prevention of Terrorism (Temporary Provisions) Act 1989 and the standards of the European Convention on Human Rights, as interpreted in *Brogan v UK* (1989) 11 E.H.R.R. 117.

Europe, was prevalent and highly developed. Such use was governed by detailed rules (due process), what Langbein calls the jurisprudence of torture. The ultimate aim was to adduce evidence that was reliable as proof of guilt. If the detailed rules were followed about the questions that it was permissible to ask, then the answers given could prove guilt because the evidence adduced could only have been given by someone guilty of the crime and thus aware of particulars relating to it.[50] In the modern era the example of torture has become the rhetorical starting point for those who wish to defend the legitimacy of acquitting persons who are guilty, but whose rights were infringed. There may be general willingness for the perpetrators of serious crimes to go unpunished, no matter how sure we are of their guilt, if the evidence necessary to convict them involved the use of torture. But it would be hard to find such widespread acceptance that, because of human rights violations not amounting to torture, serious crimes should go unpunished.[51]

As well as concentrating on the grosser forms of oppression, whose immorality is more likely to command consensus, human rights approaches also have the advantage of concrete referents, such as the Universal Declaration of Human Rights 1948, the European Convention on Human Rights 1950 (and its sub-type, the Human Rights Act 1998) and their respective investigative and adjudicative practices. These concrete referents remove some of the difficulties of trying to present the traditional practices of a single jurisdiction as the embodiment of human rights. These Conventions, which are a codification of the general standards and legal practices of modern Western liberal democracies, can be represented within a single jurisdiction as the embodiment of a higher law. There are, however, still problems, perhaps intractable problems, with how these rights will be interpreted and reconciled with each other, considerations of expediency, and how these rights can be made effective.

The right to silence can be used to illustrate our arguments here. It has recently been amended in English Law, and those amendments have been subjected to the decisions of the European Commission and Court of Human Rights. In doing so the problems of giving concrete meaning to rights have been highlighted. Are the changes made in the Criminal Justice and Public Order Act 1994, which reduce some part of the right to silence and which in practice make a difference to the advice given by lawyers to their clients, consistent with due-process safeguards? Recent decisions by the European Court of Human Rights, particularly those in the *Murray* and *Saunders* cases, give an equivocal reply. In *Murray v UK*[52] it was determined that the changes made by the Criminal Evidence (Northern Ireland) Order 1988, the precursor to the silence provisions of the Criminal Justice

---

[50] See J. H. Langbein, *Torture and the Law of Proof* (Chicago, 1977), ch. 1.
[51] See p. 30 below.   [52] (1996) 22 E.H.R.R. 29.

and Public Order Act 1994, are consistent with the right to a fair trial
(Article 6 of the European Convention). Those changes make a suspect
arrested for certain offences liable to have adverse inferences drawn against
him at trial if he fails to speak on arrest. And in *Saunders v UK*[53] it was determined that being forced by liability to sanction to answer questions under the
Companies Act did not infringe the right against self-incrimination.
However, since negative consequences might follow in a criminal case for a
defendant who speaks in response to legal obligations to do so, the rights
under articles 6 and 8 of the Convention had been infringed, such negative
consequences amounting to self-incrimination. Legal analysis might be able
to distinguish the legality of adverse inferences in *Murray* from the illegal-
ity of negative consequences in *Saunders*; however, such a distinction only
highlights the problems of giving effect to the general standards of human
rights within the law, it does not overcome them. Alan Norrie articulates
this conundrum well: 'Legal logic becomes a pirouette around a set of
necessary exclusions and inclusions designed to avoid or bridge the gap
between legal ideology and social reality.'[54]

Whereas human rights standards offer a form of argument about the
priority of one value against other values, or rights as principles in contrast
to social or economic policies,[55] they remain, in Bentham's famous phrase
'nonsense'. There is an inevitable gap between the articulation of these
rights and their practical effects. Remember that Bentham's accusation
refers to talk of 'natural rights as simple nonsense: natural and impre-
scriptible rights, rhetorical nonsense, nonsense upon stilts'.[56] The still
developing history of the interpretation and reinterpretation of the standards that in the modern world are described as human rights has little
certainty. Even at their core, in the attempts to elaborate on fundamental or
absolute inviolable rights, there is little universal agreement and much
disagreement.[57] With less than absolute rights the breadth of interpretation
available, the 'margin of appreciation',[58] remains as wide as ever. It is not
the high-sounding principles of rights that determine practical outcomes but

[53] (1997) 23 E.H.R.R. 313.
[54] A. Norrie, *Crime, Reason and History* (London, 1993), 58.
[55] R. Dworkin, *Taking Rights Seriously* (London, 1977), chs. 2 and 4.
[56] J. Bentham, 'On the Declaration of the Rights of Man and the Citizen Decreed by the
French Constituent Assembly in 1791', in B. Parekh (ed.), *Bentham's Political Thought*
(London, 1973), 269.
[57] See S. R. Chowdhury, *Rule of Law in a State of Emergency: The Paris Minimum
Standards of Human Rights Norms in a State of Emergency* (London, 1989).
[58] The phrase used by international and regional courts to allow for different interpretations of human rights standards within different national and regional jurisdictions. For a
concise statement of this doctrine in relation to the European Convention on Human Rights,
see D. J. Harris, M. O'Boyle, and C. Warbrick, *Law of the European Convention on Human
Rights* (London, 1995), 12–15. For a fuller account of the significance of this doctrine in the
developing jurisprudence of the European Court of Human Rights, see H. C. Yourow, *The
Margin of Appreciation Doctrine in the Dynamics of European Human Rights Jurisprudence*
(Dordrecht, 1996).

the commitment to particular claims. The interpretation of sections 76–8 of the Police and Criminal Evidence Act 1984 illustrates this. Those sections contain the possibility of a practical commitment to individual rights as against other objectives, but in practice they are neither uniformly nor necessarily interpreted to achieve that end. Significant latitude in interpretation and application invariably remains.[59]

The task of finding due process and rights in traditional practices can be viewed as an attempt to make moral *sense* out of history and its products. Real histories can often reveal the ex-post nature of contemporary rationalizations of existing practices. For example, suspects' pre-trial *rights* do not have their origin in any sustained theory of rights, but in the desire of lawyers and judges to protect the integrity of their traditional practices at trial from the consequences of an unrestrained growth of police powers. One history of the right to silence and its relationship to the old common law principle, the privilege against self-incrimination, relates the development of suspects' rights to maintaining the authority of the adversary process of the trial. The perceived superiority of trial practices provides a basis for organizing and criticizing pre-trial practices which threaten to subvert the trial, and for understanding the construction of accused persons' rights. This interpretation suggests that the recent history of restrictions on police powers developed in order to preserve the primacy of trial practices, and preceded the rationalization of those restrictions in their modern form as suspects' pre-trial rights, such as the right to silence. During the latter half of the nineteenth century as the role of the police was changing from that of a body required to find, detain, and present accused persons at trial, to an agency that investigated crime, new restrictions were being placed on the police. The justification for such restrictions was not only to protect suspects' rights and to ensure against the abuse of authority, but also to preserve the primacy of the trial as a mechanism for determining the guilt or innocence of the accused. The Judges Rules, first published at the beginning of the twentieth century, are the main example of this. These rules restricted the police in their interrogation of suspects by, for example, stopping the police from continuing to question suspects once they had been charged. From this historical perspective, the right of silence arose to protect an aspect of due process that may, or may not, be perceived as a right: the prosecution's burden of proof at trial. Whether or not it is plausible to interpret the development of suspects' rights in terms of the priority of adversary trial processes, it is clear that many pre-trial rules and practices are a consequence of the application of adversarial principles in general and principally their operation in the trial.[60] The adversary process

---

[59] For example, in relation to confession evidence, see Mirfield, n. 30 above, chs. 6–8.

[60] For a clear, short historical introduction to the right to silence, see S. M. Easton, *The Case for the Right to Silence* (Aldershot, 1998), ch. 1, 'The History and Development of the Law on the Right to Silence'.

gives priority to what occurs, and what evidence is produced, in court. However, whilst this key idea underpins much of the modern adversary system,[61] its consistency with a modern understanding of the values implicit in criminal justice, the current values of due process and rights, is tenuous.

The point of this short section on due process and rights is not to deny that some aspects of criminal justice, whether national, European, or international, represent ethically valuable protections against oppressive treatment; nor even that it is possible to subject the whole of criminal justice (at any of these levels) to schemes of interpretation organized around particular values. Nor do we deny that some such schemes provide a more consistent or persuasive account[62] of current arrangements than others do. But our sketch does illustrate the difficulties of developing a universal or objective account of existing practices, or one that would generally be agreed upon. Indeed most accounts of criminal justice, especially those informed by history, recognize how difficult it is to present it within a 'unified approach' since 'It may be that the demands we make of our criminal justice agencies are too varied to permit this.'[63] This points in turn to the difficulties facing the institutions which have to identify what exactly constitutes a mistake, or impropriety in the operation of the system. If there is no clear, consistent, and specific basis for identifying what constitutes a breach of due process within criminal justice, or which rights under what conditions should be given priority, how is the Court of Appeal (or any other review body) to operate? These problems become even more acute if one considers the possible relationships between the values of due process and truth.

E. THE RELATIONSHIP BETWEEN TRUTH AND DUE PROCESS WITHIN CRIMINAL JUSTICE

Whilst all of criminal justice can be understood in terms of process, it is not possible to present all of it as informed by ideas of rights or fairness. Whatever bits of it are presented as a protection of rights, or a correction of imbalance, there must remain other parts of the process (police powers to arrest, detain, question, etc.) which represent something other than these. A cynical liberal theorist might regard these other arrangements as mechanisms for social control. From this perspective, fair processes are a restraint on an indiscriminate and otherwise arbitrary exercise of state power. But a more

---

[61] Of course there are also other values that underpin the modern adversary system: the presumption of innocence, the reliance on the oath, the distrust of pre-trial procedures, the impartiality of the umpire, etc. See McEwan, n. 38 above, ch. 1 'The Adversarial Trial'.

[62] Or, in Dworkin's terms (n. 11 above), one that might fit better than others might. On the underlying values of due process, see D. J. Galligan, *Due Process and Fair Procedures: A Study of Administrative Procedures* (Oxford, 1996), Part 1, 'Procedures and Fairness'.

[63] S. Uglow, *Criminal Justice* (London, 1995), 8. We agree with Uglow's contention that 'the criminal justice system has never been planned as a "system" ' (p. 14).

attractive (and common) position is that the value other than fairness that best justifies the processes associated with criminal justice is that of truth.

Those who seek due process based on rights or fairness generally wish for the rest of criminal justice to be justified by reference to the pursuit of truth. The commitment to rights generates a commitment to individuated justice. One should not lose one's right to life, liberty, etc., except when one is factually guilty of a crime. This same commitment to rights also provides a basis for prosecution: it is only through the restraint of those who abuse rights that individuals in general can hope to enjoy rights. Thus one cannot simply have a commitment to rights or fairness. Those who advocate rights and fairness must also accept the value of truth,[64] in the sense of a need both for convictions of those who are factually guilty, and for the acquittal of those who are factually innocent. In a similar way those who advocate truth must adopt a limited commitment to rights and fairness. A utilitarian approach to coercion might have only a contingent commitment to convicting the guilty, as deterrence of unwanted behaviour might require convicting the innocent.[65] By contrast, a commitment to truth (convicting only the factually guilty) involves a commitment to a retributive theory of justice, which has at its roots some commitment to individual rights and fairness. But how are these various commitments to be reconciled?

At a rhetorical level (stated by Blackstone in the eighteenth century) it is said to be part of the law 'that it is better that ten guilty persons escape, than that one innocent suffer'.[66] Zuckerman has described other variations on this theme: 'Fortescue, writing in the fifteenth century, had a preference for a twenty-to-one ratio, while Lord Stafford preferred a thousand-to-one.'[67] Whatever the precise mathematics, these statements represent a commitment to avoid one kind of loss of truth, wrongful conviction, over another, wrongful acquittal. The argument Blackstone used to substantiate this commitment was that 'all persuasive evidence of felony should be admitted cautiously'[68] for fear of wrongful convictions. But even if one accepted (or persuaded non-lawyers to accept) this strong commitment against untruthful convictions, what room is left for the values of due process? To extend the rhetorical argument, if one lets ten guilty persons off to prevent one innocent person's conviction, does one let off a further ten in order to maintain a fair trial, the fairness of a right to silence, etc.?

[64] See H. L. A. Hart, *Punishment and Responsibility* (Oxford, 1968), ch. 1, for one of the strongest attempts to combine similar elements in the justification for legal punishment. For critique of 'Mixed Theories of Punishment' see N. Lacey, *State Punishment: Political Principles and Community Values* (London, 1988), 46–57.

[65] See the utilitarian philosopher's response, that by Smart, to such a scenario, in J. J. C. Smart and B. Williams, *Utilitarianism: For and Against* (Cambridge, 1973), 67–73.

[66] Sir William Blackstone, *Commentaries on the Laws of England (1765–69)*, iv; *Of Public Wrongs* (1769), (Chicago, 1979), 352.

[67] A. A. S. Zuckerman, *The Principles of Criminal Evidence* (Oxford, 1989), 126.

[68] See n. 66 above.

There have been those, such as Jeremy Bentham, who believed that criminal procedures should aim solely at producing accurate outcomes. He attacked the concern with due process as fairness, comparing it contemptuously with the sporting instinct of foxhunters:

Every villain let loose one term, that he may bring custom the next, is a sort of bag-fox, nursed by the common hunt at Westminster. The policy so dear to sportsmen, so dear to rat-catchers, cannot be supposed entirely unknown to lawyers. To different persons, both a fox and a criminal have their use: the use of a fox is to be hunted; the use of a criminal is to be tried.[69]

Bentham preferred a whole-hearted commitment to the pursuit of truth, a process, which he felt, required very little in the way of rules:

in principle there is but one mode of searching out the truth: and (bating the corruptions introduced by superstition, or fraud, or folly, under the mask of science,) this mode, in so far as truth has been searched out and brought to light, is, and ever has been, and ever will be, the same . . . see every thing that is to be seen; hear every body who is likely to know any thing about the matter . . .[70]

Evidence is the basis of justice: exclude evidence, you exclude justice.[71]

Those who believe that justice should involve more than truth will argue against Bentham's position. As mentioned before, a strong rhetorical argument is to ask whether one should uphold every conviction of the factually guilty whatever impropriety (including torture) was involved in their conviction.

In principle the opposite position was well put in the 'Note of Dissent' by Michael Zander in the Report of the Royal Commission on Criminal Justice,[72] in connection with the appropriate attitude to adopt towards criminal appeals in cases where convictions had been obtained through impropriety. The majority recommended that convictions obtained through procedurally defective trials should nevertheless be upheld, provided that the Court of Appeal was satisfied that the conviction was 'safe'. By contrast the dissent claimed that allowing defendants to serve prison sentences 'on the basis of trials that are seriously flawed' is to subordinate 'the integrity' of criminal justice to the conviction of particular individuals.[73] The difficulties involved in applying such a test arise frequently.[74] This is not surprising since, whatever its strength at this level of generality, this approach begs a series of questions that it is very difficult to answer. These questions concern whether, and when, breaches of due process or violations of which rights and under what conditions within the present criminal

---

[69] J. Bentham, *Rationale of Judicial Evidence, Specially Applied to English Practice*, ed. J. S. Mill (London, 1827), v: 238–9.   [70] Ibid. 743.   [71] Ibid. 1.
[72] See n. 13 above, 221–35.   [73] Ibid., para. 64.
[74] As a good recent example see the Court of Appeal decision in *Chalkley and Jeffries* [1998] 2 Cr. App. R 79.

justice process justify the quashing of a conviction and the abandonment of punishment. The difficulties of demonstrating that any particular part of criminal justice is a necessary embodiment of due process values and individual rights leads to a situation in which the quashing of convictions, or the failure to pursue prosecutions for reasons of due process alone, can be viewed as a formal, technical, and otherwise unmeritorious reason for failing to punish.

If we all believe the sceptic's position, then there can be no justice in criminal justice, and therefore no consistent conception of miscarriage of justice. As such, there is nothing in the present system to trade off. The debate between those who are committed to the present procedures and practices (or a reformed version of them) as a commitment to truth, and those seeking to defend the existing values of due process, including rights, is one between hopeless idealists.

F. GENERATING MISCARRIAGE OF JUSTICE

We hope we have presented enough material on fact and value scepticism to convince the reader that there is a significant gap between the values claimed for criminal justice and its procedures and practices. There is an enormous amount of empirical material on this, enough to write several books. But our concern is not to set out an exhaustive account of the evidence of a gap. Rather, it is to note that there is an acknowledged and even inevitable gap, and explore the implications of this for the operation of criminal justice, particularly in connection with criminal appeals.

The perceived gap between the values claimed for criminal justice and its practice points to the difficulties facing those who seek to describe and criticize it. If the gap is seen to be very large, it throws doubt on claims that values are immanent within current procedures. One cannot then ask the participants to live up to the values embodied in their institutional practices. If one denies the extent of the gap, one may appear unduly conservative. A radical reformer may prefer to record all divergence between practice and claimed values, but continue to claim the presence of such values, and the merit of seeking to close the gap. When adopting the latter position, reformers take some solace from high profile miscarriages of justice (i.e. miscarriages to which the public's attention has been drawn). When high profile miscarriages appear prevalent, then such episodes seem to affirm claims that criminal justice does (or at least should) embody fundamental values, and to provide political opportunities for reforms that close the gap. Should one then interpret wide-scale concern with miscarriages of justice as proof that the sceptics are wrong? Should one interpret that concern as demonstrating that criminal justice is an expression, or at least a partial expression, of values which it either lives up to, or through a process of possible reforms can be made to live up to?[75]

An alternative thesis is to view the rhetoric of justice within criminal justice as just that: rhetoric. By this we do not seek to assert that it is unimportant, or meaningless. Rather it is our belief that there is a strong rhetorical commitment within the legal profession, the media, and amongst politicians, to understanding the legal system as connected in important (if often inconsistent and remote) ways to the achievement of justice. This rhetoric of justice allows the legal system to present itself as more than arbitrary force. And this commitment is never merely rhetorical. Those who wish to retain the understanding that the current practices of the legal system are connected to the achievement of justice have to respond in those circumstances where criminal justice is generally understood to have failed to do this. The issue is not whether those who respond are cynics, sceptics, or committed participants. Responses are required because, to deny the need to respond is to deny the connection between the legal system and justice, which provides criminal justice with important aspects of its legitimacy. This commitment is shared between those who wish to reform the existing practices and those who wish to defend them. The defenders may seek to present the existing practices as just, or as near just as possible. Reformers will seek to make these practices more just. Neither wishes to accept the full logic of the sceptic's position: that justice is, for all sorts of reasons, unattainable, or even non-existent.

In order to maintain the rhetorical commitment to justice, paradoxically, one must have mechanisms to deal with mistakes. Whether one regards criminal justice as linked to truth, or due process, fairness, and rights, or both, one cannot deny that, on some occasion, criminal justice will miscarry. In carrying out its operations it will fail to deliver what it claims to achieve. One does not have to accept the full logic of the sceptic's position in order to accept the fallibility of criminal justice. To maintain the pursuit of justice in the face of inevitable mistakes one needs mechanisms that can rectify them. Since 1907, the main body charged with responsibility for this role is the Criminal Division of the Court of Appeal.

The Court of Appeal has an extremely difficult task. It has to define what constitutes a miscarriage of justice within a set of practices that do not, and never could, live up to the fundamental values represented by the legal system's rhetorical, if not real, commitments to justice. As we have already said, the particular injustice that it must rectify is wrongful conviction, and this is made up of both truth and due process. The Court of Appeal has the elusive task of constructing wrongful convictions and, by the same process, recognizing convictions that are not wrongful. In these circumstances, the

---

[75] For an account which attempts to understand miscarriages of justice in these terms, see S. Greer, 'Miscarriages of Justice Reconsidered' *Modern Law Review*, 57 (1994), 58–74.

interesting question, and one which informs our analysis of miscarriages of justice, is how does it maintain the rhetoric of justice, in the face of the difficulties raised by sceptics' writings? How does the Court of Appeal avoid putting criminal justice itself on trial, analysing all of its parts for their contribution to the truth of a conviction? How does it represent some aspects of procedure, or some individual rights as so fundamental that infringement warrants the quashing of convictions, even when the infringement in question did not necessarily affect the correctness, in terms of the truth, of the verdict? In carrying out this task, the Court of Appeal has had to respond to the fact that it cannot operate in isolation from other communities. Its standards of wrongful conviction will be examined by the legal community, the media, politicians, and, at second instance, the public. Whilst each of these groups share an understanding that wrongful convictions are made up of questions of truth and of due process, the attachment which they each have to these different elements is not uniform.

The legal community generally expresses a commitment to due process as a value in addition to that of truth. Whether this commitment amongst particular lawyers is a rational reaction to fact scepticism (the acceptance that if convictions cannot always be correct, they can at least be fair), or to a traditional attachment to parochial practices, or a commitment to a consistent theory of justice, is not the point. Due process provides an alternative basis to truth for deciding whether convictions are wrongful or not. Intolerance to breaches of rules, standards of procedure, and rights are presented by lawyers to themselves and to those outside the law as evidence of law's commitment to justice. Where such rules, procedures, or rights are not more widely celebrated as fundamental, or understood as contributing to truth, this justice may be seen by other communities as an example of injustice. This can lead to lawyers being vilified for their tolerance of known villains, as evidenced in a classic attack on the profession by the former Commissioner of the Metropolitan Police, Sir Robert Mark, in his Dimbleby Lecture in 1973.

The object of a trial is to decide whether the prosecution has proved guilt. It is, of course, right that in a serious criminal case the burden of proof should be upon the prosecution. But in trying to discharge that burden the prosecution has to act within a complicated framework of rules which were designed to give every advantage to the defence. . . . Most of these rules are very old. They date from a time when, incredible as it may seem, an accused person was not allowed to give evidence in his own defence, when most accused were ignorant and illiterate. . . . But it is, to say the least, arguable that the same rules are not suited to the trial of an experienced criminal, using skilled legal assistance, in the late twentieth century. The criminal and his lawyers take every advantage of these technical rules. Every effort is made to find some procedural mistake which will allow the wrongdoer to slip through the net.[76]

[76]   *In the Office of Constable* (London, 1978), 153.

It can also lead to persons who look to the Court of Appeal for an authoritative statement of their innocence being sorely disappointed. Consider the following extract from the autobiography of Paul Hill, one of the Guildford Four:

They tell me that in legal language there are conventions and formulae: one of these, apparently, is to describe convictions as 'unsafe and unsatisfactory' when they mean to say that the people before them are innocent and have been framed. They say that justice needs calm; that voices must be controlled. I say that is in itself an injustice: to fail to speak with rage about injustice is another injustice.[77]

By contrast to the legal community, the media's attachment to due process is weaker than its attachment to truth. Rights, which make no contribution to the factual correctness of a verdict, can be seen as technical and lacking merit. The media's dominant understanding of miscarriage of justice is that those who are factually innocent cannot rightfully be punished, *whatever the processes which led to their conviction*. This understanding of miscarriage of justice has the ability to threaten the legitimacy of criminal justice, and to promote a perception of crisis, because it creates the possibility of putting criminal justice itself on trial. Trials by the media of an individual can often become trials by the media of the legal system itself. The intolerance of *technical* acquittals, mentioned above, is paralleled by intolerance of the legal system's seeming unwillingness to respond to cases of (to the media) obvious or undisputed wrongful conviction of the innocent. It is these episodes which lead to a periodic perception of criminal justice in crisis.[78]

---

[77] P. Hill (with R. Bennett), *Stolen Years: Before and after Guildford* (London, 1991), 268.
[78] See our analysis in Ch. 4.

3

Remedying miscarriages of justice: the history of the Court of Criminal Appeal

A. Introduction

The Court of Appeal (Criminal Division) has the responsibility to remedy miscarriages of justice, but in order to do so it has to give meaning to what a miscarriage of justice involves. In that exercise the task of the Court of Appeal is to present the processes and practices of criminal justice as an embodiment of justice, that is, as the embodiment of values such as truth, due process, fairness, and rights. Such a task largely concerns the management of rhetoric. It is an important task but one that inevitably leads to periodic crises over miscarriages of justice. Such crises arise when commentators question whether the criminal justice process lives up to its rhetorical claims, and they are inevitable for two related reasons. First because, as we have argued in the previous chapter, criminal justice cannot live up to all of its rhetorical values at the same time. And secondly, as we demonstrate in Chapter 4, because when some commentators seriously question the practices and procedures of criminal justice they may adopt different interpretations of what its rhetorical claims imply, as well as what a miscarriage of justice means.

The seeds of these periodic crises were evident in the law and practice of criminal appeals prior to the creation of the Court of Criminal Appeal in 1907. At that time the creation of a Court of Criminal Appeal was thought to be the necessary change that, apart from remedying miscarriages, would eradicate or reduce the likelihood of further crises. For example, in commenting on the widely publicized Florence Maybrick case in 1889 and the press campaign to reverse the guilty verdict of murder against her, a leading article in *The Times* claims: 'The second reform which the Maybrick case has made a necessity is the institution of a Court of Criminal Appeal. The want of such a tribunal has been demonstrated over and over again of recent years, but until now it has never assumed the proportion of a calamity.'[1]

---

[1] 10 Aug. 1889.

Working with the rhetoric of justice the Court, since its establishment, has had to develop a manageable scheme of practices for identifying those cases when convictions can be quashed, and when not. The wrongfulness of a particular conviction may involve conclusions which, generalized to all cases, would make large numbers of convictions potentially wrongful. Or the way in which the Court has gone about establishing what is a wrongful conviction might encourage many other convicted persons to make claims that they have been wrongly convicted. The Court's everyday practices have had to avoid reaching such conclusions, whilst maintaining a rhetoric of justice and remedying miscarriages.

The problem for the Court is that there is no necessary consistency in its practices (as we will illustrate in this chapter) and no necessary congruence between its practices, and instances where other communities, most importantly the media, have come to a clear view on the wrongfulness of a conviction. The Court of Appeal (and before the Court was founded the senior judiciary) has repeatedly found itself attempting to uphold the legitimacy of its own practices, and those of the courts which it supervises, in the face of widespread criticism from the media. From its inception, the Court of Criminal Appeal has attempted to ensure that control over defining what amounts to a miscarriage of justice resides within the legal system itself, and that such control is not lost to the press. To quote the words of Lord Loreburn, the Lord Chancellor in the debates on the 1907 Act, which created the first Court of Criminal Appeal: 'events have occurred within the last twelve months, which, at least to my mind, raise the question whether there should be an appeal to the Press or an appeal to His Majesty's Judges, and for my part I have no hesitation in expressing a preference for His Majesty's Judges.'[2] Those judges who were opposed to the principle of a Court of Criminal Appeal saw the role of the press as something to be resisted rather than responded to by creating new legal machinery. Disagreeing with Lord Loreburn, in the same debate, the former Lord Chancellor, the Earl of Halsbury, said:

I protest, in the first place, against the proposition of the noble and learned Lord that this Bill is in a great measure necessary because events have occurred which raise the alternative of trial by Judges or trial by newspapers. That seems to me to indicate a weakness somewhere, to which I, for one, will not assent. I cannot understand why the legislation of the country in the most serious matter of the administration of the criminal law should be affected one way or the other because irresponsible persons think it proper to assume that they have knowledge superior to that of His Majesty's Judges.[3]

Such views were also expressed in the media. Consider a leading article in *The Times* in 1907 discussing the Criminal Appeal Bill then going through Parliament:

[2] Parl. Deb. HL 5 Aug 1907, c. 1472.   [3] Ibid., c. 1473.

Were there no other reason for creating a Court of Appeal, a strong case would be found for it in the demoralizing irregular discussions in Parliament and in the Press of the verdicts of juries . . . If there is to be no Court of Appeal, we must expect to see more and more agitations set on foot or carried on by newspapers . . . Something has to be done to counteract, as far as possible, the truly alarming ease with which nowadays a criminal who has been tried and found guilty by his countrymen can induce a large number of well-meaning persons to take for granted his innocence.[4]

When the Court was eventually set up it was given a legislative mandate which, despite the changing wording of its jurisdiction in later statutes, has not altered from its inception, namely to quash convictions where these amount to miscarriages of justice. But the basis on which the Court recognizes a miscarriage of justice can and sometimes does differ from that of the media, or other authorities such as the Home Secretary or independent review authority.[5] As such, the Court has not been able to absorb media or political concerns, to prevent pressure building up in the press or in Parliament in respect of particular cases, or to avoid the pressure for reform that can accompany sustained press and political campaigns over miscarriages of justice.[6] The creation of the Court has thus not ousted the press, or at least some members of the press, from its self-appointed role as the appeal body of last resort. But as only the Court has power to quash convictions, the role of the press cannot be separate from it. Rather, the press operates to challenge particular guilty verdicts and on occasion the Court of Appeal's own verdicts and, periodically, through the intervention of other authorities, to force the Court to reconsider cases which, according to its own routine practices and procedures do not amount to miscarriages of justice.

B. BEFORE THE CRIMINAL APPEAL ACT 1907[7]

1 STATE OF THE LAW PRE-1907

It would be difficult to describe the appellate procedures available to convicted persons, prior to the setting up of the Court of Criminal Appeal in 1907, as being greatly concerned with truth. There is evidence of a commitment to due process, but the processes due were far from rational and represent traditional practices and procedures that are piecemeal and hard to fit together under a co-ordinated scheme. Before 1907 the available

---

[4] 30 July 1907.

[5] See our analysis of newspaper reporting on miscarriages in Ch. 4, and of the new Criminal Cases Review Commission in section D of Ch. 5.

[6] Such campaigns existed well before the Court was set up and have continued sporadically ever since.

[7] For an alternative short account, see D. Bentley, *English Criminal Justice in the Nineteenth Century* (London, 1998), ch. 25 'Appellate Remedies'.

appellate procedures were very limited, the product of haphazard development rather than rational design. There were three alternative options: writ of error; motion for a new trial in cases of misdemeanour tried before the Queen's Bench Division; case stated to the Court for Crown Cases Reserved. The two former procedures were of very rare occurrence because of their extremely restricted applicability. In cases of writ of error, the irregularity to be appealed must have occurred on the face of the record of the proceedings, which comprised only the indictment, the plea, the verdict, and the judgment, and crucially omitted any detail of the process of the trial. Appeals based on misdirection to the jury or criticism of the reception of evidence or the judge's summing-up were thus excluded. Motions for new trials were likewise very infrequent for the simple reason that the vast majority of trials did not take place before the Queen's Bench Division, but at Assizes and Quarter Sessions, and so lay beyond the remit of the remedy. The use of the Court for Crown Cases Reserved was more established. Its origin lay in an informal mechanism, whereby a judge in a criminal case could reserve a point of law for discussion by his fellow judges if he felt in difficulty as to the appropriate course to follow. The deliberations took place in private and the remedy available was a pardon. Formalization into a court in 1848 improved matters by widening the jurisdiction to include cases tried at Quarter Sessions, providing for the delivery of public judgments and enabling the appellant to be declared innocent.

Yet these provisions fell far short of anything resembling an adequate court of appeal. Appeals were restricted to points of law, and to those raised at the instance of the judge who conducted the trial. The judge-led nature of the proceedings is perhaps more understandable if one considers estimates that at the end of the eighteenth century only one in six defendants appearing at the Old Bailey had legal representation. Defendants on felony charges only received the right to representation in 1836. The role of the defence at the trial (and consequently in any available appeal process) was far less central at this time. The Court for Crown Cases Reserved was not widely used. Writing in 1883 J. FitzJames Stephen estimates that less than twenty cases were heard a year.[8] These three procedures composed the totality of judicial appeals open to a convicted person. The remaining option, and the sole alternative in the area of appeals based on fact (the claim of factual error at trial or the factual innocence of the convicted person) lay in the discretionary power exercised by the executive, the prerogative of mercy.

2 THE PREROGATIVE OF MERCY

The prerogative of mercy was directly bound up with the history of capital punishment in England, and indirectly with the whole issue of social rela-

---

[8] *A History of the Criminal Law of England,* i (London, 1883), 312.

tions and paternalism. During the era of the Bloody Code, at its height during the eighteenth century, it functioned as a vital part of criminal justice. At this time, however, its role was in no sense that of an embryonic court of appeal; it was rather a method of softening the harshness and rigidity of sentencing demanded by the capital statutes. It became regular practice for trial judges to recommend the exercise of the prerogative in many cases where the severity of capital punishment grossly exceeded the seriousness of the crime, the widespread result being a conditional pardon, involving commuting the death penalty to transportation.[9] The issues at stake were less frequently the truth of guilt or innocence, and more often concerns relating to mitigating circumstances, for example the youth or good character of the offender. Until the accession of Victoria the prerogative was exercised personally by the sovereign, and normally the Crown adhered to the opinion of the trial judge. In effect the prerogative became a means to individualize and lessen the severity of the criminal code, and was fairly routine in its application.

Through the course of the nineteenth century, with the repeal of the capital statutes, the exercise of the prerogative by the Home Secretary, although still used for reasons of clemency, became more attuned to the investigation of substantive guilt or innocence, at the petition of the defendant. The Home Office's executive power was the sole means available at this time for raising questions of fact after conviction. There were three options. A free pardon, which was rarely exercised, where innocence could be proved absolutely. This raised the anomaly of pardoning an innocent man: 'To pardon a man on the ground of his innocence is in itself, to say the least, an extremely clumsy mode of procedure.'[10] A conditional pardon, which involved commutation of the death sentence, but which did not require questioning of the defendant's guilt. Lastly there was remission of sentence. This was available where, although innocence could not be proven, reasonable doubt of guilt was established. There were many more remissions awarded than pardons.

A standard practice developed in the Home Office in cases of alleged wrongful conviction, fully recounted in the Memorandum submitted to the *Beck Inquiry* in 1904.[11] This practice continued unchanged well into the twentieth century, according to the 1968 Justice Report, *Home Office*

---

[9] See Colquhoun's analysis described by L. Radzinowicz, *A History of English Criminal Law* (London, 1948), 132–6, 134: 'He first draws attention to the extraordinarily high incidence of remissions, stating that more than four-fifths of every hundred offenders condemned to death were usually pardoned, often unconditionally.'

[10] J. F. Stephen, n. 8 above, 313, and see the discussion in N. W. Sibley, *Criminal Appeal and Evidence* (London, 1908), 85 on this anomaly. Stephen's views are discussed and brought up to date by C. H. Rolph, *The Queen's Pardon* (London, 1978), ch. 1 'Forgive us our Innocence'.

[11] Report of the Committee of Inquiry into the Case of Mr. Adolf Beck, Cd. 2315 (London, 1904).

Reviews of Criminal Convictions.[12] The consequence of investigations undertaken by the Home Office was either to encourage the use of the prerogative of mercy or, after 1907, referral to the Court of Criminal Appeal in order for it to undertake a further appeal. The most notable features of such reviews were a general reluctance of the Home Office to act where no fresh evidence was offered[13] (broadly in line with the subsequent practice of the Court of Criminal Appeal), and before 1907 in cases where a police investigation did elicit new facts, the compliance of the Home Office with the trial judge's opinion as to the effect of the evidence. The Memorandum stresses the lack of judicial rigour in the Home Office processes, and its consequent deference to the views of the judiciary. Contemporary opinion varied on the relative merits of the Home Secretary's quasi-judicial role. Some felt the lack of restraint imposed by legal rules was a positive feature, enabling a more thorough investigation of a case; the opposing view criticized the effective usurpation of judicial functions by an unqualified body of civil servants, working largely in secret. And in that latter view the dangers of media involvement were a constant theme:

the one or two or three cases per annum, on which public attention is aroused and in one way or another concentrated, are fastened upon . . . This practice is rapidly growing from year to year. Whether it is based on honest misapprehension, or the deliberate intention to use sensational cases for newspaper purposes, it is a public danger and it can only be guarded against by the establishment of a Court of law such as this bill seeks to establish.[14]

The account in 1905 in the *Beck Inquiry* Report[15] adumbrates the restrained position that has been adopted by various Home Secretaries in the operation of their powers of reference under the Criminal Appeal Act of 1907, and the prerogative of mercy. Reference back to the Court of Criminal Appeal in order to undertake a further appeal has been sparingly used and often only after considerable media attention. And the use of the prerogative of mercy has substantially diminished. The use of these powers in subsequent years has reflected a continuing unease on the part of the executive in its relations with the judiciary, a concern that clearly limited the sphere of Home Office action. Nearly universal agreement that these powers have proved inadequate has led to change. Since 1997 a body quite separate from the Home Office and Home Secretary, namely the Criminal Cases Review Commission, has exercised these powers. It has taken over the power of referral (s. 3 and s. 13) and plays a

---

[12] Justice, *Home Office Reviews of Criminal Convictions* (London, 1968).

[13] Exceptions to this practice include cases involving the reassessment of expert medical opinion (see our analysis in Ch. 5).

[14] H. J. Gladstone, the Home Secretary, speaking in 1907 in the Parliamentary debates on the second reading of the Criminal Appeal Bill, Parl. Deb. HC 31 May 1907, cc. 194–5.

[15] See n. 11 above, especially xiv–xvii.

significant role in authorizing the Home Secretary to exercise the prerogative of mercy (s. 16 Criminal Appeal Act 1995).[16]

3 THE PREHISTORY OF THE ACT: FALSE STARTS AND RESISTANCE

The structure of criminal appeals was of recurrent concern in the latter half of the nineteenth century, part of the general Benthamite move to rationalize and codify the criminal law and to modernize the legal system. The years between 1844 and 1906 saw the publication of several official reports stating the need for reform, which highlighted the inconsistencies and deficiencies of the current state of the law, often in response to particular cases of alleged miscarriage and the publicity that surrounded them. Very strong criticism of the existing structure of criminal appeals came in 1845 from the Criminal Law Commissioners in their Eighth Report when contrasting the relative availability of appeal in civil and criminal cases: 'If . . . a man is to be allowed the benefit of a new trial where property to the amount of 20l. is at stake, it is hard to deny him protection to the same extent where his life is in jeopardy.'[17] They stress the absolute need for appeal on questions of fact, but judicial opinion at that time was firmly opposed. Two later reports by committees of judges in 1878 and 1892 were more positive in their recommendations, though still circumspect on issues of fact. The Royal Commission of 1878, consisting of four judges, felt that appeals against the weight of the evidence or with fresh evidence should be dealt with by new trials, not by a court of appeal.[18] The Report of the judges in 1892 envisaged appellate powers focused on the amending of sentences, with a peripheral role in assisting the Home Secretary to quash convictions.[19]

Whatever the combination of measures, none of the thirty-one Bills introduced into Parliament between 1844 and 1906 were successful.[20] They varied quite widely in their grounds of appeal, though the great majority provided the power to grant a new trial. The objections against which they foundered remained fairly consistent over the years. In 1848 concern over public cost and delay is coupled with complacency, as illustrated by Baron Parke's evidence to the Select Committee of the House of Lords considering one proposed Bill. 'I think that the complaints of the present mode of administering the criminal law have little foundation, for the cases in which

[16] See our analysis of the Commission in section D of Ch. 5. For more background on the contemporary role of the pardon, see A. T. H. Smith, 'The Prerogative of Mercy, the Power of Pardon and Criminal Justice', *Public Law* (1983), 398–439.

[17] Parl. Pap. (1845), vol. XIV, 20.

[18] Report of the Royal Commission on The Law Relating to Indictable Offences, C. 2345 (1879), Parl. Pap. 1878–9, vol. XX, 169.

[19] Report of the Judges in 1892 on the Court of Criminal Appeal (London, 1894), Parl. Pap. 1894, vol. LXXI, 173.

[20] For details of these Bills, see Return of Criminal Appeal Bills (1906), H.L. Pap. 201.

the innocent are improperly convicted are extremely rare.'[21] Complacency was not only evident in Parliament and the courts, it could also be found in the press. This can be illustrated by the way in which support for the various criminal appeal bills wavered. In *The Times*, as Pattenden shows, editorial support is given to Bills in 1847 and 1853,[22] but not in 1860:

> We believe that in our Courts of Justice innocent men never are convicted. If at long intervals some singular exception occurs to this universal rule, it is only an exception, which by its extreme rarity proves the rule ... Mr. Denman, in last night's debate, declared, as a result of many years experience as a Session's barrister, that, although he had defended many scores of prisoners, he had never seen one convicted of whose guilt he was not convinced, while he had got many off of whose guilt he felt no doubt.[23]

Such complacency tended only to be shaken by highly publicized cases of alleged miscarriage.

Persistent judicial concern centred on the granting of appeals on questions of fact. As late as 1906, when the principle of a court of appeal was widely accepted, there remained grave disquiet over the inclusion of grounds based on fact.[24] The fears usually expressed by some members of the senior judiciary and others with legal responsibilities included a number of factors that later became significant in the language of the Court of Criminal Appeal in exercising its powers, in particular, fear of the erosion of the constitutional position of the jury and of the weakening of jurors' sense of responsibility. Also the fear was expressed about opening the floodgates to a torrent of frivolous applications and the consequent consumption of judicial time. Consider this typical example from London Justices:

> Inasmuch as the punishment cannot be increased and no costs are to be allowed on either side, it is practically certain that every prisoner will appeal ... Over 2,500 prisoners are dealt with by the County of London Sessions every year ... assuming, as is probable, that the majority of the prisoners will appeal upon some one or other of the grounds open to them, the Court of Criminal Appeal would find itself unable to cope with the cases from the County of London Sessions alone.[25]

[21] Quoted in A. H. Manchester, *Sources of English Legal History 1750–1950* (London, 1984), 184.

[22] R. Pattenden, *English Criminal Appeals 1844–1994* (Oxford, 1996), 10, nn. 46 and 47.

[23] 2 Feb. 1860. These editorial comments were in response to the defeat in the House of Commons of a Criminal Appeal Bill introduced by Mr M'Mahon. The editorial also echoed concerns expressed in the debate on this Bill and regularly on other Bills about the difficulty, once a criminal appeal procedure has been established with the power to order a retrial, of limiting its use.

[24] For a typical judicial declaration of antagonism see the Lord Chief Justice, Lord Alverstone, in the House of Lords debates on the abortive 1906 Bill, Parl. Deb. HL 22 May 1906, cc. 1076–86.

[25] Evidence of Justices of the County of London to the Parliamentary Committee on the Criminal Appeal Bill 1906, reported in *The Times*, 28 April 1906.

There was concern about the inevitable delay in hearing appeals, especially problematic in capital cases. Also there were arguments about the inappropriateness of judges revising a jury's verdict without themselves hearing the actual witnesses, and fears about the loss of confidence in legal authority. Speaking of the proposed Criminal Appeal Bill in 1906 Mr Justice Bingham summarizes these judicial concerns:

It [the verdict of the jury] gave to the people a sense of security; and it placed the judgments of the Court above criticism, because it based them on the assent of the public . . . This new Bill proposed to violate it [the principle of jury verdict] by an appeal to a Court of three lawyers whose decision . . . was to have the finality which at present attached to the verdict of a jury only . . . It was, of course, conceivable that a jury might make a mistake; but such a possibility must not be allowed to paralyse justice or to delay the execution of its decrees. The faintest possibility of the improbable mistake of a jury being corrected by a court of two or three lawyers offered . . . no compensation for the mischief which the contemplated Court of Appeal might introduce. Would the public have confidence in the decisions of such a tribunal? It was not difficult to see the possibility of prejudice . . . being imputed to them . . . Again, the knowledge that their [jury] verdicts were subject to review would most certainly tend to make juries less careful than they were at present . . . Those who had experience of the workings of Courts of Appeal on questions of fact in foreign countries knew something of the abuses which these Courts created and served. They were the resort of rogues, who by money and delay tricked justice of her due.[26]

This steadfast opposition was of significance for the actual practice of the newly founded Court of Criminal Appeal and explains to some extent the narrow limits within which certain powers were construed by the judges. There is a certain unity to these concerns and fears. To establish legal procedures to question, not whether pre-trial and trial procedures have been faithfully applied, but whether their outcome is factually correct, is unlikely to uphold legal authority. Each successful appeal offers the potential to diminish rather than increase respect for the practices (criminal investigation, prosecution and trial) that make up the criminal process. At the turn of the last century, similar consequences followed from successful petitions for pardons. The momentum of press coverage of and academic and professional legal discussion about criminal appeals in the late nineteenth century was supported and reinforced by the granting of pardons in numbers of notorious cases.[27]

---

[26] A report on an address by Mr Justice Bingham to the grand jury at Manchester Assizes, *The Times*, 20 April 1906. Another reason cited by opponents of the court was that the full committal proceedings before magistrates meant that the trial itself was almost an appeal. For a summary of protections against wrongful conviction in pre-trial and trial procedure at that time, see Sibley, n. 10 above, 255–9.

[27] See Pattenden's list of such cases, n. 22 above, 13.

4 THE FOUNDATION OF THE COURT OF CRIMINAL APPEAL:
PRIVATE GRIEF AND PUBLIC PRESSURE

The pressure which finally led to the establishment of the court came from the publicity given to individual cases of miscarriage of justice, most notably that of Adolf Beck. The notoriety and increase in public awareness associated with press campaigns in relation to the Beck case and others such as those of the Stauntons in the Penge murder case,[28] Israel Lipski,[29] Florence Maybrick,[30] and George Edalji[31] provided the necessary emotive impetus to end the decades-old debate on the desirability of a court of criminal appeal. Public campaigns in all of these cases were taken up in the press. In the course of such newspaper coverage legal authority was constantly being challenged. For example, the popular newspaper *The Daily News* had taken up the campaign relating to the Lipski case. Responding to that campaign the Home Secretary had published a letter indicating that there would be a respite of one week before the sentence of execution would be carried out, to see whether any new evidence might be forthcoming and how the public would respond. A leading article uses that letter to attack savagely the inadequacies of current procedures: 'His case once more illustrates the supreme necessity of a Court of Criminal Appeal . . . It is odious to have such a responsibility thrust upon the public. If the courts as they stand are not equal to their work, new Courts should be created.'[32] By 1907 it was commonplace to find articles in the press expressing deep concerns about the implications of these cases. A leading article in *The Times* commenting on the inquiry set up to consider the Edalji case says: 'What has changed is the disposition of the public towards the administration of the criminal law. There is readiness to a degree before unknown, to believe anyone who challenges a verdict in a criminal case and who offers reasons, good or bad, for holding that the Judge and the jury have made a mistake.' Then, in commenting on the inquiry, the article goes on: 'While the course to be taken by the Home Office is inevitable in the circumstances, it is not one to be repeated; there are already, without the fresh stimulus of self-elected committees, too many tendencies to drag the administration of criminal justice into regions of turmoil.'[33] Official scrutiny of the adequacy of the Home Office as an informal court of appeal revealed serious failings that reinforced arguments for the establishment of a public judicial forum to hear cases of alleged miscarriage of justice.

---

[28] See H. L. Adam, *The Penge Mystery, the Story of the Stauntons* (London, 1913).

[29] See M. L. Friedland, *The Trials of Israel Lipski* (London, 1984).

[30] See A. MacDougall, *The Maybrick Case* (London, 1891), and J. H. Levy (ed.), *The Necessity for Criminal Appeal as illustrated by the Maybrick Case and the jurisprudence of various countries* (London, 1899).

[31] Papers relating to the Case of George Edalji, Cd.3503 (London, 1907).

[32] *The Daily News*, 15 Aug. 1887.   [33] *The Times*, 11 Feb. 1907.

The case of Adolf Beck revolved around a question of mistaken identity. Beck was twice convicted of defrauding women in 1896 and in 1904, when he was mistaken for John Smith, the real offender. When his innocence was finally established, an inquiry was set up to investigate the circumstances of his prosecution and conviction, and the subsequent failure to review it. The Inquiry's Report[34] was very thorough, but selective in its criticism, and the recommendations were narrow in the extreme. Concern with due process rather than truth was evident. It refrained from proposing the creation of a court of appeal. Since the Beck case turned on a point of law on the admissibility of evidence, it was felt that to grant an appeal as of right on questions of law to the existing Court for Crown Cases Reserved would constitute a sufficient remedy. Though their criticism of the Home Office practice of review was more trenchant, it was nevertheless felt that it remained an adequate body for reviewing miscarriages arising out of findings of fact. Some minor amendments were recommended specifically an increase in legally trained personnel, but no significant restructuring. The complacency of the conclusions does not appear to be warranted by the errors exposed in the investigation. There were faults at all stages. The prosecution had doubts over Beck's identity but still proceeded. The judge was clearly wrong to exclude crucial evidence but remained unswerving in his opinion through all subsequent consultations with the Home Office. The Home Office's investigative procedures proved gravely inadequate.[35]

The Inquiry's Report failed to satisfy the level of public outrage raised by the case.[36] The press campaign that had called for the inquiry increased, and pressure on the government for action in relation to miscarriages of justice became stronger. Fuel was added to the argument by the case of George Edalji, wrongfully convicted of maiming horses in 1903, whose cause was championed by Sir Arthur Conan Doyle.[37] He was released on licence after three years of unsuccessful petitions to the Home Office, and was eventually grudgingly vindicated in his assertion of innocence by a public inquiry initiated by the Home Secretary.[38] Again it was the role of the press in publicizing this miscarriage of justice that was significant in

---

[34] See n. 11 above.

[35] For more on the Beck case see the Report itself, n. 11 above; J. Kempster, *The Perversion of Justice by the Criminal Departments of the State* (London, 1905); Rolph, n. 10 above, ch. 3 'The Quest for Finality'; J. Pellew, *The Home Office 1848–1914* (London, 1982), 66–70.

[36] This is well illustrated in a debate in the House of Commons on the Inquiry's Report and the amount of compensation that should exceptionally be granted to Adolf Beck. Parl. Deb. HC 21 March 1905, cc. 679–704 and 1039–52.

[37] See his *The Case of George Edalji. Special investigation . . . Reprinted from the Daily Telegraph, etc.* (London, 1907).

[38] See n. 31 above. No compensation was paid in recognition of the fact that Edalji was held to be partially responsible for the miscarriage of justice. See the Home Secretary, H. J. Gladstone's letter to the chairman of the Edalji inquiry, Sir Arthur Wilson quoted in Rolph, n. 10 above, 45–6.

prompting official action. The government responded to mounting pressure with a Criminal Appeal Bill in 1906, which passed successfully through the House of Lords with two major amendments,[39] but which was withdrawn from the Commons after a great deal of criticism on its workability.[40] In 1907 the Bill that was to become the 1907 Criminal Appeal Act, which dealt with some of the criticisms, was introduced into the Commons.

C. The emergence of the Court of Criminal Appeal

It can hardly be doubted that you are practically correct in your declaration that 'A Court of Criminal Appeal . . . has become a necessity.' No one in his senses can approve of the course of things, now becoming almost normal, in which the main features are conviction, agitation by friends, investigation by a distinguished amateur, a 'boom' in the popular Press, a departmental committee of the Home Office. A Court of criminal appeal will probably be established . . . I can see, however, no reason to suppose that it will abate the evils which are now calling it into existence. The above mentioned process of conviction, agitation, & c., can go on just as well after the decision of a Court of appeal as before.[41]

The Court of Criminal Appeal was founded at the start of the twentieth century against a background of public outcry, heated press opinion, high profile individual cases of miscarriage of justice, a Royal Commission, and a public inquiry. The historical echoes resonate down the century. A tracing of the Court's interpretation of its own jurisdiction and the perennial problems encountered along the way will serve to illuminate recent debates and our concerns in this book. One word sums up the issues that have bedevilled cases of miscarriage of justice throughout the century: fact. This is the area of appeals based on questions of fact as against law and the limitations, both external and self-imposed, felt by an appellate body attempting to act as a substitute for the acknowledged arbiters of fact at first instance, the jury. The relationship between the Court of Appeal and the jury in relation to questions of fact is complicated and does not operate uniformly with respect to different types of evidence. For example, the problems of expert evidence raise somewhat different issues in arguments based on the primacy of the jury.[42] Much criticism has been levelled at the Court of Appeal over the years for its failure to overcome

---

[39] The introduction of a requirement for leave and the provision for a new trial if the verdict was against the weight of the evidence.

[40] See H. B. Polland's 'Introduction' to H. J. Cohen, *The Criminal Appeal Act, 1907* (London, 1908).

[41] The barrister, Herbert Stephen, a regular letter writer on legal questions, in a letter to *The Times*, 14 Feb. 1907, replying to a leading article in that newspaper on 11 Feb. 1907 supporting the creation of a Court of Criminal Appeal.

[42] See section B/4 of Ch. 5 where we try to analyse the relevant arguments.

deference to the jury where *the facts* demand. Indeed the recent Royal Commission on Criminal Justice premised their arguments and reform proposals about the Court of Appeal on the basis of this nearly universally accepted criticism.

In its approach to the consideration of appeals against conviction, the Court of Appeal seems to have been too heavily influenced by the role of the jury in Crown Court trials. Ever since 1907, commentators have detected a reluctance on the part of the Court of Appeal to consider whether the jury has reached a wrong decision . . . we argue in this chapter that the court should be more willing to consider arguments that indicate that a jury might have made a mistake.[43]

The controversies surrounding this issue remain in some ways as unresolved today as they were in 1907. The events and discussions spanning the years from 1845 to the present[44] reveal intermittent attempts at reform; the language and arguments separated by over a century and a half are often strikingly similar.[45]

1 THE PASSAGE THROUGH PARLIAMENT OF THE CRIMINAL APPEAL BILL

During the passage through Parliament of what was to become the 1907 Criminal Appeal Act, many of the now familiar arguments on the role of the Court were rehearsed on both sides. There was a great deal of concern over the granting of rights of appeal on questions of fact, with many speakers, drawn from both supporters and opponents of the proposed court, favouring a new trial in such cases, especially where fresh evidence was involved. The other central theme was the role of the Home Secretary; the current Home Secretary Mr. H. K. Gladstone, pressed strongly for the establishment of the new court, in order to lessen the press criticism that his decisions attracted. He felt that his powers were less than adequate for the judicial nature of the questions he had to consider.[46] Despite the Court's existence for nearly a century, in recent times Home Secretaries have expressed similar concerns. 'There are two defects in my view, which have now both emerged; one, the role of the Home Secretary; and the second that

---

[43]   The Royal Commission on Criminal Justice, the *Runciman Report*, Cm 2263 (London, 1993), ch. 10, para. 3.

[44]   For an extensive history, see Pattenden, n. 22 above.

[45]   This applies to a range of issues relating to the Court's powers and practices. If one were to consider, for example, the issue of availability of legal aid, assistance, or advice for those wishing to undertake appeals, one would find considerable similarities between the findings of the Eighth Report of the Criminal Law Commissioners in 1845 on the difficulties encountered by prisoners raising their cases with the Home Secretary (n. 17 above, 18–25) and the submission to the Royal Commission on Criminal Justice (n. 43 above) by the National Association of Probation Officers on similar problems persisting for prisoners in the 1990s.

[46]   Parl. Deb. HC May 31 1907, cc. 185–92.

of the Home Office [which], perfectly properly it seems to me, did not regard themselves as an investigative agency.'[47]

The Government's view was potentially ambiguous. And such ambiguity is characteristic of both the changing powers given to the Court of Appeal in different Criminal Appeal Acts and the way the Court has attempted over the years to operate on the basis of them. In his introduction to the Bill the Attorney General, Sir John Walton, presented the powers of the court and its aims in a manner that could lead to contradiction. His lack of certitude is understandable. His 1907 position was something of a volte-face. In 1898 he had favoured retention of the Home Office's powers. 'If you erect this Court of Appeal, which can be only enlightened in accordance with the strict rules of evidence, you will do so at the cost of a procedure infinitely more elastic, more subtle and efficient in its administration, and infinitely more in the interests of the accused person.'[48] On the one hand he held up as a model for the exercise of the future criminal appellate jurisdiction the existing civil appeal structure, in which the grounds for the overturning of jury verdicts were extremely narrow. Yet he also stressed the strong investigative powers with which the court would be equipped, and hinted at its possible activist stance: 'The Court will have ample powers to get at the truth. They will be able, if necessary, to summon fresh evidence.'[49] Later, when opposing an amendment to make provision for the ordering of new trials, he laid even more stress on the wide powers of the Court which would enable it to fulfil an equivalent investigative role to that of the Home Office, in cases of fresh evidence. He could even envisage members of the Court embarking on expeditions to hear witnesses themselves.[50] But at the same time, referring back to the civil model, he intimated that the appeal was in no sense the equivalent of a second trial, and that the anticipated exercise of powers to summon witnesses would be infrequent, being unnecessary in 'ordinary cases'.

Within such ambivalence lie the seeds of subsequent controversy over the Court of Criminal Appeal's role in deciding appeals on factual grounds. The nub of the issue was the extent to which the court was intended to fulfil the function of rehearing as opposed to review. In terms of managing the rhetoric of criminal justice, of upholding the practices of the criminal justice process (investigation, prosecution, and trial), these two functions offer very different tasks. Rehearing potentially offers the replacement of first-

---

[47] Oral evidence of Douglas Hurd MP, formerly Home Secretary, given to the May Inquiry (on Wednesday, 2 Oct. 1991) into the circumstances surrounding the convictions following the Guildford and Woolwich pub bombings in 1974.

[48] Parl. Deb. HC March 16 1898, cc. 47–8.

[49] Parl. Deb. HC April 17 1907, c. 1010.

[50] The judges proved themselves less than zealous in this respect. Examples of matters which the Attorney General felt essential for the future Court to consider included evidence not called at the trial due to the inadequate advice of defence counsel, which is precisely the sort of issue that the Court itself would later exclude from its jurisdiction.

order processes by a different process of decision-making about guilt, review does not. Rehearing distances the Court of Appeal from the practices and processes that it is meant to supervise, review confirms those practices subject to supervision and amendment. Rehearing offers little scope for maintaining the need for finality, review potentially bolsters that principle.[51] No satisfactory consensus emerged in 1907. The open-ended language of the powers of the Court did not preclude either task; the ambivalence of those who created the Court was passed on to those who were to make up the Court. The potential investigative role was cited to satisfy those who feared the loss of the Home Office's wide and flexible powers, yet when constitutional concerns as to the primacy of the jury were expressed, a more restrictive, supervisory stance was attributed to the new Court. Sir John Walton's conclusion was that time would tell: 'How the experiment would work would largely depend upon the views of the Court itself.'[52] In this he has been proved partially right. Although much of the responsibility for the narrowness of interpretation of their jurisdiction, which has been consistently highlighted by commentators in relation to individual cases over the years, must accrue to judges, one should also note tensions within the overall statute. Much press commentary (as we show in Chapter 4) is directed toward the inadequacies of individual Court of Appeal judges and the way they have chosen to exercise their powers. However, tensions within the statute constantly surface in Court of Appeal judgments, which tensions, as we have tried to argue in Chapter 2, are themselves implicit in the task before the court.[53] It is these unresolved and perhaps irresolvable issues which have haunted the exercise of the Court's jurisdiction over the years.

2 DEFEATED AMENDMENTS: ECHOES OF THE FUTURE

There were two amendments moved in 1907 of particular resonance for the future. First, an amendment to make provision for a new trial, especially in cases of fresh evidence. This was argued as being preferable for reasons of both logistical efficiency and constitutional propriety. At the stage of second reading the government's mind was not made up. However, by the time the amendment was moved, the Attorney General had decided to oppose it. Such a provision had been a standard feature of most of the previous Bills, and formed part of the 1906 Bill that was withdrawn from the Commons. The lack of such a power was of significance for the development of the Court's jurisdiction. The resistance to the hearing of fresh evidence that evolved might have been lessened if a more appropriate forum than the

---

[51] See K. Malleson, 'Appeals against Conviction and the Principle of Finality', in S. Field and P. Thomas (eds.), *Justice and Efficiency? The Royal Commission on Criminal Justice* (Oxford, 1994), 151–64.   [52] Parl. Deb. HC May 31 1907, c. 235.
[53] As illustrated particularly in section F of Ch. 2.

Court of Criminal Appeal had been available for its consideration. By 1964 when the power was finally granted the negative trend had become firmly established.[54] The lack of such a power gave a ready-made argument to those who were critical of individual judgments given by the Court. There was a reform proposal waiting in the wings.

Secondly, there was an amendment to alter the grounds upon which a conviction could be quashed to include the wording 'unsafe or unsatisfactory'.[55] When the Bill first appeared in the Commons the grounds on which a conviction could be quashed included any ground on which a verdict of a jury might be set aside in an appeal to the Court of Appeal in civil proceedings. This was in line with the use of the civil appeal structure as a model for the criminal. However it set a very high standard for the overturning of jury verdicts on the facts, for the House of Lords had held in civil cases that only a wholly perverse verdict would be susceptible to appellate reversal. The amendment was moved in order to avoid such narrow grounds. At that time 'unsafe or unsatisfactory' was rejected by the Attorney General as 'being loose to the point of obscurity and . . . being unscientific'. The merit of the civil standard lay in its 'scientific precision'.[56] But again a measure of equivocation as to the Court's intended role was apparent. The Attorney General promised to reconsider the wording because he was anxious 'that the Court of Appeal should not be fettered by rigid rules' in the exercise of its 'wide discretion'. In his next breath he stressed the essential primacy of the jury verdict.[57] In the event the amendment was rejected in favour of wording which enabled the Court to construe its jurisdiction narrowly: 'that the verdict of the jury should be set aside on the ground that it is unreasonable or cannot be supported having regard to the evidence . . . or that on any ground there was a miscarriage of justice . . .'[58]

The rejected amendment resurfaced in the reforms of 1966, its lack of precision no longer a barrier. However, the greater latitude afforded by the new wording did not radically alter judicial practice, established over more than half a century. And we would argue that its inclusion from the start would not have provided a different judicial orientation. The implicit opposition of the judges was probably stronger than the imperatives of language, as illustrated by claims in the 1966 Parliamentary debates by the Lord Chief

[54] See later discussion in this chapter for post-1964 liberalization.
[55] The wording 'unsafe or unsatisfactory' was selected from the Report of the Committee on the Edalji case, n. 31 above.
[56] Parl. Deb. HC July 29 1907, cc. 635–6. Ironically, elsewhere in the debates the Attorney General used the word 'satisfactory' in a non-specific sense to characterize the properties of a correct verdict.
[57] For a veiled prediction of judicial opposition to the Court's powers see Lord James of Hereford's speech, an ardent supporter of the Bill, during the third reading in the Lords in which he recognized the strong opposition of some Judges to the Bill. However he felt 'confident' that 'whatever might be the opinion of the Judges in respect to this legislation, they would loyally administer the Act' (Parl. Deb. HL Aug. 16 1907, cc. 1773–4).
[58] Criminal Appeal Act 1907, s. 4 (1).

Justice, Lord Parker, that their practice had always been to quash unsafe verdicts. 'This is something which we have done and which we continue to do, although it may be we have no lawful authority to do it. To say that we have not done it, and we ought to have power to do it, is quite wrong.'[59] The legal language used to capture the meaning of miscarriage of justice has proved to be fluid and nearly interchangeable. It might be that with the criminal justice's various (and potentially irreconcilable) commitments, to truth, due process, fairness, and rights, it is impossible to capture the legal meaning of miscarriage in any particular form of statutory words.

D. THE GREAT 'EXPERIMENT':[60] HOW DID IT WORK?

In assessing the Court's exercise of its jurisdiction since its inception in relation to appeals on grounds of factual error, there are two relevant areas to consider. First, appeals involving fresh evidence (normally brought under the miscarriage of justice ground);[61] secondly, appeals based on the sole ground that the verdict of the jury was unreasonable (where the evidence heard at the trial is reassessed without addition).[62] In practice the Court has never been overly specific in detailing which ground is utilized when quashing convictions, as between the unreasonable ground and the miscarriage of justice ground; this vagueness contrasts with the developing precision of its exclusionary rules on the hearing of fresh evidence. The relevant time-spans are from 1907 to the reforms of the 1960s, from the post-1966 reformed Court to the 1990s, and from the changes in the 1990s both before and after the Criminal Appeal Act 1995 to the present.

1 VERDICTS AGAINST THE WEIGHT OF THE EVIDENCE

The jurisdiction in the early days is inevitably undeveloped and somewhat inconsistent, which is unsurprising considering that there was not a great deal of uniformity in the personnel staffing the Court. The negative slant of many of the judgments is again unsurprising in view of the judicial and academic antipathy to certain of the powers with which the Court was endowed. Contemporary legal commentators did not welcome the Criminal Appeal Act 1907. In his introduction to an annotated edition of the Act, written in 1908, Sir Harry Poland was extremely critical of the reforms. He stated: 'This Act makes a revolution in the criminal procedure of this country', and

---

[59] Parl. Deb. HL May 12 1966, c. 837. [60] See n. 52 above.
[61] S.4 (1) Criminal Appeal Act, quoted on p. 54 above.
[62] The most thorough survey of cases dealt with by the Court is given by M. Knight, *Criminal Appeals: A Study of the Powers of the Court of Appeal Criminal Division on Appeals against Conviction* (London, 1970) and the later *Supplement 1969–73* (1975) which updates it.

predicted 'its consequences will be mischievous'. He strongly opposed the power given to judges to override a jury verdict, and felt that minor reforms along the lines proposed by the judges themselves would have been preferable.[63] Another commentator, Sibley, expressed a second, though less intense, set of misgivings in his 1908 treatise. In his Preliminary Essay he recounts how the Act was 'passed in the teeth of strong opposition' and encourages the judges to adopt a cautious approach to the exercise of their powers.[64] The opening judgment sets the tone and is unpropitious. In an application for leave to appeal on the ground that the verdict was against the weight of the evidence it is stated: 'There was abundant evidence to go to the jury . . . There ought not to be a re-trial where only proper evidence has been left to the jury.'[65]

These views become a constant refrain in many of the early cases before the Court: 'we are not here to re-try cases which have been heard by a jury.'[66] 'The jury are the judges of fact. The Act was never meant to substitute another form of trial for trial by jury.'[67] There were exceptions to this stance; amidst the restrictive dicta there are cases where the Court did overturn the verdict because they were not satisfied with the evidence, perhaps the most notable being that of *Wallace* in 1931: 'the case against the appellant . . . was not proved with that certainty which is necessary in order to justify a verdict of guilty.'[68] This same exception can be found in *Barnes* in 1942 in which Lord Hewart's statement in *Wallace* is approved of and the conviction quashed because 'this was not a satisfactory verdict',[69] which language pre-dates that of 'lurking doubt' enunciated by Lord Widgery in *Cooper* in 1968.[70] Such decisions are rare and are generally qualified as *exceptional*.[71] Frequently, as in *Barnes*, they involve cases where the trial judge expressed himself as dissatisfied with the verdict, though such an endorsement was not always incontrovertible.[72] They are often cases of very weak identification evidence. From his overview Knight concurs with this conclusion on the limiting approach of the Court to its own jurisdiction: 'from 1907–1966 the Court would not necessarily interfere either where the trial judge expressed his strong dislike of the jury's finding of guilt, or where the Court themselves felt it probably wrong.'[73] A fair

---

[63] See n. 40 above, 8 and 14.   [64] See n. 10 above.

[65] *Williamson* (1908) 1 Cr. App. R 3. The reference in this and other cases is to 're-trial' by the exercise of the powers of the Court, not by a jury, which possibility was not authorized by the 1907 Act. However, to some extent, the use of the phrase 're-trial' is itself confusing.

[66] *McNair* (1909) 2 Cr. App. R 2, 4.

[67] *Simpson* (1909) 2 Cr. App. R 128, 130.

[68] 23 Cr. App. R 32, 35 (Lord Hewart).

[69] 28 Cr. App. R 141, 149.   [70] 53 Cr. App. R 82; [1969] 1 All ER 32.

[71] See Pattenden, n. 22 above, 141–4.

[72] The Court of Appeal in *Barnes*, n. 69 above, goes out of its way to quote at length the judge's summing up as a strong indication that the judge was very unhappy with the evidence against the accused. See also *Hopkins—Husson* (1949) 34 Cr. App. R 47.

[73] See n. 62 above, 125.

summary of the developed position is given in the Privy Council judgment in *Aladesuru* in 1955 where Lord Tucker characterizes English criminal appeals: 'it has long been established that the appeal is not by way of re-hearing as in civil appeals from a judge sitting alone, but is a limited appeal which precludes the court from reviewing the evidence and making its own valuation thereof.'[74] He goes on to criticize the use of the phrase 'a verdict against the weight of the evidence', which appears in early reports, stress-ing that no such ground of appeal exists. Again, in *McGrath* in 1949 Lord Goddard gives a robust version of the narrow approach: 'Where there is evidence on which a jury can act and there has been a proper direction to the jury this court cannot substitute itself for the jury and re-try the case. That is not our function. If we took any other attitude, it would strike at the very root of trial by jury.'[75]

2 FRESH EVIDENCE CASES

The generally negative attitude to appeals on the ground that the verdict was unreasonable (described above) is the backdrop against which to view the more specific area of fresh evidence. The hearing of fresh evidence raises acutely many of the problems associated with the Court of Criminal Appeal carrying out its tasks of remedying miscarriages of justice and thereby dispensing justice. Prior to the 1960s reforms these problems included the Court's apparent unwillingness to substitute its judgment for trial by jury and the relationship between the evidence given at the original trial and the fresh evidence. These foci of attention have their roots in the pre-1907 dilemmas, for which our arguments in this book give a partial explanation, and can be traced in the evolution of the restrictive jurisdiction that devel-ops.[76] Commentaries on the Court's interpretation of its powers are either critical of its narrow approach or respectful of the difficult task that it faces. What we draw attention to is that both the critical and sympathetic inter-pretations, or combinations of them, recognize that whatever its powers there have consistently been strong demands for reform of the Court's prac-tices ever since its inception. When such proposals for reform are not visi-ble they are latent, but under certain conditions the latest miscarriage appears to resurrect them.

There were no specific provisions relating to the manner in which fresh evidence should be processed in the 1907 Act. From the width of the powers in Section 9 on hearing witnesses (s. 9 (b) and (c)), and appointing a special commissioner (s. 9 (d)) or an assessor (s. 9 (e)) in cases involving specialized knowledge, the potential for a broad rehearing of cases was

---

[74] 39 Cr. App. R 184, 185.   [75] 2 All ER 495, 497.

[76] For a succinct, critical summary of the failure of the Court to deal with substantive questions of guilt, including cases of fresh evidence, see G. Williams, *Proof of Guilt: A Study of the English Criminal Trial* (London, 1963), 329–4 and 114–19.

there. The crucial limitation comes with the words 'if they think it necessary or expedient in the interest of justice', since this wording gave the Court the discretion to limit its use of these powers in line with its general approach towards the overturning of jury verdicts on factual grounds. In the course of our account of the Court's construction of its jurisdiction in fresh evidence cases, it will become apparent that Section 9 was used with great discretion, and that, for example, the relevant subsections on expert evidence were hardly ever activated.[77]

A reading of the 20th edition, 1918, of Archbold, *Criminal Pleading Evidence and Practice* on the Section 9 powers does little to indicate the developing reluctance to hear fresh evidence. A series of cases are cited under s. 9 (b) in which witnesses were heard, with no recognition of the hesitance shown by the Court nor of the *exceptional* nature of each instance. By 1931 the 25th edition shows slight signs of recognizing the restrictive use of the powers in relation to s. 9 (b): 'the court will only act upon this power under very special circumstances',[78] and likewise for s. 9 (d) and (e). In the 35th edition in 1962 the fully-fledged jurisdiction is described in a detailed account in para. 899 'Leave to Call Additional Evidence', in which the lines of exclusion constructed by the Court over the years crystallize into an armoury of reasons for the rejection of fresh evidence. Any hint of positive reception is hastily neutralized and qualified by the ubiquitous tag 'exceptional': 'It is only in the most exceptional circumstances and subject to what may be described as exceptional conditions, that the court is ever willing to listen to additional evidence.'[79]

A reading of the reported cases in the area mirrors this development in the Court's interpretation of its jurisdiction, traced through the pages of successive editions of Archbold. In the early days a pattern emerges from the mosaic of individual cases of strongly worded rejections of leave to hear fresh evidence, interspersed with sporadic instances of evidence being heard. As with the earlier discussion of appeals on the ground of the verdict being against the weight of the evidence, it is not easy to discern the logic that divides the occasional admission from the more widespread refusal. One must assume that before the full rigidifying of the doctrine into its consolidated form, the potential for discretion produced contradictory conclusions in differently constituted courts.

The earliest limitation comes in *Mortimer* in 1908 where s. 9 (b) and (c) are considered for the first time, and where Lord Alverstone (a fervent opponent of the Act) somewhat arbitrarily states: 'This power was not meant to be exercised for supplementing or supporting the case made at the trial where the witnesses could have been called.'[80] It is clear from the case report that the Court was convinced of the appellant's guilt and was not

---

[77] See our analysis in section B of Ch. 5.   [78] 329.   [79] 366.
[80] 1 Cr. App. R 20, 22.

prepared to entertain the hearing of any evidence to the contrary. This view is reiterated in the same year in *Mason and Soper*[81] and in *Winkworth*.[82] Even when fresh evidence was heard as in *Betridge*,[83] it was done so grudgingly with a preference stated for ordering a new trial, and a marked distaste for assuming the role of retrying the issues. In *Gowlett (alias Woodford)*[84] the presumption against hearing fresh evidence seems to affect the outcome of the appeal, in that although the fresh evidence of an alibi is heard, the fact of its availability at the time of trial casts doubt upon its efficacy at the appeal.

In 1909 the theme of fresh evidence and new trials is again rehearsed in *Colclough* on consideration of s. 9 (b). Fresh evidence of witnesses who cast doubt on the original evidence was heard under the s. 9 (b) powers, but the Court states its reluctance to participate in the role of surrogate jury. 'If every witness who appeared at the trial were sent for, and the case gone into again, we should be substituting a trial by judges for a trial by jury—in this county a privilege of great worth to everybody.'[85] An indirect plea for the power to order a new trial follows. The case of *Perry and Harvey*[86] in the same year is a good illustration of the early dilemmas sometimes faced in the area of fresh evidence. It is a slightly more liberal judgment, which acknowledges that defendants should not be penalized for the mistaken strategies adopted by defence counsel. Liberality on this point disappears in later cases. As time passes the language of exception on the hearing of fresh evidence becomes even stronger (especially if the evidence was available at the time of trial—see *Dutt*—'in the rarest possible instance'[87] and *Mason*—'with very great caution . . . very exceptional circumstances'[88]). This hardening of attitude finds its culmination in *Parks* in 1961, by which time the discretion has been structured on specific principles: 'First, the evidence that it is sought to call must be evidence which was not available at the trial. Secondly . . . it must be evidence relevant to the issues. Thirdly, it must be evidence that is credible evidence in the sense that it is well capable of belief.'[89] In *Parks* certain evidence was, despite the strictures against admitting fresh evidence, admitted and in view of the Court's opinion that it might have cast a reasonable doubt on the mind of the jury, the conviction for indecent assault was quashed.

The principled nature of the structuring for admitting fresh evidence under Section 9 is open to question. What sometimes appear to be at stake in the cases are judicial suspicions of the appellant's motives and the implication that this might encourage prisoners to think that they might be able

[81] 1 Cr. App. R 73.   [82] 1 Cr. App. R 129.
[83] (1908) 1 Cr. App. R 236.   [84] (1908) 1 Cr. App. R 238.
[85] 2 Cr. App. R 84, 85.   [86] 2 Cr. App. R 89.
[87] (1912) 8 Cr. App. R 51, 57.   [88] (1923) 17 Cr. App. R 160, 161.
[89] 3 All ER 633, 634.

to arrange a second chance for themselves.[90] And in the context of the Home Secretary's power of reference to the Court of Appeal: 'it is clearly undesirable to encourage astute criminals dishonestly to by-pass the court after the conviction in the hope that fresh evidence, genuine or otherwise, might be got before the court as the result of a petition to the Home Secretary.'[91] In *Collins*, Lord Goddard again shows a degree of suspicion of appellants and their witnesses in explaining the limits on admission of fresh evidence. 'It is very easy after a person has been convicted to find witnesses who are willing to come forward and say this, that, or the other thing.'[92]

3 Fresh evidence and the Home Secretary

The relationship between the pre-existing powers of the Home Secretary and the new jurisdiction of the Court of Criminal Appeal was never fully worked out in 1907. There was a supposition, implicit in the debates, that the Court would supplant the role of the Home Secretary. However, by the 1950s when the restrictions on fresh evidence were fairly firmly established, certain investigative areas seem to be pushed back towards the Home Secretary, especially those involving events which occur after conviction. A line of authority evolves to the effect that the Court will not hear directly evidence of events occurring after conviction, especially confessions by third parties.[93] The alternative route is by way of reference from the Home Secretary, or as in *Rowland*,[94] an inquiry commissioned by the Home Secretary, which deals with evidence completely separate from the Court.

Linked to this point is the wider issue of whether the Court will relax its restrictions on fresh evidence when it hears referred as opposed to direct appeals. It did so in *McGrath* in 1949[95] and in *Collins* in 1950[96] (both cases contain in passing strong justifications for the Court's stance on fresh evidence). The relaxation is accounted for in terms of assisting the Home Secretary's 'wider discretion'. This is a problematic area for the Court since there is not a great logical distinction between further evidence presented by an appellant direct and evidence which comes via the Home Secretary's

---

[90] See the implications of this on leave to appeal with a view to call fresh evidence as to diminished responsibility, in *McMenemy* [1962] Crim. LR 44, and insanity, in *Dashwood* [1943] K.B. 1.   [91] *Sparkes* (1956) 40 Cr. App. R 83, 91.

[92] (1950) 34 Cr. App. R 146, 148. In any event there are still exceptions—see the inconsistency between two cases decided in the same month, October 1956, *Harrigan* [1957] Crim. LR 52 and *Musial* [1956] Crim. LR 843, and the faint liberalization in a decision like *Gatt* [1963] Crim. LR 426.

[93] See *Rowland* [1947] 1 K.B. 460, *Thomas* (1959) 43 Cr. App. R 210, *Robinson* [1962] Crim. LR 473, and for the Court's reasons the commentary on *Green* [1963] Crim. LR 840.

[94] Inquiry into the confession evidence made by David John Ware of the murder of Olive Bachin in respect of which murder *Walter Graham Rowland* was convicted, Cd. 7049 (London, 1947). See Bob Woffinden's analysis of this case, *Miscarriages of Justice* (London, 1987), ch. 2 'Walter Rowland'.   [95] See n. 75 above.

[96] See n. 92 above.

reference. The only possible difference is that in the latter case the Home Office has to some extent investigated and officially sanctioned the evidence. In *Sparkes* in 1956[97] the matter is left open, leaving the Court free to decide each case on its own merits.

Inevitably a certain tension exists in reference cases, because frequently the reference is made after an original appeal has been dismissed, and the Court's initial judgment is being questioned, even though the reference will contain matters further to those considered at the appeal. The 1968 Justice Report on this subject stresses that: 'The overriding factor governing the exercise of the powers available to the Home Secretary is a proper concern to avoid even the appearance of interfering with the independence of the judiciary.'[98] The continuing parallel jurisdiction was, as we have shown earlier in this chapter, the product of history, and developed into a pragmatic if unsatisfactory coexistence. The problems centre on the contrast between the investigative, flexible powers of dealing with evidence possessed by the executive, and the very restrictive stance adopted by the Court towards its own discretionary powers; this is highlighted by the additional restrictions imposed by rules of evidence. The result is often the creation of a lacuna between the executive and the judiciary into which prisoners fall. The liberalizing of the fresh evidence impasse brought about by the reforms of the 1960s improved the situation somewhat, but there is still the potential for friction.[99] That potential for friction as a matter of constitutional propriety might have been reduced with the creation of a new investigative body independent of the Home Office by the Criminal Appeal Act 1995. But such a change does not reduce the differences of approach to investigating or determining the existence or import of relevant evidence, and as such the potential for friction remains.[100]

From this short overview it can be seen that at some point around the 1950s the high watermark of judicial non-receptivity was reached. The various decisions on fresh evidence coalesce to produce a general situation (always with exceptions)[101] where evidence would be disallowed either if it was available at the time of the trial, or if it concerned events occurring after the conviction, e.g. subsequent confessions.[102] The developing narrowness of the Court's interpretation of its powers and the broadening criticism of its authority led to strong pressure to bring about reform and the ensuing reforms of the following decade.

---

[97] See n. 91 above.   [98] See n. 12 above, 7.
[99] See the logjam that develops over the Luton post office murder when the case is referred back four times. See Woffinden, n. 94 above, chs. 6 and 7; L. Kennedy (ed.), *Wicked Beyond Belief: The Luton Murder Case* (St Albans, 1980).
[100] See our analysis of the Criminal Cases Review Commission in section D of Ch. 5.
[101] The very inconsistency of the Court is criticized by Glanville Williams, n. 76 above, 133–6. In commenting on the shortcomings in the practices of criminal appeal he says: 'one of the greatest is the erratic way in which the court sometimes allows fresh evidence in the appeal and sometimes does not.'   [102] See nn. 93 and 94 above.

E. THE REFORMS OF THE 1960s

There were two strands to the legislative reforms effected during the 1960s. One concerned the issue of new trials generally, and in particular where fresh evidence was involved. The other strand resulted from a wider review of the whole working of the Court of Criminal Appeal, which was carried out by the Donovan Committee in 1965. The products of these reassessments were the 1964 Criminal Appeal Act (on retrials) and the 1966 Criminal Appeal Act (implementing the Donovan proposals). They were consolidated in 1968 to form the Criminal Appeal Act 1968, a complete successor to the 1907 Act.

1 THE RETRIAL POWER: A BACKGROUND

Proposals for giving the Court of Criminal Appeal power to order a retrial, as an alternative to either upholding or quashing convictions, were prevalent in many of the Bills considered before the passing of the 1907 Act, and resurfaced in an amendment to the Criminal Justice Bill in 1948.[103] The case for granting such a power centred on two particular features of the Court's jurisdiction. The first concerned cases where it was felt that guilty persons were escaping on a legal technicality, i.e. where the judge's misdirection or other irregularity had occurred at the trial but the Court felt unable to exercise the proviso[104] with confidence. The second concerned cases that involved the reception of fresh evidence. Both features shared the same worries about the relationship between the Court and the jury, and the extent to which the Court could function in the role of surrogate jury. The 1948 debates on the amendment to give the Court of Appeal a general power to order a retrial focused largely on the exercise of the proviso and the wider issue of the merits of second trials, with little discussion of the narrower subject of fresh evidence. Lord Goddard, the Lord Chief Justice, strongly advocated the granting of such a power; it was claimed in the course of the debate that the three previous Lord Chief Justices also welcomed such an addition to the powers of the Court. Opponents of the measure stressed the undesirability of allowing a defendant to stand trial twice, and the difficulty of guaranteeing a fair trial in such circumstances. In the event the Lords supported the amendment but it did not survive passage through the Commons. The next Parliamentary debate on the topic

---

[103] Shortly after the high profile *Rowland* case and the report of Home Secretary's inquiry into it, see nn. 93 and 94 above.

[104] 'Provided that the Court may, notwithstanding that they are of opinion that the point raised in the appeal might be decided in favour of the appellant, dismiss the appeal if they consider that no substantial miscarriage of justice has actually occurred' (Criminal Appeal Act 1907, s. 4(1)).

occurred again in the Lords in 1952, the occasion a motion tabled by Lord Goddard on the powers of the Court of Criminal Appeal. Here discussion centred on the issue of the handling of fresh evidence, which was the main concern raised by Lord Goddard.

The catalyst for the 1952 debate was the recent case of *Devlin and Burns*. The case is unreported but described by Lord Goddard in the House of Lords debate. In the course of his discussion he raises some of the complex problems associated with the self-perception by the Court of its practices. The key elements of Devlin and Burns' appeal from their convictions for murder in the course of burglary were alibis, an admission of perjury by a significant witness, and a confession to the murder by another person. Lord Goddard is particularly concerned with difficulties associated with the Court of Appeal considering such fresh evidence rather than a second jury: 'But how could we, without usurping the functions of a jury, which is something our Court has always refused to do.' But, beyond these usual arguments he suggests that, in relation to the key witness, had the Court considered the issue of perjury, then: 'Supposing that we had said that we did find that she had committed perjury, how could she then have been tried afterwards by a jury? The prejudice that would be against her, the Court of Appeal having found that she had committed perjury, would be so great that she could not, I should think, expect to get fairly tried.'[105] So here, as in other cases, the practices of the law create their own problems. The conditions associated with fairness apparently restrain the Court from its ability to search for the truth. In the actual case the Court of Criminal Appeal had indeed declined to consider the new evidence. In the absence of the ability to order a new trial, the evidence was not heard by the Court; the necessary but unsatisfactory compromise was the commissioning of an extra-judicial inquiry by the Home Secretary, as in the *Rowland* case in 1947.[106] This had the disadvantages for the assessment of evidence of being conducted in private, without cross-examination and not under oath.[107] In addition the witnesses to the inquiry were given an indemnity against their own prosecution. The almost unanimous conclusion of the participants in the 1952 debate was that a new trial was the appropriate forum in which to hear significant fresh evidence, especially of events that have occurred post-conviction. It was anticipated that the power would be 'used very sparingly . . . in proper cases'.[108] Caveats against granting such a new power to the Court concerned the problems of ensuring fairness at a second trial.

[105] Parl. Deb. HL 8 May 1952, cc. 747–55.

[106] Inquiry into certain matters arising subsequent to the conviction at Liverpool Assizes on 27 February 1952 of *Edward Francis Devlin and Alfred Burns* of the murder of Beatrice Alice Rimmer, Cd. 8522 (London, 1952). And see nn. 93 and 94 above.

[107] Not all inquiries share concern over these apparent disadvantages; see Sir John May's *Interim Report on the Maguire Case*, HC 556 (London, 1990) 1.5 at p. 2.

[108] See n. 105 above, cc. 758–9.

The Tucker Committee, set up in 1954 to consider the issue, concurred broadly with the feeling in the House of Lords. They decided in favour of the power to grant a retrial in appropriate fresh evidence cases, but by a majority of five to three, against a general power of retrial. Their recommendation in favour of retrials was based in part on the previous practice of the Court who 'have never considered it to be any part of their duty to substitute their verdict for that of the jury'.[109] Given this attitude they conclude that in cases where the value of the new evidence has to be weighed against the evidence given at trial, this has to be done by a jury. However, they endorse the Court's developed restrictions on the hearing of fresh evidence, even within the context of the new power, which amounts to a very conservative stance. In the debates on the 1964 Bill, there is a widespread feeling that the power to order retrials would enable the Court to adopt a more relaxed view towards the admission of fresh evidence.

This was the position taken by the second interim Report of the Justice Committee on Criminal Appeals, published in January 1964. They recommended in favour of new trials in fresh evidence cases, but their main contention was 'that the benefits of the Bill would be negligible unless the court adopted a wider interpretation of fresh evidence.'[110] In particular they highlight the problems raised by the 'not available at time of trial' requirement, which serves to exclude evidence not called due to bad legal advice or because witnesses could not be traced. In their report they stress the importance of a wider interpretation, and recommend that: 'the Court . . . should have an absolute discretion as to the nature or availability of the evidence which warrants a new trial, which should not be limited by statute or rules of practice.'[111]

2 THE REPORT OF THE DONOVAN COMMITTEE[112]

The wider reforms in 1966 were based on the recommendations of the Donovan Committee, set up in 1965 to review the working of the Court of Criminal Appeal. Its central concerns were the status and the composition of the Court, though an examination of its powers and practices also came within its remit. One of the motivations for the appointment of the Committee was the large increase in the workload of the Court after the war, and especially around the early 1960s. Between 1956 and 1963 the

---

[109] Report of the Departmental Committee on New Trials in Criminal Cases, the *Tucker Committee Report*, Cd. 9150 (London, 1954), para. 6. They conceded that there would remain a need for extra-judicial inquiries in cases where the fresh evidence was not admissible (paras. 30–2).

[110] Reprinted in the Justice Report, *Criminal Appeals* (London, 1964), para. 75. The second interim report appears as paras. 74–92 of the full report.

[111] Ibid., para. 84.

[112] *Donovan Committee Report*, Interdepartmental Committee on the Court of Criminal Appeal, Cmnd. 2755 (London, 1965).

number of applications for leave to appeal doubled and the number of appeals increased threefold.

The main focus of the report was the transmutation of the Court of Criminal Appeal into the Criminal Division of the Court of Appeal, with anticipated attendant benefits in its status and in the continuity of its composition. The actual changes were not that significant in that the Court would still be staffed by a fair number of puisne judges, with the addition of some lord justices. Criticism of lack of consistency in judgments, which partly prompted the reforms, applied more to areas of substantive law and sentencing; on such issues it could be argued that the more eminent the judge the more consistent the result. However, it is interesting to note that whereas in 1966 the source for improvement in the working of the Court was seen to lie in enhancing the status of the judges sitting, more recent debates have focused on the possible introduction of a review body, not wholly judicial in composition.[113]

The Committee reviewed the powers of the Court in relation to appeals on questions of fact, and considered the issues of fresh evidence, and of the adequacy of the grounds of appeal. Their criticisms were restrained, and expressed in the context of sympathy with the Court's problematic task in reviewing issues of fact. With regard to fresh evidence criticism of the Court's self-imposed limits on reception of such evidence did appear, and wider provision was recommended, i.e. fresh evidence should be heard if there was 'a reasonable explanation . . . for the failure to place it before the jury'.[114] However, they did not recommend legislating to this end, preferring to rely on the Lord Chief Justice's assurance to the Home Secretary on future practice, given in the course of the debates on the 1964 Act. The 1966 Bill originally contained no clause on fresh evidence; it was introduced at a relatively late stage as an amendment in the Commons by those less sanguine about judicial pledges.

On the power of the Court to interfere with a conviction the Committee did recommend changes.[115] It acknowledged the Court's refusal to usurp the role of the jury and retry cases, and felt that the language of the 1907 statute, strictly construed, prevented them from overturning a verdict if there was some evidence on which to convict. However it recognized that in individual cases the Court had been prepared to reconsider the jury verdict, and thus act as a jury. The inconsistencies between decisions and the problematic nature of the wording of the 1907 grounds of appeal resulted in a recommendation for reform, though ironically the new wording was the 'unsafe or unsatisfactory' ground rejected in 1907 for its obscurity. The major type of case which worried the Committee was that of

---

[113] Examples of such proposals are given during our analysis of newspaper reporting in Ch. 4, and at n. 167 below.   [114] See n. 112 above, paras. 131–6.
[115] Ibid., paras. 137–50.

wrongful conviction on identification evidence, and the aim of the proposed reform was to make it easier for such disputed identity cases to be re-evaluated if there had been a miscarriage of justice.[116] Another possible area of use anticipated by the Committee was in 'cases of alleged rape where there is substantial evidence of consent, which the jury reject in favour of the woman's denial'.[117]

Other recommended reforms included the rewording of the proviso to omit 'substantial',[118] on the grounds that it was superfluous. In the course of their analysis of the use of the proviso the Committee concluded that the Court had inevitably been coming to conclusions of fact in cases involving its exercise.[119] What this suggests both in relation to the Court's powers and its practices is that their authority permits them to explore facts relevant to appeals as much or as little as they wish. What restrains them is not the language of their powers but the approach that they take to what they believe is the nature of their task. They structure their approach through the legal and constitutional arguments that, in their experience, justify their practices. For example, the basic distinction in the criminal trial process between the judge's responsibility to determine the law and the jury's to adjudicate on the facts of a case encourages Court of Appeal judges to structure their deliberations so as to underpin that key device in the criminal trial. In doing so it is difficult for them, using the rhetorical arguments available to them, wholeheartedly to undertake a rehearing of the facts of the case or to have a completely open attitude to *new* facts. And, in any event, the Court of Appeal cannot simply admit new facts, but only new admissible evidence.

The contemporaneous Justice Report on *Criminal Appeals* of 1964 was far more stringent in its criticisms of the Court's failure to overturn jury verdicts, holding such limitation of their powers to be 'absurd and unjust'.[120] It stresses the fallibility and inexperience of juries, whose verdicts do not warrant such reverential treatment by appeal court judges. Its recommendation for improvement involves either a wider interpretation of the Court's present powers or the addition of a new ground: 'it would not be safe to allow the verdict of the jury to stand having regard to all the evidence.'[121] The Justice Report also contains a long discussion on the availability of legal aid, which is obviously a crucial element in appeals, especially in fresh evidence cases. The overall aim of the recommendations in the Report is: 'to unloosen some of the fetters which the court has

[116] See Justice's Report, *Miscarriages of Justice* (London, 1989) and the Report of the Departmental Committee on Evidence of Identification in Criminal Cases, the *Devlin Report*, HC 338 (London, 1976) for striking evidence that the aims of the reforms were not fulfilled.

[117] See n. 112 above, para. 150.

[118] For the wording of the proviso, see n. 104 above.

[119] The Committee also considered other arguments about other reforms not related to appeals on questions of fact.   [120] See n. 110 above, paras. 58–61.

[121] Ibid., para. 61.

imposed on itself in pursuance of the principle that the verdict of the jury should not be interfered with'.[122] The general thrust of the Justice Report's proposed reforms are similar to those of the Donovan Committee, but the tone is far more critical of the Court's practice.

3 NEW TRIALS AND FRESH EVIDENCE: THE CRIMINAL APPEAL ACT 1964

The Act implemented the findings of the Tucker Committee, allowing re-trials: 'Where an appeal against conviction is allowed by the Court of Criminal Appeal by reason only of evidence received or available to be received by that Court under section 9 of the Criminal Appeal Act 1907 and it appears to the Court that the interests of justice so require ...'[123] Logically, if the previous restrictions on admitting fresh evidence had been premised on the absence of a retrial power, the Act should allow for liberalization. But, as senior judges indicated, there were other reasons. In thé House of Lords Lord Parker, the Lord Chief Justice, justified the Court's restricting new evidence in order to prevent a prisoner keeping witnesses 'up his sleeve'[124] to use in the Court of Criminal Appeal. But he also emphasized the elasticity of the restrictions on new evidence,[125] and suggested that with the introduction of a retrial power more fresh evidence cases might be heard.[126] The debate in the Lords contained little direct criticism of the Court. The Commons were less restrained, with speakers deploring what they thought was an unduly narrow interpretation placed on Section 9, narrower than Parliament originally intended. Section 9 says only that the court shall have power to hear additional evidence. It does not say anything about it being new evidence, or fresh evidence, or about it being material, or any of the principles on which the Court of Criminal Appeal has habitually excluded fresh evidence over the years.[127]

Some speakers wanted Parliament to legislate within the Bill for the occasions on which fresh evidence would be heard, rather than leave the

---

[122] Ibid., para. 10.   [123] S.1 (1).

[124] 'A prisoner cannot, for instance, keep an alibi witness "up his sleeve" and not call him, and then go to the Court of Criminal Appeal and say, "I want to call this witness" ' (Parl. Deb. HL 14 Jan. 1964, c. 533).

[125] '... preserve within those conditions a certain elasticity' (ibid., c. 533). For cases illustrating this point see Knight, n. 62 above, 94–5.

[126] Lord Parker recognized that 'To-day a prisoner is advised that his chances of having a conviction quashed on the grounds of fresh evidence are indeed remote', so very few applications are made. Implicit in his assumption that the Bill would encourage more applications was the need for a relaxation of the stringent limitations on admission of fresh evidence hitherto imposed: 'when the Court has power to grant a retrial many prisoners who want a retrial, as they do, will not hesitate to put forward that evidence and apply to the Court' (Parl. Deb. HL 28 January 1964, c. 1103).

[127] See Parl. Deb. HC 13 February 1964, c. 591 (Mr S. Silverman). Sydney Silverman's view was well-informed. He was involved in both the Timothy Evans and Walter Rowland miscarriage cases; see R. T. Paget and S. S. Silverman, *Hanged—and Innocent* (London, 1953).

discretion to judges. But the Home Secretary, Mr. H. Brooke, adopted a hands-off approach. 'Over the years the Court of Criminal Appeal has evolved principles by which it is guided . . . It may be that the availability of a power to order a new trial will lead the court to revise the principles which it has hitherto found it necessary to apply . . . [However,] The Bill does not interfere with the court's discretion in that matter.'[128] Niall MacDermot, a member of the Justice Committee, received those assurances with scepticism. He felt that provisions were needed to ensure that: 'the discretion shall always be maintained and shall not be whittled down again by principles which purport to be laid down by the court, thereby restricting successor members of the court.'[129] In the face of these criticisms the Attorney General announced: 'I am authorised to say that it may be that if this Bill is enacted the court will consider it desirable to review its practice having regard to the provisions of the Bill.' A firmer pledge came in the Third Reading of the Bill in the Commons with the Lord Chief Justice's assurance to the Home Secretary:

He has authorised me to say that, while it is essential for the court to decide what evidence it will treat as admissible, it is not bound by its previous practice as to the admission of evidence, and that it can and will review the practice in the light of the Bill, the governing principle being to ensure so far as possible that there has been no miscarriage of justice.[130]

In addition to concern with the narrowness of interpretation given to the power to consider fresh evidence, the Commons discussed the more technical question of when a retrial would be ordered. On the law as it stood before 1964, if the Court thought, in the light of the new evidence, that the jury would have felt a reasonable doubt, they should quash the conviction. *Harding* is a good illustration regarding both the attitude of the Court to fresh evidence, 'exceptional, perhaps unprecedented, and never likely to be repeated', and defining the test the Court of Appeal then applied.

Looking at that evidence with care, and recognising the force of the rest of the evidence in this case, we are clearly of the opinion that, if this evidence had been offered in the Court below, there might have been upon the part of the jury a reasonable doubt as to the guilt of the appellant; or, to put it in another way, we cannot say that, if that evidence had been offered, the jury must inevitably have come to the same conclusion. In those circumstances the only conclusion which is possible for this Court is to say that the appeal must be allowed, and the conviction quashed.[131]

The 1964 Act changed the position in that it offered another option in cases where it was unclear what the jury would have decided; in such intermediate cases a retrial could now be ordered. It was anticipated that this would be

---

[128] Parl. Deb., n. 126 above, cc. 589–90.   [129] Ibid., c. 631.
[130] Parl. Deb. HC 30 April 1964, col. 722.
[131] *Harding* (1936) 25 Cr. App. R 190, 195 and 197. The case deals with the admission of fresh medical evidence.

especially appropriate where there was conflict between the two sets of evidence, the old and the new.[132] At that time the opportunity for ordering retrials and for reinstating the jury to its rightful constitutional position was considered the most suitable solution to the fresh-evidence dilemma and related problems. In the Parliamentary debates it was acknowledged by members of the senior judiciary that the power would be used rarely, but this expectation was thought to be due to the practices of restrictive admission of fresh evidence. With liberalization on that issue, the cases available for retrial could be expected to increase and public confidence or at least that of the press could be restored. The Lord Chancellor, Lord Dilhorne, referred directly to the press: 'I know that we introduce it to only "two cheers" from *The Times*.' Lord Silken stressed the influence of one recent high profile case: 'I imagine that even now nothing would have been done but for the case of "Lucky" Gordon.' Lord Parker organized his arguments around the need to regain public confidence: 'something which really commands public support'.[133] But the relative infrequency of the Court's use of the power over the following years, at least until the 1990s, did not fully bear out the expectations of the 1964 reform. This being the case, then, a number of questions arise. Why do the expectations associated with reform proposals appear not to achieve what their proponents anticipate? What next set of reform proposals will succeed those already enacted, and how successful are they likely to be?

4 THE CRIMINAL APPEAL ACT 1966[134]

The Act introduced a power to quash a conviction, or quash a conviction and order a retrial where the conviction is 'unsafe or unsatisfactory', or where there has been a 'material irregularity' at trial.[135] In the course of Parliamentary debate on the introduction of the 'unsafe or unsatisfactory' wording, the Lord Chief Justice claimed that the changes would not affect the Court's practice, because the Court had all along been acting in the spirit of the new legislation. Indeed in referring to the quashing of unsafe convictions he declared: 'This is something which we have done and which we continue to do, although it may be we have no lawful authority to do it.'[136]

---

[132] It has been argued (see the Editorial in the *Criminal Law Review*, Feb. 1964) that the power to order retrials worsens the appellant's position, since without it he or she would have been acquitted by the Court of Criminal Appeal directly. However, this opinion ignores the possibility that a wider band of cases of fresh evidence will be heard because of the power, instead of being dismissed for want of jurisdiction to hear the evidence.

[133] Parl. Deb. HL 14 January 1964, cc. 523, 529, 531.

[134] This Act implements the Donovan Committee's recommendations (n. 112 above).

[135] S.4 (1).

[136] Parl. Deb. HL 12 May 1966, c. 837. This judicial flexibility contrasts with a certain modesty in the Court's self-portrayal on other occasions. For example, the Court of Appeal judgment allowing the appeal of the Birmingham Six in 1991: 'The Court of Appeal (Criminal Division) is the creature of statute . . . We have no inherent jurisdiction apart from statute.' *McIlkenny and others* (1991) 93 Cr. App. R 287, 310.

Other speakers, especially in the Commons, were less complacent about the Court's exercise of its powers. In the course of the Second Reading debate it was stressed by the Government that there had been in the past a restrictive line of interpretation, and that it hoped for a more liberal attitude to the revised 'unsafe or unsatisfactory' ground. They wanted the Court to 'feel themselves more free than they have been in the past to interfere with a verdict of the jury about which there must be a considerable measure of doubt'.[137] A similar scepticism inspired the moving of the amendment on fresh evidence, which becomes Section 5 of the 1966 Act, eventually consolidated into Section 23 of the 1968 Act, together with most of the original Section 9 of the 1907 Act. The clause incorporated into statutory form the recommendations of the Donovan Committee on fresh evidence. In the Parliamentary debates several speakers referred to the need for a 'very liberal interpretation', and specifically hoped that a 'reasonable explanation' for failure to adduce the evidence at trial would not exclude reasons such as bad legal advice or misunderstanding on the part of the defendant as to the relevance of the evidence.[138] An assurance given by the Lord Chief Justice to the government spokesman that the clause 'reproduces the court's present approach' did not offer great comfort, given the vagaries of the Court's relationship with its statutory powers. The concern expressed in Parliament was justified; the cases of *Dougherty*[139] and *Shields and Patrick*[140] are clear examples of the Court's rejection of bad legal advice as a reasonable explanation. The case of *Kelly*[141] does indicate a fresh attitude to fresh evidence in the light of the 1964 Act, but the trend to that effect was not by any means sustained uninterruptedly.[142]

The other significant change in the grounds of appeal—'the material irregularity ground'—demonstrates a somewhat piecemeal approach to reform. It was introduced as a by-product of the rewriting of the proviso. The omission of 'substantial' before 'miscarriage of justice' in the wording of the proviso[143] meant that the 'miscarriage of justice' ground could no longer remain, and so 'material irregularity' was selected to replace it. There appears to have been no lengthy consideration of the nature of possible irregularities. Later, cases involving non-disclosure of evidence by the prosecution or police contrary to the current guidelines are taken to come within this ground.[144] Many speakers called for a redrafting of the whole

137   Parl. Deb. 11 July 1966 c. 1146 (Mr. Taverne).
138   For analysis of the potential difficulties arising from the wording of the section, see M. Dean, 'Criminal Appeal Act 1966', *Criminal Law Review* [1966], 534–48, esp. 544–5.
139   Discussed extensively in the *Devlin Report* (1976), n. 116 above.
140   [1977] Crim. LR 281.   141   [1965] 2 All ER 250.
142   See Pattenden, n. 22 above, 133–9.
143   See n. 104 above for the wording of the proviso.
144   See for example *Sansom* (1991) 92 Cr. App. R 115. P. O'Connor QC, who has been involved in many recent high profile criminal appeals, has demonstrated how significant undisclosed evidence has been; 'Unfair Fighting', *The Guardian Review*, 22 June 93.

of the section on the grounds of appeal, but the government felt the revisions left the section in a workable form. There was some disagreement on the overall impact of the Act, with the government claiming its measures to be 'important and radical', while perhaps a more prevalent view held that the alterations were not of enormous consequence.[145]

F. THE COURT'S DECISIONS AFTER THE 1960S REFORMS

According to most commentators an attempt to upset a jury verdict will rarely succeed if the trial has been well conducted, the relevant evidence heard, and no serious misdirections given to the jury. The impact of the 1960s reforms on this problematic area of the Court's jurisdiction seems to have been minimal, though assessment has been difficult as almost all of the judgments at this time of such appeals went unreported.[146] The uncertainty as to the level of proof employed on appeals, and the inconsistency of outcome in certain cases, reflect the problematic nature of the subjective reassessment of evidence. In the House of Lords debates,[147] which followed the case of *Luckhurst*,[148] the Court of Appeal was criticized for its implicit interpretation of the burden of proof. Although the Court acknowledged that the prosecution case contained 'considerable improbabilities', it was thought that the defence's version of events contained 'equal if not greater improbabilities'. This is to replace the notion of reasonable doubt, let alone 'lurking doubt', with the lower standard of the balance of probabilities. Ironically this case was based on unsafe identification evidence, exactly the type of appeal which proponents of the 1960s reforms hoped to facilitate.[149] Knight claims to detect some change in the language of the Court in dealing with unsafe verdicts, a shift from the earlier more forcefully negative phraseology.[150] This is indeed clearly marked in *Cooper*, where

[145] Many commentaries on the new Act did not envisage a great change in approach. D. A. Thomas, 'The Criminal Appeal Act 1966', *Modern Law Review*, 30 (1967), 64–7; M. Dean, n. 138 above; A. Samuels, 'The New Court of Criminal Appeal', *Solicitors Journal*, 110 (1966), 714–16; R. J. Walker, 'The Criminal Appeal Act', *New Law Journal*, 116 (1966), 1205–7.

[146] The leading case on the Court's approach is *Cooper*, n. 70 above. The attitude outlined by Lord Widgery in that case and his use of the phrase 'lurking doubt' as a means of identifying when a conviction is 'unsafe or unsatisfactory' has been adopted in very few subsequent cases (see discussion below).

[147] 11 March 1969 cc. 407–54, and 25 November 1969 cc. 1223–48.

[148] [1967] Crim. LR 292.

[149] See the strong criticism of the Court's decision in the case in the editorial, 'But also seen to be done', *New Law Journal*, 118 (1968), 169.

[150] See n. 62 above. Knight surveyed every judgment of the Court from October 1966 to January 1968, and in the follow-up Supplement assessed the situation post-*Cooper* from 1969 to 1973, though on a less thorough sample. His conclusions suggest no marked change in the practice of the Court, though he does point to successful appeals which pre-1966 would almost certainly have failed. (See pp.135–6 and in the Supplement pp. 63–9.) The continued upholding of other worrying verdicts, e.g. *Luckhurst*, n. 148 above, and *Jones* [1969] Crim. LR 186, counterbalances these examples.

Widgery LJ draws a line of demarcation between the pre- and post-1966 powers, and in the vaguest of subjective tests, enjoins the Court to:

ask itself . . . whether there is not some lurking doubt in our minds which makes us wonder whether an injustice has been done. This is a reaction which may not be based strictly on the evidence as such; it is a reaction which can be produced by the general feel of the case as the court experiences it.[151]

This interpretation certainly shifts the terrain from the old requirement, the supposedly objective standard of the perverse jury verdict. Yet in practice, despite the significantly different language, it appears that little had changed. Lord Widgery's new approach was 'more honoured in the breach than the observance'. Indeed according to the former Registrar of the Court of Appeal (Criminal Division), Master Thompson, whose views are recounted in the 1989 Justice Report on *Miscarriages of Justice*, 'some of the senior judges did not regard Lord Widgery's interpretation as authoritative.'[152] The phrase 'lurking doubt' has passed into the language of appellate judgments but the likelihood of upsetting a verdict on that sole ground, as representing its lack of safety, is still remote. Once again it is apparent how the general language used to try to capture or identify what amounts to a miscarriage of justice and express an open-minded attitude to it does not survive its more concrete interpretation. Such interpretation is likely to resonate more or less effectively within different systems of communication. 'Lurking doubt' may have a resonance within general social communication, or in the hands of the press, which Court of Appeal judges might well be unable or unwilling to replicate.

The constant refrain in the Annual Reports of the organization Justice, when surveying the Court of Appeal (Criminal Division) from 1965 to the 1990s, is of the limited use of the Court's powers. In 1972 the Annual Report concludes: 'that the "unsafe and unsatisfactory" provision of the 1968 Act has very nearly become a dead letter'.[153] This is partly due to the fact that the perceived negativity of the Court's stance leads to standard legal advice that, in the absence of judicial error, limited grounds for appeal exist. Many potential appellants are thus deterred from even applying for leave.[154] Again, in the 1983 Annual Report, in response to the Government's Reply to the Home Affairs Committee Report on *Miscarriages of Justice*,[155] there is strong condemnation of the self-limiting attitude of the court:

---

[151] See n. 70 above.   [152] See n. 116 above, 48.   [153] 27.

[154] The converse of that situation appears to have occurred during the 1990s. According to Lord Taylor, interviewed in *The Guardian* of 20 July 1992, the publicity accompanying recent successful appeals produced a 26% increase in the number of appeals received in the first five months of 1992, compared with the same period in 1991. See our analysis of his views as reported in the press, in Ch. 4.

[155] Home Affairs Committee 6th Report Session 1981–82, *Miscarriages of Justice*, HC 421 (London, 1982).

the Court has tied its own hands so that only a bad mistake by the trial judge in summing-up, some legal technicality, or fresh evidence, as narrowly defined by the 1968 Act, will result in the upsetting of a conviction . . . Can we expect that the Court of Appeal will now untie its own hands? Only time will tell, but our experience must lead us to doubt it.[156]

Their experience has proved right at least according to their own 1989 Report on *Miscarriages of Justice*.[157] That Report tells the familiar tale of the Court of Appeal's attitude, as frequently expressed in judgments since 1907 and regularly chastised by commentators, being one in which 'it must not interfere with the jury's verdict, as this would amount to a re-trial of the merits of the case.'[158]

In Justice's 1989 Report, some twenty years after Lord Widgery's dicta in *Cooper* in 1968, they are able to quote only six reported cases of successful appeals on the sole ground of 'a lurking doubt' over the evidence heard by the jury.[159] Of these *Pattinson and Laws* in 1973[160] and *Pope* in 1987[161] are probably the clearest examples of quashing convictions because of concern with the evidence.[162] A more typical outcome is the case of *Mycock*,[163] a conviction on problematic identification, initially refused leave to appeal because: 'the points . . . were points entirely for the jury and they were very properly left to the jury. Having considered them, the jury were entitled to convict.'[164] Commentators confirm the generally pessimistic view of the Court's role with somewhat monotonous regularity. The organization Justice believes that the Court shows extreme reluctance to quash convictions, including (pre-ESDA) cases[165] involving confessions by the appellant, or police malpractice.[166] The proposed solution to the seemingly intractable problems posed by the Court of Appeal's reassessment of jury verdicts, prevalent among reformers until the early 1990s, was to move away from a purely judicial forum towards some form

---

[156] Ibid. 11.   [157] See n. 116 above.   [158] Ibid. 48.

[159] Ibid. 49.   [160] 58 Cr. App. R 417.   [161] 85 Cr. App. R 201.

[162] See also *Arobieke* [1988] Crim. LR 314, and *Bracewell* (1978) 68 Cr. App. R 44, where despite all the grounds of appeal being individually rejected, the conviction was quashed because of the 'considerable anxiety' felt by the Court.

[163] See Justice's 29th Annual Report 1986, 17–19, and Appendix 1 to the 1989 Justice Report, n. 116 above, 87–8.

[164] Identification cases were precisely those which most concerned the Donovan Committee, and with which the reformed legislation was intended to deal. The establishment of the Devlin Committee in 1974 (n. 116 above) to investigate the problems arising from the issues of identification, especially in the cases of *Dougherty* and *Virag*, demonstrates the failure of the new grounds of appeal to deal adequately with the question.

[165] ESDA, the electro-static data analysis test, which has proved very significant in providing new evidence to overturn long-standing high profile convictions in the 1990s, such as those of the Guildford Four and the Birmingham Six.

[166] See Justice's 20th Annual Report 1977, 12, the Editorial, *Criminal Law Review*, [1983], 577–8, and A. Samuels, 'Appeal against Conviction: Reform', *Criminal Law Review*, [1984], 337–46.

of independent review body, with a wider jurisdiction and a partially non-legal membership. In a number of ways such proposals all envisage an altered role for the Court of Appeal, sometimes as a result of a new relationship with a new independent review body and sometimes by being reconstituted within such a body (a *new* Court of Appeal). The government's response has consistently been to uphold the constitutional pre-eminence of the Court, accompanied by judicial pledges from the Court's members to review their practice.[167]

1 FRESH EVIDENCE CASES

Section 23(1) of the 1968 Criminal Appeal Act[168] consists of a general discretion for the Court of Appeal to admit evidence 'if they think it necessary or expedient in the interests of justice'. In addition section 23(2) sets out a duty to admit evidence if certain criteria of credibility, relevance, and an adequate explanation for not calling it at trial are fulfilled. Section 23(2) reproduces section 5 of the 1966 Act, which was itself an attempt to incorporate into statutory form some mandatory obligations on the Court relating to the admission of fresh evidence.[169] However, the ensuing attitude towards the hearing of fresh evidence has not been consistently positive. An initially more generous approach was articulated in *Kelly*: 'In the light of the new Act [the 1964 Act], however, this court, while not laying down any strict rules, will look at each case on its merits.'[170] And other instances of an initially more liberal stance can be found in the way the Court dealt with the vexed area of evidence that was available at time of trial, such as in

---

[167] Proposals for some form of independent review body appeared regularly in Justice Reports, such as *Home Office Reviews of Criminal Convictions* (n. 12 above) and *Miscarriages of Justice* (n. 116 above). They also appeared in the *Devlin Report* of 1976 (n. 116 above), and the Home Affairs Committee 6th Report Session 1981–82, *Miscarriages of Justice* (n. 155 above). For scepticism about whether independent tribunals may be the cure-all for appellate ills, see the debate between P. O'Connor and P. Ashman, *Solicitors Journal*, 134/45 (1990), 1292–3, and B. Woffinden, 'The Independent Review Tribunal', *New Law Journal*, 139 (1989), 1108–9. Both O'Connor and Woffinden prefer fuller use of the retrial power. See also the proposal in the 1989 Justice Report, *Miscarriages of Justice* (n. 116 above) to place the subjective onus more fully on the Court by the addition of a new ground: 'they are themselves doubtful upon the evidence whether the appellant is guilty of the offence of which he has been convicted.' Such a reform is still directed towards improving the Court's performance by altering the wording of its jurisdiction through legislation.

[168] A compilation of Section 9 of the 1907 Act and Section 5 of the 1966 Act.

[169] The other significant section is section 7, the power to order a retrial. As has been argued earlier, this power should in theory have removed some of the previous objections to the hearing of fresh evidence.

[170] See n. 141 above, 229. The case was decided between 1964 and 1966, namely when the retrial power was in force but before the introduction of the provisions in section 5 of the 1966 Act. In the actual decision the fresh evidence was not heard because it was thought not to be credible.

Harris,[171] *Jennings*,[172] and *Gray*.[173] There were also signs of a more liberal approach in relation to post-conviction events such as confessions by third parties. In *Ditch* the Court of Appeal admitted the confession evidence made after conviction of one of the two people convicted of a burglary, which confession exonerated the other person who had been convicted.[174] And in *Saunders* they admitted confession evidence by someone who admitted their part in a robbery for which the appellant and seven others had been convicted, but which evidence specifically excluded the appellant from the crime.[175] In the later case of *Foster* confession evidence by a third party is admitted, but despite the extraordinary circumstances of the case, the willingness to admit it is surrounded by the language of 'exception'.[176] Indeed in the reasoning of the Court in its more liberal approach the language of exception remains a constant theme. But there are always cases that appear to fall outside whatever the Court believes amounts to *exceptional circumstances* that would have allowed for the admission of fresh evidence, based on the finest of distinctions.[177] Then in 1968 in the case of *Stafford and Luvaglio* in dealing with an application for leave to appeal and to bring fresh evidence, while commenting on the 'more liberal attitude . . . introduced by the provision in section 5', Edmund Davies LJ stresses the need for finality. 'Public mischief would ensue and legal process could become indefinitely prolonged were it the case that evidence produced at

[171] [1966] Crim. LR 102: 'the justice of the case required that it should be heard.'
[172] [1967] Crim. LR 478: 'the court felt, not without some doubt, that on the whole there was a reasonable explanation put forward . . . for failing to adduce the evidence at the trial.'
[173] (1973) 58 Cr. App. R 177, in which fresh evidence was admitted despite 'very considerable doubt whether in the circumstances of this case it can be said that such a reasonable explanation has been shown', for failure to adduce it at the trial.
[174] (1969) 53 Cr. App. R 627, 63: 'in the ordinary course of events this Court will be very careful before it will admit a confession of guilty by one of two people who have been convicted by a jury of a joint offence . . . on the other hand, there is nothing in the decided cases which in any way affects this Court in receiving such evidence in a proper case.' In this case it is clear that the Court of Appeal found that the other evidence on which the conviction was based was quite unsatisfactory.
[175] *Saunders* (1973) 58 Cr. App. R 248. The Home Secretary had referred the case to the Court of Appeal following a petition by the appellant. One member of the Court took the evidence of the accomplice under oath on behalf of the Court. The Court of Appeal admitted the new evidence and determined that the conviction was no longer safe or satisfactory. 'The evidence of accomplices can be as dangerous when used for the defence as it can when used for the Crown . . . we would not . . . accept such a submission merely on its face value without thinking about it deeply.'
[176] *Foster* (1984) 79 Cr. App. R 61, 67: 'It is rare of course to allow fresh evidence to be heard after a plea of guilty has been made. The circumstances must be exceptional. We regard this case as undoubtedly exceptional and one in which we feel entitled to admit the fresh evidence even though it comes after plea and even though in the main it relates to events which occurred after that plea was made.'
[177] See, e.g., *Williams* [1965] Crim. LR 609 where the appellant sought to introduce medical evidence as to his state of mind, which he had expressly excluded at trial; *Irvine and Wharton* [1965] Crim. LR 610 where, in order for the evidence to be received, the circuitous route via the Home Secretary's reference had to be adopted. In the area of post-conviction confessions the Court remains generally wary.

any time will generally be admitted by this Court when verdicts are being reviewed. There must be some curbs.'[178] This intimation of restriction has been confirmed by more recent cases certainly up to the early 1990s. In fact it would seem that the Court has imported the conditions of the duty of section 23(2) into the exercise of the discretion of section 23(1), thus mainly limiting the power to hear fresh evidence to cases which fulfil the criteria of section 23(2).

Section 23(2) sets out four possible bars to the duty of the Court of Appeal to receive fresh evidence. If 'the Court . . . are satisfied that the evidence . . . would not afford any ground for allowing the appeal'. If the evidence is not 'likely to be credible'. If the evidence 'would not have been admissible in the proceedings from which the appeal lies on an issue which is the subject of the appeal.' If there is no 'reasonable explanation for the failure to adduce it' in those earlier proceedings. In *Lattimore* in 1975 the conflation of sections 23(1) and 23(2) was acknowledged by Lord Scarman, and clarified. While recognizing the necessity for some limits to the admission of fresh evidence, referred to in *Stafford and Luvaglio*, he nevertheless affirms the power of the Court to admit evidence that does not always comply with the section 23(2) criteria: 'there will be cases in which, though the conditions of subsection (2) are not met and there is no requirement that the Court must receive the tendered evidence, the Court may do so, if it thinks it necessary or expedient in the interests of justice.'[179] But whilst 'there will be cases' where section 23(1) extends the jurisdiction of the Court beyond the conditions of section 23(2), the implication is that these will be rare. Of the potential obstacles created by the conditions set out in section 23(2), the most significant is the final one. The first condition has been criticized for importing into the preliminary decision, about whether the evidence can be heard, an issue that should be judged once the application to hear has been granted. The boundaries of the second of the criteria were set out in *Beresford* where the meaning of 'credible' was defined as: 'well capable of belief . . . in the context of the circumstances as a whole, including amongst those circumstances the other evidence . . . in the instant case.'[180] Delay usually undermines an appellant's ability to meet the second condition. But this is sometimes a result of the Court's reluctance to hear

---

[178] 53 Cr. App. R 1, 3. For critical reaction to this judgment at that time, see the Editorial, *New Law Journal*, 118 (1968), 1211, and Knight's Supplement, n. 62 above, 51–2. For more background on the *Stafford and Luvaglio* case, see Woffinden, n. 94 above, ch. 5, and D. Lewis and P. Hughman, *Most Unnatural: An Inquiry into the Stafford Case* (Harmondsworth, 1971). See below for the Court's attitude when the appeal is heard on reference back.

[179] *Lattimore* (1975) 62 Cr. App. R 53, 56. All the evidence on appeal from medical and fire experts could have been adduced at trial.

[180] (1971) 56 Cr. App. R 143, 149–50. The phrase 'well capable of belief' appears in the limiting 1968 *Stafford and Luvaglio* judgment (n. 178 above), which in turn was based on the 1961 criteria laid down in *Parks* (n. 89 above). As a threshold standard for admissibility its effect can be restrictive.

new evidence cases. Consider the notorious Luton post office murder case, *Cooper and McMahon*, on a reference from the Home Secretary under section 17(1)(b) asking for the Court's opinion on new alibi evidence. The reasons given for refusing to hear the fresh evidence were that it 'would not afford any ground for allowing the appeal' and that it was 'not likely to be credible'.[181] The lack of credibility was partly due to the lapse of time (over eight years) between the relevant events and the reference, but that distance was itself created by the Court's adamant refusal either to give leave to appeal initially or to react favourably in two earlier references. In cases of this nature, admittedly rare, the prolongation of the appeal process diminishes the appellants' chances of success with every passing year. But at the same time it makes it more likely that the case will be commented on in the press. There is potentially an inverse relationship between the likelihood of a successful appeal as time passes and the likelihood that a case becomes a high profile case. These factors of lessening credibility may be more or less significant in relation to different types of evidence. For example, different issues arise in the reassessment of expert evidence as opposed to the testimony of alibi witnesses (as in *Cooper and McMahon*). Indeed in relation to scientific evidence the passage of time may be helpful to an appellant with new scientific developments enabling more positive doubt to be thrown on the findings of expert forensic or scientific evidence presented at the trial. However, a different problem may arise with expert (scientific) evidence where the samples or materials which were examined, or on which tests were carried out, may have deteriorated or no longer exist.[182]

The main stumbling block in the section 23(2) conditions has remained the fourth issue of what constitutes 'a reasonable explanation for . . . failure to adduce' evidence available at the time of trial. In particular the continuance of an exclusionary attitude has applied to explanations based either on mistaken legal advice or on lack of information from the defendant resulting in failure to call witnesses at the trial. In the case of *Beresford* where an application was made to hear witnesses in support of an alibi, the limiting dictum in *Stafford and Luvaglio*[183] was again quoted. That reference implicitly supported a narrow view. 'The court has in general to be satisfied that the evidence could not with reasonable diligence have been obtained for use at the trial . . . that must necessarily include the need for the accused himself to play a proper part in assisting the preparation of the defence.'[184] An earlier case also building on *Stafford and Luvaglio*,

---

[181] *McMahon* (1978) 68 Cr. App. R 18. Given the Court's extraordinary faith in the flawed evidence of the main prosecution witness, this reasoning becomes extremely ironic. See Lord Devlin's discussion of the reasoning of the Court and their powers to determine questions of fact as opposed to 'credibility' in Kennedy (ed.), n. 94 above, and Woffinden, n. 94 above, chs. 6 and 7.

[182] See our analysis of the implications of time for the deterioration of forensic evidence in our case studies in section C of Ch. 5. [183] See n. 178 above.

[184] See n. 180 above, 149.

Quinton, disallowed witnesses in support of an alibi because of the trial lawyer's original decision to exclude them.[185] The stringency of the fourth condition was confirmed in *Shields and Patrick* in 1976 in forceful terms, though the judgment may to some extent have been aimed at altering practitioners' behaviour. For various reasons, some due to decisions of counsel, some to the defendants' own inability to locate them, witnesses had not been called at trial. The Court felt that:

there was an increasing tendency to treat the trial by jury as a preliminary skirmish rather than a trial . . . to refrain from calling witnesses who were available but whose evidence might . . . be thought dangerous to the defence and then . . . to claim that the verdict was unsafe because those witnesses had not been called . . . It was for the jury, not the Court of Appeal, to evaluate evidence . . . It would seldom if ever be a reasonable explanation for not calling a witness that the risk of calling him was at the time considered too great and counsel advised that he should not be called.[186]

The more recent case of *Gautam* confirms this view. Refusing to hear medical evidence available at the time of trial, 'the court would not permit the defendant to have another opportunity to run a defence which had been initially discussed but not run at the trial.'[187] The later trend of authority compares unfavourably with the earlier signs of liberality.[188] It also confirms the fears expressed during the passage of the 1966 Act that statutory provision was necessary to ensure a change of practice by the Court, whilst simultaneously demonstrating the ineffectuality of the section as drafted to alter their practice in all desired respects. Indeed in *Shields and Patrick*[189] it would appear that the Court excluded exactly the type of evidence at which the 1966 reforms were aimed.

The overall success of reform relating to the liberalization of the reception of fresh evidence can at best be described as partial. From that point of view there may have been some improvement, but the practice of the Court in any given instance is always difficult to assess. As Samuels notes in 1984 in his reform-based article: 'The practice of the Court is uncertain, incon-

---

[185] *Quinton* [1970] Crim. LR 91. A more sympathetic approach, exemplifying the persistent inconsistency of the Court, occurred in a similar case, *Egerton* [1970] Crim. LR 92, decided within days of *Quinton*. For an illustration of the disastrous consequences caused by the Court's attitude to bad legal advice see the case of *Dougherty*, fully examined in the *Devlin Report* (n. 116 above) and the Annual Report of Justice for 1974. In the successful appeal, on reference back to the Court by the Home Secretary, the Lord Chief Justice accepted that the Court might have interpreted its powers too narrowly.

[186] See n. 140 above.

[187] *Gautam* [1988] Crim. LR 109. For other unreported examples, see cases quoted in Appendix 1 of the 1989 Justice Report on *Miscarriages of Justice* (n. 116 above), *Martin Foran* and *Anthony Burke*. Burke's conviction was eventually quashed because of insufficient scientific evidence, but two crucial defence witnesses, not called at the trial, were refused leave to be heard on appeal.

[188] Noted by Knight in his Supplement, n. 62 above; and see our analysis of liberality above.   [189] See n. 140 above.

sistent, and unpredictable.'[190] He lists a whole range of evidence not advanced at trial, often due to ignorance or mistaken tactics on the part of defence counsel, which has been rejected as fresh evidence by the Court of Appeal. His proposals for reform include a redrafting of section 23 and fuller use of the retrial power.

2 RETRIALS AND THE ASSESSMENT OF FRESH EVIDENCE

The most notable feature of the retrial power granted in 1964 has been the infrequency of its use at least until the early 1990s. According to Knight's survey[191] it was used seventeen times between 1964 and 1968, out of a total of 18,000 applications for leave to appeal against conviction/sentence. Between 1966 and 1968 one-fifth of fresh evidence applications resulted in the ordering of retrials. This level of exercise of the power decreases over time. According to O'Connor only fourteen retrials occurred between 1981 and 1986.[192] Judicial reluctance to make use of the power for practical reasons such as lapse of time or possible prejudice to the defendant, through inability to ensure a fair trial,[193] was enhanced in 1973 by the House of Lords judgment in *Stafford and Luvaglio*. The judges in that case in effect claimed for themselves the right to consider the effect of fresh evidence on the original verdict. As Viscount Dilhorne put it: 'If the court has no reasonable doubt about the verdict, it follows that the court does not think that the jury could have one; and, conversely, if the court says that a jury might in the light of the new evidence have a reasonable doubt, that means that the court has a reasonable doubt.'[194] Before 1973 the approach when considering fresh evidence and the possibility of retrial had centred on the effect of the evidence on a reasonable jury, in keeping with the Court's stance on constitutional propriety.[195] The main authority on the procedure for considering whether to order a retrial was *Flower*.[196] Four options were available to the Court. If the Court was satisfied that the new evidence concluded the appeal it quashed the conviction. If the Court was not satisfied that the new evidence concluded the appeal, it may order a new trial, where the jury could consider the old and new evidence together. If the Court was not satisfied that the fresh evidence was true, but nevertheless thought it might be believed by a jury, it would be inclined to order a new trial. If the Court positively disbelieved the new evidence it would proceed with the appeal as if the evidence had not been tendered. Clearly in the intermediate area of doubt over the new evidence, the forum for assessment was intended to be a retrial, where a jury would consider the original

[190] See n. 166 above, 337.   [191] See n. 62 above, 96–107.

[192] 'The Court of Appeal: Re-Trials and Tribulations', *Criminal Law Review* [1990], 615–28, 622–3.   [193] See, e.g., *Pedrini* [1964] Crim. LR 719.

[194] [1974] AC 878, 893.   [195] See *Parks*, n. 89 above.

[196] (1965) 50 Cr. App. R 22.

evidence together with the additional fresh evidence. However, since *Stafford and Luvaglio* the power to order retrials has been marginalized in its significance. In that notorious case, which had been the subject of many previous legal proceedings,[197] the House of Lords was asked by the Court of Appeal to decide the following point of law:

Whether in considering an appeal against conviction referred to the Court of Appeal by the Secretary of State under section 17 (1) (a) of the Criminal Appeal Act 1968, involving the calling of fresh evidence, the correct approach of the Court of Appeal is to evaluate the fresh evidence, to endeavour to set it into the framework provided by the whole of the evidence called at the trial, and in the end to ask itself whether the verdict has become unsafe or unsatisfactory by the impact of the fresh evidence notwithstanding that it was found to be safe and satisfactory on the earlier occasion when the court refused leave to appeal.[198]

The appellants argued that the Court of Appeal had adopted the wrong approach to the assessment of fresh evidence: 'they took as the test the effect of the fresh evidence on their minds and not the effect that that evidence would have had on the mind of the jury.'[199] They argued for continuance of the authority of the test as set out in *Parks*: 'the court will . . . consider whether there might have been a reasonable doubt in the minds of the jury',[200] with the added recognition of the possibility of ordering a new trial. The conclusion reached by the House of Lords is somewhat different. They refuse to make any distinction between appeals involving fresh evidence and others, and base their interpretation of the Court's jurisdiction on the wording of section 2(1) of the 1968 Act: 'the Court of Appeal shall allow an appeal against conviction if they think (a) that the verdict of the jury should be set aside on the ground that under all the circumstances of the case it is unsafe or unsatisfactory.' They emphasize the subjective nature of the assessment involved, and while not condemning the use of the jury as a benchmark, they stress it is only one of the available approaches open to the Court. The leading judgment of Viscount Dilhorne is noticeably open-ended on the specific strategy to be adopted by the Court in regard to fresh evidence. 'What is the correct approach in a case is not, in my opinion, a question of law.'[201] What he does assert, though, is a necessary concurrence between the Court's opinion on the effect of the new evidence and that of a hypothetical jury, an assumption disputed among others by leading legal practitioners, such as both Lord Devlin and Lord Scarman, and Patrick O'Connor.[202]

---

[197] See n. 178 above.   [198] See n. 194 above, 890–1.
[199] Ibid. 880.   [200] See n. 89 above, 634.   [201] See n. 194 above, 892.
[202] See P. Devlin's arguments against 'an imperfect re-trial by judges', 'The Judge and the Jury II: Sapping and Undermining', in *The Judge* (Oxford, 1979), 148–76, and O'Connor, n. 192 above. Also see section D of Ch. 4 for analysis of the views of Lords Devlin and Scarman articulated in the press on the deficiencies of the House of Lords judgment in the *Stafford and Luvaglio* case.

In later cases the fluidity of the approach implicit in Viscount Dilhorne's judgment appears to have disappeared. In one of the unsuccessful Birmingham Six appeals, *Callaghan and others*,[203] and in *Byrne*[204] the primacy of the Court's opinion is affirmed. This has a dual impact. It implicitly negates the opportunities for ordering retrials because the views of the appellate judges on the fresh evidence pre-empt the need for a jury verdict.[205] At the same time it opens up a problematic series of questions as to the procedure to be adopted by the Court when engaged on its own subjective assessment of the evidence. A danger develops that instead of the wholesale re-evaluation offered by a retrial, the original jury verdict becomes privileged in the eyes of the Court, with the fresh evidence requiring a disproportionate weight to displace it.[206] This was certainly the case in the *Cooper and McMahon* appeals,[207] and to a lesser extent in *Stafford and Luvaglio*,[208] where strong circumstantial evidence caused problems for the defence. It is somewhat ironic that the retrial power, so long desired by many appellate judges, has apparently, once acquired, been speedily displaced by their own assumption of the jury's role. The difficulties inherent in the Court's interpretation of its jurisdiction, in relation to appeals on questions of fact, seem destined to persist whatever the attempts at legislative reform. Lord Dilhorne's words in his House of Lords judgment in *Stafford and Luvaglio* that the strategy to be adopted by the Court in regard to fresh evidence 'is not . . . a question of law'[209] have a haunting quality. If these jurisdictional and procedural questions are not law, then why do they haunt the history of the Court? Why does the repetitive need to redraft and reword the relevant statutory authority, expressed more forcefully by commentators at some times but latent at others, play its haunting theme throughout the approaching one hundred years of the Court's existence?

The combined effect of the 1964 and 1966 Acts, consolidated in 1968, appears not to have had a profound impact on the Court's exercise of its jurisdiction. Perhaps this merely confirmed the view of the Lord Chief Justice, communicated in debate, that in introducing the 'unsafe or unsatisfactory' ground the legislature would be merely authorizing an already existing practice. In the readjustment of the grounds for allowing appeals, section 2(1) (a)—'unsafe or unsatisfactory'—embraces a wide area, including appeals founded on more technical issues of misdirection. However in the narrower realm of convictions which are deemed 'unsafe' on the sole

---

[203] (1989) 88 Cr. App. R 40, [1988] 1 All ER 257.
[204] (1989) 88 Cr. App. R 33.
[205] It is ironic that this dwindling in use of the 1964 power coincides with the widening in the late 1980s of the retrial power in section 43 of the Criminal Justice Act 1988.
[206] Although it is difficult to find uniformity in the approach of the Court of Appeal, our case studies of the Court's approach to the reassessment of scientific evidence, set out in section C of Ch. 5, support this contention.   [207] See n. 181 above.
[208] See nn. 178 and 194 above.   [209] See n. 194 above, 892.

basis of the jury verdict being wrong, there is little evidence to suggest that reforms achieved through redrafting the Court of Appeal's jurisdiction and powers have marked a substantive change in its practice post-1966.

In the fresh evidence cases the availability of ordering retrials initially produced some liberalization of the (self-imposed) limits on admission of evidence. Yet the Court still places barriers on admission to a certain degree, especially if the new evidence was deliberately not called at the original trial, thus penalizing defendants for the miscalculation of their lawyers. The actual use of the retrial power has not proved frequent[210] possibly because, since the House of Lords decision in *Stafford and Luvaglio* in 1973,[211] the Court has interpreted its jurisdiction as authorizing itself to decide issues arising from fresh evidence. In so doing they have contributed few indicators as to the manner of their decision-making beyond the use of impressionistic phrases such as 'lurking doubt'.

G. The reforms of the 1990s

The changes adopted in the Criminal Appeal Act 1995 were informed by the history presented throughout this chapter, which history it continues. As described, the original statute setting up a Court of Criminal Appeal, the Criminal Appeal Act 1907, was passed against great opposition from a number of senior judges,[212] in response to a number of high profile miscarriage of justice cases. The Criminal Appeal Act 1995 has similarly been enacted in response to high profile miscarriages, although in this instance with the direct approval of the Lord Chief Justice and other senior judges. The recent high profile miscarriages of the late 1980s and early 1990s had at least one demonstrable general effect. They created a consensus (certainly in public pronouncements) on the need for reform, forcing the participants in the criminal justice process to become (but for a variety of reasons and with a variety of aims) reformers.[213] What, if anything, might there be in this latest Act which will substantially alter the practice of criminal appeals? In particular, what is likely to alter the perceived failure to remedy miscarriages of justice that certainly existed in the early 1990s, but which also existed, as this chapter has illustrated, at other times over the last 150 years? Such a perception of failure to remedy miscarriages, which we have illustrated was prevalent in the period prior to the passing of the 1907 Act and in the two decades before the 1960s reforms, was also prevalent in the

---

[210] Although after 1993 there is some increase in its use, discussed in section G below.

[211] See n. 194 above.

[212] See particularly the debate in the House of Lords on the second reading of the Criminal Appeal Bill, 1907: Parl. Deb. HL 5 August 1907, cc. 1471–84.

[213] Some of these cases and the reactions to them are described in the course of our analysis in Ch. 4.

1980s and early 1990s. Partly in response to such a perception, it should be noted that in its judgments in the 1990s prior to the 1995 Act, a *new* Court of Appeal, under the influence of a new Lord Chief Justice, had already discounted the need for reform. The Court of Appeal under its new Lord Chief Justice from 1992 had apparently adopted a *different* attitude to that of the Court under previous Lord Chief Justices.[214] The clearest example of this is the increase in the willingness of the Court of Appeal to quash convictions and order retrials. In 1989 and 1990 only one and three retrials respectively were ordered. Between 1991 and 1993 the figure was between twelve and twenty annually. For each of the years between 1994 and 1996 over fifty retrials were ordered. For 1997 the figure is thirty.[215] Two reforms adopted by the Act will be considered in this book. In this chapter we will analyse the change in the grounds of appeal, which are reduced to the single requirement that the conviction is 'unsafe'. The other major change, the transfer of responsibility for considering the safety of a conviction and referring it to the Court of Appeal (Criminal Division) from the Home Secretary's CCU (formerly C3 Division) to a new body, the Criminal Cases Review Commission, will be examined in Chapter 5. We argue that neither of these reforms of themselves will alter the practices of the Court of Appeal. With the new arrangements, as before, the important factor is the Court of Appeal's unstated (and unstateable) sense of appropriate practice, its deference to the jury, its upholding of its, and the legal system's, authority, and its concerns with finality and workability. And with these priorities the ability of the Court to satisfy some commentators, particularly commentators in the press, is limited.

In reducing the grounds for overturning a conviction to the single conclusion that it is 'unsafe' (s. 2 (1)(a)), the Act is the latest in the series of reformulations of the powers and duties of the Court of Appeal in criminal cases since 1907. It will be recalled that the original powers of the Court of Criminal Appeal under the 1907 Act gave the Court an unrestricted authority to quash convictions:

---

[214] Whether there has been a new attitude and, even more problematic, whether this attitude is recognized and adopted by all members of the Court of Appeal (Criminal Division) is an open question. See Hugo Young's account of Lord Chief Justice Taylor's views, after his first three months in office, in *The Guardian*, 20 July 92. And see our analysis of newspaper reporting of miscarriages in 1992, in Ch. 4. The Parliamentary debates on the Criminal Appeal Bill were informed by the belief that 'the prevailing climate of the Court of Appeal has altered markedly over the past few years' (Mr. D. Anderson, Parl. Deb. HC 26 April 1995, c. 935). But, as Chris Mullin MP warned, 'Many Honourable Members have remarked on an improvement of attitude following the change of personnel in that court—but they could of course change back again. The suspicion has been voiced to me that the recent liberalization may in some way be affected by the fear that something more drastic might be done to limit its powers' (Parl. Deb. HC 26 April 1995, cc. 951–2).

[215] *Judicial Statistics for England and Wales 1997*, Cm 3980 (Lord Chancellor's Department, 1998), 12.

if they think that the verdict of the jury should be set aside on the ground that it is unreasonable or cannot be supported having regard to the evidence, or that the judgement of the court before whom the appellant was convicted should be set aside on the ground of a wrong decision of any question of law or that on any grounds there was a miscarriage of justice.   (s. 4 (1)).

And the 1907 Act had no restrictions on the admission of new evidence. The Court could require the production of any document, or hear any witness that it thought 'necessary or expedient in the interest of justice' (s. 9). The Court's restricted view of what *justice* required led, in the 1960s, after earlier attempts in the 1940s, to new statutory formulae which were consolidated in the Criminal Appeal Act 1968. The 1968 Act is now amended by the 1995 Act.

The task that faced those who drafted and debated the latest Criminal Appeal Bill was similar to that which must have faced those undertaking the same tasks in the 1960s. They were concerned to encourage the Court to take a more liberal approach to appeals by the use of statutory language, against a background of existing statutory language that already empowered it to take such an approach. The 1968 Act allowed the Court to quash a conviction whenever it felt that the jury's verdict was 'under all the circumstances of the case . . . unsafe or unsatisfactory; or that the judgment of the court of trial should be set aside on the ground of a wrong decision of any question of law; or that there was a material irregularity in the course of the trial' (s. 2 (1)). The width of this power, as has been illustrated, was confirmed by the Court in the case of *Cooper*,[216] in the judgment of the then newly appointed Lord Chief Justice Widgery, in which the Court set out the doctrine of 'lurking doubt'. This doctrine allowed the Court to quash any conviction where it is not satisfied, beyond reasonable doubt, in the guilt of the accused. And the 1968 Act, in principle, still empowered the Court to hear any evidence which it thought 'necessary or expedient in the interests of justice' (s. 23 (1)), but it also had a duty to admit some evidence in some circumstances (s. 23 (2)).[217]

The 1995 Act reduces the grounds of appeal to the solitary ground that the Court finds the conviction 'unsafe' (s. 2 (1)). The duty to admit new evidence is abolished, but the power to admit new evidence is made subject to a duty to consider the same factors as limited the former duty. Those factors include credibility, relevance to the safety of the conviction, admissibility at trial, and the reasonableness of the explanation for any failure to adduce the evidence at trial (s. 4). The requirement that new evidence be 'likely to be credible' has now become only 'capable of belief', which the Report of the Royal Commission on Criminal Justice, on which this statute is based, called 'a slightly wider formula giving the court greater scope for

---

[216]   See n. 70 above.   [217]   See our analysis of this section above, in Section F/1.

doing justice'.[218] But there is nothing more in these reformulations that is likely to overcome the Royal Commission's concern that:

In its approach to the consideration of appeals against conviction, the Court of Appeal seems to us to have been too heavily influenced by the role of the jury in Crown Court trials. Ever since 1907, commentators have detected a reluctance on the part of the Court of Appeal to consider whether a jury has reached a wrong decision.

It believed that: 'the court should be more willing to consider arguments that indicate that a jury might have made a mistake . . . [and] be more prepared, where appropriate, to admit evidence that might favour the defendant's case even if it was, or could have been, available at the trial.'[219]

The Commission placed great faith in a recommendation that the ground for appeal should be 'is or may be unsafe'. It set out what it expected such a change to achieve with some care.[220] It wanted the Court to quash a conviction where it was certain that the jury's verdict was wrong, but to allow a retrial where it could not be sure that the original jury would have convicted. Where there was new evidence and a retrial was desirable but impractical, the Court should simply substitute itself for the jury, and form its own conclusion on whether the conviction was safe, or not. If it continued to believe that the conviction might be unsafe, it should acquit. If the statute had achieved what the Royal Commission wanted, this recommendation would have had the effect, in cases where retrials were impossible, of turning the Court of Appeal into a second trial court. As such it would have had to operate with the same burden of proof as was used at the first trial: a requirement to acquit unless the appellant's guilt was established beyond a reasonable doubt.[221]

Perhaps the greatest obstacle to giving effect to the Royal Commission's proposal through any statutory formula is that, according to the Court of Appeal's own rhetoric, the proposal is already law.[222] Our reading of the Court's powers under the 1907 Act, let alone under the 1968 Act coupled with the doctrine of 'lurking doubt', is that it is required to quash any conviction where the judges are not satisfied, beyond reasonable doubt, of

---

[218] See n. 43 above, ch. 10, para. 60.   [219] Ibid., para. 3.
[220] Ibid., para. 32.
[221] Ibid., paras. 32–3, and their discussion of the House of Lords decision *Stafford and Luvaglio* in 1973 (n. 194 above) at paras. 62–3. Where no new evidence was involved, and the possibility of an unsafe conviction was due to some technical error, a majority (6 to 5) of the Royal Commission wanted to quash the conviction rather than allow the Court of Appeal to substitute its own judgment on the guilt or innocence of the appellant. It is difficult to understand why convictions based on *technical errors* could not be reassessed by the Court of Appeal whilst those based on fresh evidence could. If 'technical error' really refers to fundamental flaws in procedure, and the lack of a fair trial, one wonders why this majority did not simply adopt the dissent of one of the Commissioners, Michael Zander, referred to in n. 230 below, especially para. 64.   [222] In support of this contention see p. 69 above.

the guilt of the accused.[223] After 1964 and the enactment of a retrial power, in cases where retrial was impossible, this should have been the end of the matter. The difficulties in finding a formula to require the Court to do what it already has the power to do is compounded by the perception of the current practice of the Court of Appeal in the 1990s prior to the passing of the 1995 statute. It was thought that, under the stewardship of Lord Chief Justice Taylor (and thereafter Lord Chief Justice Bingham), the Court was already acting in accordance with the *Cooper* standard, and being more willing to order retrials. Under these circumstances the problem facing Parliament was to devise a form of words which ensured that the Court of Appeal would continue to do what it was (apparently) already doing, and what, according to its own rhetoric, it had been doing at least since *Cooper* in 1968. And this was so, according to the Court, even though some commentators (particularly in the press) failed to appreciate this fact.[224] So, how do you use legislation to require the Court of Appeal to continue to apply the existing law?

The absence of any form of words that can force the Court of Appeal to do what it claims to do already was a problem of which the Standing Committee of the House of Commons, which considered the Criminal Appeal Bill, was only too well aware. Its members spoke of the need to *signal* their desire that the Court continue with its current liberal approach to appeals. Let us consider one such example of many from the Committee's discussion. 'He should consider the amendment or any other form of words that seems appropriate to ensure that we underwrite what is said to be the change in the court's approach or, where that change has not happened, give a clear signal. We want to avoid the danger of narrowing the approach or confirming the court in a previous narrow approach.'[225] The Committee's members were aware that they were in a situation where the usual conventions of Parliamentary drafting were difficult to apply. Members discussed whether deliberate use of surplus language (their view of 'or may be') might have the necessary effect. They were aware that surplus language would necessitate interpretation that has, as its starting

---

[223] This is our reading of the Court's powers. We reach this conclusion for two main reasons. First, we have not found in the case law any adequate discussion of the burden of proof on appeal. Secondly, the judges will usually articulate their concerns in terms of the safety of a conviction, rather than in terms of the guilt or innocence of the appellant. On the issue of the burden of proof see the judgment of Stuart-Smith LJ in *Maguire* [1992] 2 All ER 433.

[224] A classic example of one of the many statements, which reiterate that the Court believes that it is empowered to do and has been doing what critics are constantly urging it to do, can be found in the Government's reply (at para. 11) to the Home Affairs Committee 6th Report Session 1981–82 on *Miscarriages of Justice* (n. 155 above). 'The Lord Chief Justice [Lord Lane!] has confirmed that the Court of Appeal is very ready to use its discretion to admit new evidence under section 23 of the Criminal Appeal Act 1968, when the interests of justice so require.'

[225] Mr. D. Trimble HC Standing Committee B 21 March 1995, c. 18

point, the need to give some meaning to all the words in a statute.[226] They
were also aware of the failure in practice of much surplus language in the
1968 statute to achieve any liberal effects (material irregularity, unsafe or
unsatisfactory). In the end the Standing Committee opted for the simplest
and shortest instruction: to quash 'unsafe' convictions.[227] By deleting
grounds of appeal from the Court's statutory powers, the Committee
created a danger that the usual canons of construction might lead the Court
to read the 1995 statute as restricting the grounds of appeal. In the event,
and presumably with an awareness of the context of the amendment, the
Court of Appeal has felt able to state that the 'unsafe' test was clearly not
intended by Parliament to 'cut down the grounds of appeal'.[228] However,
the 'unsafe' test, even when it is specifically referred to in the Court's judgments, does not appear to refer to anything of particular significance.[229]
For the present at least, the Court appears to recognize the new ground as
an instruction to be (or continue to be) more liberal.

H. UNDERSTANDING REFORMULATED POWERS

The history of statutory reformulation of the powers of the Court of Appeal
in criminal cases should warn legal scholars against taking the language of
particular statutes, including the latest Criminal Appeal Act, that of 1995,
too seriously or literally. Attempting to make sense of the 1968 Act, and
then to identify what could follow from a new formulation, is a difficult
semantic exercise. For example, in reducing the grounds of appeal to the
single requirement that the conviction is 'unsafe', the 1995 Act appears to
downgrade the importance of material irregularities, or mistakes of law, as
reasons for overturning a jury's verdict. This may, at first glance, seem to be
a victory for the concept of trial as a mechanism for ascertaining truth, over
the concept of trial as a mechanism in which justice, conceived of as represented by due process and rights, is achieved. Appeals are, formally at least,
to be based on the question: is this person guilty? An alternative basis for
determining a miscarriage of justice is the question: have the rights of this

---

[226] If they were not aware of this at the start of the Committee stage they were certainly
made aware from struggling with an unpublished article by Professor J. C. Smith, quoted at
length in Standing Committee by one of its members, Mr D. Anderson (having been distrib-
uted by Sir I. Lawrence). The article has now been published as 'Criminal Appeals and the
Criminal Cases Review Commission', *New Law Journal*, 145 (1995), 533–5 and 572–4.
Earlier proposals, with an equivalent motivation, had relied on more rather than fewer words
in trying to authorize the Court of Appeal to adopt a more liberal approach: see Justice's
Report *Miscarriages of Justice* (n. 116 above), 50–1.
[227] Support for this approach was found in Lord Chief Justice Taylor's often quoted statement: 'A conviction which may be unsafe is unsafe' (Parl. Deb. HL 15 May 1995, c. 311).
[228] *Hickmet* [1996] Crim. LR 588.
[229] See the Court's reasoning in rejecting the appeal of *Mills and Poole* [1997] 3 WLR 458.

person been infringed? For many lawyers this second question is at least the equivalent of asking whether the defendant had a fair trial. Michael Zander, in his dissent in the Report of the Royal Commission on Criminal Justice,[230] believed that this change was especially significant. A willingness to uphold a conviction on the basis that there was other strong evidence on which the defendant could have been found guilty, even though his trial was not properly conducted, was unacceptable to Zander. It would remove the guilty verdict's *moral legitimacy* and make the conviction of a guilty individual more important than upholding the 'integrity' of the criminal justice process.

Despite Zander's concerns, one can also argue that the emphasis placed on the truth of guilt over rights was equally present in the statutory formula that had been repealed. Section 2 of the Criminal Appeal Act 1968 allowed the Court to decide that notwithstanding that there had been a material irregularity, the appeal should be dismissed on the basis that 'no miscarriage of justice has actually occurred.'[231] This earlier formulation (in logic if not in practice) reduced the meaning of miscarriage of justice to the single question: 'Is this person guilty,[232] regardless of the irregularity?' A 'material irregularity' might refer to an irregularity that is relevant to the guilt or innocence of the particular defendant, in which case the proviso to the 1968 Act was redundant.[233] Or 'material irregularity' may have referred to irregularities that were breaches of rules or rights that are generally important, without reference to their contribution to the decision. In this case the proviso could operate to enable the Court to conclude that, in the particular case, their breach had not affected the correctness of the conviction. Either way, the prior statute allowed the Court to uphold convictions despite serious flaws of procedure.

Kate Malleson, in her research into the Court of Appeal, found little recourse to the statutory grounds of appeal in the course of recent judgments.[234] In light of the above history, this is not surprising. But if the Court's interpretation of its role is not principally defined by its statutory authorization, then what, for the Court, generates a sufficient reason for quashing a conviction? We conclude that the standards of the Court are based on legal experience.[235] Whatever statutory language is used, the members of the Court will draw on their experience as advocates and judges in deciding what procedures are significant, and what contribution,

---

[230]   See n. 43 above, paras. 62–72.

[231]   The proviso to section 2, which had existed virtually unamended since 1907, but which was abolished by the 1995 Act.

[232]   Or, as the judges might have phrased it, would the jury still have convicted?

[233]   See Smith's article referred to in n. 226 above.

[234]   *Review of the Appeal Process*, Royal Commission on Criminal Justice Research Study No. 17 (London, 1993), 14.

[235]   In the famous words of Oliver Wendell Holmes: 'The life of the law has not been logic, it has been experience', *The Common Law* (Boston, 1881), 1.

if any, such procedures make to the accuracy of a guilty verdict. As recent history demonstrates, these standards can be tweaked in a more liberal direction in response to wide perceptions, particularly those reflected in the media, of the Court's failure to deal with miscarriages of justice. And a strong-minded Lord Chief Justice may be able to maintain a more liberal standard for at least some period after the general perception of justice in crisis[236] has dissipated.[237] Politicians in the House of Commons, and Royal Commissions, may hope to find statutory formulae to ensure that the liberal application of these non-verbal standards continues in perpetuity. Nothing in the history of statutory reform of the Court's jurisdiction suggests that they are likely to be successful.

I. CONCLUSION

In constructing its procedures the Court of Appeal relies on its deference to the original trial and the jury—that deference gives it much of its legitimacy as a legal process. It is that link, some conception of deference, which gives purchase to the Court's standards. Whereas we believe that deference is the pivot for the legal operations of the Court of Appeal, such deference is unlikely to be valued in other systems of communication such as the media. Even the Court itself has not thoroughly explored the limits and basis of such deference, which is implicit in the legal experience of its judges. In this sense it relies on what it believes to be appropriate standards.

This deference can be justified on both constitutional and rational grounds. Its constitutional aspect is that defendants should be convicted or acquitted not on the basis of what judges believe, or how judges reason, but through the judgement of their peers. The rational basis for deference is the fact that the jury see the witnesses producing their evidence, whilst the Court of Appeal does not, and is able to draw on a wider range of personal experience when reaching their verdict. In a trial which is properly conducted, where all material evidence is heard, and that evidence is not of unfathomable complexity, the constitutional and rational reasons for deferring to the jury work together. But where there is a material irregularity in the trial, the evidence is considered more complicated than a jury would be likely to understand, or new evidence comes to light, rational and constitutional reasons for deference begin to diverge. What does it mean to defer to the verdict of a jury that was materially misled by prosecution non-disclosure or biased summing up? Is this deference, or contempt? With new evidence, one cannot know how the jury might have treated it. But one can no longer be sure that the Court of Appeal is in a worse position to assess

---

[236] See our analysis of such a construction within the media in Ch. 4.
[237] See the warning by Chris Mullin MP, n. 214 above.

its reliability and probity than was the jury. And with respect to complex areas of evidence, there may be good reason to suppose that an appeal court may be better equipped to reach a verdict on the original evidence than was the jury.[238]

It is difficult for a Court of Appeal to hold on to its constitutional deference to the jury, without being made to appear irrational. No trial deals with all the evidence. Facts will always come to light, which were not known, or not used, at trial. Prosecution disclosure is always less than 100 per cent. And reserving the jury for simple cases is tantamount to abolishing it as a constitutional safeguard. When insisting upon the constitutional supremacy of the jury, the Court is either sacrificing rationality, or at least asserting that the jury's advantages continue to outweigh its own. As we have seen in its history, the Court attempts to buttress constitutional deference with rational arguments of its own. These rational arguments include the fear of manipulation of the appeal process by the deliberate withholding of evidence at trial, or that threats or inducements will be used to persuade trial witnesses to retract their evidence or new liars to come forward.[239]

A concern with miscarriages of justice points to the need to operate rationally in opposition to the arguments that seem to have underlain the constitutional deference that supports the Court of Appeal's narrow approach to its own jurisdiction. It suggests that there should be some sacrifice of deference to the jury when the Court is, rationally, in a better position to form a judgment on the guilt or innocence of the accused, even to accept the possible risk of manipulation in order to avoid the continued imprisonment of the innocent. This is, at a time of optimism, apparently the current practice. Indeed the Court is reputed to have adopted a liberal attitude in the 1990s prior to the 1995 Act. It is supposed that the new Lord Chief Justice in 1992 and the fallout from the high profile terrorist cases of miscarriage are significant factors in this change. But whatever factors have led to a supposed greater willingness to admit fresh evidence, quash convictions, and order retrials, there is nothing in the 1995 Act itself, as in its predecessors, to ensure that such liberal practices, or the reputation therefrom, will continue. The history of the Court has been one in which periods of optimism, in 1907, the late 1960s, or the 1990s, have given way to the perception of reluctance on the part of the Court to admit new evidence, or to challenge the verdict of a jury. At the heart of this history of

[238] See our analysis of the reassessment of expert evidence by the Court of Appeal in Ch. 5.

[239] We accept the possibility that apparent concern with constitutional deference and concern for defendants who manipulate the appeal process may serve to legitimate practices motivated by other concerns, such as the desire to reduce costs and to maintain the morale of the prosecution and defence. Nevertheless, such legitimations are placed under strain when they appear irrational.

reforms is the contradiction that underlies the institutional role of the Court of Appeal. One must have an appeal court, for what trial process could hope to work forever without error? An appeal court offers the opportunity for an inevitably flawed legal system still to deliver justice. But one also needs to have finality, to maintain legal authority, and to avoid appeals undermining the workability of the practices and procedures of prosecution and trial.[240] The premise, which ensures that appeals do not threaten the finality[241] of prosecution and trial, is a general belief in the probity of its actors and the accuracy of convictions obtained in accordance with normal procedures. But whilst this assumption ensures that practices and procedures remain workable, it does not tell the Court of Appeal how to identify the *exceptional* case in which actors have not acted in good faith, or normal procedures have produced a result which is widely believed to be wrong. Nor can it hope to produce reconciliation between the practices of this Court of Appeal and the demands of those who, through their own experience, entertain strong doubts both as to the probity of actors within criminal justice and the ability of its procedures to identify the factually guilty.

[240] This is but one of the tensions faced by the Court of Appeal (Criminal Division) in carrying out its appeal functions. Consider, for example, Spencer's conclusion about the pressure on appeal judges to distort the substantive criminal law or rules of evidence in order to ensure that those who are 'wrongdoers and/or guilty' are not released: 'But however admirable the conceptual foundation, the structure that case-law eventually builds upon it will never be sound until the rules of criminal appeal no longer force judges to choose in the case before them between sound law and a just outcome' ('Criminal Law and Criminal Appeals—The Tail that Wags the Dog', *Criminal Law Review* [1982], 282).

[241] For our analysis of this notion, see section C of Ch. 1.

4

Into and out of crisis: a recent history of media reporting on miscarriages of justice[1]

In Chapter 3 we endeavoured to show how the history of the Court of Appeal is intricately linked to the reluctance of the judiciary to entertain appeals on questions of fact, a reluctance that generates pressure for reform, and one which survives or resurfaces after each reform. As part of this history, we drew attention to the relevance of high profile miscarriages arising out of or reinforced by media campaigns for the creation of the Criminal Court of Appeal, and of judicial attempts to maintain the authority of the legal system in the face of reporting which questions its willingness and ability to dispense justice. In this chapter we wish to explore the relationship between the legal system and the media in relation to miscarriages of justice in greater detail.

We are not the first to claim a link between press reporting of criminal justice and reform. Indeed, there is a widespread acceptance that high profile miscarriages of justice have produced many reforms of criminal justice. One only has to think of the conviction and execution of Timothy Evans in 1950 for the murder of his baby daughter, his posthumous free pardon in 1966, and the significance of that case for the change in the law, namely the abolition of the death penalty in 1965.[2] However, such assertions are usually made by themselves, or with the support of a small selection of press cuttings and Parliamentary debates. Such claims do not explore the processes upon which they rely. There is no examination of the manner in which certain cases become high profile, of the conditions that generate them. This chapter attempts to rectify that omission.

The largest part of this chapter, beginning with section C, is a detailed

---

[1] We can find among the wealth of studies of press reporting of issues relating to crime and criminal behaviour no study specifically on the reporting of criminal appeals or miscarriages of justice, as we have undertaken here.

[2] Rolph links these two events succinctly: 'the horrifying case of Adolph Beck played the same kind of part in the ... campaign ... to establish an appeals system as that played by Timothy Evans ... in the campaign to abolish the death penalty for murder' (C. H. Rolph, *The Queen's Pardon* (London, 1978), 30). For a full account of Timothy Evans's case, see L. Kennedy, *Ten Rillington Place* (London, 1961).

study of what it meant for miscarriages of justice to become high profile during the ten-year period from 1987 to 1996. Sections D to G of the chapter set out the discourse on miscarriages of justice that occurred in one part of the media during this period. These data are presented as evidence in support of the thesis outlined in the first two sections and in the last section of the chapter. In brief, our thesis, as set out in section A, is that the media misread legal operations associated with appeals. In particular, in situations in which the media become convinced of the factual innocence of particular appellants, they approach the appellate process in the expectation that it can produce versions of the truth that accord closely with their own. The inability of the legal system to respond positively produces conditions in which reporting on disparate narratives of miscarriage of justice unite within a dominant meta-narrative of crisis. The nature and meaning of such a meta-narrative, a concept taken from media studies, is introduced in section B. The detailed study that follows these two sections demonstrates a number of propositions. It shows how there is a dominant media understanding of the role of truth within the legal system, which is different from that of the legal system itself. It shows how the creation of a perception of crisis arising from the reporting on miscarriages of justice is internal to the media; how such a perception of crisis is written into and out of existence by and within the media themselves. It also demonstrates that, while such a perception of crisis is always latent in the way the media report on miscarriages of justice, it is unlikely to be sustained over any length of time.

A. MISREADING CONVICTION, ACQUITTAL, AND MISCARRIAGE

Conviction is an operation in the legal system, and an event in the environments of other systems.[3] To the legal system, conviction in the Crown Court is a jury's acceptance, after being warned of the need for certainty 'beyond reasonable doubt', that the accused has committed the offence charged. But that acceptance is constructed *legally* through legal procedures: the trial process, rules of evidence, cross-examination, summing up, etc. Similarly, when a conviction is quashed on appeal, the legal operation is a setting aside of the conviction, with the consequence that the punishment is no longer authorized. If in prison, the appellant must be freed. If fined, the moneys paid must be returned. The appellant is restored to the legal status

---

[3] In the news media criminal convictions offer a daily diet for public consumption; see P. Schlesinger and H. Tumber, *Reporting Crime: The Media Politics of Criminal Justice* (Oxford, 1994), ch. 1. In this chapter Schlesinger and Tumber claim that 'spectacular miscarriages of justice' and the 'ensuing crisis of confidence' that 'led to the setting up of the Royal Commission on Criminal Justice' demonstrate 'good grounds for arguing that the criminal justice system is in crisis'. We find it surprising that a book dealing with the analysis of media coverage of crime should so readily accept the media's construction of these conditions. Our study applies critical analysis to this particular construction.

he had prior to conviction: a citizen who cannot legally be punished.[4] In addition the appellant might be entitled to compensation under section 133 of the Criminal Justice Act 1988 or the residual prerogative power to make *ex gratia* payments. Before punishment could recommence the appellant would have to be retried, which is one of the options open to the Court of Appeal when deciding to quash a conviction. At any such trial, as at the previous one, the appellant would commence the proceedings with a presumption of innocence, which requires the prosecution to undertake the burden of demonstrating guilt.

What meanings do the media attribute to these various legal operations? Where a trial is reported the news media present the rival arguments and testimony. Facts are *alleged*. But conviction allows the media to make a radical shift in narrative style. With conviction the news media are able to present a single, objective conclusion: the accused did what he was accused of. However, the jury do not give their interpretation of the facts, only their conclusion. Thus the report of a conviction is often a reprint of the prosecution's case, which is no longer alleged. It is not evidence. It is now *fact*. With the facts established through the authority of conviction, what *happened* can be told, and morally judged. The sentence and the judge's comments also fuel this shift in narrative style. The judge, whatever his professional doubts,[5] will defer to the jury's verdict, treat the guilt of the accused as a fact, and pronounce the appropriate sentence, supplemented by facts of previous bad character and convictions. Such additional material, inadmissible as evidence at trial,[6] helps to complete the media's story. In the post-modern world the substantiation of guilt as fact is really a remarkable achievement. With the problems of eyewitness testimony, selective memory, witness suggestibility, bias, police inefficiency, and any number of

---

[4] The entitlement to compensation depends on a number of factors that have proved controversial. Often a high profile case re-emerges in the media following dispute over the entitlement to or amount of compensation. A good example is the long controversy surrounding the compensation claimed by and awarded to the Birmingham Six; see *The Independent*, 17 July 1997 and 24 July 1997: 'The price of freedom: Six years after release the Birmingham Six are still fighting for compensation' and 'Birmingham Six to challenge "insulting" offer' (Steve Boggan). Another example is the compensation awarded to Winston Silcott for his wrongful conviction and imprisonment as a member of the Tottenham Three, while in prison for his conviction for another murder. This award became headline news and sparked considerable controversy; see the Leading Article in *The Independent*, 2 Aug. 1994 'Silcott Deserves his Money'.

[5] Any doubts may re-emerge when consideration is being given to granting leave to appeal. The judge-led nature of the possibility of a successful appeal has been of great importance, as we have shown in the early part of Ch. 3.

[6] The inadmissibility of evidence of previous convictions and bad character is fundamental to the rules of criminal evidence. The overall justification for these rules is that there is a danger in any trial that such evidence is likely to have a prejudicial effect that outweighs its potential probative value of the commission of this crime, rather than previous crimes. However, the rules are technical and there are a number of exceptions. See C. Tapper, *Cross & Tapper on Evidence* (London, 1995), chs. 7–9.

other reasons why there cannot be such a thing as an objective truth, conviction nevertheless manages, ordinarily, to produce just this, for the media and other systems.[7]

A crime reporter, however cynical or sceptical she may be about the efficacy of criminal trials as a mechanism for the production of truth, has little choice but to present *the story* represented by the fact of conviction, and the moral implications of this fact. Scepticism about the conviction, or trial processes in general, is an alternative story, but one which rarely has greater news value. To present a conviction as something less requires a reporter to report evidence. The style of reporting must continue in the form used during the trial. The narrative would be a presentation of evidence, arguments, and alleged facts. The story cannot shift from what happened to the meanings of established events: the *whys* of causation and responsibility. Thus, aside from any legal constraints represented by contempt of court, the reporter will write as if the conviction establishes the truth of the defendant's guilt. A noticeable exception to this is convictions by courts overseas. Given the lesser social authority of their trial processes in the United Kingdom and the lesser investment that the media has in their convictions as sources of news, there is a greater likelihood that conviction will fail to establish guilt as an objective fact.[8]

To adopt the terminology of autopoietic systems theory, a conviction provides a crucial moment in the *structural coupling* between the legal system and its environment. There is a substantial element of overlap, or in the terms of systems theory structural coupling, between the legal meaning of a conviction and that attributed by the media. Both systems are

---

[7] As an example of a case study of the reporting of one conviction, see Schlesinger and Tumber, n. 3 above, ch. 8 'A Tale of Conviction'. The apparent truth represented by conviction is well illustrated by the front-page reporting in most newspapers on 24 Oct. 1998 of the conviction of Michael Stone for double murder, and how that truth was bolstered by the presentation of *facts* not considered or inadmissible as evidence during the trial. The headline and first line of the front page of *The Guardian* (Audrey Gillan and Duncan Campbell) is a good example. It reads: 'Dark secrets of Russell killer. Michael Stone, the man found guilty yesterday of the double murder of Lin Russell and her daughter Megan and the attempted murder of her other daughter, Josie, had confessed to having fantasies about killing and torturing women and children, it emerged last night.' The case is noteworthy, as an example of newspaper reporting of conviction, because the apparent truth represented by the conviction was challenged within a couple of days of the end of the trial when one of the prosecution's key witnesses claimed that he had lied under oath.

[8] The reporting in this country of the trial and conviction of two British nurses for murder in Saudi Arabia, and the trial and initial conviction for murder of the former au pair Louise Woodward in the United States, are good recent examples. This is well illustrated in relation to Louise Woodward's conviction in articles in *The Guardian* on pp. 1 and 5 on 31 Jan. 97 and pp. 1, 2, and 3 on 1 Nov. 97. Also in *The Guardian* on 1 Nov. 97 the solicitor Anthony Julius debates with those who invariably represent the American criminal justice process as profoundly flawed: 'The attacks on the fairness of the trial by British newspapers have been entirely predictable.' Duncan Campbell's article in *The Guardian* 30 Oct. 97 'Jail Birds' links both cases with others in discussing the assumption that foreign judicial systems fail 'to administer justice as it would be understood in this country'.

concerned with truth. The legal system is, however, concerned with more than truth—a conviction is a finding of guilt following a fair trial—although this extra element of fairness is likely to be ignored by the media. The guilt of the prisoner is a matter of fact. The fairness of the processes that produced that verdict is assumed without comment. The facts, not the fairness of the processes that produced them, are news.[9] Thus, in the terms of systems theory, the strong coupling represented by the moment of conviction is not due to the media's adoption (or literal translation) of the legal meaning of conviction. Rather, there is a stable *mis*reading of conviction by the media. An operation that has been constructed within law through traditions, rules, practices, interests, etc., and is understood rhetorically within law by reference to the values of fairness, rights, *and* truth, is principally reported factually, i.e. as truth. Conviction, as fact, allows a stable misreading of legal processes by other systems; it facilitates the legal system's ability to interrelate, in a stable manner, with other systems.

This systems theory analysis of media treatment of conviction complements and develops other analyses of media reporting of crime. Ericson and others have written of the strong similarities between the discourses of law and news.[10] Both undertake to map order and to invest facts with significance. Ericson argues that both systems attempt to impose order in terms of morality, procedure, hierarchy, and security. Both are concerned with truth, and objectivity: 'The police, courts and legislature supply an endless number of potential items on a regular basis, and offer reliable and credible sources whose documentary or verbal accounts can be routinely *treated as facts* and easily invested with significance.'[11] Chibnall's sociology of criminal justice journalism demonstrates how those who criticize the actors (police, lawyers, or court officials) and would be inclined to question the facts represented by convictions, lose the ability to write criminal news stories as their relationship to these actors deteriorates and their sources dry up.[12] Such sceptics can be investigative journalists, but they cannot be crime reporters.[13] Many social and economic factors reinforce the stable misread-

[9] Again, this is very different from the reporting of foreign trials, even in relation to legal systems very similar to our own.

[10] As a useful introduction, see R. V. Ericson, P. M. Baranek, and J. B. L. Chan, *Representing Order: Crime, Law, and Justice in the News Media* (Toronto, 1991), ch. 1.

[11] R. V. Ericson, 'Why Law is Like News', in D. Nelken (ed.), *Law as Communication* (Aldershot, 1996), 200 (our emphasis).

[12] S. Chibnall, *Law-and-Order News: An Analysis of Crime Reporting in the British Press* (London, 1977). Hall *et al.* are able to show how 'primary definers' of events set 'the limit for all subsequent discussion' (S. Hall, C. Critcher, T. Jefferson, J. Clarke, and B. Roberts, *Policing The Crisis: Mugging, the State, and Law and Order* (London, 1978), 57–60). Such 'primary definers' are often institutional sources, sources that are unlikely to express sceptical attitudes towards the end results of the criminal process, namely convictions.

[13] In a frank article in *The Guardian* 11 Dec. 98 'Shame on the Birmingham Six', its editor, Alan Rushbridger, describes other serious restraints on journalists and editors in their attempts to question convictions, in particular as attempts to disclose miscarriages of justice.

ing of convictions as truth, with subject-matter relating to procedural fairness ignored or taken for granted. Legal constraints also explain, in part, the change of narrative style that occurs on conviction. Following conviction, the implications of libel law, contempt of court, and complaints to the Press Council are considerably lessened. The journalist is free to report conviction as fact without fear of legal sanctions. However, non-legal factors are likely to be more important. Unless the conviction is treated as an authoritative statement of guilt, the journalist is forced by the standards and practices of her profession to construct facts in the more demanding manner appropriate to the absence of such authorities: opposing accounts, different sources, and their balance. The evidence of prosecution and defence must continue to be reported, interrogated, and assessed. This style is both more demanding and it undermines the shift in narrative style (the new story) made possible by conviction.[14] A review of the safety of the conviction is more likely to appear as a future investigative journalist's report, than as the next day's headlines. The need to relate crime stories to news values also leads to a situation in which, aside from the trials of existing celebrities, the issue of whether someone has committed an offence is less newsworthy than *what* they have done. Contempt proceedings operate to prevent journalists from anticipating this news value earlier than the point of conviction.

If one looked only at convictions, systems theory might seem to offer no more than a gloss on more established forms of analysis. To represent the descriptions and conclusions of empirical studies of trial and conviction as structural coupling adds little to our understanding of these processes. But the concept of stable misreading can help to identify, inform, and explain the media's treatment of other legal operations that are closely related to conviction: acquittal and wrongful conviction. The media's ability to absorb a conviction contrasts with the difficulty that they face when attempting to report on acquittals or wrongful convictions. The media seek an alternative, equally authoritative narrative. If the accused was not convicted, the media often attempt to present this as an authoritative statement of innocence: an acceptance of the defence case.[15] Similarly, when a

---

[14] This analysis conforms to much of the literature dealing with the reporting of criminal trials; see D. Howett, *Crime, the Media and the Law* (Chichester, 1998), ch. 13 'Criminal Justice and the Media', esp. 171–4.

[15] Legally the acquittal of a defendant can mean no more than that the evidence presented did not produce a conviction. The media inevitably read more into it. So, for example, 'It's a year since the watershed trial in which Austen Donnellan was proved innocent' (*The Guardian*, 24 Sept. 94) conflates 'proved innocent' with *not found guilty*. For a case study of the reporting of one high profile acquittal, see Schlesinger and Tumber, n. 3 above, ch. 7 'A Tale of Acquittal'. Again, this may be very different from the reporting in this country of foreign systems' acquittals, a high profile recent example being the acquittal in the United States of O. J. Simpson. See A. M. Dershowitz, *Reasonable Doubts: The O. J. Simpson Case and the Criminal Justice System* (New York, 1996), esp. ch. VI 'Why Was There Such a Great Disparity between the Public Perception and the Jury Verdict?'.

conviction is quashed on appeal, the media regularly try to use the Court of Appeal's decision as an authoritative statement of innocence. In treating these legal operations as authoritative statements of innocence the media both reinforce and respond to general expectations: 'A miscarriage of justice equals, in the public's mind, innocence of the crime.'[16] The reporting of successful appeals, like the reporting of convictions, is a misreading of legal operations. To represent wrongful conviction as a condition of innocence attributes meanings to events within the legal system which differ from their legal meanings. As stated above, quashing a conviction returns a citizen to the legal condition of presumed innocence that he shares with all others: any new trial would start from this position. 'The law is, strictly speaking, unconcerned with guilt or innocence. Its concern is conviction or acquittal.'[17] But the media, and the public, can give such events a wider meaning. Acquittal and wrongful conviction are regularly taken to return an individual to an original state of grace: they *are* innocent.[18]

Even within the legal system, wrongful conviction has meanings that go beyond its narrow legal operations, but they are not the same as those of the media. The rhetorical meaning of a wrongful conviction, like the original conviction, is associated with ideas of truth *and* fairness. An unsafe conviction is one obtained on inadequate evidence and/or in breach of the procedures which are understood to construct a fair trial. As such, a quashed conviction does not mean that the individual concerned is innocent. In the overwhelming majority of cases, it means that the procedures that led to conviction were incorrect in a manner that the legal profession associates strongly with notions of fairness. Thus, to lawyers, a successful appeal is usually an acceptance that the trial was unfair. As to the factual innocence of the appellant, in response to the application of legal procedures, the lawyer can only be agnostic. This agnosticism is the logical conclusion of legal processes. That logical conclusion does not deny the possibility that many lawyers, as individuals, might believe that legal processes are likely to produce the truth, or that their clients are innocent. But such a conclusion is neither necessary nor sufficient.

Louis Blom-Cooper QC has written a remarkable book on the Birmingham Six case seeking to explore 'the public misconception about, and the professional failure to explain the function of the Court of

---

[16] L. Blom-Cooper, *The Birmingham Six and Other Cases: Victims of Circumstance* (London, 1997), 8.   [17] Ibid. 8.
[18] This is by no means easy to achieve, indeed it is rare for the successful overturning of an appellant's conviction to amount to objective proof of innocence. It certainly did so in the successful appeals of Stefan Kiszko and Patrick Phillips (see our reference to these appeals in section C/7 of Ch. 5). However this was not the case in the high profile appeals of the Birmingham Six and Maguire Seven (see our analysis of the reporting of these appeals later in this chapter and our case studies of them in section C of Ch. 5).

Appeal'.[19] He attributes the apparent lack of public confidence in the criminal justice system, which resulted from this and other leading miscarriage cases, as a product of 'undoubted confusion of thought, both among informed commentators as well as untutored citizens'.[20] The thesis which informs his book is that if the public understood the constitutional importance of trial by jury, the implications of deferring to the jury as arbiter of fact, and the commitment of criminal justice to considerations of fairness, it would not *read* quashed convictions as statements of innocence. In turn, it would not embrace explanations of why such factually innocent persons were convicted which undermine the integrity of the legal system, or press for reforms of the system designed to ensure that such convictions of the innocent never recur.

Blom-Cooper is correct to conclude that a public that shared the meanings attributed by the legal system to its own operations would not so readily treat wrongful convictions as reasons to lose confidence in the system. But his solution (education through books such as his own) shows little understanding or tolerance of the processes that lead to law being misread by the media. Nor does he discuss the benefits which, at least in the context of conviction, ordinarily follow from such misreading. By accepting conviction as a matter of fact, something which justifies punishment, criminal records, reduced access to credit and insurance, job prospects, future sentences, and general moral status, the media's misreading of legal operations exhibits a tremendous commitment and deference to law and legal processes. If conviction was understood publicly with the degree of agnosticism exhibited by lawyers themselves, these linked consequences could not follow, or at least not so smoothly. And whilst lawyers accept that trial is about fairness as well as truth, there is no straightforward consensus among lawyers about the conditions which represent fairness. Reforming lawyers want more fairness and rights in the system. If their views were accepted by the media, then even the fairness of convictions, let alone their truth, becomes contingent. In the circumstances of such informed understandings of the operation of laws, wrongful conviction in itself would not lead to the apparent crisis or loss of public confidence often referred to in the media. But neither would conviction contribute (or at least not so strongly) to stability.

In high profile miscarriages of justice, the media's search for a legal process which reverses the meaning of conviction, which points to the prisoner's factual innocence, has elements which can build into a perception of crisis.[21] The basis on which a miscarriage of justice becomes high profile

[19] See n. 16 above, 7. His book has been strongly criticized; see articles by David Pallister in *The Guardian* 29 Nov. 97: 'Outrage at Birmingham Six Book' and 'Legal Limbo of Birmingham Six'.   [20] See n. 16 above, 7.

[21] The construction of *crisis* by the media is a common phenomenon, whether or not the facts bear out such an interpretation. See, e.g., the analysis of the reporting of an 'energy crisis' by American news media: B. DeGeorge, *Interpreting Crisis: A Retrospective Analysis* (Sweden, 1987).

may contain elements of proof that the legal system refuses to recognize. Guissipe Conlan (one of the Maguire Seven and a devout Catholic) managed to enlist the support of Archbishop Hume by continuing to protest his innocence even whilst receiving the last rites. Chris Mullin MP interviewed persons who admitted to carrying out the bombings attributed to the Birmingham Six. In the case of George Edalji, the support of the renowned crime fiction writer Sir Arthur Conan Doyle played a large part in building belief in his innocence. The media rely on such *authoritative* sources for the construction of news. But the Court of Appeal recognizes no opinion as authoritative except that which it constructs for the jury. Many reform proposals understand this problem and attempt to avoid it by arguing for a Court of Last Resort[22] that is unencumbered by all the strictures of legal evidence.[23]

The Court of Appeal's deference to the jury's constitutional importance[24] is not generally appreciated or respected within the media. The narrative which the media draw from the fact of conviction is based largely on the prosecution case. Thus, if persons whom the media regard as authorities come to question important aspects of this case, the media may come to expect the conviction to be quashed. But the Court of Appeal's deference to the jury does not require it to uphold a conviction solely on the basis of the original prosecution case. If it finds other explanations for events which are compatible with the conviction, and which could have been accepted by a jury, it will continue to uphold the conviction.[25] By resisting the reversal of convictions based on the media's construction of a convicted person's innocence, a resistance which is necessary for the continued authority of the legal system, the Court of Appeal can precipitate a trial by media[26] of the legal system itself. For example, in the case of Adolf Beck, the lack of a basis for the reversal of the jury's verdict led to intense scrutiny and criticism of

---

[22] That is, an institution very different in make-up from the existing Court of Appeal. Many commentators have argued for such an alternative body. These include the influential writer and broadcaster Ludovic Kennedy, who has campaigned for such a body, and written books and numerous newspaper articles about, a number of miscarriages of justice. See his 'Reforming the English Criminal Justice System', in *Truth To Tell: The Collected Writings of Ludovic Kennedy* (London, 1991), 308–19.

[23] A good example is the clause proposed by Conservative MP Sir John Farr to be inserted into the Criminal Justice Bill 1988 to establish a tribunal to examine miscarriages of justice and look at 'evidence that was not admissible before the Court of Appeal' (*The Guardian*, 8 Apr. 88 'Tory MP Launches Fight for Bombers').

[24] We have already described this deference in the previous chapter, and deal with it more fully in section B/4 of Ch. 5.

[25] Hence Blom-Cooper's defence of the Court of Appeal's rejection of the earlier unsuccessful appeals of the Birmingham Six appellants, n. 16 above.

[26] The role of the media in publicizing alleged miscarriages has had a controversial history, but it is now generally recognized that their role has been and continues to be positive. However, the dangers of trial by media, or retrial by media, are also generally recognized, see, e.g., A. Garapon, 'Justice out of Court: The Dangers of Trial by Media', in Nelken (ed.), n. 11 above, ch. 11.

the original trial. And the legal system's resistance to a reversal of the convictions of the high profile terrorist cases (Birmingham Six, Guildford Four, and Maguire Seven) created the conditions for the appointment of a judicial inquiry into the conduct of the latter two cases followed by a Royal Commission on Criminal Justice.

B. CONSTRUCTING CRISIS[27]

In autopoietic systems theory terms, what is evoked by miscarriages of justice is a threat to the structural coupling represented by conviction. Conviction allows a stable misreading of legal processes by other systems. It facilitates the legal system's ability to interrelate, in a stable manner, with other systems. With the focus on structural coupling, the potential crisis that may be generated by miscarriages of justice comes from the threat to the stability of this coupling. It is a crisis of confidence within the media in their ability to rely on convictions to make communications about crime. Non-systems theory understandings of crisis of public confidence look at this very differently. The legal academic Zuckerman[28] and the legal journalist Rozenberg[29] and others present the crisis of confidence generated by miscarriages of justice as a crisis in the general public. They locate the crisis outside of any system, in the unstructured social world which Habermas and others call 'the lifeworld'.[30] For Zuckerman, loss of public confidence is likely to lead to reduction in the willingness of members of the public to report crimes, or to obey those in authority. It is a general weakening of the public's commitment to the normative value of the English criminal justice process. The tautology that citizens will not obey law voluntarily unless they have confidence in its legitimacy is stretched to the causal claim that miscarriages of justice will reduce the occasions on which such obedience will occur. Similar arguments appear in the Introduction to the Report of the Royal Commission on Criminal Justice.[31]

Autopoietic systems theory raises doubts over whether it is possible to read stable indicators from areas of life that lie outside of systems—areas that are spontaneous and unstructured. Such scepticism seems warranted.

---

[27] In this section we were informed by M. Fishman, *Manufacturing the News* (Austin, 1980), and particularly his analysis of the way news is constructed through organizing concepts and themes continuously reported. See the section 'Assembling a Crime Wave' in ch. 1.

[28] 'Miscarriage of Justice and Judicial Responsibility', *Criminal Law Review* [1991], 492–500.

[29] 'Only then can the system attempt to rebuild the public's shattered confidence' ('Miscarriages of Justice', in E. Stockdale and S. Casale (eds.), *Criminal Justice under Stress* (London, 1992), 116).

[30] See his *The Theory of Communicative Action*, Vol. 2, *Lifeworld and System; A Critique of Functionalist Reason* (Cambridge, 1987), ch. VI.

[31] *Runciman Report*, Cm. 2263 (London, 1993).

For example, what meaning could one attribute to surveys on public confidence in the criminal justice system, if they were to be undertaken, especially when these are conducted during a period when the media are reporting that a crisis of confidence exists? What would each person canvassed have understood by the criminal justice system? And how would one have isolated these surveys from the effects of media reporting that stated that such a crisis of confidence already existed? One must also question the ability to reason from the surveys that were carried out. For example, there are regular public opinion surveys on attitudes towards, and confidence in, the police. In a period such as that covered by our review of newspaper articles (see Section C below), a period of sustained reporting that the public should expect to suffer from some loss of confidence in the institutions of criminal justice, a drop of confidence in the police was recorded. It is difficult to show that such findings are outside of, and independent from, the media that report on them. But even if one treats them as evidence of something that exists outside of the media, how does one reason from a loss of confidence in the police, to a loss of confidence in the criminal justice system? Is a loss of confidence in the integrity of the police the same thing as a loss of confidence in the criminal justice system? While one might be tempted to claim that these ideas are linked, their exact relationship is unclear. What kind of belief must one have in the ability of the legal system's procedures to assess police evidence before a drop of confidence in the integrity of the police makes a significant contribution to loss of confidence in the criminal justice system? Journalists can reason from one to the other, only by attributing beliefs and reasoning to their audience that has not been empirically identified, and may not exist. Thus, there is actually no site of crisis outside of and independent from the media, which the media can then report upon as an *event*. References to a crisis should first be examined as an internal construction of the media themselves.

Whilst there are elements within the media that can lead them to talk of crisis, so there are even more systematically structured elements that lead them away from such communications. If all convictions were to be questioned, then actors within the media, and other systems, would have to go behind the legal code, to unravel the events which led to its application, reach their own judgments on whether the legal communication of conviction was appropriate. But this would add considerably to the complexity of the media's ability to report on crime.[32] Indeed, there is even some evidence to suggest that the production of an objectively verifiable crisis in terms of,

---

[32] Remembering that this is their everyday, staple diet. Indeed Ericson, Baranek, and Chan, n. 10 above, 341, estimate that crime, law, and justice constitute 'just under one-half of all news coverage in newspapers'. It should be noted that in Britain this may be changing with everyday stories from criminal courts declining because 'in the last 20 years, the nationwide network of court reporters which once provided blanket coverage has been slowly killed off' (*The Media Guardian*, 11 Jan. 99 'Getting away with Murder' (Nick Davies)).

for example, a significant drop in the conviction rate, would lead to a reduction in the media's willingness to report on a crisis of confidence in criminal justice. The media may have some self-consciousness of the possible consequences of their constructions of crisis, which leads them to move from an alarmist mode of reporting when the seriousness of a social situation becomes objectively apparent.[33]

Whilst the media may generate for themselves a perception of the legal system in crisis, there are good reasons to expect such crises to be both episodic and unlikely to lead to radical reforms.[34] To repeat the point, one must not forget the media's commitment to conviction. Within the media, conviction provides a rare occasion to tell an objective truth. Apparent objectivity for the media[35] is ordinarily constructed through structures of balance of information, knowledge and opinion. But a conviction, when reported, takes the form of an authoritative conclusion that the convicted person committed the crime in question. Convictions represent an occasion when, with only rare exceptions, there is no alternative authority offering a contrary view of events. There is therefore nothing to balance. A reported conviction is official confirmation of action, creating a fixed point of reference for the media's narratives. The contempt of court and libel laws provide obvious instrumental explanations for the reporting of trials and convictions. The threat of libel, or contempt of court, may account for the presentation of trial events as argument and evidence ('It is alleged', etc.). And the conviction provides the reverse position: in reporting the prosecution case as fact the media are protected against possible libel actions. The media are not alone in fixing on conviction for such purposes. Convictions

---

[33] See Ungar's analysis of media reporting of the Ebola outbreak in Zaire in the 1990s. He is able to show how the media shift from 'alarming to reassuring' when dealing with what they perceive as a crisis. They are more likely to take up the approach of reassurance when there is by most standards an existing crisis, but the approach of alarm when such a crisis is less objectively verified. As Ungar writes: 'Alarming content about risk is more common than reassuring content or intermediate content—except, perhaps, in crisis situations, when the impulse to prevent panic seems to moderate coverage' ('Hot Crises and Media Reassurance: A Comparison of Emerging Diseases and Ebola Zaire', *British Journal of Sociology*, 49/1 (1998), 36–56, 36, quoting P. Sandman, 'Mass Media and Environmental Risk: Seven Principles', *Risk: Health, Safety and Environment*, Summer (1994), 251–60).

[34] In addition to the argument we present here, some research suggests that public perception of and opinion about crime and criminals is less influenced by the press than many (particularly those in the press) imagine. See B. Roshier, 'The Selection of Crime News by the Press', in S. Cohen and J. Young (eds.), *The Manufacture of News: Social Problems, Deviance and the Mass Media* (London, 1973), 28–39.

[35] The claim to objectivity is more characteristic of television news than the press. This claim has been strongly denied in relation to both media forms; see Glasgow University Media Group, *Bad News, Vol. 1* (London, 1976), and G. Tuchman, 'Objectivity as Strategic Ritual: An Examination of Newsmen's Notions of Objectivity', *American Journal of Sociology*, 77/4 (1972), 660–79. Although there are differences between television news and newspaper news there are also strong similarities, see P. Weaver, 'TV News and Newspaper News', in R. P. Adler (ed.), *Understanding Television: Essays on Television as a Social and Cultural Force* (New York, 1981), 277–93.

can be read by other systems as similar kinds of objective facts, allowing those systems to apply their own codes: creditworthiness, insurability, employability, electability, etc. And while there may be room for judgement as to whether the particular offence, and the surrounding circumstances, justify the application of the relevant code, there is no mechanism by which these other systems can undo the event which they are seeking to interpret: a legal conviction.

The media's commitment to convictions makes it difficult for them to sustain communications about their constructions of a crisis of public confidence in the criminal justice system. On the very day of the successful appeal of the Birmingham Six being reported, normal reporting about crime based on convictions continued. A logically consistent application of any media communications on crisis to themselves should have led to a restatement of all such convictions on the basis of evidence, rather than objective truth. Once media-recognized cases of miscarriage have been recognized within the law as wrongful through a successful appeal, the pressure for reform of the legal system, based on the continued assertion that convictions are unreliable, is likely to evaporate. The media's more usual relationship with the legal system (that of an outsider which misreads legal communications for its own purposes) a system which relies on law to produce facts of guilt and innocence—is likely to return.[36] Non-systems theory approaches to the study of the media again support this analysis of any crisis of public confidence that might be represented as following from high profile miscarriages of justice. Such crises are not natural things or even agglomerations of things. They are constructs in discourse. The media talks them into and out of existence. Such talk is neither simple nor straightforward. 'Crisis, then, is not some objective condition or property of a system defining the contours for subsequent ideological contestation. Rather, it is subjectively perceived and hence brought into existence through narrative and discourse.'[37]

Hay describes the attribution of crisis to media constructions as 'a process'. In that process there are a range of 'representations and hence "constructions" of failure'.[38] At one level this involves narratives that represent newsworthy events as symptoms of failure, at another level the multiplicity of such events and the narratives that represent them create a meta-narrative of crisis. The meta-narrative integrates the multiple events. The encoding process relies on 'discursive selectivity': 'By importing such

[36] We doubt that journalists' apparent commitment to convictions represents their personal beliefs in the reliability of the English legal system, or a hegemonic (Marxist) commitment to its authority. Our use of autopoietic systems theory builds upon, and is compatible with, analysis that recognizes the factors of superficiality, narrowness of focus, competitiveness, time pressure, organizational shortcomings, etc., which surround crime reporting. See P. Grabosky and P. Wilson, *Journalism and Justice: How Crime is Reported* (Sydney, 1989), esp. ch. 4 'The Courts, Criminal Procedure and Contempt'.

[37] C. Hay, 'Narrating Crisis: The Discursive Construction of the "Winter of Discontent"', *Sociology*, 30/2 (1996), 255.   [38] Ibid. 266–7.

simplified and simplifying abstractions, a multitude of ⌐
be recruited as "symptoms" within the discourse of cris
an analysis to show how the media were influential in
'crisis-hit Britain', 'Britain under siege', 'Crisis Brita
known as the 'Winter of Discontent'; and how such ⌐
cisive in enabling Thatcherism to achieve state power
in the processes of constituting crises that new trajectories oɪ puʋ... ...
are achieved. In this sense the media are influential in determining the likely
success or failure of particular arguments for reform. Paul 't Hart puts this
well: 'The most important instrument of crisis management is language.
Those who are able to define what the crisis is all about also hold the key
to defining the appropriate strategies for [its] resolution.'[40] Thus we need
to look at not only how the media construct a meta-narrative of crisis, but
what strategies they suggest for its resolution.

In the particular context of the period covered by our survey, the crisis
was one of *public confidence*. The public that suffers this crisis is not a
statistically quantifiable cross-section of the population. According to Hall
et al.[41] the notion of 'the public' is always present in the writing of journalists. Each newspaper constructs its imagined audience, and treats that
audience as 'the public', claiming to speak to it, and for it; and even adopting a language or idiom that it attributes to it. Writing for such an audience
requires authors to make plausible claims, utilizing general points of reference that are expected to provide quick and easy ways of locating the
subject matter within the audience's understanding. Writing for such audiences presents authors with restrictions and opportunities. In constructing
a crisis of public confidence, the author can rely on persuasion rather than
empirical surveys, presenting reasons why his audience should suffer such a
loss of confidence. But the need to make an almost immediate link with the
audience's presumed level of understanding restricts the technicality or
complexity of what can be presented. In the context of reporting on miscarriages of justice, this reinforces the understanding of conviction as a statement about the truth of a person's guilt rather than about the fairness of his
or her trial. It is relatively easy to assume that an audience understands
arguments about the likelihood that a person did, in fact, commit a particular crime. Indeed, the 'Whodunnit?' crime novel or TV series is an
extremely successful and widespread form of popular culture. By contrast,
whilst some general rights (trial by jury, full disclosure, right to silence) may
be assumed to have some general level of appeal and understanding, particular infringements or restrictions on such rights require the author to
take the reader into difficult and unfamiliar terrain.

[39] Ibid. 267.
[40] P. 't Hart, 'Symbols, Rituals and Power: The Lost Dimensions of Crisis Management',
Journal of Contingencies and Crisis Management, 1/1 (1993), 41.
[41] See n. 12 above, ch. 3, esp. 60–6.

∠icson's understanding of the use of 'public interest' by the media ⅃bstantiates the above view of the nature of any media representation of crisis in public confidence. In the following quotation, 'public interest' has been deleted, and **public confidence** substituted:

Legal and news operatives do not ascertain **public confidence** through direct, systematic surveys of public opinion. In the case of both journalists . . . and judges . . . for example, knowledge of **public confidence** is derived from talking to friends, associates and other members of the deviance-defining elite. News and law are thus both orientated to particular publics, namely the regular players in their own hermeneutic circles. *The general public is only imagined as something they represent, not surveyed in a representative manner.*[42]

Our study of newspaper reporting on miscarriages of justice shows how the discourses of crisis and public confidence become a rhetorical device for questioning and challenging legal procedures, for questioning their ability to produce truth, and consequently, their moral authority. As Ericson puts it: 'political authorities are constantly faced with the risk of loss of legitimacy, of having their institutional and personal authority deconstructed by the mass media.'[43] The journalists who refer to public confidence do not carry out public opinion surveys (although they may question specific, informed individuals). If one believes (or writes as if one believes) in a failure of legal procedures to produce truth, then rhetorical logic (not empirical fact) points to there being some diminution of confidence in those legal procedures. If one describes such failures as general and systemic, there should, within the logic of rhetoric, be a crisis of confidence. If a conviction produced by police brutality is evidence that confessions are generally unreliable, or a conviction produced by poor forensic science is evidence that such science cannot be trusted, then the moral authority of the legal system is (again within the logic of rhetoric) in doubt. If legal processes do not produce truth, then how, logically, can juries convict? If other journalists write in a similar manner the objectivity of the claim of crisis is reinforced.

However, the logic of any representation of crisis is not sustained by the news media. If the legal system is in crisis, then trials of individuals are replaced by trials by the media of the legal system itself. It is no longer possible to accept a conviction as conclusive authority for what an individual has done. For to accept the inability of legal processes to produce convictions which represent truth of guilt requires the media to forgo the authoritative stories of individual wrongdoing which convictions represent. And here, what has been called the superficiality of the media comes into play. Consistency would require a media that spoke of a crisis of public confidence in criminal justice to cease publishing convictions as narratives

---

[42] See n. 11 above, 202. Our emphasis italicized.
[43] 'Mass Media, Crime, Law and Justice', *British Journal of Criminology*, 31/3 (1991), 233.

of wrongdoing. But this does not occur. Instead, reporting of miscarriages and their claimed effects on public confidence occur alongside stories of convictions. Superficiality also operates to erode perceptions of crisis engendered by high profile miscarriages of justice. As the Glasgow Media Studies Group have shown, the news media tend to focus on narratives that describe the surface of events to the neglect of reporting on their causes.[44] Thus whilst fresh individual tragedies represented by officially identified wrongful convictions will continue to make news, it is more difficult to maintain the newsworthiness of the claimed general causes of such miscarriages. Sustaining the narratives of crisis in the face of the everyday stories of conviction is also undermined by limited reforms. Part of the crisis story is the question: would this happen today? Changes in legal procedures make it more difficult to make the rhetorical logical claim that acknowledged miscarriages of justice represent a threat to the safety of current convictions. As with other stories of crisis, the antidote is likely to be rhetorical and logical rather than empirical.[45] Changes which, logically, could be expected to reduce the kinds of mistakes that are reported to have produced miscarriages undermine the media's ability to report on any continued crisis. What we see is how, as Kepplinger and Roth conclude in their study about reporting on a so-called oil crisis, 'the logic of reality differs from the logic of reported reality.'[46]

C. ANALYSING MEDIA REPORTING ON MISCARRIAGES OF JUSTICE

Autopoiesis would lead one to expect the relationship between law and the media to be a complicated one. The theory leads one to doubt the ability of different systems to *talk* directly to each other. No person, persons, or institution can expect to act as a wholly successful translator of the communications of a system. To use one of the most powerful metaphors about the theory, no communication outwards can ever escape the bubble of the system's boundaries. The best one can hope for is that the effects of such

---

[44] See n. 35 above. The particular form of knowledge represented in *the news* is succinctly described by P. Rock, 'News as Eternal Recurrence', in Cohen and Young (eds.), n. 34 above, 73–80. Rock's account is, we believe, consistent with our analysis of the implications of the everyday reporting of conviction.

[45] This argument even applies to the investigative journalist, see T. L. Glasser and J. S. Ettema, 'Investigative Journalism and the Moral Order', in R. K. Avery and D. Eason (eds.), *Critical Perspectives on Media and Society* (New York, 1991), 203–25.

[46] 'Creating a Crisis: German Mass Media and Oil Supply in 1973–74', *Public Opinion Quarterly* (1979), 296. The above analysis is borne out by other analyses of media reporting of *crisis*. Kepplinger and Roth are able to demonstrate that the way in which events relating to oil supply in Germany were reported created the conditions for a crisis, indeed encouraged a greater demand and thus the crisis itself, namely the conditions of under-supply that occurred.

communications (the shapes generated in the bubble) can be read constructively by those who seek to communicate within another system.

In the sections that follow, we have attempted to analyse the process by which law and the media mis-communicate with each other, or more specifically the way in which the media misread the particular legal communication of miscarriage of justice. In our history of the Court of Appeal, we have already noted that the media play an important role in constructing miscarriages of justice. And in the first part of this chapter, we have analysed the reasons why law and the media might be expected to mis-communicate. In the four sections that follow this one, we present systematically collected examples of this media communication about miscarriages of justice. We read articles about miscarriages of justice mainly from quality newspapers[47] in the ten-year period from 1987 to 1996. There were over 1,000 such articles. These articles all contained the phrases 'miscarriage(s) of justice' and 'Court of Appeal'.[48] Our reference to articles includes, without differentiation, news reporting, features, editorials, and even letters. We found that the large number of articles that we surveyed and the disparate kind of material that they dealt with[49] made it a less valuable exercise to try to make formal distinctions between the types of articles written than to try to present their discourse as a whole. We also made no formal distinction between articles according to their authors. Some were written by legal correspondents, general journalists, and editors, but also some by lawyers; indeed there were even articles written by former judges, television producers, victims, campaigners, etc. However, what is common ground about these articles is not so much what kinds of article they are or who the authors are, as who the anticipated audience is, and that they are newspapers' articles and therefore relatively short. Inevitably there are consequences from the simple facts that the anticipated audience is that of the general newspaper reader, that the articles are relatively short, and that they are considered to be newsworthy. Detail and technical matters are eschewed, even though in some articles by lawyers some technicalities do arise.[50]

This exercise is justified in a book on miscarriages of justice for a number

---

[47] All the articles we read were in the quality daily papers *The Daily Telegraph*, *The Financial Times*, *The Guardian*, *The Independent*, and *The Times*. We also read articles in these papers' linked Sunday broadsheets. The only other daily newspapers we read and on rare occasion mention in the text are *The Daily Mail* and *Today*. However those two papers were not part of our systematic analysis.

[48] We used the FT Profile data retrieval facility for UK News using the search string Miscarriage of Justice + Court of Appeal.

[49] Descriptions of individual appeals, narratives about particular crimes, narratives about victims of miscarriage, reform proposals, political debate, etc.

[50] Had we been concentrating on one or two specific miscarriages rather than surveying a ten-year period covering many miscarriages and related matters, the more formal distinctions between type and authorship of articles would have enabled us to present a more structured analysis.

of reasons. The idea that certain cases are high profile and capable of providing platforms for the criticism and reform of the processes and practices of criminal justice has generated a large body of writing and scholarship. Our first justification for this recent history is to unpack what this type of claim represents. Even if those reading it are left without any sense of a dominant media meaning to miscarriages of justice, or what factors make a miscarriage high profile, this at least leaves a question mark over the legitimacy of such scholarship. Whilst such deconstruction has its uses, we feel that the history we present shows that media interest in and representation of miscarriages is not so random and unstructured as this. For high profile cases to raise expectations of reforms they must not simply raise media interest due to such factors as the presence of a powerful narrative. Such cases have to be widely perceived within the media as having significant implications for criminal justice. This does not occur automatically through the intrinsic characteristics of particular cases, but is a consequence of media reporting.

We agree with Pattenden that 'Since 1988 the media have represented the criminal appeal system at Court of Appeal level as in crisis.'[51] This statement is borne out by our reading of articles about miscarriages of justice in the two-year period up to 1989, and from 1989 to 1992. However we found that the momentum of talk of crisis is lost from 1993 to 1994 and thereafter in 1995 to 1996 reporting of similar material about miscarriages is not characterized by the talk of crisis. Our history shows how the high profile cases were gradually integrated into a dominant meta-narrative of crisis, and how that narrative receded. The reader will, we hope, be left with a better understanding of the self-referential process by which miscarriages are reported as evidence of crisis. The history reveals the conditions in which those who had expectations of radical reform became optimistic, and goes some way to explaining why their optimism was so misplaced.[52] Lastly, we believe this exercise supports our view that law and the media do not share a common meaning and understanding of what constitutes miscarriage of justice. This does not mean that the authors of articles are unaware of the differences. On the contrary, we found examples of lawyers writing for an audience of journalists and general readers who expressed frustration at the media's failure to understand how law constructs convictions and miscarriages of justice. There were also examples the other way, with journalists expressing frustration at the inability of lawyers, particularly judges, to respond to what they saw as the public's understandings of miscarriage of justice.[53] We even found examples of journalists who came to understand the impossibility of reconciling the legal and public's understandings of miscarriage. Despite this, the articles we read supported our

---

[51] R. Pattenden, *English Criminal Appeals 1844–1994* (Oxford, 1996), 57.
[52] We continue this theme in Ch. 6.   [53] See particularly section H below.

view that there are different dominant meanings of or means of communicating about miscarriage of justice found in law and the media. The legal
meaning is informed by a commitment to truth and legal (current or
reformed) processes. The second meaning is based on a commitment to
truth, without commitment to legal procedures. It is the second of these
meanings, and the inability of the legal system to satisfy it, that creates the
conditions whereby particular cases of miscarriage can build into a meta-
narrative of crisis.

What we observed in these articles was an initial period in which the
authority of the Court of Appeal, and its judges, is generally respected. But
as a meta-narrative of crisis develops, tolerance of the existing system, and
of the senior judiciary's deference towards that system, deteriorates. The
development of such a general meta-narrative of crisis makes the unsatisfactory state of the processes and practices of criminal justice into an *obvious* fact. The media is the site where law's tragic choice, its sacrifice of its
fundamental values, is revealed. From this perspective, the judiciary's
apparent reluctance to recognize or respond to general perceptions of
systematic and widespread failures makes it in turn subject to virulent
attacks. After all, if the widespread failure of criminal justice to deliver
justice is obvious and the events that are treated as evidence of this failure
occurred years before, what explanation for the judiciary's attitude is there
except ignorance, bias, or institutionalized corruption? Attempts by judges
to justify their actions in terms of a more limited agenda for providing
justice than that taken up by the media fall, as autopoiesis leads us to
expect, on deaf ears. In turn, in the face of widespread criticism of the
system and itself, the judiciary responds. It takes the media seriously, not in
the sense of responding wholeheartedly to claims that criminal justice is in
need of radical reforms from top to bottom, but at the level of public relations. It is the media themselves, rather than their specific messages, which
must be taken seriously. The judges respond in a manner that leaves most
of law's institutional processes intact. They do not abandon their deference
to the jury. (With what could they replace it?). Nor do they adopt a wholesale scepticism towards prosecution processes. Instead, they address some
of the criticisms directed at themselves: that they have shown insufficient
humility, openness, or a willingness to apologize. With these changes,
together with the appointment of a Royal Commission, a new Criminal
Appeal Act, and new Criminal Cases Review Commission, and perhaps the
mere fact of time passing, *crisis* is no longer a dominant media theme, and
radical reform is no longer perceived as attainable, or necessary.

During our analysis we regularly use the phrase 'criminal justice system'.
It is the phrase most commonly used in newspapers to identify an apparent
unity among a range of disparate practices, arrangements, processes,
personnel, etc. To avoid using this phrase in our analysis would give a less
representative sense of the discourse of the newspaper articles that we read.

But, we repeat what we said in Chapter 1. Our use of this phrase does not imply that, in autopoietic terms, there is such a system, or that ordinarily that phrase should be used without considerable care. Nevertheless, it is characteristic of newspaper reporting that the phrase 'criminal justice system' or 'system of criminal justice' is used regularly and superficially, without care.

D. Before the recent crisis: 1987–8

Early in 1987 a cross-party group of MPs and Peers, including churchmen and two former senior members of the judiciary, met with the Home Secretary to express concern about and seek referrals to the Court of Appeal of the 1970s cases of the Birmingham Six, Guildford Four, and Maguire Seven. These cases had been the subject of some influential books[54] as well as a number of documentary programmes on television questioning whether the defendants were guilty of the offences for which they had been convicted.

At this stage the press is reporting on the campaigns to overturn these convictions principally as campaigns. An article in *The Times*, for example, notes 'growing public disquiet over the convictions', and the increasing pressure on the Home Secretary to make a referral.[55] But it does not suggest that the defendants must be innocent, and there seems to be no desire to identify the lessons that their wrongful convictions might have for the system of criminal justice. The article takes an optimistic view of the outcome of the campaigns. The possibility that the Court of Appeal might undertake a wider review of fresh evidence is used to imply that, if these cases were referred back to it, the outcome of the appeals might be different from earlier unsuccessful appeals. In support of this view, the article quotes a legal authority which confirms the unrestricted power of the Court of Appeal to conduct a review of all the evidence, not just new evidence, and even to consider new arguments, in deciding whether to uphold a conviction.[56] No consideration is given to the implications of taking such an open and flexible approach to criminal appeals. When the case of the Birmingham Six is referred back to the Court of Appeal by the Home Secretary, but not the cases of the Guildford Four or Maguire Seven, some of the implications of the Court undertaking open-ended reviews are considered in the press. Newspaper articles express a variety of attitudes towards this issue. Some explain the decision to refer only the Birmingham

---

[54] Particularly C. Mullin, *Error of Judgement: The Truth about the Birmingham Bombings* (London, 1986) and R. Kee, *Trial and Error: The Maguires, the Guildford Pub Bombings and British Justice* (London, 1986).

[55] 8 Jan. 87 'A Question of Justice: IRA Bombing Convictions' (Leading Article).

[56] Ibid., citing *R v Chard* (1984) 78 Cr. App. R 106.

Six case by repeating arguments about the need for finality in legal proceedings, approving of the Court of Appeal's use of its powers and deprecating some 'wild accusations of miscarriages of justice'[57] made in television programmes. At the other extreme, some articles seek to encourage the Court of Appeal to approach fresh evidence with a more liberal attitude.[58] *The Sunday Times* article on 25 January, 'Is Justice now on Trial?, is a good example of the underlying concern with the need to get to the truth. The article discusses the failure to refer the case of the Guildford Four in terms of evidence of 'proof of innocence' that has 'never been tested in Court'. It quotes sources criticizing the Home Secretary for his failure to use his powers for unacceptable reasons such as 'to prevent an avalanche of cases'. Concern with factually incorrect convictions is also clearly evident in 'Justice in the Dock' in *Today* on 25 January. That article considers the Carl Bridgewater murder case[59] in some detail following a television documentary about it, and offers the alternative story of the innocence of the four people convicted and the guilt of a named alternative suspect, namely the former ambulance driver Hubert Spencer.[60]

Some journalists and other commentators clearly believe in the innocence of the people who have been convicted in these cases and are frustrated with the failure of legal processes to quash their convictions. An article in *The Guardian* on 27 February written by the producer of a television programme about the case of the Guildford Four is a good example.[61] The author berates the political complacency behind the continued imprisonment of the Guildford Four: 'It is political. There are repercussions for legal and political careers; there are repercussions for extradition and for British justice.' Later in the year the media report on the Home Secretary's decision to establish a new police inquiry into the case of the Guildford Four, but not that of the Maguire Seven. The Leading Article in *The Times* on 15 August tries to explain this disparity despite the obvious links between the two cases. It argues that the Maguire Seven case is not suitable for further investigation since: 'The Maguires were found guilty almost wholly on the basis of forensic evidence; and precisely for that reason it has been impossible to disprove the verdict.' What the article suggests is that, in view of the impossibility of

[57] *The Financial Times*, 12 Jan. 87 'Dangers of Retrial by Television: Home Office Review of the Guildford and Birmingham Pub Bombing Cases' (Justinian).

[58] *The Times*, 21 Jan. 87 'Court must have "new" facts: Birmingham pub bombings' (Frances Gibb); *The Daily Telegraph*, 21 Jan. 87 ' "Lurking Doubts" on Bombs Trial'.

[59] The journalist Paul Foot's influential book on the case had been published the previous year; *Murder at the Farm: Who Killed Carl Bridgewater?* (London, 1986).

[60] We use this example from *Today* here to illustrate a point that will figure later in our analysis. It is that whereas some newspapers, such as *Today*, are willing to risk possible censure by naming an alternative suspect, the Court of Appeal in the course of its judgments could never do so. To do so would in itself amount to interference with the possibility of any future fair trial of that suspect. Court of Appeal judges would be only too aware of this danger.

[61] Agenda, 'The case that won't go away: Judicial shifts preventing a review of the Guildford bombings' (Grant McKee). A book published the following year by this author and

producing adequate evidence to support the widespread belief in the innocence of the Maguire Seven, the appropriate approach is for the Home
Secretary to consider use of the prerogative of mercy, namely a pardon. In
an article by Ludovic Kennedy in *The Sunday Times* on 25 October, reviewing the book *Miscarriages of Justice* by Bob Woffinden,[62] he talks about
these cases as 'only the tip of an iceberg'. Like Woffinden's book, Kennedy's
article focuses on the innocence of numbers of people convicted of offences.
He quotes Woffinden's damning conclusion: 'The shaming fact is that the
continued incarceration of the innocent is nothing less than national policy.'
When, at the end of 1987, the appeal of the Birmingham Six is being heard,
the reporting of that appeal is restrained, the narratives associated with the
guilt of these defendants being treated with respect. The reporting concentrates mainly on the human tale of the appellants, and on the evidence.
Newspaper articles talk about the evidence that was presented during the
appeal mainly in terms of the status and roles of the individual witnesses.
What the reporting seems to anticipate is a judgment expected early in the
New Year, and probably, at least from most of the reporting at that time, a
judgment likely to be in favour of the appellants.

An article in *The Times* by a legal academic at the beginning of 1988
raises the possibility of the appeal by the Birmingham Six being rejected. The
article warns that the method of appeal used in the criminal courts 'favours
appeals on technical due process points, as against genuine miscarriages of
justice, which frequently do not show up in the papers', and that 'To provide
for more appeals by way of rehearing would cost money.'[63] On 29 January
newspapers are full of stories about the rejection of the appeal. The main
wider implication addressed by journalists in their reporting on the Court of
Appeal's decision is the political consequence of its impact on Anglo-Irish
relations.[64] The case is also viewed as evidence of the need for individual
reforms to the system of criminal justice, but without any obvious link to
serious deficiencies and radical criticisms. The article by the legal correspondent of *The Times*, Frances Gibb, is a good example.[65] Her analysis links this
failed appeal with research into the number of possible miscarriages per year
by the researchers Baldwin and McConville and the organization Justice.

his fellow television documentary film-maker, Ros Franey, with a foreword by the journalist,
broadcaster, and writer Ludovic Kennedy, makes a significant contribution to the campaign
about this case; *Time Bomb: Irish Bombers, English Justice and the Guildford Four* (London,
1988).

[62] B. Woffinden, *Miscarriages of Justice*, London, 1987. We discuss the approach adopted
in this book in section C of Ch. 6.

[63] 5 Jan. 88 'When Appeals Fall Short of Justice' (John Spencer).

[64] See *The Daily Telegraph*, 'Birmingham Bomb Case: Appeal Court's Ruling Strains
Anglo-Irish Ties'; *The Times*, 'Irish Anger as Pub Bombers Lose Appeals: "Catalogue of Police
Brutality" Rejected'; *The Guardian*, 'Birmingham 6 Appeal Fails: Irish Bitterness at Working
of British Justice Intensifies'.

[65] 'Ruling Fuels Pressure for Reform.'

From this she is able to outline a number of reform proposals. The restraint shown in most of the reporting is explicable as a response to the terms of the Court of Appeal's judgment. Assuming that journalists accept the authority of the Court, then the strength of the judgment makes alternative readings difficult. Lord Lane's statement that 'the longer this hearing has gone on, the more convinced we were that the jury's verdict was correct' is regularly quoted, but not, at this stage, subjected to general vilification. *The Guardian* report by David Pallister and Joe Joyce from Dublin quotes the British Members of Parliament, Kevin McNamara and David Alton: 'the judgment would create a crisis of confidence in British justice, particularly for people of Irish extraction.' So, in this one newspaper, there is less restraint in the reporting and even the beginnings of a construction of crisis in terms of public confidence, but apparently limited to one section of the population.

Justification for the Court of Appeal's approach gradually emerges, rather than deep criticism of it. At the extreme this is represented by explaining why *the public* feel dissatisfied, but for the wrong reasons. In *The Financial Times* their legal writer Justinian presents such an explanation: 'It is the very nature of the English criminal trial that makes for difficulties in satisfying the public outside the courtroom . . . The essence of the English criminal process is that it is not tailored to the pursuit of truth.'[66] Former senior members of the judiciary, such as Lords Hailsham and Denning, also offer explanations and criticisms, which are picked up by the press. However, their criticisms are directed toward a different target, namely the media: 'Lord Denning said it was more important that public confidence in the system of justice should be upheld than that such programmes [TV documentaries questioning verdicts] should take place.'[67]

The rejection by Law Lords of leave for the Birmingham Six to appeal to the House of Lords is again reported in terms of the political consequences of its effect on Anglo-Irish relations, rather than broader legal themes.[68] Only in *The Guardian* is the technical legal debate that this ruling raises discussed. One of the barristers acting for the Birmingham Six, Michael Mansfield, is quoted making the criticism that: 'the Court of Appeal judges had wrongly taken upon themselves the mantle of retrying a case.'[69] This article also quotes alternative legal opinion. What is raised here is an issue of due process, what a system of fair trial amounts to. The claim that the Court of Appeal's role and response to appeals represents an erroneous assumption of legal authority was one shared by certain former Law Lords, whose views were later reported in the press.[70] But attempts to present

---

[66] 1 Feb. 88 'When the Truth is on Trial'.

[67] *The Times*, 22 Feb. 88 'Hailsham Call for Change on Secrecy'.

[68] *The Financial Times*, 15 Apr. 88 'Irish Voice Concern at Law Lords Ruling'.

[69] 15 April 88, 'Pub Bomb Plea Refused'.

[70] See our description of the views of Lords Devlin and Scarman about the *Stafford and Luvaglio* case, expressed on 30 November, set out in the text below.

dissatisfaction with the Court's judgment as a technical error in the Court's view of its role have, as we shall demonstrate, little resonance more generally in the press.

By the middle of the year any potential meta-narrative of crisis about the criminal justice system arising from the Birmingham Six case has dissipated. The journalist Bob Woffinden is clearly frustrated at this: the lack of media criticism and apparent loss of interest. In his Agenda article in *The Guardian* on 27 June he is very critical of the weaknesses of Home Office procedures to consider alleged miscarriages. He argues: 'The media was once properly regarded as the court of last resort, but it now seems impotent in these matters.' He proposes a new Appeal Act that he believes is 'essential if the reputation of British justice, ebbing so swiftly at present, is ever to be restored'. Having studied in depth a number of miscarriage cases and reached his own conclusion about the truth of wrongful convictions, his criticisms and frustrations are explicable. His problem is that the Court of Appeal, using its procedures, has not agreed, and neither have many of his journalist colleagues and newspaper editors.

Concerns with the appellate process arise a few months later in response to the latest police inquiry into the Guildford Four case and the expected decision by the Home Secretary on whether to refer the case back to the Court of Appeal. An article in *The Daily Telegraph* gives a detailed account of the campaign for their release.[71] Quoting from one of the books about the case the article describes how during the late 1970s and 1980s the solicitor for the Guildford Four had been frustrated because 'Despite intensive lobbying . . . no one in the British media or in British politics pursued the matter.' But, as the article shows, the campaign behind the case developed in the late 1980s, supported not only by journalists' books but also by churchmen and senior lawyers. The article anticipates that the case will be referred to the Court of Appeal, but notes the Court's earlier reluctance to find anything wrong with the verdict, quoting Lord Roskill who said at the original appeal that the case 'gives rise to no lurking doubts whatever in our minds'. However, on the same day that this article appears the Leading Article in *The Daily Telegraph* warns of the dangers of trial by media and the need for finality as well as fairness, commenting that:[72] 'television programmes are not necessarily the best forum for the forensic analysis of complex issues.'[73]

On 29 November *The Independent* anticipates the Home Secretary's referral of the Guildford Four case in temperate terms. That article talks about how 'Miscarriages of justice occur from time to time in any legal

---

[71] 19 Nov. 88 '14 Years of Doubt: The Guildford Pub Bombings of 1974'.

[72] 19 Nov. 88 'Final Decision'.

[73] A reference to the TV documentary *Death on the Rock* that analysed the death of an IRA active service unit in Gibraltar, and the very different verdict reached at the inquest. See the Windlesham/Rampton Report, *Death on the Rock* (London, 1989).

system. When they do occur they should be corrected, not swept aside.'[74] It is clear that the author is convinced that there is a prima facie case, and that the Home Secretary's powers of reference are designed for 'just such unhappy and uncertain cases as that of the Guildford 4'. The next day *The Times* publishes a long article by the former senior judges Lords Devlin and Scarman, which takes a different approach. They argue in favour of a new appeal because they disagree with the Court's approach to appeals on questions of fact. Their technical reason is their criticism of the House of Lords decision in *DPP v Stafford*. They criticize that decision because, so they argue, it usurps the power of the jury to decide on guilt or innocence. They see the importance of the jury as amounting to a basic right and the effect of the *Stafford* judgment as very damaging to such a right: 'Our constitutional ordering on which our freedoms depend has been disordered.'

Following the intervention of these ex-Law Lords, there is greater press willingness to consider whether these cases represent a major problem for the existing criminal justice system. A very good example[75] is the long article in *The Daily Telegraph* on 7 December by their legal correspondent, Terence Shaw.[76] This article starts constructing the notion of a lack of public confidence in criminal justice. It does so by relying on the views of five 'distinguished legal practitioners and expert observers' and linking their views to an interpretation of how miscarriages arise. Shaw attempts to find general lessons that run through the Birmingham Six, Maguire Seven, and Guildford Four cases. 'Yet one need not look far to find some common factors: a horrific crime attracting wide media coverage and public anger; pressure for quick arrests; actual arrests followed by confessions whose validity was subsequently questioned; claims that important evidence had emerged after the trial.' In the course of its discussion, the article asks: 'how deep are the cracks in the image of British justice?' The individual instances of deficiency it describes start to come together, but at the same time the article has an underlying message that 'Nobody we interviewed believes that the judicial system as a whole is getting worse.' So a tension arises in the article between criticism offered following the description of individual cases and the failings of particular practices and general support for the system and the values that underpin it. For example, William Goodhart, the chairman of the organization Justice, is said to be of the opinion that generally the state of British justice is not deteriorating, 'But we have been unduly complacent about aspects in the past.' And the senior criminal lawyer Sir David Napley is reported to believe that the system of British justice is 'probably better than those anywhere else in the world', but that there are

---

[74] 29 Nov. 88 'The Court of Appeal Must Judge'.

[75] See also *The Times*, 6 Dec. 88 'Correcting Miscarriages of Justice' (Peter Ashman).

[76] 'Justice—Cracks in the image: Traditionally, British criminal justice has been revered around the world. Now the key aspects are being questioned—and not only by predictable critics'.

problems with the Court of Appeal. His criticism of that body highlights the strains between justice and cost: 'I think the considered reluctance on the part of the Court of Appeal to order a new trial is a grave disadvantage and that the expense and inconvenience that a new trial involves is given excessive weight over the need to ensure that justice is done.' The article ends with more individual criticisms rather than with any attempt at linking those criticisms within the theme of a system failing. The general answer given to the general question about the state of British justice is, on the whole, reassuring: 'British justice was not seen as deeply or systematically flawed; and, if miscarriages of justice seemed more prevalent nowadays, it was because the media were more diligent in bringing cases to public attention.'

The article by Bob Woffinden, 'Justice's Handicap', in *The Guardian* on 19 December is less reassuring. The article discusses the rejection by the Court of Appeal of appeals by the Tottenham Three from their convictions for the murder of PC Keith Blakelock. Woffinden links this event with another story. 'On the same day that Mrs Thatcher ridiculed the suggestion that Father Ryan would not receive a fair trial in Britain, another high-profile case raised disturbing questions about the quality of English justice.' He also links the rejection of the appeal of one of the Tottenham Three, Engin Raghip, to the recognized and notorious miscarriage of the Confait case in the 1970s, when three youths were convicted of unlawful killing on the basis of false confessions obtained in police custody and poor forensic evidence.

Thus in 1987 and 1988 the media reacted, often superficially, to events in the campaigns to overturn certain convictions that they classified as newsworthy and thereby elevated to the status of high profile. They constructed interpretations of those events, but they were short-lived and unconfident. The possibility of a *crisis* in British criminal justice, which might necessitate radical reforms, had been contemplated but not accepted in most of the reporting. And whilst the reluctance of the Court of Appeal to overturn verdicts by juries had been noted, its ability to correct mistakes, and its general authority to pronounce on which convictions are mistakes, remained intact.

E. FROM MISCARRIAGE TO CRISIS: 1989–92

1 1989

In 1989 the Guildford Four are successful in the appeal against their convictions. The circumstances of their appeal are unusual. The appeal is arranged and expedited when, following a police inquiry ordered by the Home Secretary into the circumstances of their convictions and the inquiry's report being submitted to the Home Secretary, the Director of Public Prosecutions indicates that the Crown does not want to contest any appeal.[77] In these circumstances there is no full public review of the case nor any ordinary appeal but only a formal judgment by the Court of Appeal giving the reasons why the convictions will be quashed and statements by the appellants' barristers. Following the Court of Appeal's judgment the Home Secretary announces that a judicial inquiry will be set up under Sir John May to consider all the circumstances surrounding the original convictions. In addition the Director of Public Prosecutions announces that there will be a criminal investigation into the conduct of the Surrey police officers who had been involved in eliciting the false confessions. Such an unusual set of events makes reporting in the media difficult. What initially unites that reporting is the assumption that what had happened proves the innocence of the Four.[78] What further narrative accompanies that assumption is very varied.[79] Some reports concentrate on the statement made in the House of Commons by the Home Secretary about the case, others on the judgment given by the Lord Chief Justice in the Court of Appeal. Other reporting concentrates on what the appellants or their representatives said or what happened in or outside the Court. Commentaries by other significant persons are also reported and relied on.

Despite the wide variety of the reporting on the Guildford Four appeal at this time, gradually a meta-narrative is being constructed. Articles are not linked by the mere fact of dealing with the same events, but by investing those events with a common meaning. The meta-narrative that is emerging involves making connections between individual deficiencies arising out of the Guildford Four case and general perceptions about the system of criminal justice as a whole and the implications that might arise from those perceptions.[80] When making these links there is a tendency to involve discussion of other criminal justice systems and their practices, implying by such contrast that the English system's due processes are inadequate.[81] Within a short while, although not immediately in the wake of the Court of Appeal's judgment on the Guildford Four appeal, strong phrases about the criminal justice system being in crisis, or suffering from a loss of public

---

[77] See the Leading Article in *The Times*, 18 Oct. 89 'The Guildford Four'.

[78] This initial assumption was later contested. See *The Independent*, 14 Nov. 89 'Declaration of Innocence that Eludes the Guildford Four' (Sarah Helm). That debate continued for some time, see *The Guardian*, 11 Nov. 90 'Questions of innocence and responsibility— The Attorney General denied this week that some judges believe the Guildford Four were guilty' (Joshua Rozenberg).

[79] Even in the same newspaper, such as *The Times* in various articles about the case, 18–21 Oct. 89.

[80] For example see *The Independent*, 18 Oct. 89 'Guildford Four: Leading Judges were Connected with Case' (Patricia Wynn Davies).

[81] See *The Independent*, 19 Oct. 89 'The Guildford Four: Confession Must be Supported in Scottish Law' (Patricia Wynn Davies); *The Guardian*, 18 Oct. 89 'The Guildford Four: Scarman Cites Scottish Rules on Confessions' (Clare Dyer).

confidence,[82] start appearing—even in unlikely places. This occurs despite and alongside claims by Lord Scarman, one of those ex-Law Lords whose earlier criticisms of the Court had received wide publicity, that the decision vindicates the role of the Home Secretary, the Director of Public Prosecution, and the Court.[83]

The leading article in *The Guardian,* 'A Story Filled with Shame', on 20 October, reporting on the events of the previous day in the Court of Appeal when the convictions of the Guildford Four were quashed, is characteristic of the early construction of a meta-narrative of crisis. It starts with: 'Over fourteen years after the criminal justice system found the Guildford Four guilty, that system itself now stands, shamefaced and wriggling, in the dock.' After raising a number of linking deficiencies ('not just the conduct of the police', or 'a prosecution system so committed to securing a conviction . . . that fundamental principles of justice were jettisoned'), the article raises the deficiencies of the judiciary, as against the role of journalists: 'The judges are too ready to dismiss genuine investigations by journalists.' The authority of judges is challenged, and challenged by reference to the role of the media, whose approach to miscarriages of justice is recognized to be constructed in a more open way, and with different reference points, than its judicial construction. This marks the beginning of a media construction of a crisis of confidence in criminal justice, or even more generally in the legal system, based on a loss of respect for judicial authority and the criminal justice system's investigation, trial, and appeal processes. What always accompany such writing are proposals for reform. In this article the reform that is suggested is 'a proper investigatory body for such miscarriages of justice'. However, in keeping with the analysis in the article, there is seen to be a particular problem with such a proposal: 'the judges still resist such an initiative in the belief that it would erode the position of the Appeal Court. They, and all who profess to care about British justice, should reflect with humility and pain on the Guildford experience.'

By 23 October even Justinian in *The Financial Times*[84] is constructing a meta-narrative of crisis. Justinian's more usual approach was to offer clarification of legal processes and to explain possible misunderstanding. In this article there is a move to a different theme, the theme of deficiency in the system as a whole. 'It is vital that Sir John May in his judicial inquiry should examine the fundamental weakness of the English criminal justice system . . . Too often in the past there has been a consistently piecemeal approach

---

[82] See how David McKittrick discusses public confidence in his article in *The Independent,* 18 Oct. 89 'Guildford Four: Pressures on Police Have Caused Doubts over Safety of Convictions'.

[83] Lord Scarman's view of how this successful appeal reflects favourably on the Home Secretary, the Director of Public Prosecutions, and the Court of Appeal was given in an ITN interview and later in *The Times,* 20 Oct. 89 'A Safer Kind of Justice'.

[84] 'Judicial Inquiry Must be Thorough'.

to the problems thrown up by the system of criminal justice.' The article raises in strong terms many linked deficiencies. These include, for example, problems with trial by jury and how reliance on jury trial 'hampers a proper appellate system', problems with reliance on forensic evidence in which process 'the defence is hopelessly handicapped', and the lack of judicial control over the criminal investigation, unlike in European legal systems. Hugo Young's article in *The Guardian* the following day takes a similar, but more critical and extensive, approach.[85] He talks of the deficiencies of judicial attitudes: 'In senior judges, private arrogance has a habit of being converted into a pillar of the constitution'; 'you will have heard no word of apology or even regret from the many judges who were accomplices to the scarcely imaginable injustice.' Underlying these deficiencies is 'the frailty of the system over which they [the senior judges] preside'. Young argues that 'retrieving the reputation of the law is also a vital duty of the State'. In conclusion he is clear about what the implications of the Guildford Four case are: 'nothing less than a catastrophe for the English judicial system . . . with . . . disastrous effects on the fabric of society . . . The compromising of the system and its credibility is profound . . . Something more is needed, if we are to be convinced that the keepers of law and order understand how badly the authority of the judicial system needs repairing.'

An article by Peter Jenkins in *The Independent* carries a similar message.[86] He derides claims about the high standing of legal authority: 'the Solicitor General, Sir Nicholas Lyell, speaking for the Government, denied emphatically that the case had undermined trust in the legal system. If it has not, it should have done.' And in telling the story of how the case eventually found its way back to the Court of Appeal via the Home Secretary and a further police inquiry, he argues that: 'Constitutionally this may be very proper, but it is a formula which enables a Home Secretary to wash his hands of justice.' Jenkins's conclusion is damning of judicial authority: 'justice must not be left to old men in wigs sitting in judgement over themselves. The authority of the Court of Appeal is in ruins, as if shattered by an IRA bomb.'

At this time many articles in the press report on reform proposals being offered by lawyers and other commentators. There is a platform for the newsworthiness of what might otherwise have seemed to be rather parochial concerns. When such reform proposals are being reported on, the context is usually the need to re-establish a loss of public confidence or to earn back credibility.[87] As has been shown, a few journalists had been striving to achieve a meta-narrative of crisis linked to miscarriage cases for some time, in particular Bob Woffinden and Ludovic Kennedy. So, with the more

[85] 24 Oct. 89 'Too Much Faith in their own Convictions'.
[86] 24 Oct 89 'The Law as an Enemy of Justice'.
[87] See for example Clare Dyer's report in *The Guardian* 2 Nov. 89 'Top Solicitor Seeks Court of Last Resort'; also *The Independent* 3 Nov. 89 'Law Update: Room for Redress'.

general themes of crisis and public confidence now established, what reforms do they seek?[88] Woffinden's analysis of the repercussions of the successful appeal by the Guildford Four leads him to expect radical reform: 'the failings of the criminal justice process were systematic . . . Guildford will have had an enormous impact, not least in bringing home to the country the compound weaknesses of the UK's judicial process, and the inadequacy of the Court of Appeal as a mechanism for rectifying error.' Ludovic Kennedy, following the successful appeal, develops a damning critique of the criminal justice system, initially in a lecture to the Howard League for Penal Reform. The platform for his views and suggestions for reform is the assumption that he believes everyone then accepted that the criminal justice system was factually wrong in convicting and not rectifying the convictions of the Guildford Four for fourteen years. Just as Bob Woffinden thinks that 'the country' recognizes the failings of the system, so Kennedy feels that the public shares his view: 'When I was a boy it used to be said that British criminal justice was the finest in the world, a view held most strongly by those who had never studied any other system. Nobody says it today.' Kennedy believes that not remedying miscarriages is self-defeating since 'in the end truth will out.' But he is unwilling to trust the judiciary with the task of either determining the truth or achieving justice. 'If I say that justice is too important to be left to the judiciary, I shall not be popular in certain quarters, but I believe that their record in recent cases, both in Court of Appeal judgments and in the findings of post-appeal inquiries, shows this to be so.' The main reform that Kennedy suggests is to abandon the adversary system ('a most unsatisfactory way of attempting to dispense justice'), which in turn would necessitate a considerable number of consequential changes to be made to many of the key due-process characteristics of the current system, such as the right to silence. The need to avoid convicting the factually innocent is clearly what motivates Kennedy's concerns and proposals.

By the end of 1989 reporting on issues concerning the criminal justice system linked to miscarriages is characterized by use of the phrase 'public confidence' or some variant of it. Melanie Phillips's commentary 'Poor Judgment Fuels Unease over Guildford'[89] is a good example. She starts by reflecting on how 'the standard British response to a crisis' is to set up a judicial inquiry, with the aim that through its deliberations 'Public confidence can thus be restored and the world turned the right way up again.' However, as she sees it, the Guildford Four case, which has 'undermined public confidence in the criminal justice system itself', has also undermined faith in the judiciary, which poses a particular problem: 'But what if the

---

[88] *The Guardian* 6 Nov. 89 'Media: Investigators who Are Tried and Found Wanting' (Bob Woffinden); *The Guardian* 16 Nov. 89 'Wrong Arm of the Law' (Ludovic Kennedy).
[89] *The Guardian* 17 Nov. 89.

subject of the inquiry is the criminal justice system itself? Who then can judge the judge who has been brought in to judge the judges?' In *The Independent*, lawyers are reported as arguing for the restoration of public confidence. 'Sir John May must tackle . . . failings in the appeal system during his inquiry into the Guildford Four case if public confidence is to be restored, lawyers say.'[90] There is even an assertion that judicial reluctance to remedy miscarriages of justice might be motivated by the judiciary's concern with the effect of such cases on 'public confidence'.[91]

The claims in these articles that a fall in public confidence represents a crisis for the system of criminal justice are not based on any systematic analysis of public opinion. The authors could not point to surveys showing a drop in general levels of trust in legal processes. Nor could they demonstrate the extent of public belief in the innocence of the Guildford Four. As such, their construction of a meta-narrative of crisis is, as the media studies literature reviewed in section B of this chapter leads one to expect, essentially self-referential. Journalists could report with confidence that there is a crisis of public confidence because other journalists are reporting in a similar manner. Journalists could invest that public with a belief in the innocence of the Guildford Four because other journalists are reporting that the Guildford Four are innocent. And lastly, journalists could attribute to the public an opinion that the current criminal justice system needs radical reforms, in order to prevent innocents like the Guildford Four from being wrongly convicted.

2 1990–2

In the years 1990, 1991, and 1992 newspapers cover cases of miscarriage and alleged miscarriage, and commentary relating to them, extensively. Purely in quantitative terms newspapers during these three years contain much larger numbers of articles on miscarriages than the immediately preceding or following years.

The year 1990 witnesses a number of crucial events. There are new police inquiries initiated into the police's role in securing the convictions of the Tottenham Three and the Birmingham Six. The May Inquiry into the circumstances surrounding the Guildford Four and Maguire Seven convictions is investigating and produces its Interim Report. The Director of Public Prosecutions recognizes that the Maguire Seven convictions can no longer stand and thereafter the Home Secretary refers that case back to the

---

[90] *The Independent* 18 Nov. 89 'Appeal System Inquiry Must Tackle Failings' (Patricia Wynn Davies). Sir John May was himself reported as believing that one of the purposes of the inquiry 'is to allay public disquiet'. *The Times* 1 Nov. 89 'Inquiry Report Unlikely before 1991' (Stewart Tendler).

[91] See *The Independent* 6 Dec. 89 'Appeals Limited by Concern over Public Confidence' (Patricia Wynn Davies).

Court of Appeal. There are a number of significant television programmes dealing with the above-mentioned cases.

The presence of these events provides opportunities to develop the story of the defendants in these cases and the implications of their stories for criminal justice: when will they be declared innocent, who will pay for the wrongs which led to their wrongful convictions? But alongside a proliferation of events connected to these high profile cases, some other cases are given a higher profile than might otherwise have been expected in view of the limited past interest in them. Still other miscarriage cases produce events (such as successful or unsuccessful appeals) which pass with little or no press comment. During this period the reporting of allegations of miscarriage helps to maintain the momentum of the theme of crisis. There is wide reporting of the research by the organization Justice that suggests that between 200 and 300 wrongful convictions occur each year.[92] Such figures give a sense of the size of the problem represented by miscarriages of justice.

When events relating to the high profile cases are being reported on or discussed in newspapers there is, usually, some reference to issues of public confidence in, or at the extreme crisis of public confidence about, the criminal justice system,[93] and often some reference to reform proposals. Because of this, at that time there is a greater unity between those who report on crime or law (legal, political, or crime correspondents) and more general investigative journalists and regular columnists than usually occurs. The correspondent is likely to make a link to, at least, a reform proposal that anticipates the more critical account of the investigative journalist or regular columnist. Also there is more reporting of the reform proposals of official bodies, learned societies, or pressure groups than at other times when miscarriages are less in the news. There are also a larger number of stories relating to people closely affected by such cases, from the families of those convicted,[94] to the characters of the judges and lawyers involved in their cases.[95]

---

[92] See the article by Sir George Waller (Chairman of the Justice committee that produced their 1989 Report) *The Times* 7 Nov. 89 'Confessions that Challenge Justice'; also Clare Dyer's report in Society 'Reasonable Doubts about the Case for the Defence', *The Guardian* 22 Nov. 89.

[93] To commence a report on a particular case a sentence such as the following is very common: 'The system of criminal justice's credibility was knocked again yesterday' (*The Guardian* 15 June 90 'DPP Accepts Maguire 7 Convictions were Unsafe' (David Sharrock and Martin Linton)).

[94] As examples, see *The Independent* 8 Dec. 90 'Hope survives the seasons: Wives of the Birmingham Six face a seventeenth Christmas without them' (Nick Cohen); *The Guardian* 7 Dec. 90 (Young Guardian) 'The nightmare years of a young bride—Life has not been kind to Sharon Raghip' (Melanie McFadyean); *The Observer* 17 March 91 'Birmingham Six: Return to a Free World' (John Merritt and Dan Stanton); *The Guardian* 27 June 91 'An Unhappy Family Tied by Injustice' (David Pallister); *The Guardian* 28 Dec. 91 'Trials of Innocence' (Jeremy Hardy).

[95] Such as *The Sunday Telegraph* 15 July 90 'Judge in the Front Line/Profile of John Donaldson' (Peregrine Worsthorne); *The Independent* 30 Aug. 91 'A System Bound by Chains of Prejudice' (Alastair Logan).

What appears to have been created, after 1989, was an expectation about how such cases should be reported, and how that reporting should be constructed through a meta-narrative of crisis of public confidence or general failure in the criminal justice system. This is not a universal construction (ordinary crime reporting continues, even ordinary reporting of successful and unsuccessful appeals), but it is more likely that, especially when commenting on certain cases, definite links between these ideas will be made evident.

3 1990 AND 1991

(i) The judiciary's responsibility

The responsibility of individual senior judges for the crisis is a theme that arises repeatedly during 1990 and 1991. And at the same time articles by former judges or articles about speeches made by current judges intent on restoring public confidence are common. Some of these judicial forays seem to serve to inflame rather than dampen media perceptions of a system in crisis.

In a long article in *The Sunday Times* in February 1990 Ludovic Kennedy concludes by linking judicial failures to failures of the criminal justice system as a whole.

> I fear the harsh truth is that, just as some policemen corrupt themselves by readiness to fabricate evidence against those who they have convinced themselves are guilty, so there are judges, otherwise honourable men, who corrupt themselves by refusing to recognise police fabrication, even when it is staring them in the face. 'British justice is in ruins,' said Lord Denning after the release of the Guildford Four. But it had been in ruins for a long time . . . Yet, to be fair, it is less that the police and the judges have corrupted themselves as that the system has corrupted both of them.[96]

In his description of the system here, Kennedy is referring to the adversary system of trial. That system he believes 'invites corruption and the concealment of truth'.

Clare Dyer reports in April 1990 on the Lord Chancellor Lord Mackay's 'strong defence of the Lord Chief Justice, Lord Lane' and his criticism of the 'pressures on judges to bow to public opinion in reaching their decisions'.[97] As part of his speech Lord Mackay talks of: 'The vital task of maintaining the integrity and reputation of our system of justice, which has at times been the victim of serious misunderstandings by others of the role of the courts, judges and counsel.' In July 1990 the spotlight focuses on Lord Donaldson, the Master of the Rolls, the judge in the original Maguire Seven trial. The criticism of him in the May Inquiry's Interim Report into the Maguire Seven convictions is picked up by most newspapers, and receives

[96] *The Sunday Times* 25 Feb. 90 'I Accuse . . .'
[97] *The Guardian* 25 April 90 'Mackay Acts to Bolster Lord Lane'.

a great deal of supporting comment. This is well illustrated in the profile of him edited by Peregrine Worsthorne in *The Sunday Telegraph*.[98] The nub of Worsthorne's criticism is his belief that, like his fellow judges (quoting Robert Kee), 'He does his best to be dispassionate; he cannot see his unconscious prejudice in favour of the prosecution.' In other words, his ability to aid the discovery of the truth is hampered by the presumptions that he is working with, which unconsciously influence him. Worsthorne concludes with the hope that 'after the May report our judges would show a sharper eye for DIY evidence'.

The most senior judges are being severely attacked in 1990 and early 1991, with the main link being their role in high profile miscarriages of justice. This leads to former judges joining in the debate, proposing reforms while defending the system. The former Lord Justice of Appeal, Sir Frederick Lawton, writes two such articles in *The Times* in 1990. In July he writes in response to the Home Secretary and Director of Public Prosecution's statements that the convictions of the Maguire Seven are no longer safe and satisfactory. He attempts to explain these statements in the light of the view expressed in the judgment in the Maguire Seven appeal in 1977 in which the Court of Appeal concluded: 'No member of this Court sees any reason for disturbing any of these convictions either on the basis that any of them is unsafe or unsatisfactory or that the learned judge was guilty of any misdirection or that his summing-up in any way was unbalanced.'[99] The explanation Lawton offers reflects his view of the limitations of the procedure of the Court of Appeal, and how it 'feels obliged to accept the findings of fact implicit in the jury's verdict'. He describes how the Court of Appeal does not re-hear evidence, but deals with the appeal by a perusal of the transcript of evidence. His suggestion is that: 'The Court of Appeal would be more effective, and public confidence in it strengthened, if it were empowered by Parliament to re-hear parts of the evidence and to initiate enquiries about any aspect of the case that caused it unease.' Even with this rider (and it should be remembered that Lawton was a member of the Donovan Committee in 1965),[100] he is circumspect about his proposal since 'Finding an accident-proof jurisdiction for the Court of Appeal will not be easy.'

In September the attacks on and defences of Lord Lane reach a crescendo. When Lord Mackay is reported to have defended Lord Lane in a speech in early September, a member of the audience, a lawyer, is reported to have said: 'The Lord Chancellor's speech was, in fact, a confidence-building move. I believe that behind the scenes it was put to Mackay that he ought to speak in favour of these judges in view of the growing lack of public

[98] 15 July 90 'Judge in the Front Line'.

[99] *The Times* 17 July 90 'The Case of Unheard Evidence'.

[100] See our analysis of the recommendations of the Donovan Committee in section E of Ch. 3.

confidence in them.'[101] In an article in *The Guardian* Simon Lee concentrates on Lord Lane making it clear that, at least in the press, he has lost credibility: 'The media is indeed the battle-ground for all aspects of judicial work. It is Lord Lane's failure to come to terms with this which is his undoing.'[102] Having summarized Lord Lane's apparent shortcomings Simon Lee wants a change of style from any successor to Lord Lane, 'especially an openness to media interest in the work of the law' rather than criticism of it. Ludovic Kennedy is also reported in September to have called for the retirement of Lord Lane, but also other judges of the Court of Appeal.[103] And in his scathing criticism in March 1991 he adds to the list of those he feels share the blame: 'Roskill, Lawton, Lane, Denning, Bridge, O'Connor, Brown and others have all been examined and found wanting: collectively and individually they have gone far to undermining public confidence in the administration of criminal justice.'[104]

In October Sir Frederick Lawton writes an article in direct response to Roy Hattersley's statement at the Labour Party conference in which he claims that 'the judicial tragedies of the last 20 years have largely arisen from judges who were unable to discard their judicial prejudices.'[105] Lawton replies that: 'The charge made against the judges is wholly misconceived.' Lawton presents two main arguments. The principal one repeats his assertions in July that 'critics of the judiciary fail to appreciate the limitations which the law places on a judge' and particularly the limitations incumbent on having a jury verdict and not expecting the Court of Appeal to re-hear evidence and retry cases. He stresses that 'Reading a transcript of evidence is not conducive to raising a lurking doubt.' The conclusion he reaches casts doubt on proposals to create a new Court of Appeal or a differently constituted Court of Last Resort, which proposals had been raised by other former judges, such as Lord Scarman. His second main argument refers to numbers. He suggests that the vast majority of convictions are not wrongful: 'In those 20 years there were probably about 200,000 convictions on indictment, which were not miscarriages of justice.'

In an article in *The Guardian* in November, Joshua Rozenberg includes answers by the future Lord Chief Justice, Lord Justice Peter Taylor, to questions about the public image of the judiciary.[106] Rozenberg concludes: 'Without doubt, public confidence in the judiciary is difficult to measure.

---

[101] *The Independent on Sunday* 2 Sept. 90 'On Trial: The Judges who Daren't be Wrong' (Cal McCrystal).

[102] 10 Sept. 90 'Uneasily Astride a Fallible System'.

[103] *The Daily Telegraph* 18 Sept. 90 'Over-zealous Detectives are Undermining Faith in the Courts' (William Weekes).

[104] *The Sunday Times* 3 March 91 'Something Rotten in the Courts; Birmingham Six'.

[105] *The Times* 23 Oct. 90 'Judgments without Prejudice'.

[106] 14 Nov. 90 'Packaging the Judges'; see also his article in *The Guardian* 20 Feb. 91 'Press Gets a Wigging—The uneasy relations between the media and the judiciary as judges grow more conscious of their image'.

Although it is encouraging to hear judges like Sir Peter acknowledge that there is room for improvement.' On the other hand those same answers, to other fellow columnists, are unacceptable. Bernard Levin writing in *The Times* in February 1991 is certainly dissatisfied:

But one of the things he said still sticks in my gullet. He said that the unfair criticism was 'undermining public confidence in the judicial system' . . . it is truly terrifying for once the word is apposite that a most eminent jurist, who may shortly become the head of our judiciary, can demonstrate in public an ignorance so colossal and appalling as Lord Justice Taylor's claim that unfair criticism of the press (yes, of course that's what he put it down to) is 'undermining public confidence'.[107]

Apart from other causes, Levin sees decline in respect for the judiciary as an effect of 'the hideous growth in miscarriages of justice in recent years'. As this chapter on newspaper reporting of miscarriages shows, there had indeed been a growth in the reporting on such cases, but no evidence to suggest that there has or has not been a growth in overall numbers. It is also worth noting that Levin in this article assesses Lord Lane's 1988 judgment in the Birmingham Six appeal as representing a judge 'hopelessly, inescapably, tragically out of his depth that the proceedings might have been in Martian for all the chance that he might see what lay behind the evidence and measure it correctly'. Other features writers by no means universally support such a view.

Following criticism of Lord Lane, *The Independent* publishes a letter in his defence by a barrister with first-hand knowledge of a successful criminal appeal before him in which Lord Lane appears to have done exactly what he is criticized for never doing, namely not believing police evidence.[108] The leading article in *The Independent* two days later clarifies the issues that are being addressed so frequently at this time, and the ways in which they are being addressed.[109] The article reflects on a motion in the House of Commons calling for the dismissal of Lord Lane. The author believes that such a motion is acceptable as 'an indication of a depth of concern that cannot be ignored'. What is this concern about, especially when the author recognizes that some believe Lord Lane's 1988 Birmingham Six judgment is 'not unreasonable'? 'Lord Lane has come to symbolize the very attitudes that have created the present crisis of confidence in the judicial system.' What are these attitudes? Apparently a certain meanness of spirit such as when in allowing the Guildford Four appeal 'he was graceless and grudging'. And, in relation to the verdict by other Court of Appeal judges in the successful Birmingham Six appeal (see below), he expresses 'no word of regret or apology for the wrongful incarceration'. In conclusion the author puts forward the view that Lord Lane should 'make

---

[107]   7 Feb. 91 'In Contempt, and with Reason'.
[108]   19 March 91 'Settled and Outstanding Miscarriages of Justice' (Iain Hughes).
[109]   21 March 91 'The Case against Lord Lane'.

way for someone who visibly believes that the chief task of the law is to serve justice'. The suggestion that there is a need for a change of attitude and the link between such a change and restoring public confidence is picked up in other articles and becomes significant later in the 1990s.

(ii) Reform and public confidence

Whilst the system's perceived loss of authority and respect exposed senior judges to personal attack, reform proposals went much further than the resignation of key judges. The platform for radical criticism had been given a certain momentum, but in the writings of all but a few, such criticism is, at the beginning of 1990, hesitant and restrained. Reform proposals tend to be attached to articles about miscarriage of justice cases in which the journalist has tried to tell the story of the innocence of those wrongly convicted. However, the reform proposals are generally directed toward due process changes to the system of trial and investigation and the rights of the accused. Attempts to link the two together, as we have tried to show in Chapter 2 of this book, are difficult to advance consistently. Very few journalists, apart from Kennedy and Woffinden and to some extent Melanie Phillips, are able to maintain the logical position that their understanding of miscarriage cases precipitates. Ordinary legal, crime, and political correspondents, even with their increased interest in reform proposals and recognition in their articles of the system's fallibility, do not integrate the logic of that position into their writings.[110] And, even those journalists who try to do so, such as Melanie Phillips, have difficulty maintaining consistency.

In Phillips's commentary on *Newsnight's* review of the television programme *Inside Story* in May 1990, which dealt with the Tottenham Three trial, she is committed to the idea that the credibility of the criminal justice system 'has collapsed'.[111] *Newsnight* had rung the former Law Lord, Lord Scarman to get his response to the *Inside Story* programme, and he had obliged by saying that he thought the convictions of the Tottenham Three were unsafe. Phillips comments: 'This is all getting a trifle farcical . . . In such a climate the truth, which is more complicated than can be dealt with in sound-bites, can remain obscured.' So, she recognizes the deficiencies of trial by television news, but in similar terms also the deficiencies of an adversarial criminal justice system:

But the crisis is surely much more complex, more deeply rooted and even more alarming. It is that even when played by the book, the system is no more than a

---

[110] See the limited critical commentary and links made in the reporting on 31 March of the successful appeal by Alban Turner from his conviction for murder at the Notting Hill Carnival in 1987: *The Independent*, 'Man Jailed for Cola Killing Freed' (Patricia Wynn Davies); *The Daily Telegraph*, 'Man Jailed for Carnival Killing Freed on Appeal' (Terence Shaw); *The Guardian*, 'Man Freed in Carnival Killing Appeal' (Andrew Culf).

[111] *The Guardian* 18 May 90 'A Televised Game of Trial and Error'.

game. It is not designed to get at the truth; and that relates as much to successful appeals as to convictions at trials. It is a game played by a set of rules.

Her scepticism is definitely focused on the disjunction between the 'game' and the 'truth': 'But since that trial is no more or less than a game, since guilt or innocence can be decided simply by observing or breaking the rules of that game, then it follows that to equate the terms guilt or innocence with the truth is a terrible mistake.' And in the light of these severe criticisms her conclusion is consistent: 'Confining attention to police malpractice or the inadequacy of appeals procedure is to address the symptoms rather than the cause of the crisis. It's time that the principles of the system, the very roots of the crisis, were held up for inquiry.' However, while maintaining the talk of crisis, in her article on the Birmingham Six in September 1990, Phillips retreats somewhat from this position.[112] She recognizes that if one reads the full 169-page judgment of Lord Lane from the appeal in 1988, it has a lot to commend it: 'It is only with the luxury of hindsight that Lord Lane's judgment now seems so utterly askew. The two main witnesses who contradicted the prosecution case were hardly credible.' It is worth quoting the whole of Phillips's conclusion because it encapsulates the problem for a journalist trying to maintain some consistency in her talk of a crisis of public confidence in the criminal justice system, or the system of criminal appeal. The notion of public confidence is fluid and is difficult to link to the journalist's concentration on the truth.

Maybe there are convincing answers to all these questions that confirm the men's innocence. But there is also another possibility: that the police may well have conspired to fabricate evidence and perjure themselves in court, but that the Birmingham Six may still be guilty. The Devon and Cornwall evidence may lead to the convictions being quashed, but that doesn't prove they didn't do it. But that is a possibility the criminal justice system, and probably public opinion too, dares not entertain.

So, the criminal justice system, and particularly the appeal system, cannot win. Public confidence will only be satisfied if the truth the public (as constructed by the media) expects to hear is confirmed in the courts, even if the evidence available does not justify the statement demanded.

There was fervent media attention to the moves preceding the referral back of the Birmingham Six case to the Court of Appeal in early 1991, with judicial authority constantly being challenged.[113] And attempts by judges to respond are quickly picked up, such as Lord Justice Russell's statement in the Court of Appeal in the *Binham* case: 'Do you know of anything in our constitution or our law that enables anybody to pronounce a verdict as unsafe and unsatisfactory except this Court? It is for this Court and this Court alone to take the decision; it is not for the Crown Prosecution

---

[112] *The Guardian* 7 Sept. 90 'A Notion that Dare not be Entertained'.
[113] For example, see *The Guardian* 14 Feb. 91 'Attorney Backs Justices' (Clare Dyer).

Service, not for the Director of Public Prosecutions, the Attorney General or the Home Secretary.'[114] At the same time the press are nearly uniformly convinced that the appeal will be successful and are reporting on speculation as to how the authorities would be likely to react. The possibility of a Royal Commission gives focus to the continued reporting about reform proposals for and the lack of public confidence in the criminal justice system.[115] A good example is the set of five reforms suggested by Lord Scarman in an article in *The Times*.[116] That article is published after counsel for the Director of Public Prosecutions announced that the Crown would no longer argue that the convictions were safe and satisfactory. Few of these suggestions for reform have been implemented in the 1990s, a decade when, if one reads the quality newspapers in the early years, such reforms would seem to be a minimum response to the claimed crisis of public confidence then in existence. According to Scarman, the reforms needed include: a rule requiring that confession evidence be corroborated by other evidence; an independent forensic science service working for the courts under judicial supervision; an alternative to the Court of Appeal in a Court of Review with the judicial power to receive evidence and call for documents (akin to the European Commission of Human Rights in its relation to admitting cases for consideration by the European Court of Human Rights); a degree of judicial control over criminal investigations prior to the trial.

Further impetus is given to proposals for reform by the apparent contrast between what Sir John May and his Inquiry achieved 'with one hand tied behind their backs' and what the Court of Appeal is perceived not to have achieved, with its 'miserable performance'.[117] The multiplication of reform proposals continues. It is rare in the press for such proposals to be debated rather than listed, and many can on closer inspection be shown to have serious limitations or impracticalities. A particular tendency is to suggest that 'a limited number of cases'[118] should be re-examined using a very different set of procedures and different processes from those operating at the time, namely Home Office investigation, Home Secretary referral, and Court of Appeal hearing. But what marks out those particular cases for the different procedures is nowhere defined, although there is an expectation that the current high profile cases are among their number.

In early March 1991 the Birmingham Six appeal is heard over one week

[114] Quoted in *The Independent* 6 Feb. 91 'Appeal Judges Annoyed by Guildford Criticism' (Heather Mills).

[115] A common expression of this is 'The Home Secretary is apparently already considering whether confidence can be restored only by a Royal Commission' (*The Independent* 26 Feb. 91 'Freedom near for Birmingham Six' (Heather Mills)).

[116] 5 March 91 'Justice in the Balance'.

[117] *The Independent* 26 Feb. 91 'Full Appeal Hearing Set to Continue' (Patricia Wynn Davies).

[118] *The Guardian* 26 Feb. 91 'Birmingham Six on Last Lap to Freedom' (David Pallister).

in the Court of Appeal. The appeal itself receives a good deal of newspaper coverage and the expected outcome is reported at length with many ensuing commentaries from the day after the Court's verdict for a period of about two weeks. On the day of the verdict the Home Secretary announces the setting up of a Royal Commission into criminal justice. This piece of news focuses the attention of journalists, enabling them to link the successful Birmingham Six appeal with reform proposals and political initiatives. The leading article in *The Times* on 8 March, 'Appeals under Judgement', is typical of articles prior to the Birmingham Six appeal being heard. The article presents the argument that the case for a 'swift, time-limited Royal Commission on criminal appeals is overwhelming.' This is because public confidence depends, according to the author, on a 'sound appeals procedure'. How can the public's confidence be restored? The author answers with the contention that: 'The centre of public attention is not on the guilt or innocence of the appellants, but whether the Court can clear a pathway to the truth through the legal maze the appeal has become.' The author clearly believes that the public universally recognizes the innocence of the appellants and thus attention has to turn from the truth of guilt or innocence to the overall truth. That truth involves the story behind the innocence of the Birmingham Six including an explanation of how they came to be found guilty and had their previous appeals rejected. The expectation is that, if the Court of Appeal can establish the true story behind the Birmingham bombs and the false convictions, then public confidence will follow. It appears that the author's assessment of a lack of public confidence arises from the disjunction between the Court of Appeal's earlier judgments on the case and the story of innocence that has developed in the media, through television programmes, books, and the views of important public persons. So, in this pre-appeal article the author now expects the Court of Appeal to tell the story of innocence.

In the period after the appeal, but before the full judgment, the Court of Appeal had not yet given its version of the truth. During this period the Court's quashing of the convictions simply gives credence to the versions given by the defendants and their lawyers.[119] In her article in *The Guardian* prior to the appeal, Melanie Phillips expresses her expectations of what the appeal should represent.[120] She has a clear view about the underlying problem associated with criminal appeals: 'The current crisis of confidence in English justice has occurred to a large extent because the judges have been so terrified that admitting errors of judgement will lead to a kind of judicial apocalypse.' Hence, assuming that the appeal will succeed, she anticipates

---

[119] *The Guardian* 5 March 91 'Bombs Evidence "Withheld" from Jury' (David Pallister); *The Independent* 5 March 91 'Soap Blamed for Test that Convicted Six' and 'Six Appeal is Told of Lies and Error', and 6 March 91 'New Test Discredits Birmingham Six Scientific Evidence' (Heather Mills).

[120] 1 March 91 'If it's Human to Err, why not Admit It?'

that possibly 'far from being its blackest day, it will be the moment when the system did something right by admitting it had blundered.' She develops her argument by showing how much media criticism of the Court of Appeal leading up to this appeal has been misplaced. She even criticizes Chris Mullin MP, whose book was so influential in the campaign behind the Birmingham Six, who 'spoke ignorantly when he castigated senior judges for failing to "distinguish between innocence and guilt"'. It is an end to judicial timidity that she seems to believe is so crucial.

Where the judges go from here is a theme constantly rehearsed in newspapers following the appeal verdict in the Birmingham Six case, but before the full judgment is given. Calls for judges to resign are matched by articles defending their authority or characters, as well as reports of speeches made but really addressed for media and public consumption.[121] Louis Blom-Cooper's article in *The Observer* is a good example.[122] He is very concerned about the 'ill-informed media coverage' and the dangers of 'politicising of the administration of justice'. He believes that the necessary debate about the future of the criminal justice system must resist superficiality and 'irresponsible public pronouncements' that 'undermine a public institution far too precious to be denigrated by some momentary, strident voices'.

Newspaper commentaries after the successful Birmingham Six appeal, but prior to the full judgment, can generally be described as presenting argument in strong terms. Words like crisis and confidence appear regularly, and the adjectives 'grave', 'classic', and 'serious' tend to accompany the phrase 'miscarriage of justice'. There is also a tendency to make links between the Birmingham Six case and arguments about reform, particularly the plethora of reform proposals that had already emerged as potential evidence to the Royal Commission on Criminal Justice that had just been announced. There is a lot of discussion about the deficiencies of individual judges. There is also a greater interest in other alleged miscarriages. This appears to have been the time when newspapers are more inclined to think that other cases are newsworthy, and indeed the greater likelihood of publicity exacerbates the feeling, evident in many articles, that there are more miscarriages of justice at this time.

Consider some of the articles that follow the verdict prior to the full judgment. Robert Rice's article in *The Financial Times* talks of 'the tarnished image of British justice', which must be rectified by the Royal Commission, and 'For the sake of the British criminal justice system it cannot afford to get it wrong this time.'[123] The echo of when it got things wrong before is amplified by John Mullin in *The Guardian* on the same

---

[121] *The Times* 16 March 91 'Mackay Dismisses "Unwarranted" Calls for Lane to Resign' (Frances Gibb).   [122] 24 March 91 'Reckless Rush to Judgement'.
[123] 15 March 91 'Birmingham Six Freed by Court of Appeal'.

day; that echo being from 1960s cases. Mullin quotes a *Sunday Times* article from 1961: 'the test of a country's justice is not the blunders which are sometimes made but the zeal with which they are put right.'[124] With this echo Mullin is able to refer to current commentators who deride the system of criminal appeals, and how 'Campaigners say there can be no public confidence unless the system admits it fails from time to time.' Among the many articles concerning the Birmingham Six case in *The Independent* on 15 March are those by Patricia Wynn Davies. She describes the decision to set up a Royal Commission as indicating 'the depth of the crisis'.[125] She analyses other alleged miscarriages demonstrating how they represent, as the overall title of her article claims, 'Strong Evidence against the Court of Appeal'. She also relates a short history of the Court of Appeal suggesting that 'Eighty years on' the Court has not proved its effectiveness, and how 'The need for an effective body remains as urgent as ever.' *The Independent's* leading article on that day calls for the resignation of Lord Lane and derides the Court of Appeal: 'But most of all it is an indictment of the Court of Appeal and of those grave, intelligent but sometimes purblind men who stand at the apex of the judicial system.'[126]

Over the next week alleged miscarriages are hardly out of the news. John Mullin's article in *The Guardian* on 16 March demonstrates the current interest in other, selected cases,[127] such as those of Judith Ward, the Tottenham Three, and those found guilty of the murder of Carl Bridgewater. *The Guardian* starts a series of articles on alleged miscarriages entitled 'Justice on Trial'. This series seriously challenges judicial authority presenting evidence in such a way as to imply that the Court of Appeal must respond by recognizing the innocence of those convicted, such as Duncan Campbell's analysis of the new evidence in the Darvell brothers' case.[128] This includes evidence about how Wayne, whose admissions to the police were the basis of the evidence against the brothers at trial, was according to his former teacher at his special school 'forever confessing things he hadn't done' (his brother Paul had always maintained his innocence); evidence about a 'thick-set man' who had been seen in the entrance of the sex shop in which the manageress had been assaulted and murdered, who had 'never been traced to be eliminated from the inquiry'; evidence from the defence lawyers about their concerns that the convictions were mistaken, particularly in view of Wayne's 'bizarre' answers to questions put to him when first interviewed. Having examined the fresh evidence himself, Campbell pointedly concludes: 'the case of the two misfits has been referred back to the Court of Appeal for the fresh evidence to be examined.'

---

[124] 'Release of the Birmingham Six: Legal system "Cannot Cope with Miscarriages of Justice"'.   [125] 'The Birmingham Six: Review Confirms Crisis in Justice System'.
[126] 'The Innocent and the Guilty'.
[127] 'Suspicions Linger of Other Miscarriages of Justice'.
[128] 23 March 91 'MisfitsTrapped by Fantasy Lies'.

The Independent, in its summary of the full Birmingham Six appeal judgment, expresses concern that there was insufficient acknowledgement of the wrong done to the defendants. The title of the article is 'Court Cannot Declare Innocence on Quashing Conviction.'[129] As the press dissects the judgment, commentary concentrates on this particular deficiency, of not declaring the appellants to *be* innocent, and its implications. *The Guardian* carries a number of critical articles, such as 'Unanswered Questions and "Selected Facts" Mar Happiness',[130] quoting one of the Six, Hugh Callaghan: 'It was just as I expected. I won't lose any sleep over it. As far as I am concerned I am totally exonerated.' And in another article, the dismay of other participants is illustrated: 'The 73-page judgment, which suggested that the Court of Appeal had great difficulty in handling such exceptional cases, was not well received by the men or their solicitor. Paddy Hill said: "You can't expect more from a pig than a grunt." Gareth Peirce, solicitor for five of the men, said the Court seemed to acknowledge that it was unable to deal with miscarriages of justice.'[131]

Again, the platform given by critical commentary of the Court of Appeal's judgment in this case and others, coupled with the linking of deficiencies with talk of a crisis of public confidence, is a platform for suggestions for wide reforms. A good example is Heather Mill's article detailing suggestions for reform by one of the appellants' barristers in the Birmingham Six appeal, namely Michael Mansfield QC. He is quoted at length: 'Root-and-branch changes are needed now to confession and science evidence, if the public is to have confidence in the system. Of course, any system cannot be expected to be foolproof, but the public also do not expect people to wrongly stay inside jail for many years.' The Court of Appeal's judgment that the convictions of the Birmingham Six could no longer stand is not taken as a vindication of its role within the criminal justice system, nor as a vindication of other elements of the system of criminal justice. Indeed, quite the opposite. So, when the Maguire Seven case comes to the fore, with a preliminary appeal hearing in mid-April 1991, and later the full appeal, the reporting is again accompanied by reform proposals linked to the proceedings of the Royal Commission on Criminal Justice that had been set up.[132] There is a lot of talk of a lack of public confidence and general scepticism. The article in *The Independent* on 8 May demonstrates how the commentaries on the Maguire Seven appeal are not neutral, but structured around the preconceptions of crisis that had evolved in

---

[129]   28 March 91 (Ying Hui Tan).   [130]   28 March 91.

[131]   28 March 91 'Birmingham Six Police Report to go to DPP' (David Pallister); also *The Independent* 28 March 91 'The Birmingham Six Judgment: "Sanitised Version of the Facts" Greeted with Calm' (Nick Cohen).

[132]   For good examples see *The Daily Telegraph* 29 April 91 'Justice on Trial' (Colin Randall); *The Independent* 7 May 91 'Maguire Appeal to be Monitored by Inquiry Team' (Heather Mills).

recent times in the media in general. That article is entitled 'Why the Maguire case puts judges on trial: Patricia Wynn Davies looks at the Court of Appeal's toughest challenge'. The article ends with the following conclusion: 'The court's answer to the perceived failings in the system is that it has no power to conduct an open-ended investigation into an alleged miscarriage of justice. That, however, is no answer to its critics but rather an invitation to much-needed reform.'

Linking together the perceived inadequacies of the roles played by the Court of Appeal and the Director of Public Prosecutions, both in appeals and following successful appeals, with the underlying adversary system, Heather Mills is able to demonstrate serious contradictions implicit in the current procedures. Such contradictions are thought to be represented not only in the Maguire Seven appeal but also in other appeals.[133] Taken to one extreme those contradictions can justify a statement like that by Paul Hill, one of the Guildford Four, on hearing of the collapse of the case against the police officers involved in eliciting his false confession: 'Having spent 15 years in prison for something I didn't do, am I supposed to remain quiet while the British judicial system proves itself incapable of revealing the truth behind the miscarriage of justice which led to my frame-up and false imprisonment over those long years?'[134] Such statements abound in the press and appear to be justified by the combination of miscarriage cases and inadequacies represented in those cases, the wealth of proposals for reform, and the conditions of crisis constructed in the reporting. Nevertheless ordinary reporting of convictions continues. Even, on occasion, ordinary reporting of appeals that is noteworthy for its own reasons but not linked to the discussion of high profile cases. A good example is an article in *The Independent on Sunday* dealing with appeals following the disbanding of the West Midlands Serious Crimes Squad in June,[135] while an article in *The Guardian* dealing with the same cases only makes one tentative link to other high profile cases.[136]

The now familiar range of stories, particularly those concerning the individuals involved, characterizes the extensive reporting of the success of the Maguire Seven appeal on 27 June 1991.[137] But the fact that the appeal only succeeded on one of the six grounds of the appeal, the one conceded by the Director of Public Prosecutions, and that the appeal judgment appeared to

[133] 11 June 91 'And still they wait for justice: The Maguire family's continuing struggle to clear their names is evidence that the Court of Appeal cannot deal properly with miscarriages of justice'.

[134] *The Daily Telegraph* 12 June 91 'Guildford Four Police Win Case' (David Millward and Terence Shaw).

[135] 16 June 91 'Police Watchdog Prompts Baker to allow Appeal' (Terry Kirby).

[136] 19 June 91 'Longing for liberty—The prolonged ordeal of some of the lesser known victims of the now disbanded West Midlands Serious Crimes Squad' (David Utting).

[137] David Pallister's article in *The Guardian*, 'An Unhappy Family Tied by Injustice,' is a good example.

represent a different set of conclusions from those in Sir John May's Interim Report, gives ample opportunity for criticisms of that judgment.[138] Of course, since the appellants who were still alive were all already released from prison, the aim of the appellants was to prove their innocence and to establish their rights to compensation rather than to obtain their freedom. In that aim they were substantially disappointed and, in reporting on this, newspapers tended to associate with their aim and thus find that 'Appeal judges fail again'.[139] It is clear that the judgment does not offer a convincing narrative about the circumstances that led to the convictions, assuming the appellants' innocence. But that is the point. The Court of Appeal is not making that assumption, the media, at this time, on the whole are. Melanie Phillips's damning condemnation of the judgment uses that assumption to develop a general criticism, one that suggests that the judges, or judicial reasoning, lack common sense: 'the gap that is so often apparent between the law and commonsense'.[140] And such a criticism enables the link to a lack of public confidence to be reinforced: 'The judgment has merely helped to fuel public disquiet over the ability or willingness of the courts to see that justice is done. The judges have left a sour taste because they refused to provide a sufficiently unequivocal and ringing declaration that a serious miscarriage of justice has occurred.'

In July newspapers cover the build-up of stories relating to a new port-folio of evidence submitted by lawyers to the Home Secretary about the Tottenham Three (Broadwater Farm riot and murder case), and the new police inquiry set up into those convictions.[141] Such coverage represents ordinary reporting but with a background expectation that serious deficiencies would be shown in the criminal justice system, and public confidence would again be lost. However, such reporting does not raise the full challenge of scepticism; only a letter by the General Secretary for Liberty, Andrew Puddephatt, in *The Guardian* does that. He compares the official activity relating to the cases of the Tottenham Three and the Armagh Four (convictions referred to the Northern Ireland Court of Appeal earlier in the year) with the inactivity in other high profile cases and other allegations of miscarriage (quoting allegations in 400–500 cases). 'There can no longer be any pretence that these are isolated cases. It is clear that a sense of panic is developing that if a large number of cases are reviewed, our policing and criminal justice system will fall apart.'

---

[138]   *The Guardian* 'Court clears Maguires but casts shadow on victory' (John Mullin); *The Independent* 'A Day in the British Courts: Slur Remains after Maguire Appeal is Won' and 'Maguire ruling raises doubt over Court of Appeal: "grudging" judgment renews concerns over handling of miscarriages of justice' (Heather Mills).

[139]   Leading Article *The Independent* 27 June 91.

[140]   *The Guardian* 28 June 91 'Sense versus Blind Justice'.

[141]   *The Times* 15 July 91 'Silcott the Scapegoat? (Leading Article); articles by David Rose in *The Observer* 14, 21, and 28 July 91; *The Guardian* 26 July 91 'Broadwater Cases Go to Inquiry' (John Mullin); *The Independent* 26 July 91 'Inquiry Ordered into Silcott Case' (Nick Cohen).

In August the new inquiry ordered by the Home Office into Judith Ward's case is covered.[142] With the publicity given to particular cases, the main commentaries on criminal justice at this time continue to reflect the theme of a loss of public confidence. The article published in *The Independent* by Alistair Logan, a solicitor who acted for the Guildford Four, relating his personal loss of faith in the criminal justice system, fits well into this general atmosphere.[143] In September, the continuing work of the May Inquiry, particularly the evidence of the former Home Secretary, Douglas Hurd, and evidence being given to and expectations about the Royal Commission are constantly in the news, retaining the link between criminal justice, especially miscarriages of justice and proposals for reform.[144] Such reporting constantly questions the efficiency of the Criminal Division of the Court of Appeal.[145] By the end of September the Tottenham Three case has been referred back to the Court of Appeal and this is mainly reported on in terms of serious failings and anticipated reform.[146] However, every now and then a Court of Appeal decision is reported and commented on without obvious reference to issues of public confidence and reform, namely without recourse to a meta-narrative of crisis of public confidence. It is surprising when this occurs in relation to a case that had received some publicity and about which it is very plausible to use the adjectives 'grave' or 'serious' in describing the miscarriage, and in which serious deficiencies had emerged. The reporting of the quashing of John McGranaghan's conviction for rape is such an example. The case highlights deficiencies of prosecution disclosure, defence neglect, and problems associated with identification evidence. We can only surmise that either it is the nature of the offence that results in the reporting being so different, at this time, from other miscarriage cases, or that the case offers journalists no simple narrative associated with innocence.[147] Indeed the quashing of that conviction left a number of rape cases unsolved, and there is virtually no accompanying story about the victim of this miscarriage.

[142] *The Daily Telegraph* 13 Aug. 91 'Judith Ward's Conviction for M62 Bombing to be Reviewed' (Philip Johnston).

[143] 30 Aug. 91 'A System Bound by Chains of Prejudice'.

[144] *The Guardian* 3 Oct. 91 'Hurd Urges New Injustice Safety Net' (David Pallister); *The Times* 3 Oct. 91 'Hurd Calls for Tribunal to Investigate Unfair Verdicts' (Richard Ford and Frances Gibb); *The Independent* 3 Oct. 91 'Evidence of the need for change: Heather Mills views a barrister's proposals for drastic reform of the criminal justice system' (Heather Mills).

[145] *The Independent* 24 Sept. 91 'Inquiry "better than Court of Appeal" ' (Heather Mills); *The Times* 19 Aug. 91 'Rarely Seen to be Undone' (Ludovic Kennedy); *The Independent on Sunday* 29 Sept. 91 'How our Justice Fails to be Done' (Patricia Wynn Davies).

[146] *The Guardian* 27 Sept. 91 'Detective Suspended as Blakelock Case is Referred to Appeal' (John Carvel); *The Independent* 27 Sept. 91 'Justice System Faces Further Scrutiny after Silcott Move' (Heather Mills).

[147] *The Times* 31 Oct. 91 'Man Cleared 10 Years after Being Jailed for Rape' (David Young); *The Independent* 31 Oct. 91 'Bad Tactics and Lawyers' Errors in Rape Case' (Adam Sage); *The Guardian* 31 Oct. 91 'Judges clear lifer convicted of rapes: Blood group evidence frees man after 10 years in jail'; *The Daily Telegraph* 31 Oct. 91 'Rape Case Man Cleared after 10 years in Jail' (Terence Shaw).

Proposals to reform the criminal justice system proliferate in press articles in November 1991.[148] And other miscarriage cases continue to be in
the news, such as the Cardiff Three case (referred to the Court of Appeal in
June)[149] and the Carl Bridgewater murder case, in which a new police
inquiry is ordered.[150] But there is a crescendo at the end of November with
the decision by the Court of Appeal to quash the convictions of the
Tottenham Three. The wealth of reporting of that decision inevitably
concentrates on narratives associated with the proclaimed innocence of
those who had been convicted, implications for other cases,[151] for public
confidence in the law[152] and law reform.[153] There are some new voices in
the media, particularly those of representatives of the police suggesting that
the blame does not lie solely with them, but also with the press and the
public.[154] A meta-narrative of crisis of public confidence is clearly percep-
tible. Some of the commentaries at this time, especially in December 1991,
are damning of the existing system of criminal justice at all levels and
suggest a total lack of confidence in it,[155] or what is necessary to reform
it.[156] As we have tried to make clear, however, such commentary appears
not to make the reporting of everyday convictions significantly less reliable
as a statement of the truth of a person's guilt, except in particular, long-
standing, high profile alleged miscarriage cases. Two other matters receive
more attention in press reports at this time. One is not only the potential
number of miscarriages but also how that number could be dealt with,
namely the backlog of cases.[157] The other is the advent of the apology,
picked up by some journalists from the Appeal Court's judgment in the
Tottenham Three case: 'We wish to express our profound regret that they

[148] *The Times* 19 Nov. 91 'Lawyers Call for Appeals Shake-up' and 23 Nov. 91 'CPS Says Suspects Need New Rights' (Frances Gibb); *The Independent* 22 Nov. 91 'CPS Urges Use of Appeal Assessors' (Adam Sage) and 25 Nov. 91 'Commission Will Study Blakelock Murder Appeal' (Heather Mills); *The Guardian* 19 Nov. 91 'Solicitors Seek Appeal Tribunal' and 22 Nov. 91 'Prosecutors Call for Miscarriages Court' (Clare Dyer); *The Financial Times* 19 Nov. 91 'Lawyers in Plea to Keep Adversarial System' (Robert Rice); *The Daily Telegraph* 19 Nov. 91 'Solicitors Call for Appeals Shake-up' (Terence Shaw).

[149] *The Independent* 22 Nov. 91 'Who really Killed Lynette White?' (Rachel Borrill).

[150] *The Independent* 1 Nov. 91 'New Inquiry into Carl Bridgewater Case' (Terence Kirby).

[151] *The Independent* 28 Nov. 91 'Murder "Witness" Was not at Estate during Rioting: A flood of appeals is expected in Broadwater Farm cases after allegations that police fabricated evidence' (Heather Mills).

[152] *The Financial Times* 30 Nov. 91 'A Rapid Loss of Confidence: Public Concern over Miscarriages of Justice' (Robert Rice).

[153] *The Sunday Telegraph* 1 Dec. 91 'Calls Grow for Appeals Panel' (Valerie Eliott); *The Times* 26 Nov. 91 'Section 17 Must be Repealed' (Lord Scarman).

[154] *The Times* 2 Feb. 91 'Silcott Error Blamed on Public Apathy' (Jamie Dettmer); *The Guardian* 2 Dec. 91 'Police Chief Blames Broadwater Residents for Silence over Killing' (John Mullin).

[155] Particularly the article 'Justice on Trial' by Peter Millar in *The Sunday Times* 1 Dec. 91; also Jeremy Hardy's piece 'Trials of Innocence' in *The Guardian* 28 Dec. 91.

[156] *The Guardian* 29 Nov. 91 'A Code that will Carry Conviction' (Melanie Phillips).

[157] *The Guardian* 10 Dec. 91 'Appeals Backlog Growing' (Clare Dyer).

have suffered as a result of the shortcomings of the criminal process.' Although not entirely accurate, *The Independent*'s journalists Heather Mills and David Connett describe this statement in the following terms: 'The Court of Appeal, in an unprecedented admission of failure, apologised yesterday for a criminal justice system that kept the men wrongly convicted of murdering PC Keith Blakelock in prison for six years.' Such a statement certainly represents a change of course for Court of Appeal judgments[158] and one that, we would argue, is responsive to how the media had been reporting and commenting on recent miscarriage cases.

4 1992

The extent of reporting on miscarriages of justice does not lessen in 1992, but some of the focus changes. There is certainly a continuing flow of widely reported successful appeals, particularly those of Stefan Kiszko, Judith Ward, the Darvell Brothers, and the Cardiff Three. But somehow, as if reaching saturation point, the ability to reiterate the theme of a crisis of public confidence arising out of the latest miscarriage seems to diminish. The momentum of discussion about a loss of public confidence is still well in evidence, but the debate about reform proposals and current changes starts to take precedence over rearticulation of the talk of a crisis of public confidence. Under such conditions those who construct the debate about reform proposals become the usual commentators and are referred to by other reporters more frequently. Since such proposals tend to come mainly from those involved in the law, from judges or former judges, practitioners or academics, their comments take a more central stage. To see how this evolves, particularly concerning judges, we will look at some articles and letters in *The Times* during the year, and then link our discussion of them to other commentaries on miscarriages in other newspapers.

The deficiencies of judges, both trial court and appeal judges, had been the focus of much concern, and debate about their reform had been central to the issues reported on by newspapers in relation to miscarriages. In 1992 the judge's voice is being heard more clearly in the media, both the voice of former judges associated with the problems of the past, and the apparently new voice of judges not, or less, tainted with those problems. In *The Times* in January the former Lord Chancellor, Lord Hailsham, discusses his concerns about the deficiencies of some of the rules of criminal evidence, their 'ludicrous artificiality, complication and want of logic', and lack of common sense.[159] He recognizes that recent miscarriages of justice have arisen from the evidence of false confessions being believed by the jury and the appeal court. His solution is: 'The true safeguard of innocence must

[158] See Pattenden, n. 51 above, 181–2.
[159] 19 Jan. 92 'Bring Common Sense into the Courtroom'.

surely be logic and openness on both sides and a reliable method of trial and appeal to prevent malpractice . . . the procedure, both at first instance and on appeal, should be such as far as humanly possible to guarantee a reliable result.' Such 'apple pie' statements feed into the concerns expressed in the media in general about deficiencies in the criminal justice system. Here, innocence goes with reliability, and both require logic and common sense rather than complicated and artificial rules.

In February comes the announcement from the Lord Chief Justice, Lord Lane, that he will retire early, and that Lord Justice Taylor will become Lord Chief Justice in April. It is reported that Lord Taylor is 'pledged . . . to restore public confidence'. 'He conceded that recent miscarriages of justice had shaken public confidence and suggested that the Court of Appeal should be given powers to investigate new evidence . . . he would try to make the judicial system of England and Wales more open.'[160] The article quoting Taylor's views recognizes how the 'criminal justice system is coming under intense scrutiny and how the Royal Commission on Criminal Justice is expected to recommend fundamental reform.' Thus arguments coming from those most closely allied to the current system start to take centre stage, with the expectation of significant reforms. The former Lord Justice of Appeal, Sir Frederick Lawton, continues this theme in May. Looking at the Judith Ward and Stefan Kiszko miscarriages he concludes, rather differently from the reasons given by the Court of Appeal for allowing the appeals, that the real difficulty is the 'unsatisfactory state of the law on the relevance of evidence of mental instability in criminal trials'.[161] This argument leads him to the view that: 'There would be less chance of miscarriages of justice when there is mental instability if we had an inquisitorial system of criminal justice instead of an adversarial one.'

Five weeks after taking up his new position as Lord Chief Justice in April, Lord Chief Justice Taylor gives a newspaper interview reported on by Frances Gibb in *The Times*.[162] He had offered himself as a witness in the Judith Ward appeal indicating 'the new era of openness and greater accessibility to judges that he wants to encourage'. He also wants an 'expanded role for the Court of Appeal to order investigations, and a new independent committee to take over from the home secretary the job of looking at alleged miscarriages of justice'. And, in relation to the media: 'I am absolutely in favour of the judiciary being open to criticism by the media';

---

[160] *The Times* 26 Feb. 92 'New Law Chief Vows to Restore Public's Faith' (Frances Gibb). Colin Randall's article 'The Problems he Will Have to Face' in *The Daily Telegraph* rehearses the usual crisis arguments well in the context of the views Taylor is expressing: 'he needed no-one to tell him of the widespread belief, following a succession of miscarriages of justice, that the criminal justice system is in crisis' (26 Feb. 92). Christopher Lockwood's article in the same paper on the same day is headlined: 'Taylor and his Task: The New Lord Chief Justice Inherits a System in Crisis'.

[161] *The Times* 19 May 92 'The Mind that Matters'.

[162] 2 Feb. 92 'Chief Justice Offered to Testify in Ward Case'.

'I would like to think that, as we take steps to improve the system, and correct the failures there have been, we will get the support of the media, as well as the brickbats.' However, criticism of judges in the media at this time continues to be severe. Bernard Levin, writing in *The Times* only two weeks later, remains unconvinced by Lord Chief Justice Taylor's assurances. He writes about:

The appalling series of miscarriages that have indelibly stained our entire legal system in the last decade or so. Again and again the Court of Appeal got it wrong hopelessly, scandalously and inexcusably wrong while innocent men and women dragged out decades of prison because those wigged boobies were simply not up to their jobs. It is a mark of their unfitness for office that there has been only one judicial public apology from the bench in all the scandals.

Sir Frederick Lawton responds by letter.[163] He disputes that trial judges have been responsible for the recent high profile miscarriages, or the Court of Appeal. With regard to the latter he argues that 'Mr Levin and other critics of the Court of Appeal seem not to appreciate that it cannot act without evidence.' And, of course, he means legal evidence rather than evidence that might satisfy members of the press. He concludes: 'The recent disturbing miscarriages of justice were not caused, as Bernard Levin suggests, by the alleged inadequacies of the judges but, as our forebears before 1907 appreciated, by the fact that an appellate jurisdiction is probably incompatible with trial by jury.' Chris Mullin MP disagrees: 'The truth is that judges, both at trial and on appeal, played a large part in most of the recent miscarriages of justice and there is nothing to be gained from suggestion otherwise.'[164] Others, however, such as Ludovic Kennedy, are starting to applaud Lord Chief Justice Taylor for his policy of openness and the recent stronger and more critical judgment of the Court of Appeal in Judith Ward's appeal. 'The forthright and unequivocal manner in which the three judges gave their reasons for allowing the Judith Ward appeal (report, June 5) together with the glasnost policy of the new Lord Chief Justice, are the most hopeful signs yet that the judiciary have at last recognised and come to terms with the corruption that has disfigured so many of our criminal trials.'[165] Lord Chief Justice Taylor's speech at the annual Lord Mayor's dinner is widely reported. He again argues for more openness and responsiveness: 'Judges should "move with the times", come out of "purdah" and end their isolation from the media and the rest of the criminal justice system if public confidence is to be restored.' But at the same time he warns of the 'growing workload in the criminal courts and spoke of a "growing crisis" in the Court of Appeal criminal division, where the number of appeals

---

[163] *The Times* 19 June 92 'Rough Judgement'.
[164] Letter in *The Times* 25 June 92 'Rough Judgement'.
[165] Letter in *The Times* 17 June 92 'Miscarriages of Justice'.

against conviction was up 26 per cent on last year'.[166] This concern with numbers gradually emerges and becomes significant.

The reporting of Stefan Kiszko's successful appeal in February is a classic example of the reporting of a successful appeal, and indeed is described in the press as a 'classic' miscarriage. We use the adjective 'classic' to describe the way in which this appeal is reported because, unlike many others, it relied on evidence that proved innocence.[167] In so doing it coincided with the focus of media interest on miscarriages, a narrative based on the factual innocence of the appellant. In the judgment of Lord Lane are the words that most appellants would dearly desire to hear, but which they would never be likely to hear from a public judicial authority, and which in fact Stefan Kiszko never heard because he was in a secure mental institution at the time. These words were that 'this man could not have been the person' who committed the crime. So, the first line of one of Heather Mill's articles on the appeal in *The Independent* starts by incorporating what is in effect the paradigm of media concerns about miscarriages of justice: 'The latest in the litany of miscarriages of justice is arguably the most shocking. For even before Stefan Kiszko stood trial, there was unequivocal evidence of his innocence.'[168] Apart from the personalities involved (all the victims), the media are able to tell how the miscarriage arose through the failures of reliance on a false confession, lack of disclosure of crucial medical evidence, witnesses lying, and mistaken tactics by the defence. The only thing needed to complete the narrative is the identity of the real offender and details of his background and circumstances leading to the crime. As a substitute for this the media are able to report that the police will reopen their inquiries into the case. The *Daily Telegraph* report starts in the following way:

Police restarted the hunt for the killer of an 11-year-old girl yesterday after three Appeal Court judges decided that 40-year-old Stefan Kiszko, who had served 16 years of a life sentence for murdering her, is innocent . . . evidence, said to have been available before his original trial, showed that he could not have been the murderer.[169]

In the reporting in *The Guardian* the same emphases are found and references to how such a case should be noted by the acting Royal

[166] And Sir Frederick Lawton voices the concerns, probably shared by other judges, that such openness might lead judges into 'undesirable public controversy', in which judges might lose control to the media. *The Times* 18 Aug. 92 'The Acceptable Face of Judge Mark III.'
[167] Kiszko's impotence made it impossible for him to have been the attacker of the victim Lesley Molseed. There was indeed unequivocal proof of his innocence. Although not part of the story in the media, there were clear suspicions as to who the actual offender was; see Jonathan Rose, with Steve Panter and Trevor Wilkinson, *Innocents: How Justice Failed Stefan Kiszko and Lesley Molseed* (London, 1997), esp. ch. 22 'Who Killed Lesley Molseed?'
[168] 19 Feb. 92 'Evidence Could Have Prevented Prosecution'.
[169] 19 Feb. 92 'Man Cleared of Murder after 16 Years in Jail' (Colin Wright and Terence Shaw).

Commission.[170] While The *Daily Telegraph* article describes the case as 'a further embarrassment for the administration of justice now under review by Lord Runciman's Royal Commission on Criminal Justice' The *Sunday Times* leading article the following Sunday rehearses the usual meta-narrative of crisis of public confidence arguments. It talks of how 'sadly commonplace' it is 'for innocent people to be jailed and for guilty people to remain free'. 'The list of recent miscarriages of justice is so long it has transformed public attitudes towards the police and the judiciary from previous admiration to present contempt.' It goes on to describe the Kiszko case as 'probably the worst' of the 'recent injustices' because 'there was unequivocal evidence of his innocence.' It describes how the criminal justice system so manifestly failed, commenting that 'It is Britain's disgrace that such things can happen in a civilised country committed to the due process of the law.' It encourages the Royal Commission to report quickly and make many reforms. And it is very critical of the Court of Appeal's failure to offer an apology: 'Only the law, it seems, can ruin a man's life and never have to say it is sorry.'[171]

Whilst the Kiszko case is treated by the media as further evidence of the need for reform, other Court of Appeal decisions in the same month are reported without reference to issues of public confidence, crisis of public confidence, or reform proposals. The reporting on the appeal of Lea, Higgins, and Oliver from their convictions for murder mainly adopts the terms of the judgment as to why the convictions could not stand. 'Lord Justice Glidewell said the Court recognised that many people would feel that justice was not being done by overturning the convictions. But to uphold convictions in cases where the evidence was insufficient and the jury had not been properly directed would amount to a miscarriage of justice.'[172] Such a report gives little room for further critical commentary, except for commentary that might come close to libel or contempt. The conception of miscarriage of justice highlighted in this reporting is characteristic of legal discourse in that it is difficult to adapt to critical media commentary. The reporting on the successful appeal of Jacqueline Fletcher, who had been found guilty in 1988 of murdering her baby son, offers wider scope, the case having been taken up by the *Rough Justice* television series, but is reported on with restraint and limited commentary. The terms in which the confession in this case was elicited were reminiscent of the Kiszko case, as was the fact of the mental state of both defendants, but the reporting is very different as are the links made in that reporting.[173] The principal

---

[170] 19 Feb. 92 'Immature Man Could not Have Committed Murder' and 'Man Cleared after 16 Years in Jail' (Duncan Campbell).

[171] *The Sunday Times* 23 Feb. 92 'Justice in the Dock'.

[172] *The Guardian* 27 Feb. 92 'Appeal Court Clears Three of Killing'.

[173] *The Guardian* 29 Feb. 92 'Mother serving life freed: Court quashes murder conviction in latest "disputed confession" appeal' (Duncan Campbell).

problem that the media seem to have in reporting on these cases is their inability to adopt the focus of innocence for these appeals. Without such a focus the ensuing narrative tends to be restricted.

Where claimed miscarriages can be linked to narratives of innocence, the prevailing meta-narrative of crisis seems to encourage the situation in which such claims are likely to be published, and sympathetically reviewed. A good example is Ludovic Kennedy's article in *The Independent* about George Long. The evidence that allows Kennedy to discuss the case is Long's claim to be innocent maintained beyond the time when release on licence could arise. In other words he would probably have been released from prison, having satisfied the sentence for his conviction for murder, if he did not still refuse to admit to the crime.[174] Such behaviour, an unwillingness to accept guilt and show remorse, has a negative impact on the discretion to release on licence. However, on the other hand, it offers fruitful support to a narrative of innocence offered by a journalist. The substance of the case against Long's conviction is an allegedly false confession, which he rejected at the time and has done so ever since. Kennedy had told this story first some four years earlier, but for him the problem is that, although a number of influential people had become convinced of Long's innocence, 'there is virtually no new evidence.'[175] Kennedy makes the link in his article to evidence that 'a regrettable proportion of those in prison are innocent of the crimes for which they were convicted.' As long as there is editorial recognition of the newsworthiness of such cases, more likely at times when the media claim that there is public concern or a crisis of public confidence in the criminal justice system, the stories they offer have considerable scope. That scope easily extends to grave doubts about the accuracy of the outcomes of the criminal justice system.[176]

In 1992 the factor of numbers appealing or alleging miscarriage is constantly being discussed, as individual cases receive some publicity or comment. The meta-narrative of crisis has developed to a stage where highly publicized miscarriage of justice cases are not only reported on as evidence of the need for reform, but as evidence that other persons claiming to have suffered miscarriage are also likely to be innocent. The article by David Rose about the *Pinfold* case in *The Observer* is a good example. He talks of well-publicized cases representing only 'the tip of an iceberg:

---

[174] There are other similar cases, one which received some publicity in 1992 being that of Paul Cleeland: *The Independent* 23 June 92 'Life Prisoner Challenges "Expert" Evidence' (Adam Sage).

[175] *The Independent* 19 March 92 'If he Were Guilty, he Could be Free'.

[176] See particularly, John Carvel's article on evidence from the National Association of Probation Officers in *The Guardian* 30 March 92 'Prisoners wrongly Jailed "May Total 500": Probation officers' chief finds "lurking doubt" hangs over cases of 6 per cent of inmates at top security prison'; *The Independent* 30 March 92 'Convictions Queried by Probation Officers' (Heather Mills); *The Sunday Telegraph* 5 April 92 'Justice Put in the Dock over Miscarriages' (Christopher Elliott).

waiting in the wings of the Court of Appeal is a legion of further, less notorious but equally shocking miscarriages.'[177] Margarette Driscoll makes similar arguments in *The Sunday Times* when considering a number of recognized and alleged miscarriages following Judith Ward's successful appeal. 'Those who watched Judith Ward walk free from the Court of Appeal last week hoping it would mark the final page in an ugly chapter of judicial history should brace themselves. The legal establishment will barely have time to draw breath before the next wave of appeals washes before it.'[178] She goes on to describe how recent successful appeals will have encouraged 'many who formerly felt they would have no chance' to try again, and how the numbers are growing. The link made by Duncan Campbell in the heading to his article in *The Guardian* is also between freedom for Judith Ward and 'Home Office officials scrutinising 800 other possible miscarriages of justice'.[179] What he says about those 800 is that 'few are likely to reach the Court of Appeal.'

The theme of numbers of unresolved wrongful convictions repeats itself in many different forms. In the context of cases about which the journalist in question appears to be convinced that the person convicted is innocent of the particular crime, the implication is that a good proportion of the allegations are true but that they are unlikely to receive adequate investigation or assessment on appeal. The meta-narrative of a crisis of public confidence operates to allow journalists to imply and the reader to read in serious concerns about the possibility of large numbers of alleged miscarriages that need to be rectified. But the full implications of such concerns are not disclosed in most articles. The difficulties of investigating and reversing large numbers of convictions are not explored. Valerie Elliott's article in *The Sunday Telegraph* is a good example. She selects the case of Sammy Davis who, having served his sentence for rape, is still fighting to establish his innocence. The possibility of his case receiving adequate attention against the '700 to 800 representations each year' received by the Home Office is, by implication, in doubt.[180] The article presents a strong commitment to the innocence of Sammy Davis as attested by members of his family. The improbability that such sentiments alleging miscarriage, those of a family's commitment to the innocence of one of their number, will lead to a satisfactory conclusion in any but a few cases is noted. But there is no analysis of the difficulties of giving effect to such sentiments as legal evidence relevant to quashing convictions.

This theme of numbers (and a general sense of a large problem) arises in a number of different contexts. Judith Ward's successful appeal is reported

---

[177] 17 May 92 ' "Murderer" Waits 42 Months for Appeal after Evidence Withdrawn'.
[178] 17 May 92 'Queue Forming at the Appeal Court's Door'; on numbers, see also *The Times* 13 May 92 'Calls for New Review System' (Richard Ford).
[179] 12 May 92.
[180] 17 May 92 'Home Office Team Aiding the Search for Justice'.

on by *The Independent* with the following headline: 'Ward is 18th to be Freed in Terrorism Cases'.[181] In July a Report by Justice, the British Section of the International Commission of Jurists, indicates 'A big rise in the number of prisoners claiming to be victims of a miscarriage of justice.'[182] The tendency to report on miscarriage or alleged miscarriage cases in terms of numbers is represented in the reporting of the activities of the disbanded West Midlands Serious Crimes Squad. When *The Independent* reports the Court of Appeal's decision to quash the conviction for robbery of Delroy Hare it lists the names, convictions, and sentences relating to ten other men whose convictions had been quashed when evidence from the Squad had been contested. It also deals with another case from the West Midlands not linked to the Squad, and talks of other pending appeals.[183] As with other examples of links being made through numbers, the full implications of the theme of numbers remains unclear, other than the sense of dealing with an 'iceberg's tip'.[184] Reference to numbers feeds into media discussion about public confidence in the criminal justice system, and the crisis meta-narrative gives credence in turn to treating numbers as evidence of major problems, but the analysis is rarely developed. On a related issue Waddington thinks that the public is left 'floundering in the chasm of doubt'.[185] However, the same suggestion can be made in relation to the way the factor of large numbers is constantly implied. The reader may well be left wondering what the implications are of a large number of miscarriages. The potential implication is that the criminal justice system is failing with a large number of miscarriages providing the evidence on which a full-blown scepticism about the criminal justice system could be developed. Neither that view nor the evidence to support it is explicitly constructed in the articles that we have surveyed, although it is implicit in the way in which numbers are regularly referred to.

The reporting on the full judgment of the Court of Appeal in Judith Ward's case in early June 1992 continues to make the link between miscarriages and proposals for reform, but is generally more complimentary to the

---

[181]   12 May 92 (Heather Mills, Adam Sage and Rachel Borrill).

[182]   *The Independent on Sunday* 12 July 92 'More Prisoners Say Defence Lawyers Erred' (Adam Sage).

[183]   20 May 92 'Eleventh Man Cleared in Crime Squad Affair' (Heather Mills); see also *The Times* 20 May 92 'DPP Rules Out Action against Crime Squad' (Craig Seton). For a more detailed account of these events, see T. Kaye, *Unsafe and Unsatisfactory: Report of the Independent Inquiry into the Working Practices of the West Midlands Police Serious Crime Squad* (London, 1991).

[184]   See particularly the Leading Article in *The Independent* 2 June 92 'The Arsonists' Ordeal'.

[185]   *The Times* 21 May 92 'Coppers without Convictions'. He makes that comment in relation to the apparent contradiction that while numbers of prisoners have had their convictions quashed because of the unreliability of evidence adduced by the West Midlands Serious Crimes Squad, no police officer from that Squad would, according to the decision of the Director of Public Prosecutions, be prosecuted for alleged malpractice.

judgment itself. The reports are able to quote the severe criticisms in the judgment of many of the actors in the case, forensic scientists, police, prosecution lawyers, trial judge, even prison doctor. Also they all pick up the Court's apology and regret, and often this is contrasted with other earlier judgments that contain no such sentiments.[186] But serious doubts about the criminal justice system linger, such as that represented by the headline of the editor's article in *The Independent*, 'Why lawyers suppress the truth: The will to win has been an enemy of justice'.[187] And the possibility of utilizing the admissions of failure recognized in the Court of Appeal's judgment is soon being taken up in newspaper articles not only as a plank for proposing substantial reforms, but as evidence for other claims of miscarriage.[188] The reporting on the successful appeal by the Darvell brothers in July is similar to that relating to Judith Ward's appeal. There are links made to the overall number of appeals, to reform proposals and phrases about concern with the criminal justice system in general: 'a case which will send fresh shock waves through the judicial system'.[189] And the case gives particular encouragement to other, linked appeals, such as those by Eddie Browning (the M50 murder case), Ellis Sherwood, and Michael O'Brien.[190] But the reserved judgment itself (delivered later) rather than the story associated with the success of the appeal attracts very little newspaper commentary.

The message of the new Lord Chief Justice, Lord Taylor, delivered very publicly seems to be having an impact on the reporting of miscarriages. He talked in various speeches and interviews of how judges should be more open,[191] more willing to listen particularly to the media,[192] more vigilant about evidence and less keen 'to interpret issues of fact for the jury'.[193] And his judgments, quashing convictions and trying to set broader guidelines, are receiving a good deal of attention.[194] But at the same time he is engaged in discussing the apparent loss of public confidence in the criminal justice system[195] and crisis over appeal numbers[196] that contribute to continuing media concern with these issues and the meta-narrative theme that they had

[186] *The Independent* 5 June 92 'Judges Give Evidence Guidelines' (Heather Mills).
[187] 5 June 92 (Andreas Whittam Smith).
[188] See how the judgment was expected to be used in Derek Edwards's claim of miscarriage and breach of the right to a fair trial: *The Guardian* 22 June 92 'British Criminal Justice on Trial at European Court' (Clare Dyer).
[189] *The Guardian* 13 July 92 'Pair Contest Sex Shop Murder Convictions' (Duncan Campbell).
[190] *The Independent* 16 July 92 'Police in M50 Case "Ignored Leads"' (Terry Kirby and Adam Sage).
[191] *The Sunday Telegraph* 31 May 92 'Into the Open' (Brian Masters).
[192] *The Guardian* 'Taylor Listens as "Subversives" Discuss Miscarriages of Justice' (John Carvel).
[193] *The Guardian* 16 July 92 'Leave Facts to Juries' (Clare Dyer).
[194] *The Guardian* 25 July 92 ' "Serial Confessor" cleared of killings: Taylor signals change in law over false admissions'.
[195] *The Guardian* 2 June 92 'Open Mind Cure to Heal Legal Wounds' (Clare Dyer).
[196] *The Independent* 16 July 92 'Appeals against Conviction up 25%' (Adam Sage).

generated. That concern is encouraged by a number of newspaper reports. There is considerable interest in the batch of 111 alleged miscarriages presented by the campaign groups Liberty and Conviction to the Home Office and the successful appeal in one of those cases, that of Michael Royle and Robert Hall from their robbery convictions.[197] There is a lot of coverage of the Home Secretary's admission of his concern about the Home Office's investigative procedures into miscarriages[198] and great interest in the group some referred to as the Long Lartin 22. This is the group of prisoners serving long sentences for serious crimes 'which they all say they did not commit'[199] who had the opportunity to present their experiences to Lord Runciman, the chairman of the Royal Commission on Criminal Justice. And newspaper reactions to the latest police inquiry (the fifth) into the Carl Bridgewater murder convictions, which appears to support those convictions, was critical and full of protestations from many of those involved of their *innocence*.[200]

This marks the high-point of concerns that miscarriage cases represent a crisis for the criminal justice system. Public confidence in the criminal justice system is still a focus for many newspaper articles, but it is becoming less of a mantra. There is, at the end of 1992, a strong expectation that government action and the report of the Royal Commission on Criminal Justice will respond to the frequently expressed claim of a loss of public confidence. A group of four QCs put this well in a letter published in *The Guardian* in November:

The recent miscarriage cases should have compelled the Government to establish an independent tribunal in 1991; instead, it delayed reform for several years by the device of setting up a Royal Commission . . . A serious commitment by government to eradicate miscarriages of justice is necessary now, to restore public confidence in a system which needs that confidence if it is to perform its task of convicting those proven to be guilty.[201]

The change of emphasis is evident in reporting on the successful appeal in December of the Cardiff Three. The police's interview techniques in that case are described as oppressive and bullying and, in the words of the Lord Chief Justice, 'almost passing belief'.[202] Although police behaviour is

[197] *The Guardian* 28 July 92 'Pub robbery pair cleared on appeal: Trial judge failed to direct jury clearly over informer' (Duncan Campbell).

[198] *The Sunday Telegraph* 2 Aug. 92 'Clarke Orders Inquiry into "Rough Justice" ' (Valerie Elliott).

[199] *The Independent* 25 Aug. 92 'Judge Meets Jailed "Victims" of Legal System' (Terry Kirby).

[200] *The Guardian* 19 Sept. 92 'Police Inquiry Backs Bridgewater Murder Convictions' (John Mullin); *The Independent* 19 Sept. 92 'Dirty Tricks Claim over Paper Boy Murder Case' (Adam Sage and Terry Kirby).

[201] 11 Nov. 92 'Action in Support of Justice'.

[202] *The Guardian* 11 Dec. 92 'Cardiff 3 Murder Convictions Quashed' (Duncan Campbell and Satish Sekar); *The Daily Telegraph* 11 Dec. 92 ' "Cardiff Three" Walk Free after Court Hears of Police Bullying' (Terence Shaw).

severely criticized in commentary on the appeal, only a few references are made to other aspects of the criminal justice system. The closest example of such linked criticism is in the report in *The Times*: 'The case, the latest in a series of miscarriages of justice, will fuel criticism of police behaviour and the criminal justice system.'[203]

F. LOSING THE MOMENTUM OF CRISIS: 1993–4

1 1993

The usual events relating to miscarriages and alleged miscarriages arose during 1993. Cases are being referred to the Court of Appeal, or not being referred. Appeals are pending or on being heard succeeding or failing. Events linked to miscarriages such as new police inquiries, new trials of police officers, speeches by judges and others, television programmes, and press commentary are occurring. And, significantly, the Report of the Royal Commission on Criminal Justice is produced. But the momentum of talk about crisis of public confidence, which had started to recede towards the end of 1992, is by 1993 no longer a consistent theme implicit in so much press commentary, but only resurrected in relation to particular events. As the mantra of a loss of public confidence or a crisis of public confidence in the criminal justice system recedes, opportunities arise for some writers to present a keener analysis of the conditions that might have precipitated these notions, and to give more serious thought to what those conditions might entail. We find a number of articles, particularly in *The Guardian* before the Report of the Royal Commission on Criminal Justice is published in July, that attempt such an analysis.

In January 1993 there is some, but limited, reporting on the Court of Appeal's decision restricting the earlier Court of Appeal judgment in Judith Ward's appeal that had encouraged full disclosure of the nature of all evidence collected by the prosecution. In their decision on disclosure, in relation to the appellants known as the M25 Three, it is decided that: 'the judgment in Ward went too far in accepting [that] . . . the general rule requiring notice to the defence admitted of no qualification or exception.' Although some critical comment on this decision emerges in the press, the technical nature of public interest immunity issues in criminal cases makes such reporting difficult,[204] and not easily linked to miscarriage cases as generally understood in the media. That could not be said of the Home Secretary's decision in early February not to refer the Carl Bridgewater

---

[203] 11 Dec. 92 'Appeal Judges Free Cardiff Three over Police Conduct' (Lin Jenkins).
[204] *The Independent* 16 Jan. 93 'Judge Reverses Ruling on Disclosing Evidence' (Rachel Borrill).

murder convictions to the Court of Appeal. The campaign behind those convicted, the three television programmes, the five separate reinvestigations, and the publicity given by the journalist Paul Foot had encouraged wide belief in the innocence of those convicted, particularly with the naming of an alternative suspect. In these circumstances the Home Secretary's decision was likely to be read very critically by the media, and linked to other miscarriage cases. Even then the theme of loss of public confidence in the criminal justice system is not highlighted in most of the reporting. A comparison between the reporting on the Home Secretary's decision in *The Independent* and in *The Guardian* is illuminating.

The case is used in the leading article in *The Independent* to criticize the secretive and inappropriate procedure associated with the referral of cases from the Home Office and Home Secretary to the Court of Appeal.[205] That procedure comes under severe attack:

It should be no part of a Home Secretary's duties to sit in judgement on whether there are adequate grounds for believing that a miscarriage of justice has taken place. As long as he is obliged to do so, he should err on the side of too many referrals. In this instance, as in his decision last October to deny a posthumous pardon to Derek Bentley, Mr Clarke seems to have been keener to defend the interests of the judicial system than those of justice.

In the article by *The Independent*'s crime correspondent on the same day, reference is again made to the unacceptability of the procedure behind referral decisions, with the Labour Party's home affairs spokesman Tony Blair quoted as doubting 'the fairness of the procedures'.[206] *The Guardian*'s crime correspondent, Duncan Campbell, arranges his article so as to have a much closer focus on the claim of innocence of those convicted than on the inadequacy of the procedures involved. To give one example, he refers to how one of the detectives who took the significant confession in the case had been fined on another occasion 'for fabricating a confession'.[207] Despite the criticisms implicit in these reports, it is left to a letter published in *The Guardian* the following day to resurrect the linking theme of loss of public confidence in the criminal justice system. The letter by the Policy Officer of the organization Liberty draws attention to other alleged miscarriages, particularly the 163 cases submitted by Liberty to the Home Office the previous November. The letter claims that:

Public concern at miscarriages of justice led to the release of the Birmingham Six, the disbandment of the West Midlands Serious Crimes Squad and the setting up of the Royal Commission on Criminal Justice in March 1991. Since then a large number of other convictions have been overturned, strengthening our arguments for fundamental reform of the British judicial system.

[205]   4 Feb. 93 'An Indefensible Anachronism'.
[206]   'Bridgewater Jail Fight Goes On' (Terry Kirby).
[207]   *The Guardian* 4 Feb. 93 'Clarke Refuses Bridgewater Appeal' (Duncan Campbell).

The direct link that the letter suggests between public concern and the remedying of miscarriages goes further than any claim made in reporting on miscarriages to date. But it leaves open the question of what is the role of 'public concern' or public confidence and what part it plays, as opposed to that of the media, or politicians, or the Home Secretary or the Court of Appeal, in remedying miscarriages of justice. In his article in *The Guardian* on 16 February Duncan Campbell tries to explore that question.[208]

Campbell demonstrates historically how important campaigns are in highlighting and achieving successful appeals. At the same time he recognizes other implications of such outcomes. 'Some police officers have complained of morale dropping so low they do not bother arresting and charging offenders; of jurors who now routinely disbelieve officers who are genuinely telling the truth; of gullible appeal court judges who accept technical grounds of appeal too readily. The successful appeals, it is said, comfort criminals and depress the police.' Thus there are a range of interest groups associated with miscarriages, not one public. Indeed Campbell is critical of the potential general public when he quotes a passer-by outside the Royal Courts of Justice who on hearing that there had been a further successful appeal said: 'Oh, not another.' Campbell goes on to claim: 'His views are reflected by some newspapers which feel "that's enough miscarriages, ed.".' He is very concerned about a backlash that could arise and might fail to seek 'the simple truth', where there is 'some sort of judicial market force' that only tolerates a limited number of miscarriages.

In April Duncan Campbell is again engaging with these questions but in relation to concern about the role of television in alleged miscarriage cases.[209] The former producer of BBC's *Rough Justice* series had already criticized the new Channel Four *Trial and Error* series.[210] Now, with the showing of a television programme about the alleged miscarriage of justice in Mary Druhan's case (serving a life sentence for arson and murder), the one-sidedness of that programme comes under attack,[211] and more generally the role of television in looking at such cases. Campbell considers the issues carefully. His consideration notes how few allegations of miscarriage are appropriate for analysis in a documentary with, quoting Anne Owers from the organization Justice, most cases either 'too gruesome or too boring'. He quotes lawyers who are critical: 'the public should not believe that what they are watching is necessarily an accurate reconstruction of a crime'; 'the chief danger of mock television trials is that a "jury" may feel

[208] 'Justice Fatigue'.
[209] *The Guardian* 8 April 93 'Blind date, blind justice: If you get a raw deal from the courts go for a retrial—on television'.
[210] See *The Guardian* 1 Dec. 92 'Why We Need TV Investigations' (David Jessel); *The Times* 24 Nov. 92 'Screening a Posse of Just Men' (Sean Webster).
[211] See for example *The Daily Telegraph* 9 April 93 'Reaching an Unconvincing Verdict' (Max Davidson).

under pressure to produce what it believes is a popular verdict.' Campbell sees the role of television as potentially one of 'a court of last resort' but one which is a lottery when it comes to which cases might be selected, with encouragement for disillusioned prisoners to 'turn themselves into one-man publicity stunts' in order to attract attention. To some extent the same arguments apply to the news media. They select the news, but as Campbell would recognize such selection is structured around current ideas of what is newsworthy. An article in *The Times* makes similar points, concluding that despite the problems and limitations of retrial by television, some cases: 'no matter how good the system is . . . will always fall through the safety net.'[212] The implication is that television, and the media in general, can operate to fill in the gaps of a legitimate system of appeals, rather than to challenge that system's legitimacy. When television does the latter it generates its own conception of the public and can also generate unrealizable demands for *true* verdicts. When it does the former the cases it chooses are those that fit the needs of television production rather than those other values that might be represented in criminal trials and appeals.

The trial of police officers charged with perverting the course of justice by fabricating evidence in the Guildford Four case receives a lot of media coverage. However the verdict of not guilty poses a considerable problem. On the one hand there had been a successful appeal, on the other those who appeared to be responsible for adducing false evidence were found not guilty of criminal wrongdoing. It should be recalled that the successful Guildford Four appeal had not made public the evidence on which the appeal succeeded and Sir John May's Inquiry had specifically not delved into that evidence in public in order not to prejudice any criminal proceedings against police officers. So, it was assumed that only if Sir John resumed his Inquiry would the truth concerning the offences receive any public airing.[213] What is surprising is that despite the inconclusiveness of this situation, it did not lead to any resurrection of the theme of loss of public confidence, at least not in most of the press. The reason appears to be that, despite not having all the legal evidence, some sections of the press assumed that the story of this miscarriage had been so well publicized, and the innocence of the four so clearly recognized. However, other newspapers did not take this view. Articles in *The Daily Mail* saw this inconclusiveness as an opportunity to rethink the reasons for the 'collapse of confidence in Britain's legal system'.[214] That rethink consisted of reconstructing public

---

[212] 6 April 93 'When New Witnesses go on the Box' (Sean Webster).

[213] See *The Independent*'s articles on 20 May 93 'Defence turned case into Guildford retrial: The officers' acquittal does not undermine evidence that four innocent people were victims of a miscarriage of justice' (Heather Mills and Terry Kirby); the Leading Article 'Guildford Four still Await Justice'; also 13 May 93 'Guildford Appeal not Told Facts'.

[214] 20 May 93 'Crimes without Culprits' (Paul Harris and Suzanne O'Shea); 'Guildford Four Police Cleared of Faking Evidence: Verdict is Hailed by Lord Denning' (Paul Harris).

confidence and trust in the institutions and practices of the criminal justice system by trying to demonstrate that the so-called lack of public confidence that others had proclaimed was misplaced.

Prior to the publication of the Report of the Royal Commission on Criminal Justice in July there is a lot of build up often with commentary on leaks about what was likely to be proposed.[215] However, other events linking the media with miscarriage cases continue themes already well in evidence earlier in the year. Anticipating a new television drama documentary on the murder of Carl Bridgewater in 1978 Paul Foot sets out his explanation for the jury's mistaken decision to convict the four defendants at the trial. His convincing explanation ends with condemnation of the Court of Appeal's decision to reject the appeal in 1989: 'I could not believe that apparently serious and rational men could be so monstrously wrong.'[216] After the programme was televised the foreman of the original jury came forward to disclaim the verdict both on television and in print.[217] What the juror said was, of course, not available as legal evidence; indeed, for it to be so would have ousted some of the most basic rules supporting the institution of trial by jury. And it is noticeable in newspaper reports that comment on the case is directed to support for the campaign to encourage the Home Secretary to refer the case back to the Court of Appeal, rather than offering any analysis of the implications of what the juror had to say for the trial process. Neither is this event taken up as part of a general theme of loss of public confidence in the criminal justice system. It appears that there were severe constraints operating on the media in relation to what the juror had to say, as indeed there were. It is left to the appellants' solicitor, Jim Nichol, to draw some conclusions, his comments being published in *The Independent*.[218] He is able to show how the 'quaint rule of criminal law that says if a co-defendant makes a confession and at his trial does not give evidence, then that confession cannot be regarded by the jury as evidence against the other co-defendants' is inoperative. He goes on to say: 'Privately, lawyers know full well that juries cannot help but take these confessions into consideration. Everyone—except the judges—can see the rule is nonsense.' Nichol makes it clear that he believes that the alleged confession of one of the four defendants in practice 'convicted the others'. He goes on to discredit much of the original evidence in the case, and strongly encourages the Home Secretary to refer the case back to the Court of Appeal. But whereas other newspaper reports on this case at this stage

[215] Alan Travis's article in *The Guardian* is a good example: 2 June 93 'Concern over Miscarriage of Justice Tribunal Plan'.

[216] *Today* 29 May 93 'Now Will the Truth Come Out?'

[217] *The Daily Telegraph* 3 June 93 'Wrong Men Jailed, Says Carl Juror' (Tim Butcher); *The Guardian* 3 June 93 'Bridgewater Case Juror Recants Guilty Verdicts' (John Mullin); *The Independent* 3 June 93 'Carl Verdict Wrong, Juror Says' (Terry Kirby).

[218] 4 June 93 'Troublesome Ghosts of the Bridgewater Four' (Jim Nichol).

are strongly in favour of referral, listing the deficiencies of the original evidence and a narrative associated with the likely offender, very little is made of the implications of Nichol's legalistic argument for a fair trial process. It would of course have been possible to argue from the basis of gross deficiencies in the rules of the trial process to a lack of confidence in it in general, but that does not occur. We suggest two particular reasons, which may operate to facilitate some understanding of the nature of media logic when reporting on miscarriages or alleged miscarriages of justice. The first is that the mantra of loss of confidence or crisis of public confidence has, at this time, been exhausted. This may reflect the difficulty of sustaining such a meta-narrative or theme, or expectations associated with the imminent Report of the Royal Commission on Criminal Justice that was appointed specifically to respond to this situation. Or it may reflect growing confidence in the claimed changes in the practice of the Court of Appeal well publicized by the new Lord Chief Justice. The second reason why the continued publicity about this case does not precipitate a renewal of the perception of a crisis of public confidence at this time, in relation to the particular events being considered, is that those events reflect on issues of due process. They concern what counts as, or is implied by, the idea of a fair trial according to legal rules. It would appear that such (technical) factors have less resonance in the media than do issues concerning truth. So what could be seen to amount to a damning indictment and taken as a call for radical reform is not treated in this way.

The media are, in some ways, put on trial in the Taylor sisters' appeal heard in June. Their successful appeal against their convictions for murder is granted on two grounds, one being the deliberate lack of police disclosure of evidence and the other the potential prejudice to a fair trial of the media coverage of the trial that led to their convictions in 1992. As Heather Mills describes the judgment a few days later in *The Independent*:

In an unprecedented Court of Appeal judgment, the media were convicted of 'unremitting, extensive, sensational, inaccurate and misleading' coverage of the trial of Michelle and Lisa Taylor. Reporting was judged so bad that it created a 'real risk of prejudice'. And so bad that newspapers and television companies involved were reported to the Attorney General to see if editors should be charged with contempt.[219]

However, Heather Mills is keen to defend the media's role, preferring to attribute the wrongful conviction to the withholding by police of important evidence. 'It remains an unhappy fact that had the police not concealed crucial evidence that pointed to the sisters' innocence, perhaps the media would not have ended up in the dock.' Both of these grounds of appeal (non-disclosure and prejudicing a fair trial) principally relate to issues of

---

[219]　16 June 93 'Did the Messengers Shoot Themselves?'.

due process and rights, and it is in these terms that the Court of Appeal's judgment overturns the convictions. It does so without constructing a full analysis of the *truth* of the sisters' innocence. But since the media are concerned to do exactly that, to report on the truth, in their role as messenger of the facts of the trial, even if they might have overstepped the mark, they are reluctant to accept blame for the miscarriage. Heather Mills, in not accepting the Court's criticism of media reporting, makes no further attempt to link that reporting with any crisis in criminal justice. Failure to disclose, one of the successful grounds of the appeal is reported on by reference to earlier Court of Appeal decisions that attempt to deal with the issue and set the relevant standards, but again without any sense of crisis.[220]

In the month before the Royal Commission on Criminal Justice present their Report any momentum left of a meta-narrative of crisis of public confidence in criminal justice and the system of criminal appeal is played out, or perhaps subsides. We give three examples. Ludovic Kennedy's review of Michael Mansfield and Tony Wardle's book *Presumed Guilty*[221] in *The Daily Telegraph* lists proposals for reform made in the book together with Kennedy's own proposals, and expresses hope that the Runciman Commission 'will have listened'.[222] As one would expect, Kennedy refers to 'the gross inadequacies of our criminal justice system and the numerous miscarriages of justice which have resulted from it'. That reference is not supported by any articulation of a general loss of public confidence in it, but rather the need for particular reforms: 'the price he says we should be prepared to pay for a fairer system and fewer miscarriages of justice'. A fairer system and fewer miscarriages are assumed to go hand in hand, subject to cost. The rhetoric of justice is upheld.

The report by Duncan Campbell in *The Guardian* following a programme in the television series *Trial and Error* about the convictions for the murder of 10-year-old Wayne Keeton in 1985 does not raise the spectre of loss of public confidence.[223] But it does link that case to others about to go to the Court of Appeal and it contains echoes of past high profile cases. The best example of this is when Campbell quotes Anthony Scrivenor QC about his unease with the case because of its dependence on 'a confession which really can't be relied upon in the light of the experience we have nowadays'. The implication is that our practices should have changed, and

---

[220] In her article the day after the Court of Appeal's judgment in the Taylor sisters case, she notes how the law relating to disclosure of evidence had been 'underlined in highly publicised Court of Appeal judgments', *The Independent* 12 June 93 'Murder Trial Sisters Convicted by the Media'. The implication is that this case is an aberration, an individual miscarriage, rather than a case symptomatic of a failing system, as earlier cases were thought to have been.

[221] M. Mansfield and T. Wardle, *Presumed Guilty: The British Legal System Exposed* (London, 1993).

[222] 19 June 93 'Why 500 Innocent People are in Jail'; see also John Mortimer's review in *The Sunday Telegraph* 27 June 93 'More Justice than Injustice'.

[223] 21 June 93 'Top QC Uneasy on Murder Verdict'.

if they have (despite some rogue examples), then our system of criminal justice is basically sound.

The successful appeal of 16-year-old Ivan Fergus from his conviction for assault (stabbing) with intent to rob at the age of 13 is a clear example of the change of reporting style on miscarriages. The case is also a clear example of the change in style of an appeal judgment. The reporting on the case after the verdict had been given but prior to the full judgment relies heavily on the arguments presented on the three grounds presented by the appellant's counsel. All three grounds are successful: a miscarriage due to the weakness of the identification evidence, the misdirection of the trial judge, and failures of the defence team at the trial. But the significant part of the case highlighted in the reporting is Lord Justice Steyn's statement on quashing the conviction. 'Ivan Fergus may leave this Court knowing not just that his conviction was unsafe and unsatisfactory, but that it is our judgment that the case against him was a wholly false one and he is entirely innocent.'[224] Of course such a statement is what an innocent appellant wants to hear, but it is also what the media can readily report on, since it consistently strains to equate a successful appeal with a factually inaccurate verdict. The statement by Lord Justice Steyn adds what amounts to a translation of the legal phrase 'unsafe or unsatisfactory', in this case, into something that readily meets the expectations of other observers. The likely difficulty with this language is how it will be seen to operate in other cases. How often can it be expected that quashing an 'unsafe' conviction, to use the current legal phrase, will necessarily be equated with 'a wholly false' case and an 'entirely innocent' appellant? When the press report on the full judgment a week later they continue to rely on the unequivocal innocence of the appellant and link it not to a systematically flawed criminal justice system but a potentially effective one. 'The judges made it clear that had every professional involved in the case performed their duties correctly, this latest miscarriage of justice would not have occurred.'[225] Despite the extraordinary failings exhibited in the case, the Court of Appeal had proved that it was capable of remedying the miscarriage and in such a way as to uphold the latent justice of the criminal justice system. The repackaging seems to be relatively successful, and it is anticipated that the Royal Commission could rectify the remaining faults of the past.[226]

In *The Times* the Report of the Royal Commission on Criminal Justice

[224] *The Independent* 22 June 93 'Stabbing Case Boy Cleared in Landmark Ruling' (Heather Mills); *The Daily Telegraph* 22 June 93 'Boy's "Wholly False" Assault Conviction Quashed on Appeal' (Terence Shaw); *The Guardian* 22 June 93 'Appeal Clears Boy of Assault' (Lawrence Donegan).

[225] *The Independent* 29 June 93 'Professionals Blamed for Boy's Wrongful Conviction' (Heather Mills); *The Guardian* 29 June 93 'Lawyers Censured on Boy's Conviction' (Lawrence Donegan).

[226] *The Independent* 5 July 93 'Judges will be told to get tough with bad defence lawyers' (Adam Sage and Andrew Gliniecki).

is welcomed by Gareth Williams QC, a former chairman of the Bar Council, as 'a masterly piece of work'.[227] He recognizes that the background to the Report was 'one of cumulative unease about miscarriages of justice', but approves of all of the proposals in the Report with the exception of the proposal to remove from some defendants the right to opt for jury trial. Another article in *The Times* is also supportive of the Report and in particular their proposal to set up 'an independent tribunal' to investigate alleged miscarriages, rather than the Home Office.[228] The only sense of the previously commonplace meta-narrative of crisis of public confidence to be found in *The Times* is in an article a few day later by Walter Merricks who was a member of the previous Royal Commission on Criminal Procedure (1978–81).[229] Merricks acknowledges that 'the commission was established in the wake of a crisis' and that the expectation was for 'fundamental' reform. But he believes that such an expectation was unrealistic. He applauds the report as 'wide-ranging . . . cogently argued . . . which should stand as an authoritative benchmark'. Articles in *The Independent* are generally more critical of the Report, but any background meta-narrative of crisis of public confidence is barely in evidence.[230] It is another former chairman of the Bar Council, John Rowe QC, who raises the theme of underlying concern and criticizes the Royal Commission for paying too little attention to 'why the miscarriages had occurred'. But the momentum of talk of loss of confidence or crisis of public confidence is not part of the analysis. Articles in *The Guardian* are very similar. There is coverage of a number of the key proposals, reactions to them, and some criticism,[231] but with the exception of an article by another barrister, Michael Mansfield,[232] the theme of loss of public confidence in the criminal justice system is not present. His very critical article concludes: 'As it is, by the time of the next Royal Commission, which will undoubtedly have to be set up in 10 years time, I fear very little will have changed. This has been an abuse of an opportunity provided by the victims of miscarriages to replace confidence in the system.'

The *Daily Telegraph* article by Terence Shaw situates the Commission in the context of the successful Birmingham Six appeal and analyses some of its main recommendations.[233] It shows how some of those '352

---

[227] 7 July 93 'In the True Interests of Justice'.

[228] 7 July 93 'Independent Body to Handle Wrongful Conviction Cases' (Richard Ford).

[229] 13 July 93 'Fresh Ideas Badly Needed'.

[230] 7 July 93 'Change Sweeps the Law' (Adam Sage and Terry Kirby), and 'Royal Commission on Criminal Justice' (Terry Kirby).

[231] 7 July 93 'Howard wary on proposal to limit right to trial by jury' (Clare Dyer and Alan Travis); 'Royal Commission on Criminal Justice' (John Mullin); 'Royal Commission on Criminal Justice: Appeals Tribunal to Set its own Rules'.

[232] 7 July 93 'Justice undone: What the judicial system needs is a complete overhaul; what the Royal Commission offers is unlikely to allay public fears'.

[233] 7 July 93 'Royal Commission on Criminal Justice: Massive Shake-up Puts Law in the Dock'.

recommendations' face 'fierce opposition from the legal profession and a possible clash with the judiciary'. That article was preceded the previous day in *The Sunday Telegraph* by an article that lists a number of critical reactions to the Report.[234] The resonance of talk of crisis of public confidence, of a system failing, or a loss of confidence in it, is barely audible. The following quote from the reaction of the legal officer of the pressure group Liberty, John Wadham, gives the only such resonance: 'While some aspects of the report are welcome, others will continue to blight our criminal justice system with miscarriages of justice. There is no point in establishing a procedure to rectify miscarriages if at the same time other procedures being created are likely to result in more of them occurring.' Thus, initial reactions to the Report in the press are characterized by a very different theme from that which characterized reporting on the setting up of the Royal Commission. The theme of crisis of public confidence that had been so pronounced two years earlier has lost its momentum by the time of the Report. That theme had been built around a conception of miscarriage of justice that gave priority to factually inaccurate verdicts, with journalists' concerns that the criminal justice system was finding guilty those who are factually innocent being recognized in a few high profile cases within the legal system itself. Although the Report is introduced as having a principal concern with factually accurate verdicts and the restoration of public confidence, press commentary on it is not focused on those issues. Because the main commentaries are provided by lawyers the main theme uniting the reporting is due process and rights, the presumption of innocence, the right to jury trial, the rules of admissibility of confession evidence, etc. The one reform proposal that seems to have been given universal support is the setting up of an independent body outside the Home Office to investigate alleged miscarriages after the court system and criminal appeal system has been exhausted. In describing a Report with many reform proposals to the rules, practices, and procedures of the criminal justice system the press finds it difficult to maintain the sense of crisis and urgency that it had readily expressed in relation to other, earlier events. But if the crisis had dissipated, had it dissipated among the public, or among the press itself, and if so, what has changed? The press is at this time giving a less critical account to Court of Appeal decisions, and the Court of Appeal appears to be more likely to satisfy, in its language, the demands being made of it in the press. A renewed working relationship seems to have been established, and most of the initial reporting on the Royal Commission's Report appears to conform to it.

That new working relationship is soon put to the test. Despite the high profile campaign behind the appeal of the three appellants known as the

---

[234] 6 July 93 'Anger and Approval for Court Shake-up' (Valentine Low and Madeleine Harper).

M25 Three, their appeal fails at the end of July. The strong words of the appeal judgment are quoted without scepticism or reference back to such words in other cases. Lord Justice Watkins said of the convictions: 'there wasn't "even a lurking doubt" about their safety . . . on the contrary, the case against them was, and remains, a formidable one.'[235] But such words, as with earlier examples, hold the possibility for future media construction of a new meta-narrative of crisis of public confidence. As soon as the Court of Appeal uses strong or unequivocal language in rejecting an appeal that potential is created. When the appellant John Berry has his convictions quashed ten years after being found guilty of offences to do with making parts for terrorist bombs, the apology of the Lord Chief Justice is given prominence in the reporting of the case.[236] But Bernard Levin's scathing attack on judicial attitudes throughout the ten years of the case is less than satisfied with what the Lord Chief Justice had to offer.[237] When the trial against police officers for perverting the course of justice in relation to the convictions of the Birmingham Six is abandoned because of prejudicial publicity, the media are far from impressed.[238]

The dilemma of how judges can satisfy the press while carrying out their legal responsibilities is addressed explicitly by the Lord Chief Justice in a widely reported speech he makes at the end of November.[239] His words are worth quoting at length. He is engaging with a question about which our analysis in this chapter offers some explanation beyond his undoubted frustration at how the operation of the law is so readily misunderstood and criticized by the media.

Yet, despite the consternation and the public's sense of outrage that these miscarriages should have occurred and the determination that there should be no repetition, what do we find? That when judges exclude confessions made in breach of the 1984 Act, by oppressive interviewing, attempts are made in some quarters, not in all, to justify the conduct of the interviews and to criticise the judges. I find this attitude hard to comprehend. Do those who adopt it wish to have another group of miscarriage cases in five years time?

2 1994

A number of significant events in 1994 could have been interpreted in the media in terms of a system of criminal justice that is generally failing, or one about which the public has lost confidence. However, such an interpretation

---

[235] *The Daily Telegraph* 30 July 93 'Uproar as M25 Murder Trio Lose their Appeal' (Terence Shaw).
[236] *The Independent* 29 Sept. 93 'Man Jailed on Bomb Charges is Cleared' (Heather Mills).
[237] *The Times* 15 Oct. 93 'Long Sentences for Judges'.
[238] *The Independent* 8 Oct. 93, leading article, 'Judge's Ruling is Final Insult'; *The Times* 8 Oct. 93 'Trial Collapse Reveals Flaws in System'.
[239] *The Guardian* 27 Nov. 93 'Confession Ruling Right, Says Taylor' (Clare Dyer); *The Times* 27 Nov. 93 'Taylor Insists "Oppressive" Interrogation Must Cease' (Frances Gibb).

is barely in evidence. The meta-narrative of crisis of public confidence has given way to other themes in which miscarriages of justice are being linked to other concerns.

Throughout the year when miscarriages are being discussed in the press the main proposal of the Royal Commission on Criminal Justice, removing the power of referral of allegations of miscarriage from the Home Secretary to an independent authority, is constantly referred to. That proposal is considered to have widespread support, but it is not included in the Government's legislative programme until November. When Winston Silcott's conviction for the murder of Anthony Smith is not referred back to the Court of Appeal by the Home Secretary in January, this is reported on in terms of the need for a more independent and effective referral body.[240] Articles anticipating the final report of Sir John May's Inquiry into the circumstances surrounding the Guildford Four and Maguire Seven convictions concentrate on the weaknesses of Home Office investigations and the Home Secretary's role in not remedying alleged miscarriages. An early example can be found in *The Sunday Times* in March.[241] The apparently long delay before referral of the Guildford Four case, and even after officials from the Home Office's C3 division had advised in favour of referral, is highlighted implying that those practices were seriously deficient. When, later in March, the Home Secretary Michael Howard issues a consultation paper containing proposals for the new independent body, along the lines of the Royal Commission's Report, newspaper reports on this only tentatively echo arguments about a crisis of public confidence. Terence Shaw's article in *The Daily Telegraph* links the consultation paper to the need 'to restore public confidence in the appeal system after a series of wrongful conviction cases'.[242] He quotes the Home Secretary who said, in introducing the paper: 'On the whole, we have a system of criminal justice which results in relatively few convictions of the innocent. But one such conviction is one too many.' Despite the consultation paper producing discussion, including criticism of parts of the proposal (issues to do with legal aid, membership of the independent body, and the role of the police in carrying out investigations), it is possible for such a statement to be reported without resurrecting the previously expressed views about the implications of recent high profile cases. Before and after the publication of Sir John May's Final Report in July articles continue to link miscarriage cases to the need for the immediate introduction of a new independent body to investigate alleged miscarriages.[243] When eventually the proposal is included in the

[240] e.g., see *The Guardian* 21 Jan. 94 'Silcott Appeal Move Rejected' (Clare Dyer).
[241] 13 March 94 'Hurd under Scrutiny over Guildford Four' (Michael O'Kelly and David Leppard).
[242] 26 March 94 'Howard Outlines Independent Justice Unit'.
[243] *The Financial Times* 5 July 94 'Miscarriage of Justice Body Faces Delay' (David Owen); *The Times* 26 July 94 'Another Miscarriage of Justice?' (Michael McConville and Lee Bridges).

Government's legislative programme in the Queen's Speech in November the implication that such a body might restore public confidence is hardly audible. When it is made it is not linked to serious deficiencies in the criminal justice system or to a meta-narrative of crisis of public confidence. In fact the main reference to public confidence appears to come from an often-quoted statement by the current chairman of the Bar Council, Robert Seabrook QC: 'We believe that the inclusion of the Bill in the Queen's Speech would give a much needed signal of the Government's commitment to restoring confidence and allaying public anxieties about miscarriages of justice.'[244]

The link constantly made in the press in 1994 between miscarriage cases and the near universally supported proposal for an independent referral body seems to defuse other links. This is most noticeable at the end of 1994 when the High Court judgment is given in the case brought by six people, three of the four convicted of the murder of Carl Bridgewater and Paul Malone, Jeremy Bamber, and Sammy Davis, all having alleged miscarriages in respect of their cases over a long period. The decision concerns the information acquired in the Home Office when investigating alleged miscarriages and whether it should be disclosed to potential appellants. The judgment favours disclosure, and disclosure of evidence acquired during the investigation before the Home Secretary's final decision on whether to refer. Reporting on what could be interpreted as a very significant judgment that could have re-established the theme of systemic failure tends not to do so. Use of numbers, such as the estimated 200 other allegations to which the ruling would apply, could easily have added to that theme. As it is, the links made in the reporting were mainly to the anticipated new independent body to investigate miscarriages, but also to other issues that involved the Home Secretary with the Courts.[245] The link to other miscarriage cases is much less pronounced than the link made in the reporting to the other examples in 1994 of when the Home Secretary had been the subject of judicial reviews and, mainly, defeated in the Courts.

At the beginning of July Sir John May produces his long-anticipated Final Report into the circumstances surrounding the convictions of the Guildford Four and the Maguire Seven. His Interim Report had been produced when the meta-narrative of crisis of public confidence was

[244] *The Independent* 16 Nov. 94 'Independent Body for Miscarriage of Justice Claims'; (Donald MacIntyre and Jason Bennetto); *The Financial Times* 17 Nov. 94 'The Queen's Speech: Ministers Plan Body to Probe Miscarriage of Justice Claims' (Robert Rice).
[245] *The Times* 29 Nov. 94 'Convicted killers may win right to see secret files' (Frances Gibb); *The Daily Telegraph* 29 Nov. 94 'Appeal Battle: Hopes Rise for Six in Fight to Lift Conviction' (Terence Shaw); *The Financial Times* 29 Nov. 94 'Howard suffers Court defeat on miscarriage appeals' (John Mason); *The Guardian* 29 Nov. 94 'Secrecy ended in appeal rejections: Court ends Home Office secrecy on appeal referrals' (Duncan Campbell); *The Independent* 29 Nov. 94 'Judges Deal New Blow to Howard' and 'Judges Halt Secrecy in Appeal Cases' (Heather Mills).

embedded in media reporting. It could be argued that the strident criticisms in his Interim Report contributed to that meta-narrative since it was thought that the Report included criticisms of nearly every element of the criminal justice system. Similarly it could be argued that the less strident criticisms represented in the Final Report were less likely to contribute to a renewal of any meta-narrative of crisis of public confidence, as the criticisms were not only less strident but also more specifically directed to the particular actions of individuals. However, we feel that this interpretation is less persuasive than the one proposed in this chapter, namely that the meta-narrative of crisis of public confidence had not been sustained in the media and that by the time of this Report it had receded. In most instances the criticisms contained in the Report are taken at face value, as criticisms of individual actors and their individual failings rather than more generally of the criminal justice system.[246] In a few articles such an approach is criticized, and that criticism resonates with the earlier themes of systemic failing and loss of public confidence, but that resonance is muted.

A good example is Robert Kee's article in *The Observer* 'Cocklecarrot's Law Lets Bad Justice off the Hook'.[247] Wondering what the purpose of Sir John May's exercise was, Kee constructs a sense of public expectation: 'The person on the Clapham Omnibus had vaguely felt it to be to get at the truth of this dreadful affair.' He suggests that such an expectation was not met by the Report and particularly so because of the Report's approach to the meaning it gave to miscarriage of justice. Kee notes that although the clear conclusion in the Report is that a miscarriage of justice had occurred in the Guildford Four case, nevertheless to the Report that specifically means: 'When the result of criminal proceedings is one which might not have been reached had a specific failing in the criminal justice system not occurred in connection with or in the course of those proceedings.' Such a conception of miscarriage is at least, according to the Report, fair and correct, and compares favourably to 'the use of a crystal ball with its undefined notion of justice'. For the Report it is clear that the determination of actual, factual guilt or innocence went beyond its remit. The Report's orientation mirrors that of a Court of Appeal judgment, giving priority to correct procedure and, to some extent, the protection of rights. That orientation is found lacking by Kee. The Report, he argues, is unsatisfactory: 'The rest of us, it seems, will just have to go on gazing for justice in our crystal ball.' What this means is taken up by Paul Foot in *The Guardian*.[248] He quotes from the Report:

In some representations made to me, reliance has been placed on some abstract notion of justice, by reference to which it has been argued that the convictions of the Guildford Four were clearly wrong and should never have occurred. Such

---

[246] *The Guardian* 1 July 94 'Individuals Blamed for Jailing of Guildford Four' (Alan Travis); *The Independent* 1 July 94 'Guildford Four "Plot" Dismissed' (Terry Kirby).
[247] 3 July 94.   [248] 4 July 94 'Not for Truth, Justice, and the British Way'.

reliance is impractical. Without any defining criteria, my personal view of what is just may well differ from that of lay commentators or the producers of media programmes.

Paul Foot finds the discrepancies between the Interim and the Final Report striking. He describes the first as 'incisive, clear, at times even angry', while the second is 'rambling, vague, complacent'. Linking his arguments to other high profile miscarriages, he states in unequivocal terms: 'they didn't do it', and of the Guildford Four and Birmingham Six: 'All were entirely, and demonstrably, innocent.' And he raises the issue that, to date, 'not a single person has been punished for these injustices.' His criticism ends with condemnation: 'The dreadful and inhuman treatment of all these people continues as an affront to the very word "justice", and is compounded by the weasel reaction of the political and judicial authorities, of which Sir John May's report is the most recent example.' These criticisms are motivated by a conception of miscarriage at some distance from the conception espoused in the Report and characteristic of Court of Appeal judgments. Even then the attacks on the demonstrable deficiencies exhibited by these cases are directed widely, rather than being brought together under the theme of a system of criminal justice in crisis. That meta-narrative, upon which construction a platform for radical reform only recently appeared to be inevitable, had dissipated.

Throughout press reporting on miscarriage cases in 1994 the principal links being made are between such cases and reforming the system of referral, as well as other sporadic themes. These other themes include the continuing discrepancy between the commitment of certain journalists to the simple truth of the innocence of particular victims of miscarriage and the reluctance of various figures of authority to comply with such statements. Rather than statements of innocence, official sources now more readily issue statements of apology, which at times are singled out for commentary by the press. The criminal justice system and its traditional practices also continue to offer fruitful information and controversy for newspaper articles. A notable example, which receives an enormous amount of newspaper coverage, is the award of compensation made to Winston Silcott for his false conviction as a member of the Tottenham Three. However, what is clear from reading newspaper articles on the theme of miscarriages in 1994 is that, with very few exceptions, any momentum behind the set of organizing ideas about a system in crisis has been lost. Other linking ideas have arisen but it is less possible for them to coalesce to form any meta-narrative and in particular any meta-narrative of crisis.

G. AFTER THE CRISIS: 1995–6

In the years 1995 and 1996 'crisis' is no longer a common epithet utilized in newspaper articles to refer to the state of the criminal justice system or public confidence in it. Despite this, many alleged miscarriages remain in the wings awaiting publicity, while others receive some coverage in various forms in the media. Not only is the word 'crisis' no longer utilized but there is much less reference to and resonance with previous high profile miscarriage cases. In 1995 highly publicized allegations of miscarriage arise in relation to the murder convictions of Winston Silcott,[249] Ian Simms,[250] Sara Thornton,[251] Glen McCallion,[252] and Paul Esselmont,[253] and there is the highly publicized successful appeal of Kevin Callan[254] and the unsuccessful appeal of Sheila Bowler.[255] Newspaper reporting on the last two cases is striking for its lack of resonance with other recent high profile cases. The Callan case offers fruitful evidence for deep scepticism about the use of expert evidence in the criminal trial, but it is not interpreted in that way. The Bowler case includes the type of Court of Appeal statement that has haunted its recent past. 'The idea that the old lady could have walked the distance unaided and without falling over was "quite incredible", said Lord Justice Swinton Thomas', in 1995.[256] In 1997 following a further appeal by Sheila Bowler the Court of Appeal quashes the conviction and orders a retrial, having accepted as fresh evidence that 'old people suffering from dementia did sometimes perform unexpected feats of strength when they found themselves in strange or frightening surroundings.'[257] The media do not comment adversely on this change, the Court's willingness now to accept the defence's version of events, which it had so unequivocally rejected in the past.

Also during 1995 the Criminal Appeal Bill is published, debated, and then passed. Although it receives quite a lot of publicity the technical nature of the changes receive limited consideration. The major change, the adoption of a new independent authority to direct investigations into miscarriages and take over the Home Secretary's role in deciding on whether or not to refer cases to the Court of Appeal, does receive some attention. But

[249] *The Independent* 21 Jan. 95 'Howard to Review Winston Silcott Conviction' (Heather Mills).
[250] *The Independent* 28 Jan. 95 'Burden of Proof: No Body, no Witness, no Motive' (Bob Woffinden).
[251] *The Guardian* 5 May 95 'Stabbing that led to Calls for a Change in the Law' (Alan Travis); *The Independent* 5 May 95 'Sara Thornton Granted Murder Case Appeal' (Heather Mills).
[252] *The Observer* 21 May 95 'Anxiety of Trial Judge at Killer's Conviction' (David Rose).
[253] *The Daily Telegraph* 17 Nov. 95 'Child Killer's Appeal Delay Unlawful' (Terence Shaw).
[254] *The Guardian* 7 April 95 'Self-taught Expert Wins Murder Appeal' (John Mullin and Clare Kitchen); *The Independent* 7 April 95 'Inmate Studied his Way to Freedom' (Heather Mills).
[255] *The Guardian* 6 May 95 'Woman Loses Appeal over Aunt's Death' (Duncan Campbell).
[256] Ibid.
[257] *The Guardian* 6 Feb. 98 'Woman Jailed for Murdering Aunt Cleared in Re-trial' (Clare Longrigg). At the retrial in 1998 the jury appeared to accept the fresh evidence and found Sheila Bowler not guilty.

such attention as that proposal receives is generally either optimistic about the new authority's more satisfactory status, its independence of politics, and its hoped for greater effectiveness, or critical of certain aspects of its powers and eventual make-up. Neither approach is underscored by the sort of meta-narrative that had been so evident only a few years earlier, despite some of the headings of the articles.[258] The conditions of the crisis, as they had been constructed in the media, had exhausted themselves.

Apart from the usual range of stories about criminal appeals, two particular issues offer journalists a continuous source of information about the inadequacy or potential inadequacy of the system of criminal justice and its system of appeal in 1996. Both issues could have renewed the theme of crisis of public confidence and renewed the discussions that such a theme can entail in the media. But neither did so in any significant sense, and in not doing so the relevance of recent history about miscarriages starts to wane while the sense of history over a longer time span is virtually lost completely. The two issues are the continuing events in 1996 surrounding the Carl Bridgewater murder case and the implications of the finding that there is contamination in machinery at the Forensic Explosives Laboratory near Sevenoaks where forensic evidence for many explosives (especially IRA) trials had been produced.

The Bridgewater Four case campaign receives a lot of publicity. There is a new television documentary and a new book by Jill Morrell, who had campaigned so effectively for the release of hostages in Lebanon.[259] Following the High Court ruling about disclosure at the end of 1994[260] leaked information demonstrating the inadequacy of Home Office investigation practices is well publicized.[261] Then there is the long hesitation by the Home Secretary in deciding whether or not to refer the case to the Court of Appeal,[262] and then the decision in July to do so.[263] The case has all the

---

[258] *The Independent* 24 Feb. 95 'Miscarriage of Justice Body fatally Flawed' (Heather Mills); *The Guardian* 24 Feb. 95 'New Body to Assess Criminal Appeals' (Alan Travis); *The Times* 24 Feb. 95 'Howard Proposes Independent Body on Injustice Cases' (Richard Ford).

[259] Jill Morrell, *The Wrong Men*, published by the Bridgewater Four Support Group, London, 1995. It is interesting to compare two reviews of the book by Melanie McFadyean in *The Guardian* 19 Dec. 95 'Some Other Campaign', and the barrister Helena Kennedy in *The Independent on Sunday* 25 Feb. 96 'Trying to Write a Few Wrongs'. McFadyean's review is dominated by a notion of injustice, of how different groups of innocent people can be wronged. Kennedy is less convinced by the connection between hostages and those who are victims of miscarriage, and as a lawyer she is more concerned to link the Bridgewater Four case to other miscarriages and the faults in due processes that allow such events to occur. She writes: 'It is as though in these cases the burden of proof shifted to the accused. "Prove to us that you are innocent" was the unspoken demand, and the protections which should be there for all of us were absent.'

[260] See our reference to this on p. 161 above.

[261] *The Independent* 6 Aug. 96 'Bridgewater Four inquiry conducted by one man: Hard-pressed officers worked at weekends, leaked papers reveal' (Michael O'Kelly).

[262] *The Guardian* 11 April 96 'Untrue Confessions' (Jill Morrell).

[263] *The Independent* 27 July 96 'After 17 Years, Hope Flickers' (Jason Bennetto).

hallmarks of a high profile miscarriage: a very strong campaign built up over many years, including the refusal by the appellants to accept blame, thus causing them to remain in prison when otherwise they could have been released, and their extraordinary rooftop protests. The campaign is fuelled by the strong words from the Court of Appeal judgment in 1989 rejecting the appeal and the decision in 1993 by the Home Secretary not to refer the case back. Also, and what contributes to the newsworthy nature of the long saga, there is a definite story, a potentially clear narrative about what in fact happened and how 'The Wrong Men' (the title of Jill Morrell's book) came to be found guilty.[264] With all this, the main focus for critical comment in the newspaper reporting is directed to the Home Office, the Home Secretary, and the lack of government commitment to remedying miscarriages as demonstrated by the limited resources made available to do so. But more general scepticism about the criminal justice system and the current Court of Appeal hardly arises, with the exception of Helena Kennedy's review referred to in note 259 above. The continuing high profile reporting of this case is characterized by the specific injustice that it represents and, to some extent, the apparent reluctance of those in political authority to respond. However, the major reform enacted in the Criminal Appeal Act 1995 *apparently* reduces the relevance of such criticism.

There was little possibility that the evidence of contamination at a forensic laboratory could be treated as an individual injustice rather than as potentially involving a number of miscarriages arising from a general failure. As Richard Ford explains in *The Times*: 'At least 12 people may have been wrongly convicted of terrorist offences on the strength of tests at a government laboratory where equipment was contaminated with explosives, the Home Office admitted yesterday.'[265] Although the article describes the political controversy that this admission precipitated, how it was 'a big embarrassment' for the Government, there is no link made to deficiencies in the criminal justice system as such. In only two articles can we find any reference to general concerns linking these events to other deficiencies in the criminal justice system. Heather Mills in *The Independent* talks of how 'The criminal justice system was dealt another blow',[266] and Alan Travis and John Mullin in *The Guardian* refer to how 'Confidence in the British criminal justice system was dealt a devastating new blow' by these revelations.[267] However, both of those articles and others[268] do not

---

[264] *The Observer* 4 Aug. 96 'The Bridgewater Four' (Nick Cohen). This article takes the story even further by describing what has happened to other key actors in the case over the last seventeen years that the three appellants have been in prison, the fourth having died in prison. For the full story see P. Foot, n. 59 above, *The Final Story* (London, 1998).

[265] 15 May 96 'Lab Tests Cast Doubts on IRA'.

[266] 15 May 96 'Semtex Error Could Free 12 IRA Men'.

[267] 15 May 96 'New Doubts on IRA Bombs'.

[268] *The Daily Telegraph* 15 May 96 'IRA Bomb Cases Cast into Doubt' (Philip Johnston); *The Guardian* 16 May 96 'Bombers' Lawyers Re-examine the Semtex Evidence' (John Mullin); *The Guardian* 16 May 96 'Legal Hurdles to Overturning Convictions for Bombings' (Alan Travis).

raise doubts about whether the system for remedying any resultant miscarriages is likely to prove deficient. Neither the inquiry set up to consider the implications of this information for convictions nor the system for remedying any potential miscarriage that might arise from the inquiry's deliberations is subjected to critical scrutiny. What the reporting concentrates on are the difficult tasks ahead of unravelling the implications of this information for individual cases. Despite the seriousness of this situation it does not lead journalists into linking themes of deficiency out of which a more general theme of loss of confidence or crisis of public confidence could arise. For the moment the structuring of newspaper articles around such a meta-narrative has passed.

H. Underlying patterns

From the perspective of the legal system, the above reporting represents so much *noise*. It is a perturbation. A disturbance that is addressed to its procedures and practices but cannot be directly integrated into them. For example, the experience of the Birmingham Six, as constructed in newspaper articles, cannot be introduced as evidence in other cases involving false confessions, whether at the trial court level or in the Court of Appeal. The system's inability to respond is not simply a function of the conservative attitude of its most senior personnel: the Lord Justices of Appeal and Law Lords. The Court of Appeal cannot operate on the basis that the system of prosecution and trial suffers from major flaws. To preserve a legal system the Court of Appeal has to limit itself to rectifying the system's mistakes. And its definition of what constitutes a mistake cannot equate with the level of criticism represented by the media narrative of crisis. The media can put criminal justice on trial, and find it wanting. They can criticize judges who fail to acknowledge and respond to the meta-narrative of crisis that the media have constructed. But the Court of Appeal, and the senior judges, cannot treat prosecutions, trials, and convictions as generally suspect. The media can treat the stories of *innocent* prisoners as truth, accept that the claims of other prisoners are likely to be true, and seek reforms designed to reverse their convictions and prevent further such convictions in future. And it can do so while still reporting on, and demanding, that criminal justice produces routine, truthful convictions.

The distance between the media and the legal system is captured in the contrast between the arguments in one newspaper article by the former senior judge and Master of the Rolls Lord Donaldson in 1994,[269] and those in one letter in *The Times* in 1996 by the producer and presenter of Channel 4's *Trial and Error* series of television programmes, David Jessel.[270]

---

[269] *The Mirror on Sunday* 28 Aug. 94 'The Scales of Justice Should not Aid the Guilty'.
[270] 29 April 96 'Criminal Appeal System Questioned'.

Lord Donaldson uses his article to express his frustration with the general public, including journalists, who have such a poor understanding of the basic rules and principles of the criminal process. He quotes Professor Michael Zander, a member of the Royal Commission on Criminal Justice: 'The question of whether someone is innocent or not is not one that is addressed in a criminal trial in our legal system.' What, then, is the trial about? It is about the presumption of innocence, exclusionary rules of evidence, an elaborate code governing confession evidence, identification evidence, and other evidence obtained by the police, the different duties of prosecuting and defending lawyers, the duties of the judge and jury, in sum those rules and practices that make up the criminal trial process. It is about the conditions, as set down in the law, for a fair trial and the protection of rights. Lord Donaldson is even frustrated at the recommendation by the Royal Commission on Criminal Justice to set up an independent Criminal Cases Review Authority to investigate alleged miscarriages after the normal processes of appeal have been exhausted. He criticizes the Royal Commission for this proposal, believing that 'it has not explained what it means by a miscarriage of justice': 'Does it mean that information that was not before the jury might have enabled the accused, although probably guilty, to get away with it? Or does it mean that subsequent information shows that he was probably innocent?' He favours the view that 'The true role of the new authority should be to identify the *few* cases in which the innocent are convicted',[271] even though he admits that such a task might require the authority 'not to be blinkered by the strict rules of evidence'. What Lord Donaldson has done is capture the relationship between the trial and the appeal system, how upholding the authority of the trial (first-order determinations) conditions the usual approach adopted by the other (the Court of Appeal's second-order determinations). He expresses his frustration with those who do not structure their communications about criminal justice on the basis of the same priorities.

David Jessel's letter to *The Times* is in response to comments made by Lord Chief Justice Taylor in 1996 in his Court of Appeal judgment which rejected the appeals from their convictions for murder of Gary Mills and Tony Poole.[272] Jessel also expresses his frustration, but it operates in the opposite direction. After detailing the main arguments against the safety of the convictions of Mills and Poole, Jessel concludes:

Having spent three years investigating the case of Mills and Poole with the Trial and Error television team, I plead guilty to the Lord Chief Justice's charges against those in the media who 'do not shrink from substituting their assessments for those made by the Court'. The difference is that my assessment is mere criticism; theirs puts people in prison for life.[273]

---

[271] Our emphasis.   [272] David Jessel, *The Times*, 16 April 96.
[273] See also his strong defence of the role of the *Trial and Error* series in exposing miscarriages and criticism of misplaced judicial rebukes; 'Clued Up', *The Guardian* 19 Nov. 96.

Others in the media, who have spent a lot of their time investigating alleged miscarriages of justice, have expressed a similar frustration more fully. A good recent example is the analysis by Peter Hill, the journalist who originated the influential *Rough Justice* television series in 1980. In presenting his arguments he contrasts 'The legal determination of the truth' with 'The journalistic determination of the "truth" '. His sense of frustration with the former is clear, although he is also willing to criticize some parts of the media for their irresponsibility and bad reporting that 'hardly serves the "public good" '.[274]

We are not suggesting that senior judges simply respect the existing system and wish to preserve it from change. In the above history, we saw former Law Lords writing in support of high profile prisoners because of their view of the proper relationship between the jury and the Court of Appeal. From these judges' perspectives, reversing the *Stafford* decision would be an important change, which would bring criminal justice closer to actual justice (fairer, and more likely to be correct). But such issues, bound up as they are with technical rules of due process and rights, have little purchase in the media. The fact that former Law Lords are criticizing the legal system in support of high profile prisoners assists the construction of a meta-narrative of crisis, but the particular arguments that they make are not taken up. Later, when the meta-narrative of crisis has generated a vilification of judges who fail to recognize and respond to it, we see one of the same Law Lords seeking to defend his successors from unjustified criticism. Similar situations arise with other suggested reforms. While those perceived as legal radicals have greater access to the media while there is a meta-narrative of crisis, no consensus builds up around their suggested reforms of the system of prosecution, trial, and appeal. The consensus that criminal justice is in crisis, that the authority of the legal system can be freely challenged, and that radical change is needed, does not produce agreement on what exactly needs to be done.

When the meta-narrative of crisis has passed, deference towards the legal system's construction of criminal justice (the only workable basis for appeals) once again becomes acceptable. Evidence for this conclusion, apart from that presented in this chapter, is given by the journalist David Rose in his book *In the Name of the Law: The Collapse of Criminal Justice*. Rose writes: 'On investigating a case of this kind, one first fights to convince one's newspaper executive that the subject is worthy of space: a battle which, in the late 1990s, is increasingly hard to win, as miscarriages of justice no longer command the mainstream of political debate.'[275] The high

---

[274] P. Hill, 'The Role of the Journalist', in C. Walker and K. Starmer (eds.), *Miscarriages of Justice: A Review of Justice in Error* (London, 1999), 281. We undertake a critique of the arguments that Hill presented in a shorter form in an earlier publication, in section C of Ch. 6.

[275] D. Rose, *In the Name of the Law: The Collapse of Criminal Justice* (London, 1996), 34.

profile cases remain mistakes of the system, and continue to be points of reference for media discussion of criminal justice issues. But the mistakes are no longer reported as evidence that the system needs root and branch reform. Instead, the reform that commands consensus is an improvement in the ability of the system to deal with its mistakes: a reform of the jurisdiction of the Court of Appeal and the system of referral to that Court. Thus we find a repetition of the pattern which gave birth to the Court of Criminal Appeal. High profile cases, widely reported as the wrongful imprisonment of innocent persons, draw attention to the conditions that make such wrongful convictions likely. To quote Woffinden's conclusion again: 'the continued incarceration of the innocent is nothing less than national policy.'[276] High profile cases also provoke intolerance of the legal system's inability to recognize and remedy these mistakes. The reform produced is, as a sceptic would anticipate, not root-and-branch reform, but changes intended to reassure the media of the legal system's ability to deal with its mistakes. In 1907, this was the creation of a Court of Criminal Appeal. In 1995 it is the creation of a new Criminal Cases Review Commission. In 1995, as in 1907, the new body inherits a problem which it cannot hope to solve, and a role which will make it part of the next crisis of public confidence.

[276] See p. 113 above. Woffinden, *Miscarriages of Justice*, 346.

5

Scientific evidence and investigation by the new Criminal Cases Review Commission: the scope for further miscarriages of justice and crisis

A. Introduction

As we have shown in Chapter 3, the task facing the Court of Appeal (Criminal Division) when adjudicating on potential miscarriages of justice has not changed since the creation of that Court, despite the various reforms to its jurisdiction. And as we have shown in Chapter 4, the conditions that precipitate high profile miscarriages of justice have not altered, namely the systematic misreading by the media and other systems of the legal operations of quashing or upholding a conviction. In these circumstances are there, or have there been, any other changes likely to ameliorate the effects of the combination of these factors? In this chapter we rely on our analysis of the history of criminal appeals and our analysis of the recent history of press reporting of miscarriages of justice to consider two potentially significant changes.

The Royal Commission on Criminal Justice that was set up directly in response to the convictions of the Birmingham Six being quashed by the Court of Appeal proposed numerous reforms. Those proposed reforms were generally intended to achieve various improvements in the criminal justice process, to reassure the public that miscarriages of justice would be less likely to occur and that those which did occur would be more effectively rectified. The Commission particularly recognized the benefits of the increasing reliance on scientific, technical, forensic, and expert evidence, especially in the context of those miscarriages that were widely believed to have resulted from police malpractice and false (and enforced) confessions.[1]

---

[1] Royal Commission on Criminal Justice, the *Runciman Report*, Cm 2263 (London, 1993), ch. 2, paras. 43–7. See also P. Roberts, 'Forensic Science Evidence after Runciman', *Criminal Law Review* [1994], 780–92.

A number of their proposals are directly linked to the greater availability of technical evidence, such as audio and video recording, and the increasing potential for using scientific evidence such as DNA evidence. To this end they recommended reclassifying samples such as plucked hair and saliva from mouth swabs as non-intimate for the purposes of permitting the police to acquire them, in some circumstances, without consent.[2] And in order to facilitate the greater use of DNA evidence, they recommended that, beyond the arrangements for retaining fingerprints from convicted offenders, DNA profiles should not be destroyed if a suspect is acquitted or not proceeded against, but should be retained for statistical purposes.[3] One of the other key proposals made by the Royal Commission was the recommendation to abolish the Home Secretary's role in investigating alleged miscarriages of justice and the replacement of the Home Office's CCU (previously C3 division) who carried out this work by an independent Criminal Cases Review Authority.[4] The latter body was expected to overcome the Home Office's well-evidenced reluctance to refer cases to the Court of Appeal.[5] The anticipated outcome would be a likely increase in the number of cases that will be referred, and greater numbers of miscarriages of justice thereby remedied without the long delays and public disquiet that had occurred in the cases which had led to the Commission's appointment.

In view of these recommendations we consider the implications for miscarriages of justice of the development and greater reliance on scientific/expert evidence in the criminal trial, in terms of its reassessment by the Court of Appeal. We also consider the significance of having a new body empowered to investigate and refer on alleged miscarriages of justice to the Court of Appeal. Does greater reliance on new types of evidence and the way that the Court of Appeal approaches such evidence, namely its reassessment of expert/scientific evidence on appeal, reduce the likelihood of high profile miscarriages of justice? And does a different body with authority to investigate alleged miscarriages of justice and refer those cases on to the Court of Appeal make miscarriages less likely and their resolution more probable or at least less likely to precipitate *crisis*? If the answer to all of these questions is no, then the conclusion can only be that further crises will emanate as a response to existing structures and the conditions of their operation. Even more, such crises, like those resulting from natural occurrences, cannot be fully defused by human endeavour. In other words, attempts at legal and political change cannot in

---

[2] 'Because, however, DNA profiling is now so powerful a diagnostic technique and so helpful in establishing guilt or innocence, we believe that it is proper and desirable to allow the police to take non-intimate samples (eg saliva, plucked hair etc) without consent from all those arrested for serious criminal offences, whether or not DNA evidence is relevant to the particular offence, and so recommend' (The *Runciman Report*, n. 1 above, ch. 2, paras. 25–38, 35).
[3] Ibid., paras. 36–8.   [4] Ibid., ch. 11, para. 11.
[5] Ibid., ch. 11, and esp. para. 9.

themselves alter the conditions under which such events arise, even though they might achieve other aims.[6]

B. Legal authority and scientific authority

1 The increasing reliance on expert evidence

Throughout the twentieth century, human testimony, particularly witness and confession evidence, has been shown to be suspect as a basis for criminal conviction. This fact does not imply that it is always unreliable as evidence leading to conviction, but that it is always potentially unreliable and, in accordance with the fact sceptic's account,[7] it may precipitate wrongful convictions. At the same time, during the twentieth century, while the potential unreliability of forms of witness and defendant evidence has become clearer so the greater reliance on expert, scientific, and technical evidence in criminal trials has increased.[8]

The admission of expert/scientific evidence in a criminal trial is not that dissimilar from any other evidence, namely that the evidence is relevant and has probative value.[9] Technically the rule of admissibility of expert evidence is usually stated in its negative form, as an exception to the inadmissibility of evidence of opinion as opposed to fact. But, of course, expert evidence may be evidence solely of fact or a mixture of fact and inference from fact, namely opinion, or opinion *per se*.[10] What is really characterized by the admissibility rules relating to expert evidence is the notion that experts because of their expertise can present their facts or opinions in ways that go beyond the experience of the ordinary lay person. Theirs is knowledge less susceptible to the problems associated with evidence from other forms of human testimony. It is knowledge of the expert, based upon a person's expertise; objective knowledge established using standards normally, but

---

[6] In autopoietic terms, the conditions of legislative and political failure. See G. Teubner, 'Social Order from Legislative Noise? Autopoietic Closure as a Problem for Legal Regulation', in G. Teubner and A. Febbrajo (eds.), *State, Law, and Economy as Autopoietic Systems: Regulation and Autonomy in a New Perspective* (Milan, 1992), 609–49.

[7] Set out in section C of Ch. 2.

[8] It should be noted that one of the main constraints on the developing use of such evidence is budgetary; see the Royal Commission's recognition of this, n. 1 above, ch. 2, para. 45.

[9] As T. Hodgkinson states in his practitioner text: 'Expert evidence on a particular matter is admissible if it has both relevance and probative value in relation to issues in the case' (*Expert Evidence: Law and Practice* (London, 1990), 4). The whole of Hodgkinson's introductory chapter is useful background to the arguments we present here.

[10] Some writers doubt the classification of expert evidence as evidence of opinion. Rather, for them all forensic science evidence can be viewed as evidence about inference from facts. See, e.g., B. Robertson and G. A. Vignaux, *Interpreting Evidence: Evaluating Forensic Science in the Courtroom* (Chichester, 1995), esp. ch. 11 'Implications for the Legal System', 195–202.

not invariably, associated with science.[11] However there is one key limitation to the admissibility of expert evidence, which has now been formally removed in relation to civil cases,[12] but not criminal cases. It is the common law rule (which currently has an unclear scope and effect[13]) that experts cannot be asked to give their evidence in such a way as to determine the ultimate issue, the actual question of fact that needs to be decided by the jury. Such a rule attempts to uphold legal authority against another form of authority, scientific authority. Despite the unclear scope of this rule,[14] its implications underlie the admissibility and use of expert or scientific evidence throughout the criminal trial and appeal processes.

When scientific or expert evidence leads to conviction there is an appearance that, at least initially, the conviction is *safer*. This flows from the perception that scientific evidence has particular authority: the defendants had handled explosives; the blood traces from the defendant were only compatible with his having attacked the victim, etc. Such forensic evidence, once accepted by a jury, provides the media with convincing *facts* that explain and justify the jury's verdict. The sworn evidence of eyewitnesses, even if these are not policemen, has less cachet. And, as Blom-Cooper has observed, to convict on the basis of *circumstantial* evidence has been taken by some 'both serious and amateur commentators' as almost an apology, an admission that the verdict could be wrong and that others might have decided otherwise.[15] But an awareness of the processes by which forensic science evidence is produced reveals that the certainty that it might appear to offer to the truth of any conviction can be quite temporary. As Roberts and Willmore conclude in their research for the Royal Commission: 'Our research suggests that the potential for error resides in all cases in which forensic science evidence is utilized. Defence solicitors and triers of fact, in particular, should be made aware of its limitations.'[16] Later experts may

---

[11] Some writers dispute this caricature of scientific knowledge as objective knowledge, particularly in its applied forms, such as forensic science. See, e.g., C. Jones, *Expert Witnesses: Science, Medicine, and the Practice of Law* (Oxford, 1994).

[12] By s. 3 of the Civil Evidence Act 1972.

[13] '... in *R v Stockwell* [(1993) 97 Cr. App. R 260, 265] the Court of Appeal adopted the view expressed in the previous edition of this text that the expert should be permitted to give his opinion on an ultimate issue, subject only to a direction to the jury that it is not bound to accept the expert's opinion' (C. Tapper, *Cross and Tapper on Evidence* (London, 1995), 553).

[14] See J. D. Jackson, 'The Ultimate Issue Rule: One Rule too Many', *Criminal Law Review*, [1984], 75–86.

[15] L. Blom-Cooper, *The Birmingham Six and Other Cases: Victims of Circumstance* (London, 1997), 21. Blom-Cooper's argument, on the other hand, attempts to demonstrate the real value of circumstantial evidence, which is in his opinion much higher and potentially more reliable than many commentators are willing to admit.

[16] P. Roberts and C. Willmore, *The Role of Forensic Science Evidence in Criminal Proceedings*, Royal Commission on Criminal Justice Research Study No. 11 (London, 1993), 143. The same conclusion can be found in H. Miller, *Traces of Guilt: Forensic Science and the Fight against Crime* (London, 1995) published to accompany a television series on forensic science evidence. Miller concludes that 'the police and the courts must view the claims of

offer different opinions. Standards and processes change. In these circumstances the Court of Appeal faces a difficult task in forming a view as to when a conviction obtained with the assistance of expert, scientific, or forensic evidence can continue to be upheld. The extra cachet provided by the original forensic evidence at trial can increase the media perception that the conviction can no longer stand when its reliability is later thrown into doubt. The media can shift easily from an acceptance that scientific evidence used in a case was reliable to a view that it was not. The Court of Appeal cannot shift so easily. The Court of Appeal has to review scientific evidence with the awareness that it is used routinely to secure convictions (and acquittals). If forensic science evidence is to be used extensively in trials, it cannot simply be abandoned on appeal whenever another expert is willing to challenge it. Thus, it is not enough for expert witnesses to offer new and different opinions, for this can occur in connection with any conviction obtained through the use of scientific evidence. The case of *Steven Jones* is a good, recent example of the difficulties faced by the Court of Appeal in deciding whether or not to admit new scientific evidence. Exceptionally in this case new scientific evidence was admitted and considered by the Court, but the appeal against conviction for murder was nevertheless dismissed. Lord Chief Justice Bingham's judgment rehearses the technical legal arguments well.

The Court in the past accepted that section 23 may apply to expert evidence, and we would not wish to circumscribe the operation of a statutory rule enacted to protect defendants against the risk of wrongful conviction. But it seems unlikely that the section was framed with expert evidence prominently in mind. The requirement in subsection (2)(a) that the evidence should appear to be capable of belief applies more aptly to factual evidence than to expert evidence, which may or may not be acceptable or persuasive but which is unlikely to be thought to be incapable of belief in any ordinary sense. The giving of a reasonable explanation for failure to adduce the evidence before the jury again applies more aptly to factual evidence of which a party was unaware, or could not adduce, than to expert evidence, since if one expert is unavailable to testify at trial a party would ordinarily be expected to call another unless circumstances prevented this. Expert witnesses, although invariably varying in standing and experience, are interchangeable in a way in which factual witnesses are not. It would clearly subvert the trial process if a defendant, convicted at trial, were to be generally free to mount on appeal an expert case which, if sound, could and should have been advanced before the jury.[17]

If the new evidence is admitted, the Court of Appeal has to establish whether the errors illustrated by the new evidence or changes in scientific procedures that have occurred warrant quashing the conviction. This task

---

forensic scientists with far more caution than they have done in the past' (p. 188). See also P. Roberts, 'Science in the Criminal Process', *Oxford Journal of Legal Studies*, 14 (1994), 496–506.

[17] *Steven Jones* [1997] 1 Cr. App. R 86, 93.

is quite different from the routine work of the Court, which requires it to assess whether legal procedures, rooted in traditional understandings of fairness, have failed to operate, as they should. Here, the Court is required to review the integrity and meaning of scientific procedures. As such, it is likely to be involved in assessing the integrity of scientific evidence using methods that are not themselves scientific.[18] Where this leads to the Court rejecting new expert/scientific evidence, and upholding a conviction, it may face considerable difficulty in convincing some members of the scientific community or the media that its decision carries authority.

The analysis in this chapter starts with another short history: the history of reassessment of expert/scientific evidence on appeal. This history demonstrates that cases involving scientific evidence are subjected to the same constitutional constraints as other cases, namely that the Court of Appeal seeks to maintain the primacy of its own legal operations, which are informed by a rhetoric of deference to the jury. The commitment to the jury's decision to convict restricts its willingness to admit and assess new scientific evidence, particularly in those cases where it was available at trial. The Court limits its willingness to hear such evidence to *exceptional* cases. Having demonstrated this relationship of deference we proceed to examine the difficulties which it creates for the ability of the Court of Appeal to present its practices as rational. We argue that while scientific evidence at the level of trial offers the prospect of more accurate outcomes, and hence fewer miscarriages of justice in particular as these are generally understood by the media, it may increase the possibilities of generating crises of confidence at the level of appeal. To demonstrate the particular difficulties faced by the Court of Appeal in reconciling its own procedures with the expectations generated by scientific evidence we use two case studies. These studies deal with two of the cases that were most significant in creating the last crisis of confidence: the Birmingham Six appeals (1987/8 and 1991) and the Maguire Seven appeal (1991).

2 A HISTORY OF THE REASSESSMENT OF EXPERT EVIDENCE ON APPEAL

Appeal cases that involve the more specialized area of fresh expert, originally almost invariably medical, evidence follow the pattern of the more general cases,[19] but with an even more steadfast refusal to hear new/fresh evidence. During the twentieth century the number of reported applications to hear fresh expert evidence has been relatively few, perhaps reflecting the lesser significance of forensic evidence in the earlier years of the century.

[18] See Roberts and Willmore, n. 16 above, ch. 4 'Legal Adversarialism and the Forensic Expert'.
[19] See particularly sections D/2, E/3 and F/1 of Ch. 3.

They fall into three main groups. There are cases where the expert/medical evidence at the trial is contested on appeal, mostly involving issues as to cause of death. Secondly, applications to introduce evidence in support of the defence of insanity, in cases of convictions for murder. Finally, cases involving handwriting issues.

(i) Attempts to contest the expert/medical evidence heard at trial, on appeal

The earliest reported case where an expert witness was allowed to give fresh evidence as to cause of death was in 1909 in *Joseph Edwin Jones*.[20] At that time the rigidity of the rule that the evidence should not have been available at the time of the trial was not fully established. A gun-maker, an expert in firearms, gave evidence that it was possible, from the nature of the gunshot wounds, for the victim to have committed suicide. In the context of the other evidence, this opinion was insufficient to overturn the conviction. By 1921 the attitude to fresh scientific evidence was following an increasingly exclusionary line. In *Starkie*, there was an appeal from a conviction for administering and supplying drugs with intent to procure an abortion. Despite there having been a misunderstanding at the trial, the defence was not permitted to call scientific witnesses to establish the nature of certain drugs, because it was held that the witnesses could have been called at the trial. The Lord Chief Justice made the usual determination: 'If counsel deliberately refrains from calling witnesses at the trial the Court will be slow to call them on the appeal, and will only do so in exceptional circumstances.'[21] In *Thorne*, subsections (d) and (e) of section 9 of the Criminal Appeal Act 1907 were considered in the context of reassessing medical evidence given at the trial. The defence argued that the conflict in medical evidence over the victim's cause of death made it a suitable case for reference to 'a special commissioner' under 9(d) or an 'assessor' under 9(e). The response of the Court was predictable, in upholding legal authority. It stressed the primacy of the role of the jury, and was clearly opposed to transferring: 'to a medical expert, or medical experts, the determination of a question on which a jury, having conflicting views before them, has arrived at a unanimous conclusion.' At the same time it acknowledged its own powers: 'Undoubtedly the Legislature has armed this Court with the widest possible powers for the purposes of investigation, and in a proper case this Court would not refuse to make use of the powers which are contained in these paragraphs of s. 9.' The question is begged as to what is 'a proper case' for the exercise of 'the special and exceptional powers provided by s. 9',[22] though the implication is that such a case will be rare. The use of these powers does not appear to have been raised again in reported cases.

---

[20] 2 Cr. App. R 88 and 102.　　　[21] *Starkie* (1921) 16 Cr. App. R 61, 63.
[22] *Thorne* (1925) 18 Cr. App. R 186, 187 and 188.

Two later cases had more positive outcomes on fresh medical evidence, though both are hedged around with the language of the *wholly exceptional*. In *Ellen Harding*, fresh medical evidence as to the cause of death was heard and the appeal was granted. It was stressed that the hearing of such evidence was wholly exceptional—the circumstances being 'quite exceptional, perhaps unprecedented, and never likely to be repeated'.[23] The precise nature of the exceptional circumstances was not specified. The case did turn on the conclusions that could be drawn from the medical evidence, and the defendant was a young mother whose conviction had been accompanied by a strong recommendation to mercy from the jury conveyed to the Secretary of State by the judge. The role of the Court in assessing the fresh evidence was to judge whether: 'if this evidence had been offered in the Court below, there might have been upon the part of the jury a reasonable doubt as to the guilt of the appellant'.[24] The stance of the Court in 1936 was clear to the extent that the logic of the *exceptional* was understandable.

The issue of fresh medical evidence occurred again in *Jordan* in 1956. At stake was the cause of death, whether due to the stab wound or to the later abnormal hospital treatment. In this judgment the issue of fresh scientific evidence is placed firmly in the context of the main fresh evidence cases, when justifying 'why such applications should be granted only with great restraint'.[25] As in *Ellen Harding*, the obvious indecision of the original jury and the recommendation to mercy that accompanied their verdict seemed to affect the inclination of the Court of Appeal to hear the further evidence and reconsider the verdict. The issue for the Court 'is not whether we, if we were a jury, would have accepted and acted on the opinions those gentlemen expressed, but whether the jury in all probability would have allowed their verdict to be affected by them'.[26] The test for new scientific evidence, like that for all other new evidence, is altered in 1973 by the House of Lords decision in the case of *Stafford and Luvaglio*.[27] In view of that judgment the members of the Court of Appeal must consider whether the new scientific evidence alters *their* confidence in the safety of the verdict. As we shall show in our case studies, this standard allows the Court to uphold jury verdicts which, had the new scientific evidence been available at trial, might not have been reached by the original jury.

(ii) Insanity cases

The general response of the Court in such cases was to divert this jurisdiction back to the Home Secretary whose 'large powers ... remain untouched'. This was the reply to the first suggested use of section 9(e) to

23 *Ellen Harding* (1936) 25 Cr. App. R 190, 195.   24 Ibid. 197.
25 *Jordan* (1956) 40 Cr. App. R 152, 154–5.   26 Ibid. 156.
27 [1974] AC 878. Discussed above in section F/2 of Ch. 3.

assess the sanity of the appellant in *Victor Jones*.[28] Later cases reiterated this view: in *Loake*[29] a report was received under section 9 from the Lunacy Commissioners, but the extreme rarity of such an event was stressed the following year in *Lumb*. 'The circumstances under which this Court would enter upon an enquiry under s. 9 of the Criminal Appeal Act are very special. It did so in Loake, but I am not aware that it has ever allowed expert evidence to be called after the trial.'[30] The pattern was followed in *Perry* (fresh evidence was heard but 'it must not be taken as a precedent'),[31] and in *Holt* (where an application for a surgical examination under section 9(d) was refused).[32]

(iii) Handwriting cases

These cases are merely illustrative of the somewhat unscientific role of experts at the start of the Court's jurisdiction. In both *Brownhill*[33] and *Rickard*[34] the Court itself examined the handwriting, substituting an assessment by the Court for an assessment by experts. The nature of expertise and science are a constant theme. Doubts about credibility justify the appeal court being wary of so-called expertise and requiring expert evidence, like all other evidence, to be subjected to the rigors of the adversary process.[35] As has often been noted[36] this method, examination and cross-examination, is not the method of science, with its principal reliance on hypothesis and testing.[37]

Reassessment of expert evidence by the Court was restricted in the formative years of its jurisdiction. The use of the subsections (d) and (e) of section 9 of the 1907 Act, which gave the Court its own wide investigative powers, was so minimal that when the legislation was reformed in the 1960s, these powers disappeared without comment.

3 AFTER THE 1960S REFORMS

In relation to the admission of fresh expert/scientific evidence the post-1966 liberalization on reception of evidence has not been of vast significance, though in recent years the Court's wider discretion under section 23(1) of the Criminal Appeal Act 1968 has been brought into greater prominence.

---

[28] (1910) 4 Cr. App. R 207, 218
[29] (1911) 7 Cr. App. R 71.
[30] *Lumb* (1912) 7 Cr. App. R 263, 264.
[31] *Perry* (1919)14 Cr. App. R 48, 56.
[32] *Holt* (1920) 14 Cr. App. R 152.
[33] (1913) 8 Cr. App. R 258.
[34] (1918) 13 Cr. App. R 140.
[35] For recent examples of new scientific techniques being subjected to legal assessment, see the Court of Appeal judgments dealing with 'facial mapping': *Stockwell* (1993) n. 13 above and *Clarke* [1995] 2 Cr. App. R. 425.
[36] And as we have tried to demonstrate in section C of Ch. 2.
[37] See the 'Introduction' in R. Smith and B. Wynne (eds.), *Expert Evidence: Interpreting Science in the Law* (London, 1989), 1–22.

The most frequently cited authority on the admission of fresh expert evidence is *Lomas*[38] where fresh medical evidence from a pathologist was heard, the circumstances of that case (as usual) being deemed exceptional by the Court. The medical evidence centred on the intention of the accused to cause serious injury and the possible consequent substitution of a conviction for manslaughter rather than murder. At the trial, the prosecution expert went unchallenged due to the inability of the defence to produce a sufficiently experienced pathologist. On appeal counsel for the Crown argued that the fresh evidence should not be heard on the ground that no reasonable explanation was available for its failure to be adduced at trial, and so the criterion in section 23(2)(b) was not fulfilled. Due to the particular facts of the case, that the medical opinion proffered by the prosecution went to the foundation of the charge and that the physical evidence on which the opinion was founded was very slight, the Court decided to hear the newly commissioned evidence for the defence. Following the objective line of reasoning, i.e. predicting the effect of such evidence on the mind of the jury, it concluded that the conviction for murder was 'most unsafe and unsatisfactory'. The countenancing of the fresh expert evidence in this case was accompanied by a strongly worded anti-precedent-forming warning: 'we regard this as an exceptional case depending on its own special facts and not as a decision giving any encouragement to similar applications in other cases in the future.'[39] Thus in its immediate post-1968 judgment the face of the Court was firmly set against the reopening of cases to allow for the reappraisal of expert/scientific evidence. The limiting factors were introduced via an interpretation of section 23 that envisaged *the normal case* of fresh evidence to involve 'a question of fact, where, for example, some eyewitness or alibi witness not previously available has later been discovered'.[40] Generally fresh expert evidence of scientific or medical opinion, though admissible, would be heard with extreme reluctance. A further limit on the reception of expert evidence was sometimes argued for by imposing the section 23(2) criteria, especially the reasonable explanation for non-availability at trial, and ignoring the wider discretion of the Court in section 23(1).[41]

In cases involving expert opinion on appeal the evidence frequently fails to pass the section 23(2) hurdle, in that there is no reasonable explanation for the failure not to have adduced the evidence at the trial. In cases such as *Merry*[42] and *Lattimore*,[43] however, where expert opinion was of crucial importance to the outcome of the appeal, the expert evidence was heard under the section 23(1) discretionary power, the unfettered nature of that power being firmly emphasized by Lord Scarman in *Lattimore*. Again,

---

[38] [1969] 1 All ER 920.
[40] Ibid. 923.
[42] (1970) 54 Cr. App. R 274.

[39] Ibid. 924.
[41] For the text of s. 23, see section F/1 of Ch. 3.
[43] (1975) 62 Cr. App. R 53.

exceptionally, in *Frankum*[44] and *Morgan*[45] additional expert evidence was heard under section 23(1). In the former case the appellant, who had been found guilty of manslaughter by reason of diminished responsibility, wanted to introduce further medical evidence as to the toxic effects of a drug prescribed to him for treatment of a peptic ulcer. Although admitting the further evidence the Court of Appeal approved the verdict of the jury who had been asked and given an answer to the specific question of whether the abnormality of mind was due to inherent causes or a side effect of taking the drug. In *Morgan* new evidence was admitted about whether a shoe impression found at the scene of the crime came from a shoe belonging to one of the defendants. The significant evidence from the prosecution's scientist at trial had been that the impression *was* made by the defendant's shoe, the new evidence said that it only might have been, this new evidence having come about following an initiative taken by the Director of Public Prosecutions. Having admitted the new evidence and considered it, the Court allowed the appeal.

On the method of evaluation of the evidence the cases differ. In *Merry* the issues involved the possible causes of a particular pattern of blood-staining on the defendant's suit. The Court refused to hear experts for the Crown challenging the new defence evidence: 'if we were . . . to assess the weight of the evidence on both sides we would be abrogating to ourselves the functions of a jury, which is not proper.'[46] A retrial was ordered, providing an opportunity for each side to call evidence as they desired. *Merry*, occurring roughly midway between the 1960s reforms and the watershed judgment of *Stafford amd Luvaglio*,[47] presents a restrained view of the Court's responsibility *vis-à-vis* the reassessment of expert evidence. By the end of 1975, when *Lattimore* was decided the issue of retrial was not considered in the judgment. Fire experts and pathologists on both sides were heard at the appeal (mainly experts who had testified at the trial) and the Court participated in the reassessment of the medical evidence as to the time of death. The assumption of the role of reassessment was in line with the post-*Stafford* view of the Court's function, though in this case it may also have been affected by the wording of the Home Secretary's reference to the Court: 'he hereby refers the whole of the cases . . . for determination.' This approach, which allows the Court itself to undertake the reassessment, is continued in the later cases of *Frankum* and *Morgan*.[48]

On the separate issue of the hearing of fresh medical evidence to introduce a plea of diminished responsibility after the trial, the Court has opposed the introduction of wholly new evidence, unrelated to issues raised at the trial. In *Melville*[49] a plea of diminished responsibility was argued for

[44] [1984] Crim. LR 434.
[46] See n. 42 above, 278.
[48] See nn. 44 and 45 above.
[45] *The Times*, 9 June 1978.
[47] See n. 27 above.
[49] [1976] 1 All ER 395.

on appeal on the basis of mental abnormalities observed after the trial. The Court decided that such evidence could be heard only if it were 'over-whelming'. The responsibility for supervision of prisoners after trial was said to lie with the Home Office and not the Court of Appeal. However, in later cases in the 1990s the Court has been willing to admit new psychiatric evidence and on that basis to order retrials. In *Campbell*[50] the Home Secretary referred the appellant's conviction for murder to the Court to undertake a further appeal in view of fresh evidence about his state of mind due to epilepsy. At both the trial and the initial appeal the expert psych-iatrist for the defence had been unable to raise evidence of abnormality of mind. At the new appeal the evidence of two psychiatrists with special expertise in epilepsy was admitted. The Court drew the distinction between a tactical decision by the defence at trial not to advance a particular argu-ment and being unable to support such an argument due to inadequate expert evidence. On the Court deciding that the case fell into the latter cate-gory, the new evidence was admitted and since it 'might well have succeeded' a retrial was ordered. In *Hobson*[51] the Court ordered a retrial after the admission of new psychiatric evidence bearing on a conviction for murder in 1992. The circumstances of the case were consistent with 'battered women's syndrome' but it was not until 1994 that such a condi-tion had been recognized as part of what was described in the case as the British Classification of Mental Disease. That new classification allowed for the possibility of the defence of diminished responsibility and not merely that of provocation, which defence had been rejected at the original trial.

4 CONSTITUTIONAL RELATIONSHIP WITH THE JURY—DOES SCIENTIFIC EVIDENCE MAKE A DIFFERENCE?

The above short history, and that in Chapter 3, has demonstrated that the Court's relationship to the jury is one of deference. Reform proposals have veered between requiring greater or lesser deference, just as interpretation of the cases permits such an analysis, namely that of greater or lesser defer-ence by the Court of Appeal in its relationship with the original jury and its verdict. Whichever way this is argued, the inescapable fact is the recogni-tion that, at some level, deference to the jury is implicit in the role of a Court of Appeal. It might be that the explicit expression of deference by the Court is, in some situations, a camouflage for other interests: to reduce costs, to maintain the morale of the prosecution and the police, to avoid admitting to inadequate practices, etc. But even then it is impossible to avoid the conclusion that deference is an implicit part of the Court of Appeal's role in upholding and exercising legal authority. Scientific evidence, however, puts the Court's deference to the jury under particular

[50] [1997] 1 Cr. App. R 199.   [51] [1998] 1 Cr. App. R 31.

strain. Where evidence is complicated, it is hard to accept that the jury will understand it any better than would an appeal court. Indeed, as our case studies below show, where appeals involve a reassessment of scientific evidence the Court of Appeal may proceed on the basis that the scientific evidence was not understood, and yet still manage to uphold the jury's verdict. To the extent that new scientific evidence is objective, it is not open to the objections made to other kinds of witness evidence, namely that it will be distorted by the deterioration of memories or even the appellant's ability to secure perjury. Its objectivity also undermines one of the major practical advantages that the jury is supposed to possess, namely the ability to assess the credibility of witnesses on the basis of their demeanour. Demeanour is logically irrelevant to the scientific aspect of an expert's evidence. The *expert* nature of scientific evidence also makes it less plausible to suspect that failure to obtain it before trial, or a decision not to use it at trial, was the result of a deliberate attempt to manipulate the appeal process.

Not all science is complex and technical, but to the extent that it is, and yet is relevant to verdicts, the arguments that justify a review of evidence on appeal apply more strongly to scientific evidence than other forms of evidence. This is particularly necessary if, as occurred in our case studies (see below), the scientific evidence operates as a crucial linchpin in the prosecution's case. Scientific data provide facts (the defendant had been in contact with explosives) around which the explanation of events must be organized. Explanations that do not fit in with those facts are likely to be discounted. Where a defendant's explanations are inconsistent with scientific facts, those facts may provide a starting point on the more general question: whom do you believe?

One must be careful not to exaggerate the differences between expert/scientific and other forms of evidence. Scientific evidence is likely to be presented as objective knowledge, indeed that is its peculiar strength as a form of evidence. 'To say of something that it is "scientific" is to encourage the view that it is altogether respectable and must be taken seriously . . . The popular wish to be thought scientific is of course the result of the enormous power and prestige that science (whatever it may be) enjoys in our society.'[52] In reality, science is neither as objective, nor as precise, as lay people or judges are likely to believe. But science is likely to be presented at trial in a manner that accords with its popular perception. What is crucial at trial is not the methods, hypotheses, and doubts which underlie a scientist's interpretation of data, but his conclusions. And it is these conclusions, typically that there is an X per cent probability of the defendant having handled explosives, been at the scene of the crime, etc., which is debated

[52] S. Richards, *Philosophy and Sociology of Science: An Introduction* (Oxford, 1987), 7.

before the jury. This process of closure hides many of the aspects of scientific evidence that make it similar to other forms of evidence. Conclusions are often reached on the basis of tests that cannot be repeated by other scientists (with forensic science the samples are often small and deteriorate with time). Conclusions are not simply logically deduced conclusions, but are often based upon a particular scientist's experience. At one extreme, the only thing one might assume from the fact that a particular piece of evidence is scientific is that it is independent. But even that is questionable, with evidence that scientists who work permanently or mostly for the prosecution may lose their neutrality, and the common practice especially in civil law, but also applicable to criminal law, of experts selling their opinions to whichever side hires them, and varying those opinions accordingly.[53] Justice and the Council for Science and Society considered the problems of partisanship in their Report, *Science and the Administration of Justice*. Despite these problems, they rejected the various proposals to create a 'neutral expert' in criminal cases.[54] The solution adopted by the House of Lords Select Committee on Science and Technology was, when both sides in a criminal trial intend to offer scientific witnesses, for a 'pre-trial review' to be arranged, supervised by the trial judge, 'to resolve the disagreement or at least to define it as narrowly as possible'.[55] Such a solution remains controversial and, at this time, it is not likely to be implemented.

In the face of the subjectivity of much of science one possible reaction is to dismiss the claims that it needs to be treated differently. On this assumption it could be argued that the jury should assess it with the same reliability (or lack of it) as other forms of evidence. Thus, for example, if scientists are expected to vary their conclusions depending on who hires them, why not allow the jury to choose which one to believe on the usual unscientific basis: their assessment of the respective scientists' demeanour, experience, and impression as a witness?[56] This reaction is, in our view, untenable. One cannot proceed from an acceptance that science is not wholly objective to a conclusion that scientific evidence has the same status as autobiography.

[53] See the concerns expressed in the *Runciman Report*, n. 1 above, ch. 9. See also Jones, n. 11 above, ch. 10 'The Impact of Advocacy', and the extraordinary American examples of partisanship recounted by H. L. Klawans, *The Trials of an Expert Witness: Tales of Clinical Neurology and the Law* (London, 1991).

[54] Justice and the Council for Science and Society, *Science and the Administration of Justice* (London, 1991), ch. 7. See the debate on this between M. N. Howard, 'The Neutral Expert: A Plausible Threat to Justice', *Criminal Law Review* [1991], 98–105 and J. R. Spencer, 'The Neutral Expert: An Implausible Bogey', *Criminal Law Review* [1991], 106–10.

[55] House of Lords Session 1992–93, 5th Report, Select Committee on Science and Technology, *Forensic Science*, HL Paper 24 (London, 1993) 5.20 at 46.

[56] The reasoning in the civil case of *Joyce v Yeomans* [1981] 1 WLR. 549, where expert evidence was crucial to the decision about the amount of damages, support this argument. The Court of Appeal felt that it should uphold the view of the trial judge on which expert's evidence to prefer because, having seen the experts and heard their testimonies, the trial judge was in a better position to decide.

Our current understanding of the world is based upon the acceptance of the primacy of scientific explanations over other forms of knowledge. When assessing the guilt or innocence of the accused, or whether a conviction involves a miscarriage of justice, the primacy of scientific knowledge forms part of that assessment. We do not intend to debate the relative merits of scientific knowledge over other forms of knowledge or even to identify exactly what scientific knowledge is. But we do suggest that the qualities on which science is generally based, such as rationality, consistency, objectivity, verifiability, and accuracy have become the indices against which all other forms of knowledge are measured. So the trial itself, or an appeal, or a miscarriage of justice, is assessed *scientifically* by looking for the rational, consistent, objective, accurate, etc., explanations of any set of events. As such, science itself, the body of knowledge which has come to dominate our general ways of thinking about other things, including the legal system, must invariably be given primacy.

But while one cannot easily ignore the fact that scientific evidence has features that are likely to make it a superior form of evidence, its actual strength, in a particular case, still has to be assessed. And in assigning the task of making this particular assessment to a jury, one has to deal with the jury's likely perception of science. There is a difference in allowing a jury to rely on evidence which the jury know, on the basis of their own experience, may be distorted by bias, memory, or mistaken perceptions, and allowing them to rely on evidence which they believe, incorrectly, is wholly objective. In cases where the scientific evidence is unchallenged, it is very likely to provide a linchpin against which to assess the strength of other kinds of evidence. In the absence of scientific evidence, there is more likely to be a holistic basis to the jury's assessment of what took place. Witnesses who were initially seen as independent and credible may have their evidence subsequently discounted when it is found to be inconsistent with other evidence. But scientific evidence may operate as a bedrock of objective fact to which all other explanations have to be reconciled, with the result that the only explanation that is compatible with the scientific evidence has to be accepted, even though a jury's own experience of life must have told them that this was highly improbable.[57] The danger that a jury may invest science with too much objectivity is not limited to cases where scientific evidence is unchallenged. Even when there is a conflict in the evidence of different scientists, this is not likely, by itself, to shake the jury's perception that science is *scientific*. Instead, one will, we suggest, have a peculiar situation in which, on the basis of their respective performance as witnesses, one of their interpretations is treated as having the same objective qualities as if they had been the only scientific witness. And all explanations of events have to be reconciled with the preferred witness's scientific *facts*.

[57] The Maguire Seven case is a clear example of this (see our case studies below).

The difficulties involved in constructing an appropriate legal forum for the assessment of scientific evidence raise a question which is relevant to any use of science outside of the scientific community: how does one ensure that one's own system is rational and logical in its use of science? In particular, how do non-scientists know whether what they are getting from scientists is scientific? Although scientific values have penetrated most other forms of knowledge, scientific knowledge is not readily available to the non-scientific community and, conversely, the manner in which science is used in other systems (including the legal system) remains alien to most scientists. This is partly due to the technicality of and speciality within science and other systems. But it is also due to the fact that knowledge, within any social system, is not solely based upon values, but also upon practices. Thus, what counts as knowledge within the scientific community is not simply a result of rationality, consistency, objectivity, etc., but of the practices of members of that community. These practices include the manner in which experiments are expected to be carried out, the number of times they need to be repeated, the extent to which one can safely extrapolate, on the basis of logic, from any particular set of results. These matters are not themselves established through logic or rationality, nor are they consistent as between sciences, or even within particular branches of science. Sound scientific knowledge is founded upon the consensus within the scientific community as to what constitutes sound scientific knowledge and, whilst that consensus is built upon the values of rationality, consistency, objectivity, etc., these are not the whole story. Inevitably there are elements within science that appear irrational and arbitrary. This is partly the consequence of the need for standards. Accepting accuracy does not tell you how accurate to be, nor does consistency tell you which contrary results can safely be ignored. But that science might appear irrational, is also in part a result of the different types of reasoning contained within science. Science is both deductive and inductive. Deductive reasoning tends to involve a closed system of logic whereby a rule is established for the conclusions which must, inevitably, follow from the presence of certain facts. But inductive reasoning works on the basis of hypothesis and falsification. Think of a hypothesis, and then work out tests that can falsify that hypothesis. The more tests that fail to falsify the hypothesis, the more willing scientists are to rely on it to develop hypotheses in other areas. Eventually a hypothesis may reach such a level of general acceptance that it operates, within the scientific community, as a rule. As such, all scientific knowledge is contingent. There is a theoretical possibility that any of the rules or laws of science may later be disproved. It is simply that, at a given time, the weight of evidence is assessed by scientists to make the disproving of some hypotheses no more than a theoretical possibility, which they feel can safely be discounted.

The irrational aspects of scientific knowledge, those based not upon evidence alone but convention, are often screened from the jury, who cannot penetrate the technical information required for an assessment of the objectivity of the evidence. As such they must necessarily take science, or rather the scientist, on trust. In the case of conflicting scientific evidence, they must decide which of the scientists to trust. The claim that scientific evidence has led to a miscarriage of justice is, in essence, a claim that this trust was, for some reason, misplaced.

The difficulties involved in introducing scientific evidence at trial are not limited to those created by the role of the jury. Even in the absence of a jury, science is distorted when used in a trial. There are significant problems involved in using science forensically. First, until quite recently the Home Office employed most forensic scientists in the United Kingdom. Forensic scientists are quite a small community, and the wider scientific community does not always share some of its standards of what counts as good practice.[58] Secondly and more generally, the procedures for presenting evidence at trial are completely different from those used to present test results to the wider scientific community. The latter are likely to be written and usually published. Peers will assess the quality of the results claimed by their ability to reproduce the data for themselves. By contrast, test results are presented at trial orally, and subjected to cross-examination to assess their probability and relevance to the unique events which are the subject of the prosecution. The 'adversarial scepticism of legal processes' is distinct from 'the normal consensual discourses of scientific expertise'.[59] The House of Lords Select Committee on Science and Technology put this dilemma clearly.

We perceive a fundamental clash of cultures between science and the law. The process of the courts seeks definite answers to questions put by counsel who are required to be learned only in the law; these answers are delivered extempore in an adversarial setting before a jury unlikely to contain anyone with relevant scientific knowledge. The scientist, on the other hand, is accustomed to dealing with conclusions which, to satisfy standards of scientific precision, must often be qualified by limits of probability. These may have precise statistical meanings; but they are not easily understood by the non-scientist, and the values will change as knowledge and techniques advance. It may therefore be that the best scientist will appear the most prevaricating witness.[60]

5 SCIENTIFIC EVIDENCE ON APPEAL

When appeals to the Court of Appeal involve a review of scientific evidence, the problems set out in the previous section (B/4) have to be managed by

---

[58] See the *Runciman Report*, n. 1 above, ch. 9.
[59] R. Smith and B. Wynne (eds.), 1991, n. 37 above, 15.
[60] See n. 55 above, 5.14 at 45. The arguments presented in this quotation are particularly relevant to the way that we have organized the information in our case studies below.

that Court in a manner that retains both its own authority and that of the trial court. As noted before, there is no particular reason for a jury to be better able to assess the evidence of experts than the Court of Appeal. Indeed, if the jury's ignorance of the processes that create scientific knowledge is accepted, members of the Court may be better placed to form an assessment. However, those who urge the Court to reconsider scientific evidence, and those who comment on such appeals, may still wish the Court to ask itself how the original jury would have reacted to the doubts which have now been raised. As our case studies set out below show, where the Court admits new scientific evidence, and as we have indicated there are many self-imposed restraints on it doing so, it does not limit itself to such an assessment. This can lead to situations where the evidence presented to the appeal would, if it had been available at trial, have left the original prosecution case in tatters, but the Court is still able to uphold the conviction (as we show below). In such cases, the Court of Appeal is in danger of appearing both irrational and unresponsive.

Very little attention has been paid in the literature on the use of expert/scientific evidence in criminal cases to the practices of the Court of Appeal when called upon to undertake some reassessment. This is not surprising since the topic lies between two bodies of knowledge. A great deal is written about expert evidence, but as a perusal of Hodgkinson's practitioner text illustrates, very little comment is specifically directed towards criminal appeals.[61] It is assumed that the same rules of evidence largely can and should apply at any appeal stage as they do at the original trial.[62] The same lack of focus on appeal courts is equally apparent in context studies that evaluate the use of science in the courts and in the writings of forensic science practitioners. Studies of criminal appeals, although they will include consideration of expert evidence cases, do not separate out such cases for particular discussion. This is perhaps not surprising historically in view of the limited number of such cases that have arisen. However it would appear that the number of such cases is increasing.[63] Thus in order to understand the manner in which scientific evidence is reassessed on appeal we undertook our own study. We examined the treatment of this evidence in two high profile appeals: the Birmingham Six appeals in 1987/8 and 1991 and the Maguire Seven appeal in 1991. This required us to obtain copies of the transcripts of the evidence and the *full* judgments of the Court of Appeal, to see how the evidence was presented, and what role it played in the final appeal judgments. These two cases were, as we have illustrated

---

[61] See n. 9 above; the specific references to criminal appeals are at 117–18 and 211–12.

[62] For example, in the Report by Justice and the Council for Science and Society, n. 54 above, despite constant references to Appeal Court cases, no consideration is given to whether any different questions arise in relation to scientific evidence rather than other evidence.

[63] See the Home Office Memorandum to the Royal Commission on Criminal Justice (1991), *Forensic Science Memorandum*, especially at 4.2.

in Chapter 4, very significant in the media and their construction of a crisis of public confidence in criminal justice.

C. TWO CASE STUDIES: THE BIRMINGHAM SIX APPEALS 1987/8 AND 1991, AND THE MAGUIRE SEVEN APPEAL (1991)[64]

These two cases arose out of bombing incidents in Birmingham, Guildford, and Woolwich in 1974 in which twenty-eight lives were lost. The legal responses to what was unquestionably part of the IRA's terrorist campaign in England were the enactment of anti-terrorist legislation (the Prevention of Terrorism (Temporary Provisions) Act 1974) and the attempts to bring the perpetrators to justice. The defendants in the B6 case were tried for charges that amounted to the claim that they were the ones who actually carried out the Birmingham bombings. The M7 defendants were charged with offences of illegal possession of explosives which, it was thought, in some way or other linked them to those who had carried out the Guildford and Woolwich bombings.[65] The principal pieces of evidence at trial[66] in the B6 case were the forensic evidence that showed that some of the defendants had been in direct contact with nitroglycerine (NG) and the confession evidence that followed arrest and detention by the police. Both strands of evidence were strongly contested by the defendants at their trial and at the various appeals, in various campaigns, and through the civil courts. The principal and for all practical purposes sole piece of evidence at trial in the M7 case was forensic evidence which showed that each of the defendants had handled NG, which handling could not have been brought about innocently, i.e. by innocent contamination. The defendants denied this at their trial and appeals, during the whole period of their imprisonment and since their release,[67] the successful appeal in 1991 taking place after their release.

At the B6 trial, Dr Skuse, a Home Office principal scientific officer, gave evidence that, on the basis of Greiss tests undertaken by himself, he was 'Ninety-nine per cent certain'[68] that some of the defendants had been in contact with NG. He also gave evidence that the presence of NG on one of the defendants had been confirmed by tests carried out by Dr Drayton, a Home Office senior scientific officer. However Dr Drayton had not been called as a witness at the trial. Dr Skuse's evidence was challenged by Dr Black, a scientist and former chief inspector of explosives at the Home

---

[64] Hereafter, in this chapter, referred to as B6 and M7.
[65] One of those tried for the actual Guildford bombings (that is, one of the Guildford Four) was the nephew of one of the M7 defendants and the son of another.
[66] The significance of the other circumstantial evidence has remained controversial. Contrast the account of the trial by C. Mullin, *Error of Judgement: The Truth about the Birmingham Bombings* (Dublin, 1997) 175–247, with Blom-Cooper, n. 15 above, ch. IV.
[67] Except for the one defendant who died in prison.
[68] Mullin, n. 66 above, 189.

Office. He questioned the specificity of the Greiss test, and was not satisfied with Dr Skuse's failure to reproduce the positive results when the
samples in question were subjected to other tests. These other tests included
Thin Layer Chromatography (TLC), which is 100 times more sensitive than
Greiss, and Gas Chromatography/Mass Spectrometry (GC/MS), 1,000
times more sensitive. Dr Black was also unconvinced by the single positive
result recorded by Dr Drayton. This result had been produced using a
GC/MS that identifies the atomic masses present in a sample (through the
MS) and reveals these masses at different times for different substances
(through the GC). Of the three masses contained in NG, only one had been
confirmed, although that had occurred at the time expected for NG. This
result was not confirmed by another GC/MS test carried out by Dr Black
on the same sample.

At the M7 trial Mr Elliott, a Home Office scientific officer, gave evidence
that extensive tests on the Maguires' house, which it was claimed was a
bomb factory, had produced no evidence of bulk explosives or detonators.
However, TLC tests on the defendants' hands, under their fingernails, and
on one of the defendant's gloves, had proved positive for NG for each of the
defendants, but negative for other members of the Maguire household who
were not charged with any offences. Mr Higgs, a Home Office principal
scientific officer, and Dr Hayes, a scientific officer, supported Mr Elliott's
interpretation of the TLC tests[69] as proving the presence of NG, and the
incompatibility of these results with any innocent contamination. In reply to
the question at trial: 'from the presence of nitroglycerine under the nails . . .
what deduction or inference does that cause you to make?' Mr Elliott said:
'My assessment of that would be that the explosive containing nitroglycerine had been handled, or, if you like, kneaded, to use the bakery term, rather
than just touched with the hand . . . contamination under the fingernails
does not arise from you touching objects.'[70] Mr Higgs also claimed that the
TLC test was unique for NG. Of the chances that some other substance
might produce positives he said: 'In the real world, they are millions to
one.'[71] Mr Yallop, formerly head of RARDE's forensic laboratory, disputed
this. He believed that an ordinary non-explosive substance in everyday use
(substance x) might exist, which could have produced positives in the tests
carried out. In his opinion, the possibility of substance x's existence, together
with the general circumstances of the case, which made the handling of
explosives by these defendants improbable, made it wrong to conclude that
NG was present on the defendants' hands. He also questioned whether the
TLC test should be relied upon without a confirmation test. Further, along

---

[69] All three scientists worked at the Ministry of Defence's research laboratory at
Woolwich, RARDE (the Royal Armament Research and Development Establishment).
   [70] M7 Appeal transcript of evidence, Friday 17 May 1991, 21.
   [71] R. Kee, *Trial and Error: The Maguires, the Guildford Pub Bombings and British Justice*
(Harmondsworth, 1989), 209.

with Mr Clancy, also a former head of RARDE's forensic laboratory, he was unwilling to rule out innocent contamination through the defendants' handling of something which had earlier been in contact with NG.

It was clearly forensic science that underpinned the findings of guilt at trial in both of these cases; indeed played a pivotal role not only in the trials but also in the investigative processes that preceded them. Then how does the Court of Appeal reassess such scientific evidence on appeal? To what extent is that reassessment *scientific* in nature? In order to examine this process we look first at the basis upon which counsel chose to challenge the scientific evidence at the appeals, and then at how the Court of Appeal treated the scientific evidence.

1 THE BASIS FOR CHALLENGING SCIENTIFIC EVIDENCE AT THE APPEAL

In both cases new scientific evidence (principally tests carried out since the trials) was brought to bear on the former scientific evidence, to question whether that former evidence could any longer support the convictions. In addition, a large proportion of the questioning of witnesses by appellants' counsels addressed the credibility of the scientific evidence presented by the prosecutions' witnesses at the trials. This questioning was directed at a number of discrete issues. A first issue concerned whether there had been *full disclosure* of the scientific evidence at the trials. The issue of full disclosure is complex in relation to scientific evidence because so much scientific knowledge is interdependent. The ideal situation, which is probably impossible to live up to in practice, has been outlined by Ormrod.

It should be the right and duty of experts to exchange their reports before trial and, if they wish, consult together and it should be a rigorous obligation on all experts to give the court, as clearly as they can, the limits of accuracy of their evidence, whether it is experimental or theoretical, and to disclose, if it be the fact, that other views exist in their profession. It should also be their duty to the court, to indicate what inferences cannot properly be drawn from their evidence.[72]

As a part of the difficulty with whether it is possible to live up to these ideals, there is a further practical problem with the obligation of full disclosure. It concerns how well experts are trained in what needs to be disclosed to the court for legal purposes. An example of this can be given from the questioning of Mr Higgs at the M7 appeal.

Mr. Butterfield QC (for the Crown): This morning in answer to Mr. O'Connor you said to my Lords that you had no standards of full and frank disclosure. You agreed with that. I want to understand what you understood by the question and what you thought you were agreeing to.

---

[72] Ormrod, 'Scientific Evidence in Court', *Criminal Law Review* [1968], 240–7, 246.

Mr. Higgs: I thought that by 'standards' you implied that there was some written instruction with respect to how one should present evidence in court, what sort of information one should give in the court and from what point of view. We had absolutely nothing.

Mr. Butterfield: Did you receive any training as forensic scientists about your proper duties in this respect?

Mr. Higgs: Indeed not, no. I was transferred from what was, virtually, a research laboratory straight into the forensic laboratory and left to swim.[73]

There is clear legal authority that failure to disclose information to the defence or the Court can, in some circumstances, amount to a material irregularity (using the Criminal Appeal Act 1968 wording) on the basis of which an appeal against conviction will be successful.[74] The changed wording of the Criminal Appeal Act 1995, which no longer uses the phrase 'material irregularity', does not alter the substantive situation. Now, a failure to disclose can make a conviction 'unsafe'.

The first issue addressing the credibility of the scientific evidence at trial, that of full disclosure, arose in these appeals in the following terms. In the M7 case, did the scientists in their evidence at trial fully disclose to the jury all the tests undertaken and the results of those tests, even those tests that did not appear to support the prosecution case? With respect to the B6 case, did Dr Skuse disclose in full the manner in which his Greiss tests had been carried out? A second issue was that of reliability: were the tests used by the prosecution scientists sufficiently reliable, then, or now? A third issue was that of competence: were the specific tests relied on at trial carried out in a manner, and by personnel, whose competence could be trusted? The common theme which underlies all of these issues is that the jury would not, or might not, have convicted if they had been made aware of the deficiencies of the original scientific evidence.

At the original trials, there had been no pretence that the jury, or even the judge, would be able to pronounce scientific judgement on the dispute between the prosecution and defence scientists. This was well demonstrated in the judge's summing up at the B6 trial.

Members of the jury, the resolution of scientific argument of this sort is difficult, particularly difficult for a jury of lay people, and I say once again that I am not going to try and go into the technicalities in detail because I would be in grave danger of misleading you. The only way that you can resolve these differences is by your impression of the witnesses. Use any technical knowledge that you have, but in the end you will judge it primarily by your impression of the witnesses, and secondly perhaps by a comparison of their relative experience.[75]

---

[73] Transcript of evidence, Monday 20 May 1991, 68.

[74] For examples see *Lawson* (1990) 90 Cr. App. R 107 and *Sansom* (1991) 92 Cr. App. R 115.

[75] Quoted at the 1991 appeal by Lord Gifford, transcript of evidence, Tuesday 12 March 1991, 47.

In other words the trial judge encouraged the jury to worry less about the details of the expert evidence than to decide, on the basis of the witnesses' demeanour and experience, whom to believe. On appeal, the Court could not question the jury's assessment as to which scientist had a superior demeanour at trial, nor would it have been particularly scientific for it so to do. Relative experience might seem more relevant to the question of which expert the jury ought to have believed. However, this would probably put no more than a gloss of rationality upon what, at best, was an irrational trial process.

At the 1991 B6 appeal one of the counsels for the appellants, Lord Gifford, did not limit himself to the implications of new scientific evidence. He offered, as a standard by which to assess the inadequacies of the original scientific evidence, his own version of the summing up that he suggested ought to have been given to the jury.

Members of the jury, you have heard two conflicting interpretations from the expert witnesses of the tests which Dr. Skuse carried out. You may think it right to approach the prosecution evidence on this aspect of the case with a degree of caution. You will bear in mind that there are three tests for the presence of nitroglycerine on hands and no one of the positive tests is confirmed by any of the others. Dr. Skuse suggested a reason, namely that the nitroglycerine had been fully absorbed by the time of the subsequent tests.

Dr. Black, on the other hand, testified that with competent handling that should not have happened. The fact remains that the verification which a careful scientist would wish to find before making a firm diagnosis was not there.

While Dr. Skuse was 99% certain that a positive Greiss test alone was proof of nitroglycerine handling Dr. Black said that other substances might give the same result. While he could not name them with certainty, no one can say that some future scientist might not one day identify a commonly handled substance which could test positively for Greiss.

In the result you may think it right to concentrate your deliberations first and foremost on the evidence that these men made as confessions and not to base your conclusions on the scientific evidence alone.[76]

What this model summing up represents is an assertion that, with the benefit of scientific knowledge, the trial court judge or the jury would have realized that the scientific evidence was fatally flawed and should not have been relied upon. Whilst Lord Gifford may be correct, the Court of Appeal's adoption of such criticism poses considerable problems for the authority and finality of any trial process which relies upon contested scientific evidence. Trial judges are not greatly more able to assess contested scientific evidence than juries. When Mr Justice Bridge in his original summing up refused to sort out the technicalities of the scientific evidence for fear of further confusing the jury, there is no reason (or at least no reason for the

[76] Ibid. 49.

Court of Appeal) to suppose that he was being anything other than genuine. Lord Gifford was in effect proposing that judges should compensate, through the summing up, for the lack of scientific knowledge of the jury. More importantly, where they fail so to do, this should form the basis of an appeal against conviction. In the event, the Court's reaction to this submission was simply to observe that any criticism of summing up had already been dealt with at the original application for leave to appeal in 1974, and that this hearing was, rather, directed at the substantive merits of the convictions. The implication of this reaction is that a review of the substantive merits of a conviction, and a consideration of how the original summing up might have misled (or at least failed sufficiently to assist) a jury, are not the same thing.

This problem arises starkly with respect to the use of DNA (Deoxyribonucleic acid) testing as evidence in a criminal trial. Following the Court of Appeal's decision in *Adams*,[77] the admission of expert evidence by a statistician to help the jury to evaluate the DNA evidence is strongly discouraged. Rather, as suggested in the leading Court of Appeal judgment in *Doheny and Adams*, in which procedures are set out for adducing and interpreting DNA evidence, the trial judge's summing up should give guidance and 'dispel any obfuscation that may have been engendered'.[78] Such a procedure, excluding further reliance on expertise at trial but relying on the trial judge's summing up, has been strongly criticized, such criticism being exemplified in an article in *New Scientist*.[79] The focus of that article is: 'If juries are not allowed to use mathematical theories to interpret evidence and instead have to fall back on their common sense, the wrong people may well end up behind bars.'[80] Since statistical computation is so relevant to the inferences that can be drawn from DNA evidence, withdrawing expert statistical evidence from consideration at trial appears to some writers to be highly questionable.[81]

To return to our case studies, the general reaction of the Court of Appeal to attempts made by appellants' counsel during all these appeals to discredit the original scientific evidence, as represented in their judgments at the end of each appeal, was unsympathetic. This indicates to us that themes such as the extent of disclosure made by the original Crown's scientific witnesses and their general reliability and competence did not form the basis of the Court's reassessment of the scientific evidence.

---

[77] [1996] 2 Cr. App. R 467.

[78] *Doheny and Adams* [1997] 1 Cr. App. R 369, 375.

[79] R. Matthews, 'Tipping the Scales of Justice', *New Scientist*, 13 Dec. 1997, 18–19.

[80] See also the appeal, following retrial, *Adams (No. 2)* [1998] 1 Cr. App. R 377, and the critical comment on that decision by B. Robertson and T. Vignaux, 'Explaining Evidence Logically', *New Law Journal* (Expert Witness Supplement), 6 Feb. 1998, 159–62.

[81] See generally C. G. C. Aitken, *Statistics and the Evaluation of Evidence from Forensic Science* (Chichester, 1995), and B. Steventon, *The Ability to Challenge DNA Evidence*, Royal Commission on Criminal Justice Research Study No. 9 (London, 1993).

Whilst it may have been necessary to question the integrity of the original scientific evidence, it was not, as the reaction of the Court of Appeal shows, sufficient. This is in marked contrast to the approach adopted by Sir John May in his *Interim Report on the Maguire Case*. One of his conclusions, after hearing evidence of the deficiencies (particularly concerning the lack of full disclosure) of the scientific evidence at the M7 trial was that: 'In my opinion it has been shown that the whole scientific basis upon which the prosecution was founded was in truth so vitiated that on this basis alone the Court of Appeal should be invited to set aside the convictions.'[82]

2 THE JURY'S TREATMENT OF SCIENTIFIC EVIDENCE: WHAT TO REASSESS?

In both of these cases the Court of Appeal's reassessment of the scientific evidence was, on one level, more rational than the trial process. Instead of concentrating on the method by which the jury had chosen to accept scientific evidence, it concentrated on the conclusions that the jury may be taken to have accepted, and asked itself whether those conclusions were, in the light of all the available evidence, supportable. The reason why it is not rational to concentrate on the method by which the jury has chosen to accept scientific evidence is because there is considerable doubt as to the ability of juries to understand complex scientific evidence. Not all informed opinion unequivocally supports this proposition, but a lot of it does, particularly in the context of the adversary trial process. For example, in describing a situation of conflicting expert opinion, Regis Professor of Forensic Medicine J. K. Mason takes for granted that 'plausibility essentially becomes not a matter of scientific logic, which the jury cannot understand, but of a combination of many totally extraneous factors.'[83] And of those 'extraneous factors', Phillips and Bowen suggest: 'the jury may erroneously accept an expert witness who has become something of a good advocate for his or her cause, as against the expert witness who remains objective in attitude and dispassionate in manner.'[84] The question at these appeals was thus, quite rationally, not whether the jury for valid reasons accepted the scientific conclusions, but whether those conclusions could now be supported.[85] The

---

[82] Sir John May, *Interim Report on the Maguire Case*, HC 556 (London, 1990), 51.

[83] J. K. Mason, 'Expert Evidence in the Adversarial System of Criminal Justice', *Medicine, Science and the Law*, 26/1 (1986), 8–12, 10.

[84] J. H. Phillips and J. K. Bowen, *Forensic Science and the Expert Witness* (London, 1985), 6. See also S. Shaw, 'The Law and the Expert Witness', *Proceedings of the Royal Society of Medicine*, 69 (1976), 83–9, and L. J. Lawton, 'The Limitations of Expert Scientific Evidence', *Journal of the Forensic Science Society*, 20 (1980), 237–42.

[85] Significantly, we believe that the differences between the conclusions of the Court of Appeal and those of Sir John May in his *Interim Report on the Maguire case* (n. 82 above) are principally based on the differences of approach of the Court of Appeal and Sir John May to

presumed irrationality of the jury's assessment of scientific evidence was built into the appeal process.

In its 1988 B6 judgment, the Court of Appeal concentrated not upon the reliability of Dr Skuse's tests, or his evidence about them, but upon the reliability of his conclusion that some (or definitely one) of the defendants had been in contact with NG. Proceeding on the basis that none of the evidence presented by Dr Skuse was reliable, and relying instead on the evidence of Dr Drayton (who carried out the 1974 GC/MS test but was not a witness at the trial) the Court of Appeal was still able to conclude:

That fact [that the positive Greiss tests were not confirmed by other, more sensitive tests] in the context of the evidence, as it stood at trial, did not persuade the jury that it was in any way unsafe to accept Dr Skuse's conclusion that these two men had been in recent contact with commercial explosives. That fact, in the context of the whole of the evidence, including that produced before us, does not persuade us that there is anything unsafe in accepting Dr Skuse's conclusion.[86]

Much of the appellants' evidence and argument failed to anticipate the Court's ability to separate the conclusions reached by the prosecution's trial experts from the methods by which those conclusions had been reached. Appellants' counsel Mr Mansfield, at both the 1987/8 and 1991 B6 appeals, attacked the reliability of Dr Skuse's methods and, in particular, their failure to meet the criteria of interverifiability, namely the ability of other scientists to know exactly how tests have been carried out in order to satisfy themselves as to their accuracy, and the reasonableness of any conclusions drawn from them. Indeed some form of verification is part of all analyses of what makes for good science or good scientific tests, although it is by no means all that is necessary. As Giere argues: 'It must be possible, at the appropriate time, to verify whether the prediction is in fact true or false. This is required because the truth or falsity of the prediction is going to provide part of the justification for our conclusion concerning the hypothesis.'[87] Armed with this irrefutable standard, Mr Mansfield's assumption seems to be that, once you have shown that the methods of a scientist are unreliable, his results and conclusions are discredited. But the 1988 judgment proceeded on the basis that although Dr Skuse may have been an unreliable witness, who may have repeatedly lied as to his methods,

this issue. For example, Sir John May's conclusions include the following statement in dealing with the survey of hand test kits. 'By itself this may not be a fundamental point, but the evidence clearly supported the alleged exclusivity of the test upon which the Crown case was based, and I feel could well have had an important effect upon the *jury's mind*' (our emphasis, 14.6 at 51).

[86] Transcript of full judgment, dated Thursday 28 January 1988, 162.

[87] R. Giere, 'Justifying Scientific Theories', in E. D. Klemke, R. Hollinger, and A. D. Kline (eds.), *Introductory Readings in the Philosophy of Science* (New York, 1988), 264.

his test results still have to be explained, and the available explanations support his conclusions.[88]

The M7 appeal had a similar thrust. Much of the questioning of the experts about their evidence at trial[89] was directed at the reliability of the TLC tests that had been carried out, or the interpretation of those tests given by scientists to the jury at trial. These tests had indicated that NG was present either on one or both hands or under the fingernails of one or both hands of all of the defendants, or on the plastic gloves of one of the defendants. There was considerable evidence that some of Mr Elliott's scientific views were flawed. First, that Mr Elliott and Mr Higgs had confused the jury about the difference between the extent to which the TLC tests were positive as opposed to specific for NG. Secondly, that some confirmatory tests were carried out which were not disclosed in the evidence, which tests would at least have demonstrated to the jury that the prosecution scientists were less certain about their evidence than it might otherwise have appeared. Thirdly, that with respect to the notorious exhibit 60, the prosecution's scientists had misled everybody. The legal particulars of the charge against the defendants specifically alleged possession of NG. Exhibit 60 was the document that came to light toward the close of the trial. The document suggested that the prosecution's scientists knew all the time that the TLC test used could not specifically identify NG, since NG and at least one other explosive substance, PETN, could not be distinguished by it. Of all the scientists only Mr Elliott seemed to have retained the view, prior to his death, that he could distinguish NG and PETN using the TLC test, and that his personal experience with the test allowed him to do so.[90] None of these alleged deficiencies in the prosecution's scientific evidence or in the competence of the prosecution's scientists either individually or collectively determined the Court of Appeal to decide in favour of allowing the appeal.[91]

As with the B6 appeals the Court of Appeal seems able to separate the scientific conclusions assumed to have been accepted by the jury from the processes by which those conclusions had been reached. The Court of Appeal listens to and admits evidence on the wide-ranging criticisms of the

---

[88]   In some respects this comes close to the movement in modern science known as holism, which insists that 'single hypotheses are never tested in isolation but are always tested as a part of larger complexes or wholes. It thus denies that one can speak . . . about single hypotheses or theories being "well tested" or "confirmed" or even "corrigibly falsified." Holism insists that it is only rather large systems of hypotheses which are open to empirical scrutiny' (L. Laudan, *Science and Relativism: Some Key Controversies in the Philosophy of Science* (Chicago, 1990), 70–1).

[89]   The main scientific witness, Mr Elliott, had died before the 1991 appeal, so questioning was directed to his colleagues and some of it to their interpretations of his evidence and notebooks.

[90]   Because of his death it was not possible to assess his view fully.

[91]   *Maguire* (1992) 94 Cr. App. R 133. The approach taken by the Court of Appeal, as illustrated by its judgment, is clearly different from that of Sir John May, as expressed in the Conclusions to his *Interim Report* (n. 82 above).

scientists involved (their procedures, opinions, and approaches to their responsibilities as witnesses), but, short of evidence of bad faith, is unwilling to respond positively. Without bad faith or dishonesty (rather than inefficiency, mistakes, or economies with the truth) there appears to be a great reluctance to accept that the test results recorded by the prosecution's scientists, and their conclusions, cannot survive.[92] The scientific conclusions accepted at trial retain their pivotal importance for upholding the convictions. And, as a result of this, the possibility of recognizing and enforcing standards for *good science* or for the good scientific witness in a court of law are avoided. To the extent that the appellants' counsels concentrated their reassessment of the expert scientific evidence on the methods, practices, or standards used by the scientific witnesses at trial, rather than their conclusions, they were probably working on incorrect assumptions. It might be that, as far as the M7 appeal is concerned, the experience of counsel at the May Inquiry[93] led them to such erroneous assumptions. Short of bad faith it would appear that the claimed observations of expert scientific witnesses would not be ignored despite evidence of their incompetence as either scientists or expert witnesses. This in turn leads to a discussion of whether the conclusions drawn from those observations were justified.

In principle there is nothing irrational about taking conclusions and seeing whether they are supportable, whether such conclusions are those of a lay person or a discredited scientist. One can be right about something for the wrong reasons. The scientific question is how one goes about deciding whether those conclusions can be supported. What does and does not count as acceptable evidence? In particular, if those conclusions can only be sustained on the basis of scientific evidence, of what does this consist? As the next section will show, the Court of Appeal's separation of the scientists' conclusions from their evidence is a logical precondition for the reassessment of evidence that they have undertaken. So too is their decision not to reconstruct the admittedly irrational processes of the jury. However, their approach to deciding whether the scientific conclusions can be supported in these cases, to a scientist, might well appear to be wholly inadequate and unscientific.

---

[92] With bad faith the scientist's conclusions don't survive, which is what amounted to one of the successful grounds of appeal in *Judith Ward*'s case (1993) 96 Cr. App. R 1. The judgment in that case is remarkable for a number of reasons. It upholds all the grounds of the appeal, it expresses criticism of many of those involved in the original prosecution in strong terms, 'Our law does not tolerate a conviction to be secured by ambush', and it expresses regret to the appellant. The circumstances surrounding the prosecution and those that led to the appeal are also remarkable, see J. Ward, *Ambushed: My Story* (London, 1993).
[93] See n. 82 above.

3 HOW DOES THE COURT OF APPEAL REVIEW SCIENTIFIC CONCLUSIONS?

(i) Theory versus practice

In their review of scientific evidence the Court of Appeal, in both the B6 appeals and the M7 appeal, demonstrate problems of reconciling the theoretical knowledge and methods of the scientific community with forensic practice. This problem of reconciliation, which is never easily overcome, allows theory and practice to diverge. This divergence can reach the stage where the Court accepts the evidence of a practising scientist, rather than evidence of the science upon which her practice is based. This process may be the unavoidable consequence of a legal system that seeks to use science for its own purposes. Nevertheless there is some indication, at least in these cases, that Court of Appeal judges have a bias in favour of matters practical, which can make the divergence between the knowledge and methods of the general scientific community and that of forensic practice more acute.

(ii) Good Science

At the 1974 B6 trial, Dr Hugh Black gave evidence of the cumulative nature of the tests used for NG. As a scientist, he would not have accepted single positives unconfirmed by other tests. Even with the GC/MS test, which is the most sensitive, he would not have accepted a single test, which confirmed the presence of one mass. He wanted all three masses associated with NG to be confirmed. In his evidence to the 1987/8 appeal Dr Black was fairly uncompromising in asserting that the tests which had been carried out were insufficient, and that he did not himself have to carry out such tests in order to reach this conclusion.

Black: it is no good saying to me that this is NG at 46 . . . If a chemist says to me, it is 46; it is no good him saying to me that this is what I've got when I know perfectly well it is not or may not be.[94]
Counsel: So you were coming to these particular tests on the GC/MS tests relatively fresh in experience, is that right?
Black: Well, in the sense you are describing, yes, but I am a qualified chemist and I don't need to have to prove all the facts of chemistry all over again. I could interpret the evidence which is put before me, which in fact I did; just indeed with respect you are doing now.[95]

On Dr Black's view neither the evidence of Dr Skuse, who had none of his Greiss test positives confirmed by any other test, nor of Dr Drayton, who had done only one run and seen a mass of 46 at a time associated with NG, would suffice. The Court of Appeal never accepted Dr Black's view even

[94] Transcript of evidence, Monday 9 November 1987, 72.   [95] Ibid. 52.

though two other scientists at the 1987/8 appeal supported it.[96] And even at the 1991 appeal the Court accepted that the single GC/MS result must mean something, and only rejected it when a plausible innocent explanation was provided. Whilst the 1991 Court formally accepted Dr Black's view on the need for Greiss tests to be confirmed,[97] this was largely lip service; they concentrated on the presence of an alternative explanation for the Greiss test results, rather than rejecting them as inadequate data.

The M7 appeal included a similar question relating to *good science*. Dr John Yallop's view of the TLC test results at trial was that, for a number of reasons, they should not be relied on. One of the reasons was that the TLC test was devised as an identification test rather than as an exclusion test, i.e. it was originally developed in the presence of known explosive material to determine the identity of the particular explosive.[98] In view of the practical adaptation of the TLC test for its use as a test to confirm the presence of explosives, Dr Yallop's scientific opinion was that the TLC test should not be treated as reliable without confirmatory tests and/or corroborative evidence. At trial the jury were told by the scientific witnesses for the prosecution that the samples were not large enough to allow for confirmatory tests to be carried out either by TLC but using a second eluent, or by using an alternative test. Even in the 1991 appeal after it had become clear from the questioning that adequate samples did exist so that confirmatory tests were possible (and some had been done but not disclosed to the jury), the Court of Appeal was not willing to readdress Dr Yallop's view. The practical outcome of the original tests was upheld. The conclusion that the TLC tests identified NG (very probably), but if not, then PETN (another explosive substance), was allowed to stand, since no experimental tests had contradicted it, even though the scientific values of accuracy and objectivity were thereby devalued. New evidence of possible innocent contamination by NG was accepted as the only basis for overturning the convictions. 'On the ground that the possibility of innocent contamination cannot be excluded and *on this ground alone*, we think that the convictions of all the appellants are unsafe and unsatisfactory . . .'[99]

(iii) Forensic practice

At the 1987/8 B6 appeal, the Court of Appeal upheld the convictions. One of the key ingredients in its decision was its acceptance of the evidence of Dr Drayton, who conducted the original GC/MS test. Dr Drayton was recognized to be a sincere witness, who could be relied upon to conduct

---

[96] Dr Brian Caddy and Mr David Baldock.

[97] 'Although the Greiss test is no longer in use, the better view has always been that it was no more than a preliminary screening test subject to confirmation by some other test' (the B6 judgment, *Richard McIlkenny and others* (1991) 93 Cr. App. R 287, 300).

[98] See the discussion on pp. 205 and 207 below.

[99] *Maguire*, n. 91 above, 152–3 (our emphasis).

tests in a competent manner. She gave evidence that she was satisfied that a mass of 46 coming through her machine at 4.2 minutes was consistent with NG and no other material, and that none of the suggested reasons why a false positive might be recorded had occurred. How could the Court of Appeal prefer this evidence to that of Dr Black, Dr Caddy, and Dr Baldock, that this one test result was an inadequate basis upon which to be satisfied as to the presence of NG?

The Court of Appeal's approach was to favour practical considerations over theoretical and methodological ones.[100] In its judgment the Court of Appeal state that 'there are no grounds at all for questioning' the accuracy of Dr Drayton's observations.[101] This, at first glance, seems something of an overstatement, given the evidence of three other scientists that they would not have been satisfied with identification based upon this one test result. But the Court supports this statement with two practical devices. First, with its observation that Dr Drayton had greater familiarity with the machine used to carry out the test than did other scientists. She knew it, they said, 'like one's own car'.

We have no doubt that Dr. Drayton was the real expert on GC/MS. She was a very impressive witness and commonsense tells us that despite the views held by Dr. Caddy and Dr. Baldock there are no grounds for questioning the retention times of 4.2 minutes fixed by Dr. Drayton for NG on her machine on 27th November 1974.[102]

The second way in which the Court justifies relying on Dr Drayton's evidence is to place on the other scientists the burden of explaining what the test result represents, if the substance tested is not NG. By demanding an alternative plausible answer the Court displaces good scientific practice: the fact that other scientists would not be satisfied with this basis of identification. Whilst the scientists can adduce some practical explanations for the result, these are dismissed on the basis of insufficient evidence before the Court. In the absence of such explanations, the only correct scientific answer to the question 'what else is it if not NG?' is 'I do not know'. But, with the reversed burden of proof, such an approach is not sufficient to conclude that Dr Drayton's evidence is unsafe. Mr Mansfield describes this process in his address to the Court of Appeal in the 1991 B6 appeal:

The problem that it appears has faced Dr. Black in the first place and Drs. Caddy and Baldock in the second, is that they are scientists with, if I put it this way, immaculate theory. They are right, but because they have not been able to produce an example, the court, in a sense has turned its back on that.[103]

This emphasis upon practical considerations, coupled with a reversed

---

[100] Their approach in this respect duplicates much of what occurred at trial.
[101] Full judgement transcript, n. 86 above, 155.
[102] Ibid. 155.
[103] Transcript of evidence, Monday 4 March 1991, 59

burden of proof, allows the divergence between scientific theory and methodology and forensic practice to become acute. The 1987/8 and 1991 B6 appeals provide a number of further examples of this.

Example 1. In 1987/8 the Court is asked to discount the Greiss test results, in view of the failure to provide positives for TLC and GC/MS (100 and 1,000 times more sensitive respectively). Dr Black, in his appeal evidence, takes a rigorous view of the need for scientists to retain enough of a sample from one test to allow for retesting with more rigorous tests: 'I have to assume that Dr. Skuse is a competent chemist. I have to assume that he stores his samples properly. I can't ask him: "Look, did you do your job properly?" That is not a question I can put to Dr. Skuse. I assume that he did, just as he must assume I did.'[104] This approach contrasts with that of the Court of Appeal which accepted that forensic scientists may not have enough of a sample to retest it, given delays, repeated handling, and deterioration due to other substances present in the sample tested. It asks whether it is possible for sufficient NG to disappear to make confirming tests impossible, and are assured by Dr Thomas Hayes, a forensic scientist, on the basis of his practical experience, that it is.

Lord Chief Justice: Would the evaporation or decomposition rate be greater or less if there were adventitious material in the sample?
Dr. Hayes: My experience tells me it would be very much greater . . . I know that because in the course of very many analyses I have experienced just the situation I describe, in other words, where a known extract, a real world extract, which I have examined by thin layer chromatography, and when attempting to carry out subsequent confirmatory tests I have had difficulty in identifying further residues when the sample has been spoiled through a period of time.[105]

In their judgment, the Court accounted for the lack of confirmation on the basis that the quantities of NG were too small, given all the circumstances of their handling by the forensic service, to be confirmed by the more sensitive tests.[106] The underlying reasoning appears to be that, if forensic practice makes good scientific standards impossible to apply, it is the standards that have to give way.

Example 2. The preference for practice over theory applied not only at the 1987/8 appeal, where the convictions were upheld, but also to the use of science in the 1991 appeal, where they were quashed. Dr John Lloyd had conducted tests to see what might produce a mass of 46 when passed through a GC/MS. Various substances were found to produce this mass at times similar to that recorded for NG. This evidence invited the Court to repeat the approach taken in 1987/8 and at the trial, which was to enquire whether any of these identified substances had been in contact with the

---

[104] Transcript of evidence, Monday 9 November 1987, 78.
[105] Transcript of evidence, Wednesday 18 November 1987, 71.
[106] Judgment transcript, n. 86 above, 161.

appellants. The possibility that an unknown substance might produce this result had been put to Mr Baldock at the 1987/8 appeal.

Lord Justice Stephen Brown: If it could not have been nitrocellulose, could it have been anything other than nitro-glycerine?
Mr. Baldock: I do not honestly know. There are an awful lot of organic nitro compounds. I cannot eliminate the possibility that somewhere, out of the many thousands, that one of them would produce a retention time of 4.2 and would give that particular fragment.[107]

In their judgment this was described as part of a process of thinking of 'every conceivable theoretical possibility for questioning those results'.[108] Now contrast the 1991 approach. In the course of identifying materials that produced similar reactions to NG in the GC/MS, Dr Lloyd had found that an unknown substance in a swab taken from a smoker had produced an identical result. The Court of Appeal described this particular result as 'crucial'.[109] It provided the concrete example of what in 1987/8 had been described as a 'theoretical possibility': that there is an unidentified substance that could produce an identical result in a GC/MS to NG.

(iv) In defence of practice over theory

Although the Court of Appeal appears to exhibit a preference for practical experience and plausible explanation over general qualifications and theoretical possibilities, this does not mean that it always prefers *bad practice* to *good science*. There are questions on which the less qualified person, with greater experience, is better able to express an opinion than the more qualified person whose understanding of the area is through his general theoretical knowledge.[110] To put this in an extreme way, there are questions that the laboratory assistant is better able to answer than the professor. Consider for example the effects of different strengths of caustic soda on the sensitivity of the Greiss test, one of the major areas of dispute in the B6 appeal. A person like Dr Skuse, who regularly does such tests, and periodically alters the strength of the caustic soda, is better able to express an opinion on the likely consequences of those changes on the sensitivity of that test than a better-qualified chemist like Dr Black. Here is a relevant extract of evidence, from Mr Mitchell (for the Crown) examining Dr Black on his knowledge of the tests carried out by Dr Skuse.

Mr. Mitchell: The position then is that at this trial in June and July of 1975, you did

---

[107] Transcript of evidence, Wednesday 11 November 1987, 19.
[108] In response to an answer given by Mr Baldock under cross-examination, see judgment transcript, n. 86 above, 154.
[109] See n. 97 above, 302.
[110] The proposition that a less eminent expert's evidence may be preferred because of his or her practical involvement in the issues of the case has old legal authority; see *Brock v Kellock* (1861) 3 Giff. 58.

not appreciate the significance of the alkali concentration and the use of a solvent in relation to the sensitivity of the test.

Dr. Black: I had no reason to appreciate it one way or the other at that time.[111]

The Court of Appeal is only obviously wrong to prefer the evidence of someone like Dr Skuse (assuming he is a competent forensic scientist) if one of two conditions apply. First, if the only evidence that counts as *scientific* is based not on experience but on tests that can be reproduced.[112] Whilst this may be an ideal within science, it is not a practical proposition within general science, let alone within forensic science, for the samples are not always available (and this standard also ignores the role played in science by interpretation). The second basis on which the Court would be clearly wrong to prefer the evidence of the more experienced witness is where the superior experience of the preferred witness is not directly relevant to the question that needs to be addressed. To use an example from the B6 case: the experience of the relative sensitivity of Greiss tests is not relevant because they cannot be relied upon by themselves, and the sensitivity of the tests required to confirm them is greater by such a magnitude that precise knowledge of the parameters of Greiss is simply not relevant. However, if in most situations it is not possible to dispense with experience in favour of something thought of as *pure* science, the Court of Appeal is left with a crucial question. How, without being scientists themselves, do judges in the Court of Appeal know when the experience of the scientist before them is relevant, or superior, to others?

4 THE COURT OF APPEAL'S VIEW ON THE ROLE OF THE
   SCIENTIST AT COURT: SCIENCE IN CONTEXT?

At the 1976 M7 trial one of the key scientific witnesses for the defence, Mr Yallop, was severely criticized by Sir Michael Havers, the prosecuting counsel, for his scientific approach. He was accused of stepping outside his role as a scientist by taking the factual context into account when giving his opinion on the conclusions that could be drawn from the prosecution scientists' tests. This was said to be 'taking into account non-scientific matters'. These included the absence of any explosive being found in the Maguires' house, the use by only one of the defendants of gloves, and the bizarre pattern of comings and goings from a house in which the defendants were engaged, according the prosecution, 'all hands to the pump'[113] in disposing of the explosive material. At one level, the criticisms directed at Yallop make some sense. In interpreting scientific results, one should not think about other facts that might point towards the guilt or innocence of the

---

[111] Transcript of evidence, Monday 9 November 1987, 58.
[112] What Mr Mansfield described as the principle of interverifiability; see p. 196 above.
[113] Sir Michael Havers, quoted in R. Kee, n. 71 above, 200.

accused. The danger is all too obvious. Facts that point to the guilt of the accused may result in scientific tests being interpreted more readily as proof of guilt, so that the scientific evidence in question loses its objectivity. However, good scientific practice does not allow scientific results to over-whelm all other factual evidence.[114] To put this another way, the less consist-ency there is between the conclusions indicated by test results and other data, the more suspiciously one should look at one's test results. So, although Yallop was accused of acting unscientifically, he was in fact acting, on one level, in a highly scientific manner. There is clearly a choice for scien-tists in postulating their scientific statements as the truth, or as a pos-sible/probable interpretation/understanding of it. Such a choice goes to the heart of considerable debate in the philosophy of science.[115]

At the 1991 appeal the Court was asked to adopt Mr Yallop's approach: to reassess the scientific evidence in the light of other evidence; to be scep-tical about the probity of the scientific evidence in the light of the improb-ability that the defendants could have undertaken what the scientists claimed their tests indicated (that because NG had been found under their nails they must have been kneading bulk explosive). But the Court was not being offered a simple choice between a scientist who insisted on placing science in context as against scientists who insisted upon forming opinions without reference to the surrounding facts. Indeed it emerged at the appeal that the Home Office scientists had not been as indifferent to the context of the evidence they had given at trial as it had previously appeared. Evidence on this emerged during the cross-examination of the Home Office forensic scientist Dr Hayes, who was forced to admit that RARDE might alter the acceptable parameters of a test for NG, depending on how the sample in question was labelled. So, for example, test results for a sample taken from the scene of an explosion would be interpreted differently from a sample taken from a suspected bomb store, on the basis that the first sample requires an answer to the question, 'what explosive has been used?' whilst the second requires an answer to the question, 'is explosive present?' What Dr Hayes's cross-examination reveals is not that RARDE scientists were unscientific, but simply that the evidence that they had given to the jury simplified the processes by which their conclusions were reached. They, like Mr Yallop, were altering their interpretation of test results in response to surrounding data. They were simply not prepared to go as far in this as Mr Yallop was prepared to do.

At appeal, the Court was thus not being asked to choose between scien-tists who take context into account and those who do not, but to judge which of them had formed the correct view of the relationship between test

---

[114] This is certainly the case with Bayesian probability reasoning. See C. Howson and P. Urbach, *Scientific Reasoning: the Bayesian Approach* (Chicago, 1993).
[115] See, e.g., the essays in Part 4 of Klemke *et al.* (eds.), n. 87 above.

results and the general context, or, to put this another way, between the objective evidence, and the interpretation they gave to it.[116] As such, it is not perhaps surprising that the Court was not prepared to adjudicate on the appropriate contextual (Bayesian) approach to the scientific evidence.[117] The Court was spared from having to form such a judgment by the results of new scientific tests that showed that the contamination did not require contact with bulk explosive.

In our judgement the Crown's case that all the Appellants must have been knowingly handling bulk explosive was highly improbable. But the force of these criticisms in relation to the finding of NG largely, if not entirely, disappears on the hypothesis that there was a primary source of contamination of NG in the house and that some, if not all, the Appellants may have been innocently contaminated by it.[118]

We cannot know for sure whether the Court would have rejected the prosecution's scientific evidence on appeal solely on the basis of its inconsistency with other evidence. However, we have considerable doubts as to its ability, or willingness, to do this. For a start, the Court of Appeal's judgment deals separately with the 'non-scientific' and the 'scientific' evidence, whereas Mr Yallop's point (and the point implied by the evidence of RARDE's practices) is that this divide is not necessarily scientific. What is clear from the Court's treatment of Mr Yallop's evidence is that, regardless of its attitude to the need to put scientific evidence in context, this is not something that it feels needs to be put to a jury. Part of the M7 appellants' case was that RARDE forensic scientists had failed to reveal their own doubts as to the specificity of the TLC tests. Some of this evidence related to their failure to disclose the need to eliminate PETN, another explosive substance, which the Court felt able to dismiss on the basis that the exact identity of the explosives, although relevant to the precise charge, was not important to the justice of upholding a conviction for possession of explosives. But other parts of this evidence related to the prosecution's failure to reveal its own uncertainty about whether TLC tests might produce positives from *innocent* substances, and the tests it had carried out to investigate such possibilities, even as the trial was proceeding. As with the B6 appeals (discussed above), the Court of Appeal's approach was not to ask itself whether the jury formed its opinion of the forensic issues on the basis of good scientific evidence, but whether its conclusions could now, in light of all the scientific evidence, be supported. The Court of Appeal quashed the M7 convictions solely on the basis of new tests, which showed that the prosecution scientists' conclusions were unsupportable (that innocent contamination was incompatible

---

[116] See R. F. Coleman and H. J. Walls, 'The Evaluation of Scientific Evidence', *Criminal Law Review* [1974], 276–87, 287.

[117] See, as one of many examples of this approach, M. O. Finkelstein and W. B. Fairley, 'A Bayesian Approach to Identification Evidence', *Harvard Law Review*, 83 (1970), 489–517.

[118] M7 appeal full draft judgment, dated 26 June 1991, 43.

with NG under suspects' fingernails).[119] In reaching their decision the Court of Appeal seemed to indicate that the relevant question in the M7 appeal was, like that in the B6 appeals, not whether the jury were misled by the original evidence, but whether the conclusions offered to the jury by the prosecution remained supportable. The implication is that, as far as the Court of Appeal is concerned, the jury need not be made aware of the contextual factors which influence a scientist's interpretation of test results. The image of a pure scientist emerges as the model scientific witness. Such an image is a fiction disguising the complex reality whereby scientific evidence is produced, interpreted, and communicated to a court.

5 How does the Court of Appeal approach changing science?

> There was material available to me which suggested that in the 14 years or thereabouts since the convictions scientific knowledge and experience in the relevant fields had developed substantially. (Sir John May)[120]

Science moves on but the stages of that movement are often uncertain and can involve detailed and complicated controversy. The issue at the M7 trial was primarily about questioning the reliability of the TLC tests that proved positive in the case of each of the defendants. The prosecution's forensic science evidence was based on the claim that these tests were reliable and that the choice of one particular TLC test was uniformly reliable. It also depended on the suggestion that it was neither possible nor appropriate for the forensic scientists to undertake confirmatory tests at the time. The prosecution evidence further claimed that the TLC test was specific or, if not specific then at least positive[121] for NG or another explosive substance. It also relied on an explanation[122] that innocent contamination could not produce these test results. Moenssens, Inbau, and Starrs state: 'Thin-layer chromatography, (TLC), is a rapid, inexpensive and sensitive method which is widely used to identify traces of explosives in extracts from the debris from an explosion scene . . . TLC, being primarily a separation technique, should be used prudently and cautiously, in the identification of compounds.'[123] Evidence on appeal confirmed that the general attitude of

---

[119] See the final sentence of the M7 appeal judgment, quoted in the text at n. 99 above.

[120] *Interim Report*, n. 82 above, 1.6 at 2.

[121] Much of the evidence at the appeal dealt with whether, and to what extent, answers by the prosecution's forensic scientists were misleading in that they confused the issue of whether the test was specific for NG, with whether it was positive for NG (but also positive for some other explosive substances).

[122] It is best described as an explanation or perhaps an interpretation since it was clearly not based on detailed experimental work or knowledge prior to the trial.

[123] A. E. Moenssens, F. E. Inbau, and J. E. Starrs, *Scientific Evidence in Criminal Cases* (New York, 1986), 145.

the scientific community to the overall reliability of the TLC test as an exclusion test lessened during the period between the original M7 trial and the 1991 appeal. New more sensitive tests were used such as Gas Chromatography[124] and later, High-Powered Liquid Chromatography. The importance of some confirmatory tests became more generally recognized and new procedures made the use of confirmatory tests (either a different test, or the same test but using different solutions) obligatory, as a matter of good scientific practice. The difficulty of demonstrating at any given time what is and what is not within the bounds of good scientific practice becomes clear during the cross examination of Dr Hayes, at the M7 appeal. The value or otherwise of confirmatory tests, even what confirmatory tests may or may not confirm, is, in this area of science, a complicated issue. Science does not necessarily develop scientifically. Consider Dr Hayes's answer to a question about how the standard of 200 nanograms for determining whether a positive for NG would be recorded came about: 'It came about historically because some time prior to my joining the laboratory that was actually the limit of detection. As techniques improved so the detection level was lowered to about 100 nanograms in 1974 and it has dropped considerably lower since that time.'[125] Nevertheless the standard did not change, so that only results which were as strong as those produced by a 200 nanograms control sample would be recorded as positives.

Some of the appellants' new evidence consisted of an attempt to show that the original basis of conviction was unsound, due to diminishing faith in the specificity and reliability of TLC. The issue of specificity remained a difficult question throughout the 1991 appeal. The TLC test was demonstrably not specific for NG, although, like Dr Skuse's persistent attitude to the Greiss test, Mr Elliott might, if alive, have continued to argue that from his personal practical experience he could show that it was. The Crown throughout the appeal insisted that TLC was specific for a limited number of explosives. They discounted two other possibilities. The first is the speculation that TLC might react identically to the molecular structure of a non-explosive substance. Secondly, that specificity is made even more problematic by the possibility that some of the other explosive substances, apart from NG, might have non-explosive uses and therefore people might come into contact with them apart from their use as explosives. Indeed, one non-explosive use of NG, in a heart tablet, was tested by the Crown, but found to have insufficient NG to produce a TLC positive. In cross-examination, Dr Higgs was referred to his testimony before Sir John May's Inquiry:

(Q) Mr. Higgs, would you not agree that in the circumstances of this case confirmatory tests should be taken on the TLC plates?

---

[124] Indeed most laboratories had the gas chromatograph available and were using it at the time of the trial, but the Woolwich establishment did not.
[125] Transcript of evidence, Wednesday 22 May 1991, 46–7.

(A) There was no reason at all at the time to consider a confirmatory test. In hindsight it may be acceptable and perhaps this is so but at the time we did this test there was no means of doing so or grounds for doing so.[126]

There is no indication in the Court of Appeal's judgment that changing scientific knowledge or practices are, by themselves, likely to alter its view of the safety of a conviction. The fact that scientists would not, today, conclude with the same certainty that NG had been present solely on the basis of one TLC test is not referred to in the judgment. Again, the focus is on whether the original scientific conclusions can be supported. The basis for concluding that they cannot be is, as with the B6 appeals, not an acceptance that the original evidence was insufficient, but the presence of new tests that show how, and why, those conclusions might be wrong.

The Court of Appeal's approach has something to recommend it. If every improvement in the standards required from expert witnesses at trial made every conviction obtained through the earlier use of lower standards automatically unsatisfactory, this would either deter the use of scientific evidence or the improvement of standards or both. Not only would such a conclusion be unwelcome, but it is also unnecessary. For one has to ask what the improvements mean in terms of the reliability of the earlier evidence. The answers to this question may range along a spectrum. At one extreme new standards in the circumstances of the case in point may simply indicate that the scientific evidence at trial was slightly less credible than was originally believed. At the other, the earlier evidence may form a wholly unsatisfactory basis for conviction. The problem for the Court of Appeal is to locate the particular change in standards along this spectrum. Simply telling it that today's scientific community would no longer give evidence on the basis of yesterday's tests provides it with an insufficient basis upon which to tell whether a conviction is safe or not.

6 How does the Court of Appeal respond to uncontested science?

At the 1991 B6 and M7 appeals, the new scientific evidence included agreed reports that the Crown did not wish to contest. In these circumstances, the scientists who prepared those reports were not subjected to the usual process of cross-examination. In both cases, the Court expressed disquiet at this. In the B6 judgment, the Court stressed the importance of an adversarial system that exposed witnesses to cross-examination:

We doubt that there is a better way of exposing the weaknesses in a prosecution case, whether the witness be a policeman, scientist or bystander, than by cross-examination. . . . [But] for an adversarial system to work, there must be an adversary. One of

---

[126] Transcript of evidence, Friday 17 May 1991, 13. A confirmatory test was in fact carried out, which proved negative, but was not disclosed to the jury.

the difficulties in the present appeal has been that we have listened to the fresh evidence of Dr. Scaplehorn and Dr. Baxendale without the benefit of hearing any cross-examination ... [T]he effect of [the Crown's] decision [not to contest the appeal] was, inevitably, that we have not heard the other side put, if indeed there is another side.[127]

In the M7 appeal judgment, the Court's concern was apparently even greater. They had felt the need to undertake some of their own cross-examination of scientific evidence, even though significant questioning by judges pursuing their own lines of enquiry is actually contrary to the adversarial process.

Indeed it had been suggested by counsel for both sides that we should simply read [Professor Thorburn Burns's] report as containing his evidence. However ... we considered that there were a number of questions which were raised which required to be investigated before we could properly discharge our responsibilities ... In so doing we were obliged to adopt a more interventionist approach than is usual or desirable in our adversarial system of justice. However, such is the inevitable consequence of the present procedure where the Crown do not contest an important issue, unless we are to relinquish our responsibility.[128]

Unless the evidence of scientists is subjected to cross-examination, the process of appeal is relinquished to other bodies than the Court, namely the prosecution service and the scientists. Within the adversarial process, as we have stressed in Chapter 2, cross-examination forms an essential part of the technique whereby *legal truth* is established. It allows the scientist's view of what is relevant to the issue of guilt to be challenged. Without it, scientists can identify what is required to establish whether appellants may have been wrongly convicted. The Court's attempt to challenge a scientist's view of what is relevant to the question of guilt, and its frustration at the lack of an adversarial process, is well illustrated by the Court's interrogation of Dr Hayes at the M7 appeal.

At the M7 appeal, the agreed new scientific evidence was a compilation of work carried out before 1982 and more recent scientific tests. Mr Higgs, one of the prosecution's witnesses at trial, had in 1982 been one of four scientists to publish a paper confirming that (in contradiction to the evidence he had given at the M7 trial) innocent contamination could lead to the presence and persistence of NG samples under the fingernails.[129] The more recent tests were undertaken at the instruction of Sir John May. He appointed an analytical chemist, Professor Thorburn Burns, to review the relevant literature and to undertake relevant experiments.[130] Professor

---

[127] *Richard McIlkenny and others*, n. 97 above, 312–13.

[128] Full draft judgment, n. 118 above, 31.

[129] J. D. Twibell, J. M. Home, K. W. Smalldon, and D. G. Higgs, 'Transfer of Nitroglycerine to Hands during Contact with Commercial Explosives', *Journal of Forensic Sciences*, 27 (1982), 783–91.

[130] Sir John May said of Professor Thorburn Burns work: 'Without it, I could not properly or fully have completed this part of the Inquiry' (*Interim Report*, n. 82 above, 3).

Thorburn Burns's research was presented to the Court of Appeal as an uncontroversial piece of new scientific evidence. Having read this evidence, the Court attempted, through their own questioning of Dr Hayes, who had conducted one of the original tests on Mrs Maguire's gloves, to explore an alternative conclusion to that reached in the agreed report. Could the amount of explosives found on the hands of each of the M7 appellants undermine the conclusion that some or all of them had been innocently contaminated?[131]

Lord Justice Stuart-Smith: You said yesterday . . . that you were struck by what you saw on those plates . . . If the contamination resulted from handling a towel you might expect a varying level but not if they were all handling explosives . . . You were struck, as I understand it, here by what apparently was a high and consistent level of contamination.
Dr. Hayes: That is right, yes.[132]

This line of questioning (whether the amounts and pattern of positive results was better explained by something other than innocent contamination) was followed up by the Court asking a further fourteen questions, and subsequently taken up by the Crown in their re-examination. In response to counsel for one of the appellants, who declared his disquiet at these questions, the court felt compelled to justify its intervention.

Because the Crown has taken the attitude that it has, it has fallen to the court to have to investigate these matters, at any rate to the extent that we understand properly what we are doing, we understand the nature of the evidence, the inferences which are to be drawn from it and that we can properly come to the conclusion at the end of the day, that the convictions are unsafe and unsatisfactory . . . We have to explore the thing [the hypothesis of innocent contamination] so that we understand what the position is.[133]

The difference that a full cross-examination might have made to this new scientific evidence is illustrated by Professor Thorburn Burns's response to questioning at the May Inquiry. Because Dr Hayes questioned the relevance of some of the findings of Professor Thorburn Burns's experiments to the facts of the M7 case, Professor Thorburn Burns was asked (particularly by the Crown's counsel) to extrapolate from his specific findings to an interpretation of the test results in the M7 case. Professor Thorburn Burns's position, which may have appeared obstinate, but was clearly *scientific*, was to refuse to extrapolate. His tests proved the possibility of innocent

---

[131] Professor Thorburn Burns's scientific evidence contained five conclusions, the fourth of which was that 'NG contamination at the levels expected to have been reported as "acceptable positive" from a communally used hand towel is a distinct possibility, but presupposes the presence in the house at some stage of at least one person who had significant contact with nitroglycerine' (The May Inquiry, News Release, 1 June 1990).
[132] Transcript of evidence, Wednesday 22 May 1991, 47.
[133] Ibid. 66.

contamination, but not whether there was in fact innocent contamination in the M7 case. As he makes clear: 'I was just asked to look at a possibility and a possibility was looked at. If someone wished to finance a whole new research, I would be delighted to do it.'[134]

The questioning of Professor Thorburn Burns illustrates how easy it is, by cross-examination, to show the gaps in experimental data and use those gaps to cast doubt on the whole of a scientist's evidence. But this is exactly what is so problematic about expert scientific evidence. It suggests certainty, but, if it is good scientific knowledge, cannot be stated as certain. All interpretations need careful qualification. Professor Thorburn Burns consistently recognized the limits of his experimental data and was unwilling as a scientist to extrapolate beyond it. As Dr Hayes admitted, the approach that the Court of Appeal wished to explore at the appeal involved the scientist in 'playing detective': 'I well recall a situation at Sir John May's Inquiry where I ventured to suggest a point and was told, in no uncertain terms "not to play the detective"! Where the line is drawn between detection and forensic science, I am at rather a loss to determine.'[135]

7 MISREADING THE COURT OF APPEAL

As we have tried to illustrate, the approaches identified by our case studies have their own institutional logic. If an appeal court hearing is not a retrial, it must seek to uphold the conclusions of a trial court whose procedures are neither unusual nor unacceptable. If the jury are not expected to understand the processes by which scientists reach their conclusions, there is little point in simply re-examining those processes on appeal. The Court, quite rationally, looks to the conclusions that the jury are understood to have accepted to see if those conclusions can stand. This is part of a wider process whereby the Court concentrates on the verdict, to see whether, on the basis of all the available evidence, this can be upheld.

By concentrating on conclusions, rather than the processes that produced those conclusions, the Court avoids having to retry the scientific evidence. The fact that the defence would, by the time of a much later appeal, be able to damage or even demolish the prosecution evidence at trial is not, as our case studies show, necessarily sufficient to justify quashing the conviction. And this applies even in cases where scientific evidence was crucial to the prosecution's case at trial. Asking scientists to provide plausible alternative and innocent explanations for evidence accepted at trial operates as a reversed burden of proof and in subjecting their explanations to cross-examination increases the difficulty of discharging that burden. In doing this, the Court insulates the jury's verdict from the consequences of scien-

---

[134] Transcript of evidence to the May Inquiry, Monday 4 June 1990, 129.
[135] Transcript of appeal evidence, Wednesday 22 May 1991, 70–1.

tific reassessment of the scientific evidence provided at trial. Changes in scientific standards, proof that the tests used would not meet with the approval of the wider scientific community, and even discrediting the professional reputation of original witnesses is not necessarily sufficient to justify quashing a conviction.

Writing of the B6 appeals Blom-Cooper argues for the need to educate the public into the constitutional and evidential considerations that inform the Court of Appeal's practices.[136] He believes that this is necessary in order to diffuse media and public perceptions that high profile miscarriage of justice cases represent failings in the criminal justice process, especially within the Court of Appeal. The logic of his position is that any person charged with the responsibilities of the Court of Appeal, who understood the need for and nature of deference to the trial court's role, would adopt practices similar to the Court of Appeal. In our view, although Blom-Cooper's arguments have logical force, they underestimate the strength of the alternative understandings that the media use and promote as to the nature of miscarriage of justice.[137] When the original prosecution case is destroyed, it is difficult to convey the processes by which the Court of Appeal has nevertheless managed to sustain the conviction.

In the context of appeals involving scientific evidence, there are, we would claim, even greater difficulties for the Court of Appeal in sustaining its relationship of deference to the jury. The media look to the scientific community for facts and truth. Whilst law insists that scientists cannot pronounce on the guilt or innocence of the accused at trial, the media respect no such boundaries when they focus on cases where a miscarriage of justice is suspected. When scientists insist that the evidence that is believed to have led to the conviction of an appellant was fatally flawed, the media are likely to conclude that the *conviction is* fatally flawed, i.e. the appellant should, at trial, have been acquitted, and is innocent. On this basis, they also expect the Court of Appeal to confirm the appellant's innocence. But cases where science can demonstrate to the Court of Appeal's satisfaction that the appellant was innocent (that innocence is the only conclusion consistent with the known facts) are rare. This conclusion did arise in Stefan Kiszko's successful appeal[138] and also that of Patrick Nicholls in 1998. The reporting on the latter appeal uses the description 'one of the gravest ever miscarriages'. His conviction for murder was, twenty-three years after that event, overturned because the pathologist's evidence on which it was primarily based was, in the light of new scientific evidence, thought to be deeply flawed. The victim had actually died of natural causes, so no crime had been committed by anyone, let alone

---

[136] See n. 15 above. We have discussed this argument in section A of Ch. 4.
[137] See our analysis throughout Ch. 4.
[138] See the description of Stefan Kiszko's appeal, and the reporting of it, in section E/4 of Ch. 4.

Patrick Nicholls.[139] This conclusion, that innocence is the only consistent interpretation of the known facts, does not follow from the reassessment of the scientific evidence in the B6 and M7 cases. Hence the continuing difficulties experienced by the successful appellants who remain concerned that they have not cleared their names. Despite the severe challenges to the scientific evidence in the B6 1987/8 appeal, the convictions were upheld. Some scientists and some in the media regarded both the scientific evidence and the Court of Appeal's judgment as seriously deficient. And even when the B6 convictions were quashed and those of the M7 following the introduction of new scientific evidence in 1991, the Court's judgments appeared, according at least to many in the media at that time, to be grudging and minimal, with the Court still seeming to fail to recognize the tattered state of the original prosecution cases. Whilst the Court subjects appellate evidence, including scientific evidence, to a reversed burden of proof, the media provide the Court with another reversed burden of proof. Since the original evidence at trial is no longer considered *scientific*, can the Court explain, to the satisfaction of the media, why the original conviction is safe? Blom-Cooper assumes that, with sufficient explanation by lawyers, this task can be accomplished. We, by contrast, doubt that this can be done. This makes the Court's constitutional practice, especially in cases involving the re-examination and reassessment of scientific evidence on appeal, likely to generate the conditions for fresh crises of confidence, in the role of the Court of Appeal, in the future.[140]

Our analysis of the Court of Appeal's approach to reassessing scientific evidence on appeal can be restated in terms of autopoietic systems theory, which has informed it. The Court of Appeal is not a panel of scientific experts. It is a court of law; it has a given history, certain powers, procedures, rules, and approaches, and it has its rhetoric. It is not a court of first instance. It has a relationship with the trial and the jury that we have described as deference. It has a role to play within the system of law, not apart from it. It works with rules that are systematically organized to uphold the authority of law for the purposes of achieving legal judgment. An example is the common law rule referred to at the beginning of this chapter, which disallows putting to an expert witness the actual question that the jury needs to decide. Legal authority is constructed through ideas which allow for law's closure,[141] the finality and workability of its prac-

---

[139] See 'Innocent—after 23 Years in Jail', *The Guardian* 13 June 98 (Duncan Campbell). In a later article in *The Guardian* on the same day, 'Mistake Led to 23 Years of Regret' Duncan Campbell and John McManus offer a narrative explaining how this *mistake* could have arisen. However, a more sinister interpretation is suggested in the same newspaper a few days later by Paul Foot, 'The Sussex Mystery', 16 June 98.

[140] We believe that recent decisions by the Court of Appeal trying to come to terms with the complexities and controversies surrounding DNA evidence are a good example of this potential. See p. 194 above.

[141] In systems theory terms, it's normative closure.

tices, against the openness of its operations to its environment,[142] which has the potential to threaten that authority.

At the level of the trial, forensic evidence is an application of science and as such, inevitably, a misreading of science,[143] but one that offers law (with the appearance of support from the authority of science) an apparently greater likelihood of *rightful* conviction. At the level of appeal the misreading of science is more dynamic. To the outside world a miscarriage of justice based on new scientific evidence can easily be interpreted as proof of innocence. On rare occasions this is the only consistent conclusion, as demonstrated by, for example, the Kiszko and Nicholls cases.[144] Even in these circumstances, in law, the conclusion of these cases was that the convictions were no longer 'safe'. But, if one looks at other cases, indeed most cases where scientific evidence is reassessed on appeal, the appellants remain disappointed with the result that, even though they may have succeeded in the appeal, their innocence has not been proved.

D. LEGAL AUTHORITY AND INVESTIGATION: THE CRIMINAL CASES REVIEW COMMISSION

1 INTRODUCTION

The previous sections in this chapter were organized around consideration of the relationship between legal and scientific authority, particularly as that relationship impacts on the process of appeal. The criminal law relies on science as evidence for the purposes of its own operations. The Court of Appeal is called upon in individual cases to assess the acceptability of that reliance, and to do so not scientifically, but in a manner which upholds the role and authority of the criminal process, the jury, and itself. There are two standards operating here. Problems can arise when those standards are perceived to be in conflict, or at least to challenge each other. Invariably in a court of law it is legal authority that will prevail, but at a potential cost. That cost is likely to include criticism from other actors, whether scientists, investigative journalists, or politicians. The Court of Appeal is a legal authority whose processes are structured in a self-referential way to answer legal questions, and with a general responsibility to uphold the legitimacy and the claimed benefits of legal authority. Faced with any conflict with scientific authority it may be less successful in legitimizing legal authority at the end of the twentieth century than it appeared to have been at the beginning.

---

[142] In systems theory terms, it's cognitive openness.

[143] In systems theory terms, the misreading of the true/untrue binary code of scientific discourse by the legal/illegal or acquittal/conviction binary code of law's construction of criminal justice.

[144] See p. 213 above.

A second challenge to legal authority is that associated not with the dictates of science but with other methods of inquiry into facts relevant to convictions. Such methods are less constrained than legal method, less rule-bound and procedurally sensitive, but nevertheless parasitic on legal authority. Such a challenge was in the past represented by the powers of the Home Office to direct investigations into alleged miscarriages and, as a consequence, on occasion to authorize a formal pardon or to refer the conviction back to the Court of Appeal to undertake a further appeal. In extreme cases a conflict between these authorities based on a different method of work became significant. Indeed, in the Luton post office murder case the Home Secretary referred Cooper and McMahon's appeal back to the Court of Appeal on four separate occasions, on each of which the Court turned the appeal down. Finally the Home Secretary on his own authority released the prisoners and issued a pardon.[145]

A major change almost universally supported in evidence to the Royal Commission on Criminal Justice and enacted in Part II of the Criminal Appeal Act 1995 was the creation of a new body to direct investigations into and refer alleged miscarriages of justice on to the Court of Appeal. Such a body might answer some constitutional problems associated with the activities of the Home Office and the Home Secretary, but it does not eradicate the potential conflict between legal authority and the practices of open investigation. But perhaps this new authority, an 'executive Non-Departmental Public Body'[146] independent of the Home Office, can diffuse the conditions that generate periodic perceptions that criminal justice is in crisis, which the activities of the Home Office, appeared not to be able to do?

2 THE CRIMINAL CASES REVIEW COMMISSION

The Criminal Appeal Act 1995 removes the power of the Home Secretary (administered through the Criminal Cases Unit, formerly C3 Division of the Home Office) to investigate and refer convictions to the Court of Appeal under section 17 of the Criminal Appeal Act 1968.[147] The Act transfers this task to a new authority, the Criminal Cases Review Commission, made up of lawyers and lay members.[148] The new body also has the final say on who can be pardoned, although responsibility for deciding whether someone's case should be investigated with a view to offering a pardon still lies with

---

[145] See B. Woffinden, *Miscarriages of Justice* (London, 1987) chs. 6 and 7, and L. Kennedy (ed.) *Wicked beyond Belief: The Luton Murder Case* (St. Albans, 1980).

[146] Criminal Cases Review Commission handout, Introducing the Commission.

[147] Section 3.

[148] With a composition of at least eleven members, at least one-third being legally qualified and at least two-thirds having 'knowledge or experience of any aspect of the criminal justice system' (s.8).

the Home Secretary.[149] There appears to have been a unanimous view that such an alternative body should be set up, although little unanimity of view about its powers and responsibilities. The reasons for this unanimity are various, but the underlying reason is probably that related by Chris Mullin MP in 1992: 'Sir David Napely told the Home Affairs Select Committee, in 1982, that he was not aware of any miscarriage of justice that had been corrected as a result of an initiative by the C3 department. I do not know if much has changed in the ten years since that remark.'[150]

Reformers were looking to the new body to act in at least three ways that were different from C3 Division and the Home Secretary. First, in its investigative role, they wanted it to have greater resources so as to become more proactive. There is some possibility of this, since undoubtedly the Commission does have greater resources than C3 Division.[151] However much depends on the burden on the Commission resulting from the number of petitions that it receives. In view of the short period of the Commission's operation, it is difficult to estimate what the number of petitions is likely to be year to year, after the early years of its operation; nevertheless we give the current figures later in this section. Previous experience suggests at least 700 annually.[152] Concern has been expressed, however, that the responsibility of the Commission to decide whether to refer sentences to the Court of Appeal (s. 9(1)(b)), as well as convictions (s. 9(1)(a)), might lead to the Commission being overwhelmed by petitions. A second hope, also related to its investigative role, is that the Commission would adopt a less sceptical view towards claims of police and prosecution malpractice. However, its similar reliance on the police to undertake all large or routine investigations makes any increase in such scepticism unlikely. Throughout the (fierce) debates in Parliament, the Government sternly resisted proposals that investigations, apart from those involving expert opinions or tests, should be carried out directly by the Commission's staff rather than the police, even in those cases where serious allegations of police misconduct were being alleged. The Commission was only left with the responsibility for determining what should be investigated, and the limited right to reject the appointment of a particular police officer as investigating officer.[153] The Government's view relied heavily on the Royal Commission's conclusion that there was 'no practical alternative to the police carrying out the investigation'.[154] The practical effect of changes to the Bill's provisions that came about following amendments moved during debates in the House of Lords

---

[149] Section 16.
[150] C. Mullin, 'D. N. Pritt Memorial Lecture', *Socialist Lawyer*, Spring 1992, 17.
[151] See sections 19–22.
[152] The *Runciman Report*, n. 1 above, ch. 11, para. 23.
[153] See the speech of the Home Secretary Michael Howard, moving the Second Reading of the Bill, HC Deb. vol. 256 cols. 26–7, 6 March 1995.
[154] The *Runciman Report*, n 1 above, ch. 11, para. 28.

was clarified by the Parliamentary Under-Secretary of State for the Home Department during the final stages of the Bill's passage through Parliament.

The Government has no intention of funding a team in the commission whose job would be to operate as a mini police force, duplicating work which could, and should, be done by the police or other public bodies . . . I have made it clear that we do not envisage the commission carrying out large-scale investigations. We envisage its doing investigative work from time to time but, generally, the right people to investigate will be the police or other bodies.[155]

The third hope was that the Commission might be staffed by persons who, through their knowledge of criminal justice or other specialist knowledge, and their commitment to preventing miscarriages of justice, would take a more robust approach than C3 Division and the Home Secretary in referring cases to the Court of Appeal.[156] One needs to question that assumption, namely whether such a body, however staffed, could help to introduce or maintain a robust approach and thereby encourage a *liberal* attitude by the Court of Appeal to miscarriages of justice.

The Royal Commission based its recommendation to set up an independent referral body 'on the proposition, adequately established in our view by Sir John May's Inquiry, that the role assigned to the Home Secretary and his Department under the existing legislation is incompatible with the constitutional separation of powers as between the courts and the executive'.[157] The Royal Commission felt that the Home Secretary's desire (as a member of the executive) not to be perceived to interfere with the role of the judiciary was leading to a reluctance to exercise the power of referral, and to the prerogative of mercy falling into disuse. Being more 'independent of the Government' than the Home Secretary, the new body was expected to take a more proactive role. Although the Royal Commission sought to avoid a problem of conflict between executive and judicial authority, it may have failed sufficiently to consider the condition that this conflict led to. Since the creation of the Court, the evidence suggests preponderantly that the Home Secretary has not sought to challenge the authority of the Court but, quite the contrary, has been dominated by the Court. Home Secretaries have principally sought to anticipate the Court's likely approach and only to refer cases that have a good chance of success. Although this deference may have been caused by the Home Secretary's awareness of the constitutional problems of challenging the Court's authority, the fact that the new

---

[155] HC Deb. vol. 263 cols. 1371–2, 17 July 1995. For an alternative view and approach see Justice Report, *Miscarriages of Justice* (London, 1989), 68–73.

[156] The deficiencies of the former practice of referrals under section 17 Criminal Appeal Act 1968 are summarized by M. Tregilgas-Davey, 'Miscarriages of Justice within the English Legal System', *New Law Journal*, 141 (1991), 668–70 and 715–17. *Runciman Report*, n. 1 above, gives the figures of referrals for the years 1989–92 in ch. 11, para. 6: '3 in 1989, 7 in 1990, 10 in 1991, 8 in 1992'.

[157] See n. 1 above, ch. 11, para. 9.

body is not part of the executive does not, by this fact alone, make it willing to challenge the Court's authority. Indeed, the Royal Commission was quite clear that the Court should continue to carry out its present constitutional role: 'we do not see the Authority as coming within the court structure. Nor, equally importantly, would it be empowered to take judicial decisions that are properly matters for the Court of Appeal.'[158] The Government had explicitly accepted this view in rejecting the call in the Sixth Report from the Home Affairs Committee Session 1981–2, *Miscarriages of Justice*, to establish an independent review body outside the court system. 'As a matter of constitutional principle it should primarily be for the courts and the judicial process to review convictions and, if necessary, upset them.'[159] The decision not to constitute the Commission as a Court is, we would argue, not simply a political expedient but almost a logical necessity. No body can undo a legal determination of conviction, to *unconvict* as opposed to excuse through a pardon, except another legal body. Any such legal body, which appropriates the functions of the Court of Appeal, becomes the Court of Appeal. It is in these terms that we approach the many proposals to create a 'Court of Last Resort'.[160] If the Court is to be left with the judicial role and powers, what is a non-court body, with equivalent powers to the Home Office's C3 Division, likely to achieve? Why are investigations supervised by a quango likely to result in a more productive relationship with the Court of Appeal than a government department? Indeed why should constitutional factors have made the Home Office reluctant to exercise its power to investigate claims of miscarriage? Investigation as opposed to adjudication, at least in our adversarial system, is not seen as a court function. From 1907 until the 1960s reforms, the Court had this power, but rarely exercised it. And since then until the 1995 Act came into operation, it did not even have the power to carry out or direct others to carry out investigations. The original power to direct others to investigate can be found in section 9(d) of the Criminal Appeal Act 1907. The 1960s reforms resulted in this power being, by implication, repealed, since the then new statutory provisions did not include it. However, we can find no reference in the Parliamentary debates as to the reason why it was not included. We surmise that this was because it was never used. The

[158] Ibid., para. 15. [159] HC 421 (London, 1982), para. 7.
[160] See, e.g., C. Mullin MP, n. 150 above; Sixth Report from the Home Affairs Committee Session 1981–2, n. 159 above; Justice Report, *Miscarriages of Justice*, 1989, n. 155 above; P. O'Connor, 'The Court of Appeal: Re-Trials and Tribulations', *Criminal Law Review* [1990], 615–28; P. Thornton, A. Mallalieu, and A. Scrivener, *Justice on Trial: Report of the Independent Civil Liberty Panel on Criminal Justice* (London, 1992). An attempt to establish an independent review body was formally defeated after debate in the House of Commons on 16 June 1988, by 121 votes to 45, on an amendment to the Criminal Justice Bill then before Parliament. Some proposals mix the idea of an independent review body and the Court of Appeal. See, e.g., Lord Scarman's proposal to set up a 'court of review' with a Law Lord as its president: 'Section 17 Must be Repealed', *The Times* 26 Nov. 91.

power is now re-established by section 5 of the 1995 Act, in that the Court of Appeal can direct the Criminal Cases Review Commission 'to investigate and report to the Court'.

The reason for the Home Office's tardiness to investigate was, we suggest, apart from its lack of resources, that it saw no point in making investigations where the basis of enquiry was to form a different opinion from that reached by the Court. There was no point in gathering evidence that simply allowed an investigator to reach a different opinion from the trial court if there was no likelihood that the Court of Appeal would adopt a similar approach, and share that opinion. In particular, what was the point of forming a different view of the merits of evidence that had already been considered by the Court of Appeal, which had then upheld the conviction? In the Home Office Discussion Paper, *Criminal Appeals and the Establishment of a Criminal Cases Review Authority* (1994), the justification for this approach is clarified.

Given that the courts will remain the ultimate arbiters of the safety of convictions, it would be inappropriate for the Authority to refer cases purely in order to express disagreement with conclusions which the courts had reasonably drawn on previous occasions from evidence and argument fully and properly exposed to them. To do so would suggest that the Authority was seeking itself to act as a kind of higher appellate court, and the courts would be placed in an invidious position in responding to the reference.[161]

The only alternative to curtailing investigations in anticipation of their reception by the Court was to embark upon investigations and to make referrals in order to put pressure on the Court to alter its procedures or conclusions. And it is here that the constitutional aspects of the relationship enter. Such a procedure would create a potential challenge to the Court's legal authority. If the Court repeatedly rejected Home Secretary referrals, the media could adopt one of two positions: the Home Secretary and Home Office were incompetent in forming their judgment of what appeals were likely to succeed, or the Court's procedures for assessing appeals was flawed.

It is not surprising that the Home Secretary and Home Office were reluctant to expose themselves to charges of incompetence, or of seeking to usurp judicial functions. With responsibility for maintaining law and order, there may even have been some awareness that widening the basis of appeals would threaten the criminal justice process's ability to deliver convictions. Changing to a quango eliminates some of these constitutional factors. But is there really an alternative role for a referral body other than one of deference? While a quango is not so directly a Government body, it

---

[161] At para. 42. References cannot be made unless 'an appeal against the conviction, verdict, finding or sentence has been determined or leave to appeal against it has been refused' (s. 13 (1)(c)).

is still not a court, and runs the risk, if it challenges the legal authority of the Court of Appeal, of being accused of incompetence, or seeking to influence a judicial function. In defending itself against the latter charge, it lacks the political authority of the Home Office. The Court may feel far freer to criticize unsuccessful referrals from a body with less authority. As such, a quango may actually feel less able to refer hopeless cases, and put pressure on the Court, than did the Home Office and Home Secretary. When the Commission sends a case on to the Court it will have undertaken an investigation and will have expended some energy. The new Commission will wish to avoid a general perception that such expenditure was wasted and that it is failing. In terms of reputation and consequent repercussions this is an area of law and politics in which failure is a sanction.

In the Criminal Appeal Act 1995, the subordination of the new Commission to the Court of Appeal is set out clearly. Under section 13 the Commission shall not refer a case to the Court of Appeal unless it considers that there is a 'real possibility' that the Court of Appeal will quash the conviction. It is not given an authority to undertake an independent assessment of lurking doubt, or to assert its own view of what procedural errors are unacceptable. This is so even though the enquiries that the Commission directs an investigating officer to undertake are solely for them to decide, as long as they are reasonable (s. 20 (1)). Instead, it is given a parasitic standard, to refer only those cases which, unless exceptional (s. 13 (2)), will meet the Court of Appeal's unarticulated standards of what constitutes a miscarriage of justice. It has also been signalled by the word 'real' to err on the side of caution in deciding what to refer to the Court. Mere possibilities are not enough, only 'real' ones will suffice. Whilst neither are objective standards, any response to 'real possibility' at least increases the Commission's ability to avoid censure for appeals which the Court pronounces as hopeless.

Even if the subordination of the Commission were not set out in the Act, it would, as with the Home Secretary and C3 Division, have arisen from the need to refer cases to the Court for convictions to be quashed. So it is interesting to note that the first period of the Commission's existence resulted in a number of cases being referred, all of which were successful when the appeal was heard by the Court of Appeal.[162] The transfer of cases from the Home Office to the Commission had been completed by 31 March 1997 and thereafter the Commission started its work. The Commission's first annual report covered its workload up to 31 March 1998.[163] That Report gave the following statistics about alleged miscarriage cases: '284 transfers and 1,096 new cases had been received; 308 had been completed, including twelve referred to the relevant courts of appeal; two appeals had been heard

[162] Five referrals resulting in five successful appeals up until November 1998.
[163] Criminal Cases Review Commission, *Annual Report 1997–98* (18 June 1998).

and had been successful.' Although it is unclear from the Report, the suggestion is that a good proportion of the caseload completed refers to cases deemed ineligible. The gradual build-up of cases and the priority given to transferred cases meant that, 'intensive review' of new cases had only begun in forty-nine cases, with five 'referred to the courts' and thirty-eight 'still under review'. Eight hundred and fifty-one cases were awaiting review. The Report highlights the disparity between the number of cases requiring review and the availability of staff to undertake such reviews. In the circumstances it argues that approximately a doubling of the staff of case-managers would be required to meet the demands of the average of 4.4 new cases per day being received.

The First Report of the Home Affairs Committee of the House of Commons, Session 1998–9, into The Work of the Criminal Cases Review Commission[164] brings the statistics on the Commission's first annual report more up to date. Of the 2,325 cases received by the Commission, 282 had been transferred to the Commission from the Home Office and Northern Ireland Office, with 2,043 being new applications from April 1997 to February 1999. Some 1,727 had been deemed eligible for review, with 170 still awaiting assessment for eligibility; 1,428 of the 1,727 were still under consideration, 259 had been rejected and 40 referred to the Court. Twenty-seven cases referred to the Court of Appeal had not been decided by the Court, 10 had been successful (8 convictions quashed, 2 sentences reduced) and 3 unsuccessful (2 convictions and 1 sentence appeal).[165]

Just as there appeared to be universal support for the setting up of such a body, so there seems to have been nearly universal commendation for the work it carried out in its first year.[166] The House of Commons Home Affairs Committee, in considering nearly two years of the Commission's work, has supported these views. 'We note the good start which has been made by the Commission and its staff in respect of those cases which it has examined, particularly as regards the professionalism, independence and openness which it has brought to bear on its work.'[167] And when the Court of Appeal quashed the first conviction referred to it by the new authority, that body, it was reported in the press, was described by the Court as a ' "necessary and welcome" body without whose work the injustice might never have been identified'.[168] The same newspaper report accepted, without criticism, the Court of Appeal's claim that justice could be delivered provided that 'all concerned . . . observe the very highest standards of

---

[164] HC 106, 23 March 1999.   [165] Ibid. vi.
[166] *The Independent* 30 March 98 'Justice will be done: In just a year, the Criminal Cases Review Commission is beginning to convince defence solicitors that it means business' (Grania Langdon-Downs); *The Guardian* 21 March 98 'Justice Watchdog Gets Favourable First-Year Verdict' (Duncan Campbell).
[167] See n. 164 above, ix, para. 19.
[168] *The Guardian* 25 Feb. 98 'Seaman wrongly Hanged in 1952' (Duncan Campbell).

integrity, conscientiousness, and professional skill'. Thus, although doubts linger about some cases, the creation of the Commission has assisted the press in general to report without scepticism as to criminal justice's ability to achieve its rhetorical aims, namely justice.[169] But how long will this last?

3 WHERE THE COMMISSION IS STARTING TO FAIL

So far there have been two unsuccessful appeals against conviction following referral by the Commission to the Court of Appeal. These rejections did not result in significant publicity. The press did not interpret these unsuccessful referrals as evidence of any failing by either institution.[170] The thesis we present in this book anticipates that, at particular times, the press response will be critical and will be linked to other 'serious deficiencies'.[171] Meanwhile, the Commission is already beginning to be criticized for its failure to refer cases, and the delay in making referrals. Cases deemed inapplicable for referral already exist, and the response of the media to them is an indication of the tentative nature of the willingness of some commentators to accept the new remedial system's operations. To illustrate this we will refer to press coverage of the Commission's decision not to refer Winston Silcott's appeal from his murder conviction of Anthony Smith to the Court of Appeal. It should be remembered that Winston Silcott, as one of the Tottenham Three, had already had one conviction for murder, that of PC Keith Blakelock, quashed on appeal.

In his article in the Saturday Review of *The Guardian* on 28 November 1998 Jeremy Hardy discusses Winston Silcott's case and the decision by the Criminal Cases Review Commission not to refer it back to the Court of Appeal. He demonstrates serious doubts about the conviction and thereby his serious doubts about the Commission's decision. From the premise that its decision is wrong comes his critique of the Commission's approach. The Commission has decided that the Court of Appeal would not believe the witnesses who support Silcott's appeal based on self-defence, and that their

---

[169] See n. 166 above. The same can be said for the current work of the Court of Appeal itself. Some of its judgments are being commended in the press, particularly its willingness to make robust statements on quashing convictions, such as statements of apology. See our comment on the recent use of apology by the Court in section D of Ch. 6.

[170] In the Home Affairs Committee Report, n. 164 above, two cases are noted from the Commission's second year of operation in which referral has resulted in convictions being upheld. These are the cases of Clovis Gerald (November 1998) and Graham Walker (January 1999). Following these rejections by the Court, neither case has featured significantly in the press.

[171] See as an example the article by Bob Woffinden, 'Why the Wheels of Justice Grind so Slowly' in *The Times* 30 March 99. In that article Woffinden refers to Walker's case (n. 170 above) but without criticism. However, in reviewing the Commission's work Woffinden implies serious deficiencies in the practices of criminal justice which might 'make them [miscarriages] more likely'. He even makes one tentative argument that 'the commission's mere existence may be helping to create miscarriages'.

evidence would in any case not be admitted as new evidence. Hardy, who believes the evidence, claims that the Commission is wrong in failing to make a reference, and criticizes the Commission for seeking to anticipate the Court's decision. As a sign of things to come, Hardy describes the Commission as a 'quango' and expresses the view that 'The Home Office's C3 department, which the commission replaced, was in some ways preferable.' A newspaper article by Paul Donovan had anticipated such a criticism. In making this criticism Donovan quotes the former Secretary of State for Scotland as to why such a quango should not be set up for Scotland, namely that referral decisions should be subject to Parliamentary scrutiny and accountability.[172] Hardy's frustration with the Commission is not due to its failure to investigate. The Commission has found the relevant witnesses, and explored the new defence (self-defence) which differed so radically from the one advanced by Silcott at trial (I was not involved in the assault). If this defence and evidence had been put to the jury at the original trial, it might have been believed. Hardy wants Silcott's new defence to go to the Court of Appeal, on the basis that the Court might believe it. He perceives a definite reluctance by the Commission to refer cases on this liberal basis, and he may well be right. The Commission is likely to anticipate the Court's response. It might well doubt the willingness of the Court of Appeal to quash convictions (and to order retrials) whenever there is an argument or piece of evidence which, had it been put to the original jury, might have made a difference to the outcome. However, neither the reasons for the Court's reluctance nor the Commission's anticipation of it are a satisfactory basis for the Commission not referring cases or for the Court rejecting them, at least to some members of the press.[173]

The advantages of the Home Office identified by Hardy and Donovan go straight to the conditions that generate high profile miscarriages of justice. The Home Office, through Parliament, can be subjected to political pressure. Despite its constitutional difficulties, it can be forced to refer cases that have little or no hope of being accepted by the Court. As such, it can be forced to recognize as miscarriages cases that those responsible for maintaining the legal system do not see as *exceptional*. In her oral evidence to the Home Affairs Committee Gareth Peirce, a solicitor with wide experience of miscarriage cases, makes this point.

Curiously, the Home Office, faulty as it was, would sometimes make that quantum leap on the basis that possibly the CCRC now would not, where it had very little to go on but, for some reason or another—and it may have been a reason dictated by other kinds of pressures—nevertheless the Home Office, possibly because of its lack of resources, would sometimes refer cases where then the preparation for the appeal revealed far more and totally justified the reference.[174]

---

[172] *The Guardian* 7 Aug. 96 'Cold Comfort for Victims of Injustice'.
[173] See our analysis of the views of Woffinden and Hill in section C of Ch. 6.
[174] See n. 164 above, 1.

The exceptional aspect of such cases, and we would remind the reader of the significance of the epithet 'exceptional' in the reasoning of the Court throughout its history, has little or nothing to do with legal processes. They are identified as such, extra-legally, when journalists and other campaigners take a different view of the guilt of the defendant than that of the original jury. Whilst the Home Office may have been reluctant, as a political body, to interfere with the legal system, its constitutional inclinations could, given sufficient pressure, be overcome. Hence one could have the spectacle of the Luton post office murder case being referred to the Court four times. By contrast, the Commission, as a 'quango', is not subject to the same political pressures as the Home Secretary. Nor, in those cases where there is concern in the media about the safety of the conviction, does it have the same political clout if it refers such a case to the Court, only to have the case rejected and its own judgment questioned. And the likely basis of such criticism will be that it has misunderstood the meaning of s. 13 (1), and failed to restrict itself to cases with a 'real possibility' of success. Whilst the Home Office and Home Secretary could be accused of bringing politics into law, the Commission was at least spared the accusation that it was legally incompetent.[175] The major substantive recommendation of the Home Affairs Committee Report is that a formal review of the wording of the test of referral (s. 13 (1)) should take place after five years of work by the Commission. They make this suggestion because, despite admitting that there have been too few cases investigated to make such an assessment, they conclude that 'there may be problems with the statutory test laid down in the Criminal Appeal Act 1995.'[176] Once again the need to change the statutory formula emerges as the potential solution to the long-standing perceived problem of how to create effective remedies for miscarriages of justice.

The work so far undertaken by the Commission points to the difficulties it faces, and the kinds of criticisms that it can expect. Whilst being complimented for its 'meticulous' investigations, which have resulted in a small number of successful referrals to the Court of Appeal, it is beginning to be criticized for the serious and developing backlog of cases awaiting review, and the times such reviews are taking.[177] Indeed the Home Affairs Committee Report describes the 'present situation in respect of delays' as

[175] A criticism made by Louis Blom-Cooper in *The Guardian* 1 Dec. 98, in his response to Hardy's article. However, Silcott's solicitor Adrian Clarke defends Hardy against this charge, concluding: 'Lawyers should be cautious about criticising journalists who take the trouble to elucidate serious concerns about the way the law is framed and applied' (*The Guardian* 13 Feb. 98 'Silcott Solicitor Quashes Opinion on Legal Commission').

[176] See n. 164 above, x, para. 24.

[177] The Home Affairs Committee Report, n. 164 above, says: 'we are concerned about the growing backlog' (xx, para. 72) and 'we believe it ought to be possible to process most cases with greater speed than is presently the case' (xxi, para. 75). For developing criticism of the Commission, see Bob Woffinden's article 'Justice Delayed' in *The Guardian* 6 Oct. 98.

'unacceptable', and 'deteriorating'.[178] As Hardy's response demonstrates, those who look to the Commission to improve on the Court's record for rectifying miscarriages of justice do not expect this backlog to be removed by a process that leads to the majority being rejected. Those who are impatient with the delay would like the Commission to lower its standards of investigation and its threshold for referral. In her oral evidence to the Home Affairs Committee, Gareth Peirce expressed concern, to which the Committee gave some support, that 'the CCRC is substituting itself for the Court of Appeal and in effect having to make a judgement on the case itself.'[179] In other words, that the interpretation that it is giving to its responsibilities of investigation in order to satisfy the standard of only referring cases to the Court where there is a 'real possibility' of a successful appeal, is too demanding. More cases should be referred, and more of the groundwork should be left to those preparing the cases for appeal. But with at least four new cases arriving each day, such a policy would create tremendous pressure on the Court of Appeal. If the Court was unwilling to expand its workload dramatically, or maintain its tolerance of referrals which did not fit the Court's standards for quashing convictions, criticism of the Commission by the Court could be expected to follow. The Commission occupies an uncomfortable position between the Court and the media.

The Commission's chairman and the Home Affairs Committee have called for more resources and extra funding has been announced,[180] but how are these resources likely to be used? Will they result in an increase in the speed with which the Commission can demonstrate (to the parties and the media) the reasonableness of rejecting cases? Or will they result in an increased number of referrals to the Court? Probably both. But the ratio of the two outcomes is unlikely to satisfy those who look to the Commission to correct the Court's poor record of quashing convictions on appeals based on issues of fact. If the Court's standards of what is exceptional and what constitutes new evidence continue to be high (and unless the Court in turn is to be overwhelmed, they must be high), the threshold adopted by the Commission will either disappoint the Court's critics or lead to a conflict between the Commission and the Court. In such a conflict, the Commission could be expected to lose, not least because the Commission's case for further increased resources will be undermined if the Court criticizes it for exceeding or misunderstanding its jurisdiction.

The need to avoid clashing with the Court of Appeal also goes some way to explain the reason for delay. The Court is reluctant to substitute its opinion for that of the original jury, and this reluctance is particularly acute in

---

[178] See n. 164 above, xiii, para. 36.

[179] Ibid., x, para. 26 and see p. 224 above.

[180] See n. 164 above, xvi–xviii, paras. 51–8. The Report comments that further additional resources will be required beyond the additional resources already announced.

cases where there is no new evidence. This makes it difficult for the Commission to act on the basis of a review of the cases brought to its attention. Rather than rely on doubts generated by its assessment of the original evidence at trial, or evidence already considered by the Court of Appeal, it is likely to seek new evidence. To avoid confrontation with the Court, it is driven to move beyond a process of review, to one of investigation. By trawling back through police and court files, it can hope to come up with evidence which, even if not sufficient to succeed, will at least head off the appearance of an outright disagreement with conclusions reached in earlier judicial proceedings. The need to do this must inevitably lead to delays and expense.

The pressure to seek new evidence also creates difficulties for the Commission in knowing how to focus its resources. How does one prejudge the likely outcome of further investigation? The weakness of the original evidence may indicate that a small amount of new evidence might prove sufficient to quash the verdict. But a complete reassessment of the process of trial and investigation is a time-consuming and expensive exercise. This is likely to push up the threshold for assessing what is a weak case, worthy of further investigation. There is a danger that the press will form different judgements of which cases are prima facie worthy of further investigation than the Commission. There is also likely to be a difference of opinion over the scope of such investigations. And if the Commission is to realize its potential as an alternative to investigative journalism, as a body that will assist the hundreds of prisoners who do not attract press attention, it must not allow its agenda for investigations to be set by the media. It has to defend its own authority.

This is not to say that the Commission cannot undertake valuable work on behalf of those who have been wrongly convicted. The present arrangements do allow for successful appeals when there is cogent evidence not available at trial. The history of many of the high profile cases is one of extraordinary efforts to find that evidence, motivated by a belief, even in the absence of such evidence, that the prisoners should never have been convicted. For those who cannot enlist journalists, family, or friends to undertake such investigations, the Commission offers some hope, and will result in some successful referrals that would not otherwise occur.

Our analysis of these two developments (the increasing reliance on scientific evidence and the establishment of a new investigative and referral body, the Criminal Cases Review Commission) is that they will not diffuse the conditions that generate high profile miscarriages of justice. In the case of scientific evidence, the authority of science may actually increase the media's willingness to put the *irrational* procedures and judgments of the Court of Appeal on trial. In the case of the new Commission, this quango may serve to deflect media criticism from the Court to itself, but is unlikely to maintain media confidence in itself as a body capable of remedying high profile miscarriages of justice. Our reading of the future that is likely to result from these changes follows a pattern identified in the history of criminal appeals in Chapter 3, and our analysis of media reporting in Chapter 4: a perceived reluctance of the institutions responsible for remedying miscarriages of justice, which has the potential, in high profile cases, to generate a media construction of criminal justice in crisis. In the next chapter, we attempt to articulate our general conclusions on the nature of appeals within criminal justice and their relevance to attempts at institutional reform: that miscarriages of justice, within a routinely imperfect criminal justice process, represent an inescapable tragic choice.

6

From understanding miscarriage of justice to reform

I realize I am a voice crying in the wilderness, but I believe that the innocent are convicted far more frequently than the public cares to believe, and far more frequently than those who operate the system dare to believe. An innocent person in prison, in my view, is about as rare as a pigeon in the park.[1]

We wish to debate with what we called in the introductory chapter to this book the rationalist tradition of law reform. This is the tradition that sees changes in criminal justice, including the creation and reform of the Court of Appeal (Criminal Division), as a progressive solving of problems and an increase in the ability of criminal procedures to convict the guilty and acquit the innocent. When this tradition seeks to utilize miscarriages of justice in order to promote appropriate reform, it argues that the reforms sought will reduce miscarriages of justice. We wish to consider the extent to which and manner in which legal reforms can prevent miscarriages of justice, and remedy the perception of crisis, especially a perception of crisis constructed in the media, which high profile miscarriages can produce. The history of miscarriages of justice in the twentieth century is told within the law, in appeal cases, and the various statutes that set out the changing arrangements that apply to such appeal cases. But this history is also told in the media, in their interest in some appeal cases and the campaigns that surround them as newsworthy, and in their construction of some cases as high profile. Although the rationalist tradition of law reform may draw on materials from the media, in presenting arguments about appropriate reform, it does not analyse the media's relationship with law. As such, it fails to consider the implications of the media taking the rhetoric of law's construction of criminal justice seriously. We would argue that it is not enough simply to note that the media generate pressure for change. One also needs to consider the implications of such pressure if, as we have argued in Chapter 2, the rhetorical values of law's construction of criminal justice cannot be expressed in its practices, and the demands of a media which accept them (even, or perhaps especially, in an altered form) are potentially insatiable.

---

[1] The Reverend James McCloskey, quoted in M. Yant, *Presumed Guilty: When Innocent People are wrongly Convicted* (New York, 1991).

A. *TRAGIC CHOICES*[2] ANALYSIS OF THE IMPETUS TO REFORM MOTIVATED BY HIGH PROFILE MISCARRIAGES OF JUSTICE

The trial judge, Mr Justice Bridge, in his summing up to the jury in the trial of the Birmingham Six in 1975, said that if the defendants were telling the truth then the police had been involved in a conspiracy

unprecedented in the annals of British criminal history . . . consider the scale of the conspiracy in terms of those involved. It ranges, does it not, from detective constables and police constables right up through the police hierarchy to . . . Assistant Chief Constable . . . If the evidence of the defendants is true, it shows the police not only to be masters of the vile techniques of cruelty and brutality to suspects. It shows them to have a very lively and inventive imagination.[3]

In the Court of Appeal Lord Denning MR regarded the attempt by the Birmingham Six to bring civil actions against the police and others for assault as a potential indictment of the whole practice of criminal justice:

If the six men win, it will mean that the police were guilty of perjury, that they were guilty of violence and threats, that the confessions were involuntary and were improperly admitted in evidence, and that the convictions were erroneous . . . This is such an appalling vista that every sensible person in the land would say: 'It cannot be right that these actions should go any further'.[4]

These statements imply that an acceptance of the innocence of the Birmingham Six would necessitate wholesale reform of criminal justice. By contrast, the Court of Appeal (Criminal Division) in the second appeal (the first reference from the Home Secretary) was reluctant to accept the appellants' claims to have had confessions beaten from them by large numbers of police, with the knowledge and complicity of their seniors.[5] By the third appeal (the second reference), in which the convictions were quashed, the appellants still had not persuaded the Court of Appeal to accept that evidence of widespread police abuse justified quashing the convictions.[6] But what they could show was that a small number of police officers had not kept a contemporaneous record of interviews, despite having claimed to have done so whilst giving evidence under oath. The evidence of such

---

[2] G. Calabresi and P. Bobbitt, *Tragic Choices* (New York, 1978), as explained in Ch. 1.
[3] Quoted in C. Mullin, *Error of Judgement: The Truth about the Birmingham Bombings* (Dublin, 1997), 226–7.
[4] *McIlkenny v Chief Constable of West Midlands Police Force* [1980] 2 All ER 227, 239–40.
[5] *Callaghan and others* (1989) 88 Cr. App. R 40.
[6] The evidence that the defendants had been assaulted shortly after their arrest was known at the time of their trial, and indeed was recognized by the trial judge who indicated that those responsible should be brought to justice. However, such brutality was not considered at the time of their trial, or later at their appeals, necessarily to make their confessions unreliable.

malpractice justified quashing the convictions.[7] Lord Justice Lloyd said immediately at the end of the appeal hearing: 'In the light of the fresh evidence that has become available since the last hearing in this court your appeals will be allowed.'[8] The full judgment delivered later makes it clear that it was the fresh evidence 'that Superintendent Reade, D.S. Morris, D.C. Woodwiss and D.C. Langford were at least guilty of deceiving the court' that was crucial to the decision of the Court of Appeal. It was this fresh evidence that allowed the Court of Appeal to speculate that the original jury might have viewed the scientific evidence and the police's evidence of the admissions differently. However, the Court of Appeal specifically rejected the suggestion from appellants' counsel that the scientific evidence or the confession evidence was by the end of the appeal, in principle, inadmissible or irrelevant.[9] Were it not for the widely held view that the Birmingham Six were innocent, this could have been seen as an example of a judiciary who are willing to release guilty persons in order to uphold procedural standards; over-zealous police officers, who in trying to disguise their procedural errors, lied under oath. That this story was not the dominant one reported in the media was a result not of any fault in the Court's technique, but of the widespread belief in the claims of innocence of the Birmingham Six that already existed. As such, the Court of Appeal's decision to quash their convictions was not received as the correction of a regrettable but relatively limited error, but as authority for the acceptance of the claims made by the Birmingham Six of extensive abuse and corruption. To the extent that there was reporting and understanding of the much narrower admissions contained within the successful grounds of appeal, the Court itself came in for criticism. The following statement by Paddy Hill (one of the Six) as he left the Court of Appeal, implying wholesale deficiencies in criminal justice, was widely reported: 'Justice—I don't think them people in there have the intelligence or the honesty to spell the word, never mind dispense it. They're rotten.'[10]

Another widely reported quotation which accompanied the quashing of these convictions was the view expressed by Lord Lane, given at the end of his judgment in the unsuccessful 1987/8 appeal, that: 'The longer this hearing has gone on the more convinced this court has become that the verdict of the jury was correct . . . We have no doubt that these convictions are both safe and satisfactory.'[11] But, since the second and third appeals in 1987/8 and 1991 were based on different new evidence, which new evidence was the reason for the appeal's success, there is no logical reason

---

[7] *McIlkenny and others* (1991) 93 Cr. App. R 287.
[8] See n. 3 above, 398.
[9] *McIlkenny and others*, n. 7 above, 317–18.
[10] Front page, *The Independent*, 15 March 91.
[11] See n. 3 above, 351; an incomplete summary can be found in the reported judgment, n. 5 above, 47.

why Lord Lane's view was incompatible with the decision in the third appeal. Nevertheless, Lord Lane was vilified in the media for expressing this view.[12] Just as the third appeal was treated as an endorsement of the appellants' claims to be innocent, the second was a crushing rejection. If the third judgment was taken as correct, the second must have been chronically wrong. The fact that the Home Secretary announced the setting up of a Royal Commission to look broadly into criminal justice on the day that the convictions of the Birmingham Six were quashed was also no coincidence. The Home Secretary too recognized that the Court of Appeal's decision would be read by the media as an endorsement of stories of the innocence of the Birmingham Six and, conversely, the guilt of the police force, trial process, forensic science, and Court of Appeal. Since stories of the innocence of the Birmingham Six had been published and broadcast for so long, and so often, it only required a favourable decision by the Court of Appeal for them to become orthodoxy.

In the face of the Court's inability to convince *the public* that this and other successful appeals represented only limited mistakes, and the consequent attention to the operation of criminal justice practices and processes, reform became necessary. Justice had to be preserved as the overall value, and criminal justice repackaged and re-presented as the embodiment of that value. The widely reported crisis of confidence in criminal justice, which accompanied the release of the Birmingham Six, led to a climate of optimism amongst those arguing for reforms. The Royal Commission on Criminal Justice was the hoped-for vehicle for turning high profile miscarriages of justice into changes in criminal justice that it was claimed, with varying degrees of plausibility, would prevent such miscarriages of justice from recurring.[13]

This episode can be re-examined using *Tragic Choices* analysis. Let us remind the reader of the nature of this analysis, set out already in Chapter 1. Although criminal justice is understood as an expression of fundamental values, its institutional arrangements for the investigation and prosecution of crime will necessarily sacrifice those values.[14] A process of appeal attempts to disguise this sacrifice by treating miscarriages of justice as an occasional and remedial mistake in the routine workings of criminal justice, rather than an inevitable and routine consequence of its institutional arrangements.[15] From this perspective the second and third Birmingham Six appeals must represent two of the least successful attempts by the Court of

---

[12]   As we have demonstrated in section E of Ch. 4.

[13]   See our article 'Royal Commission Buys Time for British Justice', in *The Irish Times*, 14 June 91.

[14]   See our analysis in Ch. 2 for an account of how this occurs, and how miscarriages of justice are thereby generated.

[15]   We have given a historical account of this process that supports this conclusion in Ch. 3.

Appeal to present outcomes that are an inevitable consequence of institutional arrangements as if they were accidental mistakes. The Court of Appeal tried to leave open the possibility that, but for the police's mistakes described above, and those of forensic scientists (outlined in Chapter 5), these *terrorists might* have been properly convicted.[16] Meanwhile the Birmingham Six and other terrorist cases have provided a platform, especially in the media, for reasons for having 'lurking doubts' not only as to the safety of these convictions, but the safety of criminal justice itself. The publicly expressed concerns of the Irish government bolstered these doubts by giving support to those who claim that suspect communities are susceptible to systematic disregard of rules of procedure.[17] And quashing the convictions of the Birmingham Six appellants lent credence to their personal stories,[18] the implications of which have already been highlighted in the above judicial statements.

What is interesting in the context of *Tragic Choices* analysis, and a cause of despair to those lawyers, professional and academic, who proposed radical reforms, is how few changes for which they argued have in fact been made. The expected instrument for change was the Royal Commission on Criminal Justice, but that body's Report and its reception by the Government in 1993 has been accused of strengthening police powers, and actually increasing the possibilities for systematic abuse of procedure and incorrect verdicts.[19] *Tragic Choices* analysis indicates why such a groundswell of concern with fundamental values could lead to so little in the way of radical reforms. As shown in Chapter 4, the crisis generated by high profile miscarriages of justice is a crisis in the ability of actors, within law but most importantly within the media, to continue to use the rhetoric of fundamental values. There is, for the reasons explored in Chapter 2, no possibility of eliminating the gap between such values and the practices of criminal justice. There is no value, or combination of values, which is obviously immanent in the existing practices of criminal justice. The values that inform rhetorical commitment against miscarriages of justice are unattainable,

[16] Which is what L. Blom-Cooper argues in his book, *The Birmingham Six and Other Cases: Victims of Circumstance* (London, 1997).

[17] See, e.g., P. Hillyard, *Suspect Community: People's Experience of the Prevention of Terrorism Acts in Britain* (London, 1993), and B. Dickson, 'The Prevention of Terrorism Acts', in C. Walker and K. Starmer (eds.), *Justice in Error* (London, 1993), ch. 9.

[18] Such as that told by Hugh Callaghan, *Cruel Fate: One Man's Triumph over Injustice* (Dublin, 1994).

[19] Royal Commission on Criminal Justice, the *Runciman Report*, Cm 2263 (London, 1993). As examples of critical reaction to the Report see M. McConville and L. Bridges (eds.), *Criminal Justice in Crisis* (Aldershot, 1994), esp. chs. 1–4; S. Field and P. Thomas (eds.), *Justice and Efficiency? The Royal Commission on Criminal Justice* (Oxford, 1994), esp. the chapters by Field and Thomas, Bridges, and Hodgson; R. Reiner, 'Investigative Powers and Safeguards for Suspects', *Criminal Law Review* [1993], 808–16; A. Ashworth, 'Plea, Venue and Discontinuance', *Criminal Law Review* [1993], 830–40; P. Thornton, 'Miscarriages of Justice: A Lost Opportunity', *Criminal Law Review* [1993], 926–35.

incoherent, and inevitably traded off against non-values such as institutional interests and costs. But the powerful rhetoric of miscarriage of justice, which has generated the media's perception of crisis, does not allow a target to be set of acceptable numbers of failures. Perhaps in the worlds of education and even health it may be possible to have a statistical target for, respectively, illiterates and deaths. Tragic choice occurs when one focuses on the mechanism by which a particular individual is chosen to be illiterate or to die. With criminal justice, the analysis operates at a prior stage. The current rhetoric of justice does not allow one to accept that a particular aspect of criminal justice will lead to a known statistical number of persons being wrongly convicted. And even if statistical targets could be set, which they cannot be, every appeal is potentially an individual miscarriage of justice and every miscarriage of justice is individually unjustifiable.

At first glance, acknowledged miscarriages of justice offer fertile ground for reforms to criminal justice. There is a common commitment to the rhetoric of miscarriage of justice among lawyers (radical and conservative), the media, and politicians. Thus, one does not suffer from the same fragmentation of values that might inhibit reforms in other areas. But against this, one must recognize that there is no limit to the resources that can be expended in the pursuit of these values, no prospect of actually achieving them in practice, and plenty of competing uses for the resources required. The media are willing to report that criminal justice falls short, even hopelessly short, of the media's understanding of justice. But this does not mean that they will report favourably on the spending which will occur (or even the convictions which will not take place) if politicians made the prevention of miscarriages their sole or dominant spending commitment.

In these circumstances, the realizable tasks of those involved with reform are twofold: to reduce the number of likely miscarriages, in terms of incorrect verdicts, or unfair procedures, or both, and to increase the ability of the legal system to use, and the media to report on, the rhetoric of justice. The second of these is likely to be given priority over the first. There are a number of reasons for this priority. First, where the reform process is a response to the media reporting a crisis of public confidence, changes which the media interpret as likely to restore public confidence remove the pressure for further change. By contrast, changes which, however statistically likely to improve accuracy or fairness, are *not* interpreted to reduce miscarriages (remembering that the media's dominant understanding is in terms of truth and not fairness), thus will not reduce the pressure for reform. This is something that is often overlooked by those proposing radical reforms. The media's dominant construction of miscarriages in terms of the accuracy of verdicts does not easily lend support to reforms linked to concepts of due process and rights. Rights and processes that make no *obvious* contribution to the accuracy of verdicts are difficult to defend in the media. This may even lead a reform process generated by high profile miscarriages of justice to result in a reduction in the rights of suspected persons.[20] Secondly, there are the issues of cost, and institutional interests. Changes which restore the media's confidence can be found which are much cheaper and face less opposition from groups like the police, the Home Office, or the Treasury than changes which are likely to contribute significantly to the accuracy or fairness of verdicts.

The factors which steer reforms towards changes which respond to media concerns have consequences for reform generally and for the reform of the Court of Appeal in particular. The role of the Court of Appeal, from the perspective of *Tragic Choices* analysis, has not changed since its creation. It has had to utilize a rhetoric that is impossible to realize through the existing practices of criminal justice: indeed, which could not be realized within any set of practices. At the same time, it is not itself a mechanism for reform, or at least this is not its dominant role. As the body responsible for correcting the mistakes of criminal justice, it is inevitably committed to a relationship of deference to the existing institutional arrangements and practices. To put this another way, in order to correct the mistakes of the existing institutional arrangements, it cannot treat those arrangements, or even significant elements within them, as a mistake. This does not prevent it from admitting to the inevitability of mistake. Indeed, the obviousness that any institutional arrangements for criminal justice will make mistakes formed a powerful argument in the campaign that led to the Court's creation. But if the task of investigation has been given by Parliament to a police force with given institutional practices, and the task of assessing evidence has been given to a trial court with its own practices, what exactly is left to a Court of Appeal? How does that Court, with its responsibility for correcting all inaccurate and unfair verdicts, deal with all the unfair and inaccurate verdicts which any given set of institutional practices will inevitably produce, without making the procedures for investigation and trial unworkable?

B. MANAGING INEVITABLE MISCARRIAGE OF JUSTICE—THE ROLE AND REFORM OF THE COURT OF APPEAL

1 THE COURT'S ROLE

From a *Tragic Choices* perspective the central role of the Court of Appeal, as a second-order institution, is to develop a workable set of practices for

---

[20] A recent example is appropriate. To the extent that the Criminal Justice and Public Order Act 1994, which among other things dealt a severe blow to the so-called right to silence, can be understood as linked to the Royal Commission's Report and the high profile miscarriages that precipitated the setting up of the Royal Commission, this argument is made out. See our discussion later in this chapter, at section E.

constructing miscarriage of justice. Its constructions of miscarriage of justice must uphold fundamental values, without providing evidence of a need for radical reform. The open-ended nature of this task is well illustrated by the legislation. Since the Court of Appeal has always had the discretion to rectify anything that it felt constituted a miscarriage of justice, the problem for the Court is not a lack of statutory power. It is finding a way to exercise that power without undermining the stability of the whole existing arrangement. No responsible Court can really apply the maxim: 'Fiat justicia, ruat coelum' (Let justice be done though the heavens fall). And the Court has developed a number of techniques that work very well. First, what gets to the Court has, in most cases, to receive the leave of a single judge. What actually constitutes a sufficient abuse of procedure or likelihood of error to warrant a referral to the Court is based on the experience of the judge in question. In practice, little reason is given for refusal, and virtually none for acceptance.[21] The organization Justice has criticized this and recommended reform to remedy the inadequacy of lack of reasons being given for refusal.[22] But an alternative view is that it is often not possible to articulate what exactly constitutes an appealable case or not. In this view we recognize echoes of Karl Llewellyn's teaching, of the understanding of law jobs as crafts. 'Skill in juristic method, by man's good fortune, cannot only be a personal attribute, but a tradition; . . . By man's bad fortune, skill in juristic method has not as yet been reduced to readily communicable form.'[23] Like much of the law, a strong case is no more than an experienced view of how another body of judges is likely to react to it. So long as there is general confidence in the procedures for leave, the ability to have a case reviewed by a single judge can successfully dispose of a large percentage of allegations that a guilty verdict was a miscarriage of justice. The self-limiting nature of these arrangements is clearly demonstrated by K. Malleson's research. She concludes:

it is clear that the system operates so as to focus on a relatively small number of disproportionately heavy-weight cases. This practice is in accordance with the Court's original design and is perpetuated by the limited resources of the appeal courts. Moreover, its bias is rarely acknowledged because the popular image of

---

[21] See K. Malleson, *Review of the Appeal Process*, Royal Commission on Criminal Justice Research Study No.17 (London, 1993), 35. There is considerable evidence, documented over time, to suggest that adequate legal advice on undertaking an appeal is often unavailable. See e.g., J. Plotnikoff and R. Woolfson, *Information and Advice for Prisoners about Grounds for Appeal and the Appeals Process*, Royal Commission on Criminal Justice Research Study No.18 (London, 1993), and M. Zander, 'Legal Advice and Criminal Appeals: A Survey of Prisoners, Prisons and Lawyers', *Criminal Law Review* [1972], 132–73.

[22] Justice, *Remedying Miscarriages of Justice* (London, 1994), 8.

[23] K. Llewellyn and E. A. Hoebel, *The Cheyenne Way: Conflict and Case Law in Primitive Jurisprudence* (Norman, 1941), 309. The procedure for leave is set out by M. McKenzie in 'A Guide to Proceedings in the Court of Appeal Criminal Division' [1997] 2 Cr. App. R 459–91, 461–5.

miscarriages of justice consisting of a few high profile and serious cases reflects and reinforces the Court's priorities.[24]

A second technique is to work with a set of rules and exceptions. The Court of Appeal has rules that reduce the number of cases that can expect to succeed, and also operates exceptions to those rules, which if generally applied, would make the process of appeals unworkable. The best example of this is the 'lurking doubt' principle. This is the ultimate safety valve. A case that is appealed on the basis of lurking doubt offers no precedent for further appeals. 'This is a reaction which may not be based strictly on the evidence as such; it is a reaction which can be produced by the general feel of the case as the court experiences it.'[25] Unfortunately, at the same time, it offers no precedent for excluding appeals either: every case is potentially a lurking doubt case. The Court's application of this principle has commonly been thought to be inconsistent.[26] The resolution of this problem is the use of this general discretion on an exceptional basis. *Normal* appeals must identify errors of procedure or show new evidence. Only exceptional (high profile, where no *normal* errors are available) cases need to be disposed of on a lurking doubt basis. A third device is constitutional rhetoric. The Court of Appeal, as the upholder of fundamental values, has to locate those values somewhere in the trial process. And the principal location of trial justice in the rhetoric of the Court of Appeal is, as we have tried to show throughout this book, the jury. Here we have an institution that is inarticulate, which decides on the guilt or innocence of the accused. If the verdicts of juries can be defended, the trial process can remain relatively stable. The rhetoric of the Court of Appeal allows its judges to present their commitment to the normal practices of trial courts (normal, within an acceptable margin of error, established by the judges' own experiences) as a constitutional commitment to the opinion of a body other than themselves: the jury. A refusal (usually) to undertake open-ended review of the safety of a conviction is presented as a constitutional form of justice: the judges' deference to the jury.

This process of review requires the Court of Appeal to identify how a conviction might have been constructed by the jury rather than simply administering justice (or identifying miscarriages of justice). This is an inescapable consequence of the Court of Appeal's relationship to the trial. At trial, convictions are constructed. McBarnet, in her seminal book *Conviction*,[27] explored the processes by which convictions are constructed,

---

[24] K. Malleson, 'Miscarriages of Justice and the Accessibility of the Court of Appeal', *Criminal Law Review* [1991], 332.

[25] Widgery LJ in *Cooper* (1968) 53 Cr. App. R 82, 86, discussed above in section F of Ch. 3.

[26] Samuels gives a clear account of this inconsistency, contending: 'One judge may feel a lurking doubt, another may not' (A. Samuels, 'Appeals Against Conviction: Reform', *Criminal Law Review*, [1984], 337).

[27] D. McBarnet, *Conviction: Law, the State and the Construction of Justice* (London, 1981).

noting the apparent gap between law in action and the rhetoric of law. She found that management of this gap was not an aberration, a falling off from practical standards. Rather, management of this gap was part, indeed a major part, of the practice of law at the trial court level. For example, a criminal trial requires the jury to be instructed in the rhetoric of 'beyond reasonable doubt' whilst at the same time being steered towards reaching a decision on the basis of limited evidence and restricted possibilities. Thus, whatever might in science or through common-sense assessments made outside of a court room pass for knowledge 'beyond reasonable doubt', a jury is allowed to make decisions on the basis of what, for the legal actors, in their own forum, passes as *sufficient* evidence of guilt.[28]

Juries have to be convinced beyond reasonable doubt—but they cannot choose the issues that they have to be convinced about: sufficiency and credibility are distinguished in law. The law defines how much evidence constitutes 'sufficient' to prove a case and it is the judge's role to decide that this standard has been met. The jury's role is to decide whether they believe it. But the legal demands involved in 'sufficiency' are often rather lower than one might expect. Indeed from judges' summing-up addresses it seems clear they recognize they have to persuade juries—whose only knowledge of the law is after all the rhetoric—that *enough* evidence is not as much as they might think.[29]

Although the legal system espouses the values of truth and fairness, the practices of trial are designed, as McBarnet observed, to achieve closure. The trial court operates to manage the gap between rhetoric and apparent practice. The gap between the standards of the court and the rhetoric of justice is not a simple gap between practice and rhetoric, practice and rule, or law in action and law in the books. Managing the gap is itself part of the practice of law.[30] McBarnet concentrates on the ability of the higher courts to manage the gap between rhetorical statements about rights and the experience of defendants. Claims that English justice recognizes rights such as the right to silence, or to full disclosure, are riddled in case and statute law with exceptions. Thus whilst appeal court decisions and statutes provide the framework for broad rhetorical statements on the standards necessary for a just trial, they also provide a means for relaxing such standards in particular cases. Case law doctrine and statutory interpretation (both examples of legal practice) allow rhetorical standards and the failure to achieve them to coexist.

Our thesis is a continuation of that propounded by McBarnet. The Court of Appeal plays a strategic role within criminal justice, by managing the

---

[28] As Rock shows in his description of the Crown Court, a jury has to apply common sense in a situation that lies outside the common experience of lay actors; P. Rock, *The Social World of an English Crown Court* (Oxford, 1993), ch. 2.

[29] McBarnet, n. 27 above, 13.

[30] This is certainly recognized by McBarnet, n. 27 above.

same apparent gap between rhetoric and practice. At both levels, the trial and the appeal, the gap has to be managed in order to construct conviction, and miscarriage. Rationalist approaches to criminal justice reform find a standard by which to appraise the practices of the Court of Appeal in its rhetoric about miscarriages of justice. The ensuing reform proposals attempt to encourage the Court of Appeal to live up to that rhetoric. An alternative view is that the Court of Appeal is simply a court of review, and what it reviews is a legal system in which fundamental values are both celebrated and not achieved at the same time. Whilst McBarnet's review of appeal courts' doctrines concentrates on the rhetoric of due process, our study has been more concerned with the gap between the practices of the legal system and its rhetorical commitment to truth. The management of the gap between actual practices and both of these values poses a formidable task for the Court of Appeal. If the basis of its review were an open-ended and unrestricted pursuit of the values of justice, it would not be a court of review. It would simply undo what trial manages to achieve. Its lesser brief is to examine how the trial court has managed the gap between rhetoric and practice; that is, in McBarnet's terms, how it has constructed a just conviction using limited resources, sufficient evidence,[31] and current versions of traditional procedures.

Where a conviction may be factually incorrect the Court of Appeal may have difficulty in overturning the conviction and at the same time managing any apparent gap between its and the trial court's rhetoric and practice. It is here that media and public, and perhaps even political conceptions of miscarriage of justice, tend to diverge from the Court of Appeal's self-perception. For example, the judge's statement of the standard of proof is one of the most important rhetorical aspects of the trial, an affirmation of justice which exists alongside practices which do not match up to it. A trial judge's failure to make the usual statement can be seen as a classic case of mismanagement of the coexistence of rhetorical values and lesser practices. By contrast, since a large part of the function of a trial is to reduce the number of possibilities that need to be considered and to make the introduction of evidence manageable, a court of review cannot take a completely open-ended approach to the re-examination of the truth of a defendant's guilt or innocence. If the defendant has been (whatever phrase was used in the summing up) convicted on the basis of evidence that was sufficient to persuade a jury, the Court of Appeal cannot (without undoing the trial process) impose the much higher standard of *no reasonable person could doubt*.

This perspective may throw some light on the Court of Appeal's apparently greater willingness to quash convictions where there has been procedural error or something that can be presented as a procedural error,

---

[31] See p. 238 above.

compared with its reluctance where such errors are absent. Where there are due-process failures the Court of Appeal has a less difficult task to manage the gap between its rhetoric and its practice in quashing the conviction. The Court of Appeal has created a body of doctrine whereby general rights are qualified by exceptions. Where traditional procedures are not followed to an acceptable degree, the quashing of a conviction represents an opportunity to demonstrate a rhetorical commitment to due process and rights. Where the infringement is not considered sufficiently serious, the Court might identify the claimed breach of a right as coming within one of the numerous exceptions or, formerly, within the proviso (thus asserting its commitment to truth). The statement that the Court is *more willing* to respond to such appeals needs qualification. The standards of due process, whilst they may appear technical (both because they prioritize fairness and rights over truth, and because legal rights, being riddled with exceptions, *are* technical) provide a workable basis for a routine appeal process. Practitioners can predict when an appeal is likely to be successful, and can usually do so solely on the basis of a transcript of the trial and the judge's summing up. Appeals based on fact have no such benchmarks. They cannot be routinized in the same way. The absence of a procedural error means that the trial has been routine. The process for identifying truth has been followed. The Court of Appeal has the difficult task of identifying why the trial's routine operation has, nevertheless, and in this particular case, produced an erroneous outcome. Alternatively Court of Appeal has the even more difficult task to identify parts of criminal justice (police practices, forensic tests, eyewitness evidence) that can be expected routinely to produce errors. The latter situation, if adopted by the Court, would create the expectation of routine rehearings or retrials. The greater willingness of the Court to hear due process appeals lies, in the end, in the logic of law as a system. Due process appeals can be made routine. They can relatively easily operate within an existing legal system. Appeals based on fact threaten the ability of the processes of criminal justice to continue to operate routinely, and to exist as a stable site of inter-system coupling.

Our thesis may help to explain much of the opposition of the judiciary to the formation of the Court of Criminal Appeal. In the latter part of the nineteenth century judges had already witnessed significant reforms designed to make trials fairer and more likely to reach a correct verdict. Such reforms included, among other things, improvements to the practices of summary trial and trial procedure in general, extension of the opportunities for legal representation of defendants, extension of the right to elect for trial by jury, greater use of solicitors as police prosecutors, and the significant change at the end of the century brought about by the Criminal Evidence Act 1898 of allowing defendants to testify at their own trials.[32]

---

[32] See generally, D. Bentley, *English Criminal Justice in the Nineteenth Century* (London,

The legal system was perceived to be much less likely to make mistakes by the end of the nineteenth century than it had been at the beginning. For many senior judges, the residual number of mistakes could not justify the creation of a tribunal that would, inevitably, be required to put the legal system itself on trial. Remember that it was the role of such a court in dealing with evidence that principally concerned the judiciary. And it is in this role that a court of review finds itself forced to repeat and reassess the investigative and interpretative job of the trial process. It has responsibility for a task that has, at a first-order level, already been undertaken. If it regularly assumes the work of the trial court, and even more so if it goes beyond the routine practices of the trial court and places the investigative process and trial process on trial, it will tend to undermine the existing institutions of criminal justice.

Much of the thesis presented here simply repeats what other writers have called a commitment to finality.[33] This appears to be a commitment to verdicts as conclusive. But the real commitment to finality is a commitment to the processes by which verdict has been produced. This commitment to processes may go some way to explain judicial statements about jury verdicts that can appear as logical absurdities. What did it mean for the Court of Appeal to insist before 1966 that it could not substitute its decision for that of the jury when hearing new evidence? Consider, for example, Lord Goddard's statement in *McGrath*: 'Where there is evidence upon which a jury can act and there has been a proper direction to the jury this court cannot substitute itself for the jury and re-try the case. That is not our function. If we took any other attitude, it would strike at the very root of trial by jury.'[34] Surely it was clear that the opinions of the members of the Court were the only basis on which a decision to quash or uphold a conviction could have been reached.[35] However, this may not have been an absurdity.[36] The Court's members are committed to the practices (evidence, cross-examination, argument, and summing up) which enable a jury of lay persons to take responsibility for stating whether someone should be liable to punishment or not. And there is no reason to expect the practices of the Court of Appeal (generally) to provide a superior basis for such decisions.

1998). And, in relation to the last example given, see C. F. H. Tapper, 'The Meaning of Section 1(f)(i) of the Criminal Evidence Act 1898', in id., *Crime, Proof and Punishment: Essays in Memory of Sir Rupert Cross* (London, 1981), 296–322.

[33] See our understanding of this conception set out in section C of Ch. 1. With respect to criminal appeals, see K. Malleson, 'Appeals against Conviction and the Principle of Finality', in S. Field and P. Thomas (eds.), n. 19 above, 151–64.

[34] [1949] 2 All ER 495, 497.

[35] 'It was only in *Stafford v DPP* [1974] AC 878 that the House of Lords eventually concluded that it was for the Court of Appeal to determine for itself the weight to give to fresh evidence, rather than concern itself so much with the question as to what effect it might have had on a jury' (The *Runciman Report*, n. 19 above, ch. 10 para. 62).

[36] See the discussion of the *Stafford and Luvaglio* decision by P. Devlin, *The Judge* (Oxford, 1979), ch. 5 (II) 'Sapping and Undermining'.

This leaves the Court with the task of deferring to a system for constructing convictions which is seen as superior to its own, whilst at the same time
continuing to affirm a rhetoric of justice which expects some verdicts to be
mistaken, and requires the Court to correct such mistakes. With this task,
the question for the Court is not whether its individual members agree with
the jury's verdict. To accept that their opinion on the guilt of an accused,
reached on the basis of their practices, was as good as that of a jury might
show respect for scientific truth, but it would show no respect or commitment to the practices by which convictions are constructed at trial. To show
respect, they have to accept that their own opinion, reached through their
own practices, is not, in and of itself, enough of a reason to reverse a jury's
verdict. Thus, despite assertions in *Stafford*[37] and *Cooper*[38] that the Court
will use its own judgement, the elements of deference which were the bases
for the earlier seemingly absurd statements remained, and the Court continued to be criticized for its excessive deference to jury verdicts.[39] Whether
the Court of Appeal in the new millennium under Lord Chief Justice
Bingham, the successor to Lord Chief Justice Taylor, will be able to maintain a reputation for taking a liberal attitude towards appeals and a corres-
pondingly less deferential attitude towards jury verdicts remains to be seen.
But for the reasons that we have given throughout this book, we expect
accusations of excessive deference to reappear.

A rationalist critique presents the role of and reforms to the appeal
process as relying on the assumption that the practices that are being
appealed against are themselves rational. A different approach accepts that
trial court practices are parochial, and largely traditional. They are an
outcome of history. And while rational argument and reform may have
played a part in that history, rational reform cannot eliminate the irrational
elements of those practices. To use the most obvious example taken from
Chapter 2, whilst the right to elect jury trial has been presented rhetorically
as a cornerstone of justice by English lawyers,[40] neither Scotland's legal
system nor many in Europe embody such a right, nor is it enshrined in the
European Convention on Human Rights. Thus deference to a jury's decision in one legal system cannot easily be defended on rational grounds,
without seeming to be imperialistic. For example, claims that the removal
of the right to elect jury trial would undermine justice lead Maher to state:
'assessed by the critics' comments quoted above the Scottish Criminal
process is one which has done away with fundamental freedoms and funda-

---

[37] n. 35 above.   [38] n. 25 above.
[39] See, e.g., Justice, *Miscarriages of Justice* (London, 1989), 48–51, and the *Runciman
Report*, n. 19 above, ch. 10.
[40] See G. Maher, 'Reforming the Criminal Process: A Scottish Perspective', in M.
McConville and L. Bridges (eds.), n. 19 above, 59–68, 64. Although rhetorically a cornerstone
of justice what such a right amounts to remains controversial. See, e.g., Ashworth, n. 19 above,
832–3, who regards this *right* as a claim that it should be for the defendant to decide when the
consequences are so serious that Crown Court trial is appropriate.

mental civil liberties, and has a system of jury trial which is completely worthless.'[41] It is not what one defers to which forms an essential part of an appeal court's function. Rather, it is the inescapable necessity for deference. An appeal court and trial courts cannot coexist without deference from the former towards whatever practices constitute the latter. If the rhetoric of trial justice has truth and due process (fairness and rights) elements, the practices of an appeal court have to be presented as embodiments of these values. This presentation will continue, however much an awareness of the contingency of knowledge, or the parochial nature of justice, forces us to accept that any particular set of practices must make mistakes, and cannot *be* fair.

2 THE COURT'S REFORM

Reform of the Court of Appeal has been explained as a process in which the judiciary's reluctance to overturn the verdicts of juries can be overcome or at least be reduced by rational reforms. Where those reasons are institutional, the Court's practices can be changed. An alternative or supplementary explanation concentrates on the personnel involved, who are felt to suffer from a complacent lack of commitment to justice, or an irrational confidence in the institutions and practices of criminal justice (despite all evidence to the contrary). Where this explanation is offered, the rational solution is a change in the staffing of the Court.

Given the history of reasons for judicial reluctance to entertain appeals, one may argue that we are running out of institutional explanations for it, and therefore also running out of rational reforms to overcome it. Let us clarify how a potted rationalist history of reform of the processes of criminal appeal reads.[42] In the first half of the nineteenth century the inadequacy of criminal appeals was due to lack of adequate trial records and experienced judges. In the second half of that century it was thought to be a job which was better done by the Home Secretary. When the Home Secretary's role came into disrepute at the end of the nineteenth century the Court of Criminal Appeal was established. In the first half of the twentieth century the perceived reluctance to quash convictions was thought to be due to a lack of power to order retrials. With the power to order retrials established in the 1960s, constitutional conflict between the role of the executive and the judiciary made the Home Office's investigative department C3 and the Home Secretary too reluctant to send cases to the Court, and the Court too hostile towards those sent.[43]

Other parts of this history concentrate on the personnel involved. Let us

---

[41] Maher, n. 40 above, 64.
[42] Such as that written by R. Pattenden, *English Criminal Appeals 1844–1994* (Oxford, 1996).
[43] Hostility extended by the Court towards the media where it perceives trial by media.

give two examples spanning this period. To Pattenden, the complacency of senior judges in the mid-nineteenth century appears obvious and disagreeable. She describes how, while applauding current criminal procedures, they complacently disapprove of reform.

In 1848 Baron Parke, who by then had twenty years' experience as a criminal judge, told a Select Committee of the House of Lords that he was not personally acquainted with any case in which a person really innocent had been punished. His views were unchanged in 1864 when he told the Capital Punishment Commission that he had never tried a case of murder in which there was a conviction where a new trial could properly have been ordered ... Baron Bramell, told the same Commission that 'people in England are never convicted except, in my judgment, upon the very clearest evidence'. Other judges said the same.[44]

For a more recent example, we have already commented in Chapter 4 on the vilification of the senior judiciary for their perceived reluctance to accept errors in the criminal justice process. In the case of Lord Lane this resulted in his early retirement and replacement by Lord Chief Justice Taylor in April 1992, a judge with a more *liberal* reputation.

There may come a point where one might simply accept that the judiciary have, and will always have (at least according to some sections of the media), a *perceived reluctance* readily to accept appeals against guilty verdicts in the absence of any error of law. If that point has been reached it may be time to look to other, less rational ways of understanding this. Much of what we are saying is not new. Rational historical analysis acknowledges the presence of conflicting values and conflicting approaches in the appeals process. Pattenden, for example, reaches the conclusion about the Court of Appeal (Criminal Division) that it is 'confused and inconsistent about the values it promotes'.[45] Over the years many commentators have made similar arguments. Both the practices of the Court of Appeal and proposals for its reform tend to be criticized in terms of the inconsistency of the values espoused. These values include truth and fairness (their amalgamation in justice), the constraints of cost, and the need for finality. On the premise of confusion about values, Pattenden calls for legislation to sort out and rank the Court's aims and priorities, and particularly to determine 'What is more important: upholding convictions, or minimising miscarriages of justice?'[46] However, *Tragic Choices* analysis draws attention to the unavoidability of such apparent confusion, and to the task faced by institutions which must grapple with it. Devices that can be described as mechanisms for achieving a system's values can also be described as mechanisms to disguise and displace the inevitable sacrifice of

---

[44] Pattenden, n. 42 above, 16–17.   [45] Ibid. 210.

[46] Ibid. 210. Others have tried to reinterpret this contrast as representing respectively a greater commitment to crime control values rather than those associated with a due process model. See A. Sanders and R. Young, *Criminal Justice* (London, 1994), ch. 9.

those values. The Court of Appeal has a Janus-like quality: it celebrates the value of remedying the mistakes of miscarriages of justice, but also, and at the same time, manages inevitable injustice. As such there is not a policy here, to be identified by Parliament, which will produce a stable trade-off between fundamental values.

C. ALTERNATIVE EXPLANATIONS OF THE ROLE OF THE COURT

We are by no means the first commentators to observe patterns in the history of the Court of Appeal: legislation offering the prospect of remedying greater numbers of miscarriages, followed by *conservative practices* leading to eventual crisis. Nor are we alone in pointing to the crucial role of the media in generating general certainty as to the innocence of particular individuals, and consequent frustration with the Court's failure to respond to this. But we differ in our explanation of these patterns.

Bob Woffinden, a journalist who has been writing about miscarriages of justice for over twenty years, recognizes such patterns in his book *Miscarriages of Justice* published in 1987.[47] The book, which analyses a number of leading miscarriages post-1945, presents a severe indictment of the processes for remedying miscarriage. As a journalist specializing in miscarriages of justice, writing at the time when the hoped-for benefits and promises of the 1960s reforms had not been fulfilled, he rightly anticipated the crisis generated by miscarriages of the late 1980s and early 1990s. He was able to look back and quote those who had reached similar conclusions to him during earlier periods in the twentieth century and the nineteenth century. He criticizes the criminal appeal process for its failure to exhibit a wholehearted commitment to truth. As he says with bafflement and consternation in his Introduction: 'Why, after I and perhaps millions of others had become genuinely convinced of the innocence of a convicted person, and after public and parliamentary pressure had been exerted, were the authorities hardly ever able to do anything about it?'[48] And in his Conclusion, after reviewing a number of cases in depth he contends: 'Truth does periodically surface in the judicial review process (as in the Confait case), but it is very much the occasional luxury, certainly not a built-in feature.'[49] The final paragraph of his book highlights his moral outrage.

It is wrong to keep innocent people in prison. That is a truth so basic that no amount of politics, of bureaucratic expediency and judicial casuistry, can alter it. Yet the shaming fact is that the continued incarceration of the innocent is nothing less than national policy. There can be no sadder reflection on the state of Britain today

---

[47] B. Woffinden, *Miscarriages of Justice* (London, 1987).   [48] Ibid. xi.
[49] Ibid. 345.

than that there seems to be no one in the legal or political hierarchies with the moral fibre, with the simple human decency, to want to do anything about it.[50]

Woffinden recognizes the underlying problems facing the Court of Appeal in carrying out its tasks, and admits that those problems motivate the Court to view its task narrowly. He also recognizes the need for finality to avoid criminal justice deteriorating into a process in which repeated tribunals reassess the same issues, which he admits, would be 'self-defeating, impractical, and also absurdly expensive'.[51] He accepts the fear that an appellate body that failed to place restrictions upon the cases it was willing to reassess would be overwhelmed. He also sees the danger that defence lawyers would treat a trial as a mere rehearsal of their 'full' case. Lastly, he cites 'the critical reason', the need to avoid undermining the role of the jury. Woffinden regards these points as 'incontestable'. But he goes on to claim that it is 'nevertheless unpardonable that appeal judges have allowed such considerations an overriding importance, with the result that the channels of judicial review have effectively been sealed'.[52]

To us this seems to be a classic statement of tragic choice, and a good example of the greater emphasis placed on considerations of truth over those of due process by many commentators in the media. The real need to restrict appeals is 'incontestable', whilst allowing such considerations to override the need to correct miscarriages of justice (in terms of truth) is 'unpardonable'. Woffinden is scathing in his comments on the judiciary, whom he accuses of abject moral cowardice in preferring to conceal the 'valetudinarian' state of criminal justice. But while one may agree that a more liberal set of judges might impose fewer restrictions on appeals than conservative ones, and be more willing to use their authority to effect some reforms in the procedures for investigation and trial, the task which he poses for these 'cowards' is far from easy. As a sceptic, he is convinced that the causes of miscarriage go far beyond mistakes in the current procedures, the correction of which he denigrates as 'ascertaining that trial etiquette had been properly observed'.[53] For him, miscarriage of justice cases require one to admit 'to a catalogue of serious errors in the detection of crime and the administration of justice'. And in this admission he does not share the respect shown by the judiciary or some radical lawyers[54] for the role of the jury and its 'essentially amateur deliberations'.[55]

As far as Woffinden is concerned, the Court of Appeal has 'ducked the responsibilities which Parliament prescribed for them and which the country expected of them'.[56] But is this a satisfactory interpretation of the

---

[50]　Ibid. 346. A short section of this quotation was given in section D of Ch. 4 when considering Ludovic Kennedy's review of Woffinden's book.

[51]　Ibid. 322.　　　　　　[52]　Ibid. 340–1.　　　　　　[53]　Ibid. 323.

[54]　See, e.g., the newspaper article by Michael Mansfield QC, 'Civil Rights Now, Please' *The Guardian* 13 Nov. 98.

[55]　Woffinden, n. 47 above, 323.　　　　　　[56]　Ibid. 323.

Court's mandate and failings? Parliament has delegated to the Court the task of defining and correcting miscarriages of justice. But is this really a mandate to demonstrate a commitment to truth that is incompatible with existing standards of investigation, advocacy, forensic science, jury perceptions and intelligence, etc.? This mandate places an enormous political responsibility upon the judiciary in terms of a substantial reduction in the number of supposed criminals who can be dealt with through the courts. It also undermines the Court's role in enforcing due process.

Legal academics have written similar critiques of the role of the Court. According to Pattenden in her book on criminal appeals, 'since 1988 the media have represented the criminal appeal system at Court of Appeal level as in crisis.'[57] This is due, Pattenden believes, to its perceived failure to carry out its intended functions and in particular that of rectification of erroneous convictions. Pattenden examines the various roles of the Court: lawmaker (changing first-order determinations), corrector of due process errors, corrector of erroneous convictions (jury errors), and guardian of rights, noting that the Court has failed to develop a consistent set of principles to underpin its practices. She also notes that lay conceptions of miscarriages concentrate on the factual innocence of the accused, whilst criminal lawyers are 'aware that a no less important function of an appeal in the English legal system is to protect the right of the defendant (whether guilty or not) to a fair trial conducted according to law'.[58] Her explanation of the Court of Appeal's inconsistency is partly that the personnel who sit in the Court vary, and partly that the Court has failed to develop a consistent set of aims and values to guide the different judges. Her suggested remedy is for legislation to provide consistent aims and priorities.[59] She also holds out the hope that increasing the resources of the Court of Appeal would allow it 'to discharge its intended role efficiently and effectively'.[60] Although the range of factors listed in her explanation for the Court of Appeal's reputation about its failings and disproportionate priorities[61] has some merit,[62] that explanation is underpinned by the rationalist assumption that reforms and increasing resources can produce the sort of changes required. With greater resources miscarriages can be, if not reduced, at least adequately identified and remedied. Pattenden even wonders whether the

---

[57] Pattenden n. 42 above, 57, and see our commentary on this statement in section C of Ch. 4.

[58] Ibid. 57–8. [59] See p. 244 above.

[60] Pattenden n. 42 above, 79.

[61] Disproportionate in the following terms: 'the Court of Appeal in its present form is an inadequate forum for righting wrongs. It is an adequate forum for correcting errors of law, but it has failed signally to identify miscarriages of justice' (P. Thornton, A. Mallalieu, and A. Scrivener, *Justice on Trial: Report of the Independent Civil Liberty Panel on Criminal Justice* (London, 1992), 24).

[62] In presenting her arguments Pattenden (n. 42 above, 69–82) takes issue with the explanation for this reputation offered by Malleson (n. 33 above), who views these practices as representing the Court's strong commitment to finality.

Court of Appeal's reputation for resisting appeals based solely on fact is already changing in the 1990s.[63] We find this explanation generally unconvincing. The Court of Appeal has always had a reputation for over-zealously preferring due process over truth and has been subjected to academic criticism for this,[64] although at some periods criticism of the Court in the press for failing to give sufficient attention to truth has dwindled. What is at issue is the Court's reputation.

Aside from the fact that the pattern of media-generated perceptions of crisis is much older than 1988, our analysis leads us to be extremely sceptical about the suggestion that such patterns of crisis can be cured by rational reforms: in particular, that the Court's reputation as inefficient and ineffective at remedying factually incorrect convictions can be overcome by reform, whether those reforms are of the processes of the Court through legislation, or by increasing the resources made available to it. Adopting a meaning of miscarriage of justice in terms solely of truth is a consistent aim and one that may enable the Court to bring about a change in its reputation. But such a consistent aim is corrosive of any commitment to due process. This can be illustrated by looking at the very different meaning of *finality* offered by Peter Hill, an investigative journalist and originator of the influential TV series *Rough Justice*.[65]

Hill writes in the *New Law Journal* about the case of Anthony Steel, convicted of murder in 1979, mostly on the basis of his own confession. The confession was retracted by Steel, and lacked any independent corroboration. Nor did it contain any special knowledge that would ensure that it could only have come from the murderer. Despite this, it was accepted by the jury, who presumably rejected Steel's alternative explanation: that he confessed after hours of interrogation simply in order to be allowed to call a solicitor. Hill gives this case as an example of the legal system's failure to achieve finality. He gives this term an unusual interpretation. He accepts that the obstacles placed in the path of persons claiming miscarriage of justice serve to ensure the finality of most verdicts. But what he appears to mean by finality is the failure of the legal system to produce verdicts that are incapable of raising doubts, which settles the matter, once and for all,

---

[63] Pattenden, n. 42 above, 78.

[64] Such criticism takes a number of forms, which are likely to be reflected in the Court's reputation. Woffinden (n. 47 above, 341) quotes the legal officer of Justice, Peter Ashman, to develop one such criticism. The implications of such a priority are thought by Ashman to be counterproductive: 'the kind of appeal actually conducted by the Court of Appeal [i.e. on errors of law] undermines trial by jury far more than appeals judged on merit. What it generally means is that someone who is clearly guilty can get off on a technicality, while someone who is clearly innocent, and in whose case the jury simply arrived at the wrong verdict, has his appeal dismissed.'

[65] P. Hill, 'Finding Finality', *New Law Journal*, 146 (1996), 1552–4. Some of the *Rough Justice* cases are published in the books by M. Young and P. Hill, *Rough Justice* (London, 1983), and by P. Hill, M. Young, and T. Sargant, *More Rough Justice* (Harmondsworth, 1985).

for all reasonable and impartial persons. In the Steel case his concern is the fact that there was evidence, not put to the jury, that threw additional doubt on the reliability of the confession. The murdered girl could have used two paths to get to where she was killed. Steel's confession was only compatible with her having used one of these. The victim's family had provided statements that she favoured the other, shorter route. These statements were produced by the police, but not used by the defence, who had concentrated on a somewhat unattractive medical defence: that even if Steel attacked the girl, it was her doctors who had killed her by turning off her life support machine. Hill wants the matter reheard, with the additional evidence of the victim's preference for the second route fully considered, on the assumption that this (together with unspecified 'other' evidence throwing doubt on Steel's confession) might lead to his acquittal. Hill has also carried out an enquiry into the police investigations. He can show that a series of accidents led the police to commit themselves to a version of the murder involving the less likely longer route. The implication (not fully spelled out) is that Steel's confession involved an unlikely route because it came from suggestions put by the police during the interrogation. As Steel's retraction must have forced the jury to consider that his confession was a response to police questions, the *accident* by which the police adopted their version of events is new, previously undisclosed, corroboration of Steel's explanation for his confession.

By itself and from the perspective of any appeal court committed to finality (and respect for trial court proceedings) this is a pretty thin basis for overturning a jury's verdict. If one starts from a position of deference to *that* jury it requires one to assume that the jury's assessment of Steel's retraction hung in a delicate balance. If that jury had heard evidence of the greater convenience of the shorter route, the victim's preference for it, and the accidents that caused the police to believe that the victim had taken the longer route, they might have believed Steel's retraction and assumed that his confession came from suggestions put to him in interrogation. But a general assumption that the verdicts of juries are reached on such fine balances is simply too threatening to the legal system. There is an enormous potential to rehear cases using unused evidence and unstated arguments. This is not solely a consequence of errors by the defence at trial or their general lack of resources. Sometimes arguments and evidence have to be sacrificed deliberately in order to strengthen a defence case. Laymen, as members of juries, are likely to react adversely to a defence that reads like legal pleadings: 'I was not present at the crime, but if I was present I did not attack X, but if I did attack X others struck the fatal blow', etc. And even within one line of argument a defence team must choose which of their witnesses are likely to perform better at trial. Calling more witnesses to make a single point does not only create a risk of unnecessary repetition. Plausible evidence by a strong witness can be undermined by implausible evidence from a weak one. Many commentators have likened this process of selection and tactics to a game. Hill wishes to overcome the limitations of such a game by playing it again, and again, until every possible version of the defence case has been properly assessed. His standard is that of *best evidence*. He envisages a system where nothing goes wrong, and every aspect of a case is fully explored and assessed.

Hill proposes that miscarriage cases are not simply reheard, but reinvestigated, and the processes of reinvestigation and rehearing should not be limited by any restrictions or principles. Any evidence must be reconsidered which, on the balance of probabilities, is worthy of consideration within an individual case. Such rehearings and reinvestigations must be approached without commitment to the integrity of current procedures for investigation or trial, for we 'must not flinch from facing up to the two most reprehensible possibilities in a court room—the prejudiced jury and the crooked, incompetent or simply over-worked police officer.'[66] This sceptical approach, reflecting many of the problems identified as fact scepticism in Chapter 2, goes beyond the approach likely to be adopted by any appellate court. There is no commitment to the original jury's verdict. Indeed, in recognition of the inappropriateness of current trial practices to an inquiry of this kind, Hill concludes that: 'Inevitably, such a process will have to be more inquisitorial than adversarial.'[67] Single trials, at least in cases involving serious crimes, would be the exception rather than the norm, as these 'have become too complex to be necessarily *finalised* at one hearing at one particular point in time. Finality in some cases may have to be the result of a longer process than a simple trial.'[68] Although this procedure is to be limited to 'problem cases', the standard of best evidence and the generally sceptical approach to jury verdicts and police practices argue for a system in which the only verdicts that cannot be appealed against are those which achieve finality in the sense that no reasonable person could doubt the prisoner's guilt.

Hill's commitment to truth leads him to construct a criminal procedure shaped by his own practices as an investigative journalist. He illustrates how the issue of finality is not simply a question of trading off truth and cost. Finality goes to the possibility of the legal system existing as a stable system, with definite borders. For Hill, a trial is too simple a mechanism for getting at something as complex as truth. Indeed, any structured and routine institution would lack the necessary flexibility. We need an open process of enquiry, unlimited by restrictions of principle, uncommitted to traditional practices. This argument goes beyond issues of cost, though these are likely to make it unacceptable to any rational policy forum. It requires the legal system to surrender its authority to decide on the guilt or

---

[66] 'Finding Finality', n. 65 above, 1554.   [67] Ibid.
[68] Ibid. (our emphasis).

innocence of individuals with *any* finality, thus presenting a challenge to the authority of any legal system. All verdicts (including, although Hill neglects this point, acquittals) are only contingent. If challenged, closure is postponed whilst there is further investigation and rehearing. Fresh challenges, including renewed scepticism towards those who adjudicated at earlier hearings, should produce further investigation and hearings. And lastly, unpinning all this is only a qualified scepticism. Hill believes that these best procedures will produce finality, meaning incontrovertible truth. But if one accepts the full fact sceptic's position, no verdict is ever *final* in the sense in which Hill uses this term.

While Hill seeks truth, Pattenden, as a liberal academic lawyer, seeks a consistent interpretation of miscarriage of justice that pursues truth *and* due process. But she does not sufficiently explain what mandate would achieve this. Without restriction, the pursuit of both goals must be at least as unrealizable as Hill's pursuit of truth. As such, Pattenden's second suggested remedy (increasing the resources made available to the Court) is unlikely to prevent high profile miscarriages from arising. However, if due process means a commitment to traditional (or stable) practices and principles, and as a consequence a willingness to sacrifice the pursuit of truth, Pattenden's formula would be more practical than Hill's; though such a sacrifice opens the legal system to journalists' criticisms that innocent people are sacrificed to lawyers' *games*.

We believe that *Tragic Choices* analysis offers a better explanation for the criticisms levelled at the Court than rational analysis that assumes that there is a practical problem that can be solved by (even radical) reforms. If the Court has managed to achieve a general reputation for *excessive* attention to errors of law this is, we would argue, the result of the difficulties which the legal system has in presenting due process as a value independent of truth within the communications of other systems. And if the Court's general reputation is of an insufficient commitment to the value of truth, this is due to its consistent inability to present its commitment to the existing practices for obtaining convictions at the first-order level as a commitment to truth.

D. AFTER THE LAST CRISIS

Recent judgments of the *new* Court of Appeal exhibit the same tensions and management of those tensions as previous Courts of Appeal. But, at the same time, the authority of the Court of Appeal is being reconstructed under the influence of changing personnel, new statutory powers, a new procedure for referral and a constant threat of crisis from the construction of miscarriages within other systems, particularly the media but also politics. If, as we suggest, that reconstruction is not simply a rational response to miscarriages, then what new elements does it involve? A rational response would set a target for reducing the number of wrongful convictions. We have argued that this is not a plausible task. *Tragic Choices* analysis sees the task differently, as reconstruction for the purposes of disguising the sacrifice of fundamental values. We would argue that the Court of Appeal has always operated with an eye to its audiences, which audiences include its construction of the public. The new elements, in response to the latest crisis and reforms, include a more concentrated commitment to reinforce legal authority by responding directly to a particular audience, namely the media. The constant refrain against trial by media goes hand in hand with a greater willingness to satisfy media-generated demands. This can be illustrated in a number of ways.

Before the Royal Commission on Criminal Justice had even reported, a new Lord Chief Justice (Lord Taylor) had presented himself as a man more willing to look sympathetically at miscarriages of justice. In order to convince the public of this new approach, the Court promptly reached some decisions that had some, albeit limited, implications for the general conduct of criminal trials. In *Ward*, the Court strongly criticized many of the key actors including the police and the forensic science service, indicating that standards of procedure and requirements for disclosure should be significantly higher than occurred in that case, in the knowledge that new practices had already been introduced.[69] In the *Cardiff Three* case[70] the Court suggested that standards of oppressive questioning by the police could extend to aggressive and repetitive questioning. And in the *Taylor Sisters* case,[71] the Court of Appeal questioned the ability of the jury to overcome extensive and prejudicial media reporting. But increasing confidence in a system by using the second-order mechanism to change the first-order allocation is a process that is difficult to maintain, remembering of course that the first-order allocation is a sacrifice of fundamental values. There are no procedures that can embody truth and fairness (or justice) without sacrificing one to the other, and both to cost. It is, as the Royal Commission correctly understood, but may have been naive to state, all a question of 'balance'.[72] Stability of first-order allocation is better achieved by changing the main second-order mechanism itself, reforming the Court of Appeal.

In the Criminal Appeal Act 1995, as outlined in Chapter 3, we saw the latest in the series of reforms of the Court of Appeal's powers. The Royal

---

[69] *Ward* (1993) 96 Cr. App. R 1.   [70] *Paris and others* (1993) 97 Cr. App. R 99.
[71] *Taylor* (1994) 98 Cr. App. R 361.
[72] The *Runciman Report*, n. 19 above, ch. 1 para. 27. A critique of the use of the metaphor of balance, when considering the criminal justice process, that approximates to some of the conclusions presented in this chapter, is presented by G. Maher, 'Balancing Rights and Interests in the Criminal Process', in A. Duff and N. Simmonds (eds.), *Philosophy and the Criminal Law* (Wiesbaden, 1984), 99–108. And see our trenchant criticism of the use of this metaphor in section E of Ch. 2.

Commission had wanted the Court to adopt a less restrictive approach to the quashing of convictions. Its research showed that most convictions were quashed on the basis of error at trial, usually in the trial judge's summing up.[73] It wanted the Court to adopt a less deferential approach to the verdicts of juries and to be ready to accept that a jury might have made a mistake, even where no procedural error had occurred. To encourage this more liberal approach, they sought to find a form of words for a reformulation of the Court's powers, which offered *guidance* to the Court. In addition, as we have described in Chapter 5, it recommended that the responsibility of the Home Secretary's C3 Division to investigate and refer cases to the Court of Appeal should be replaced by a new *independent* authority. Both these recommendations were enacted, with minor modifications, in the Criminal Appeal Act 1995. The reasons given for abolishing Home Office investigations and the Home's Secretary's power of referral to the Court were mainly constitutional: the Home Secretary, as a member of the executive, was reluctant to usurp the constitutional functions of the Court of Appeal. A non-government body could be expected to take a more robust attitude to investigation and the referral back to the Court of Appeal of cases that had already been the subject of appeal. By presenting the reluctance and limitations of the Home Secretary and C3 Division as a constitutional problem, one was able to seek a constitutional answer.[74] The new powers of the Court of Appeal are a far less substantial change. Indeed, as becomes apparent from reading the Royal Commission's Report, and even more so from the debates in Parliament, there is a definite sense of rearranging the emperor's clothes.[75] As we have shown in Chapter 3, the Court of Appeal has always had the formal statutory power to define whatever it saw fit as a miscarriage of justice, to be as liberal as it wished towards new evidence, and to be as disrespectful as it should choose towards the verdicts of juries.

A second example of the greater willingness of the Court to speak directly to the media is the new role given to apology within the judgments of the Court of Appeal. Apology has had a very limited role in traditional judgments of this Court. Even in *classic*[76] miscarriage cases, such as that of Stefan Kiszko, where medical evidence was able to prove innocence, the apology was grudging.[77] There is good reason for this. What does it mean for the Court of Appeal to apologize? Are they, like a parent, apologizing for a child's misbehaviour? Shouldn't it be for others to apologize for what

[73] See n. 19 above, Royal Commission, *Runciman Report*, ch. 10, paras. 3 and 35.
[74] See our analysis in section D of Ch. 5.
[75] See D. Schiff and R. Nobles, 'Criminal Appeal Act 1995: The Semantics of Jurisdiction', *Modern Law Review*, 59 (1996), 573–81.
[76] See our explanation for the use of this adjective, with reference to Kiszko's case, in section E/4 of Ch. 4.
[77] See Pattenden, n. 42 above, 372, n. 203.

they have been responsible for? Gratuitous apologies can be easily criticized, while acceptable apologies are not easy to construct: 'The production
of a satisfactory apology is a delicate and precarious transaction.'[78]
Recently, however, the Court of Appeal has started to offer apologies more
frequently and less grudgingly. As Pattenden suggests: 'There were
complaints in the 1980s that, when the CACD quashed a conviction
because of an unsatisfactory verdict, it did so grudgingly and without
expressing regret that the appellant had been the victim of a miscarriage of
justice. All this has now changed.'[79] And the media latch on to statements
of apology to enrich their stories. A good example is the reporting of the
successful appeal on behalf of Hussein Mattan who was executed for
murder in 1952; the first case referred to the Court of Appeal by the
Criminal Cases Review Commission. In the Court's judgment was an
expression of 'profound regret': 'The court today can only hope that its
decision will provide some crumb of comfort for his surviving relatives.'[80]
Apologies resound well in the stories that the media tell. But whilst the
media might give support to calls for apologies, they are not necessarily
convinced of the genuineness, or benefits, of such apologies: 'But, in an era
where everything from Bloody Sunday to the ghost of Derek Bentley may
be disinterred for apologies, when it is all too late; when every certainty of
today is tomorrow's shame: don't hold your breath.'[81] Relying on new
devices to reinforce authority and demonstrate a commitment to the
rhetoric of justice also has the risk of creating further incentives for those
seeking to show that their convictions were wrongful. Alongside the oft-
sought declaration of innocence that the Court of Appeal is ill-equipped to
provide, they may seek the Court's apology for the institutions and persons
that it does not control nor, in any meaningful sense, can be held responsible for.[82] In 1998 the Court of Appeal apologized in the following terms
for the fifteen years of imprisonment suffered by a man who was revealed
by psychological tests only carried out in 1994 to have a weak personality
likely to lead to a false confession. 'A grave injustice was done to Mr.
Roberts. We are conscious that the unreserved apology we offer him for it
and our profound regret that it should have occurred will not give him back
those lost years of life and liberty.' In making this apology, Lord Justice
Henry added that medical science and the law had advanced since the
conviction. He was apologizing for a system that was 'human and fallible'.[83]

---

[78] N. Tavuchis, *Mea Culpa: A Sociology of Apology* (Stanford, 1991), Preface.
[79] Pattenden, n. 42 above, 181.
[80] 'Seaman wrongly Hanged in 1952', *The Guardian* 25 Feb. 98 (Duncan Campbell).
[81] 'Conspiracy of Truth', *The Guardian* 3 Aug. 98 (Peter Preston).
[82] There may be parallels with medical negligence cases where many plaintiffs claim that
their main motive is to achieve a full explanation and an apology, rather than damages.
[83] 'Innocent Man Spent 15 Years in Jail', *The Guardian* 20 March 98 (Duncan Campbell).

E. A TRAGIC CHOICES AND AUTOPOIETIC SYSTEMS THEORY ANALYSIS OF CRIMINAL JUSTICE REFORM

We are confident that the history of periodic crises of confidence, and its relationship to the inability of the Court of Appeal to respond fully to the media's interpretation and construction of miscarriage of justice, is better understood through the analysis provided by Calabresi and Bobbitt's *Tragic Choices*. In this final section, we offer the hypothesis that autopoietic systems theory, combined with *Tragic Choices* analysis, gives insights into the failure of high profile miscarriages of justice to produce radical reforms of criminal justice. In particular, we believe that those who seek radical reform of criminal justice often exhibit two failings. First, whilst they welcome the work of the media in establishing orthodox examples of miscarriage of justice they pay insufficient attention to the media's own understanding of what constitutes miscarriage. They hope to hijack examples of incorrect verdicts in order to strengthen the rights of suspects throughout the processes and practices of criminal justice. Systems theory points to the mismatch between the discourses of the media and radical lawyers. Secondly, radical reformers are unwilling to consider the implications of *Tragic Choices* analysis for the practicality and feasibility of their proposals for change.

At the end of the twentieth century, just as at the beginning, miscarriages of justice pose a problem for rational law reform. At its simplest this problem can be simply stated. Despite the century's reforms and progress in criminal justice, despite the attempts to move criminal justice closer to justice, miscarriages continue. At the end of this century, as at the beginning, further reforms, probably through legislation, are required to prevent further miscarriages from occurring in the first place, and to create an appeal process that is capable of correcting them efficiently if they do occur. Such an approach is well represented in the Report of this latest Royal Commission on Criminal Justice. Their approach to law reform falls within the tradition of argument for rational reform. Such a tradition sees no intrinsic reason why the different elements of and values in criminal justice cannot be brought together in such a way as to improve it. Interestingly, the main critics of the Royal Commission share the same general approach, although they disagree strongly on many of the particular suggested reforms. Whereas there is talk about fairness and rights throughout the Commission's Report, its guiding principle, terms of reference,[84] and its one *definite* standard are the correctness of verdicts in terms

---

[84] The Royal Commission's principal terms of reference were: 'to examine the effectiveness of the criminal justice system in England and Wales in securing the conviction of those guilty of criminal offences and the acquittal of those who are innocent, having regard to the efficient use of resources' (The *Runciman Report*, n. 19 above, iii).

of truth. The standards of many of its critics are less geared towards truth and more focused on fairness and rights.

The critics are right in thinking that the problem with referring to factually correct verdicts as the leading guide to reform is that the ensuing discussion leaves many aspects of the present practices and procedures of criminal justice, and many of the demands of those who seek radical reforms, hard to justify. In order to achieve truth one has to rely on evidence. An approach to evidence that has as its single goal the outcome of truthful verdicts is, as Bentham has shown in relation to what he called free proof,[85] best undertaken without reference to rules or rights. All one needs are impartial, totally rational adjudicators, of superior intelligence. But there is little reason to believe that, for example, the jury fits this ideal, or many aspects of the adversary process of trial.[86] When truth is treated as an objective and rational value, rights that conflict with truth appear irrational and often subjective. Thus it should not surprise radical lawyers when pressure for reforms generated by miscarriages of justice leads to a decrease in rights that cannot demonstrate a convincing link to the reliability of evidence or verdicts. For example, despite assertions that the miscarriage cases that generated the recent crisis demonstrated the need to strengthen suspects' rights, the last Government was able to dilute the right to silence. In the Criminal Justice and Public Order Act 1994 the caution was changed to warn suspects of the likelihood of adverse comment being made at trial if they failed to reveal facts relevant to their defence when arrested. The Government, on the basis of the standard adopted by the Royal Commission, justified this reform: that it would not decrease the frequency with which the innocent would be acquitted, but would increase the frequency of *the guilty being convicted*. The Royal Commission had found it difficult, using its terms of reference, to uphold the right to silence, or at least to show why its protection was consistent with more truthful convictions. What it ended with was a proposal that further eroded the right to silence, although not one that went as far as abolition. And it failed to recommend any other form of protection, such as a corroboration rule for confessions.[87] This is even more striking since the Royal Commission's sponsored research study presents evidence that is clearly supportive of the need for corroboration of any confession not made under judicial supervision.[88]

---

[85] Arguments about this conception are discussed by L. J. Cohen, 'Freedom of Proof', in W. Twining (ed.), *Facts in Law* (Wiesbaden, 1983), 1–21.

[86] See our analysis in section C of Ch. 2.

[87] This failure has been strongly criticized by many. See, e.g., A. A. S. Zuckerman, 'Bias and Suggestibility: Is There an Alternative to the Right to Silence?', in D. Morgan and G. Stephenson (eds.), *Suspicion and Silence: The Right to Silence in Criminal Investigations* (London, 1994), ch. 8.

[88] M. McConville, *Corroboration and Confessions: The Impact of a Rule Requiring that no Conviction can be Sustained on the Basis of Confession Evidence Alone*, Royal Commission on Criminal Justice Research Study No. 13 (London, 1993).

However, one should not conclude that the strength of the rhetoric of truth leaves no room for rights, so that the process of reform will gradually strip all rights from criminal justice. Truth cannot be found in legal processes without confidence in the veracity of the institutions and actors of criminal justice. In law (as in science[89]) such confidence is reliant upon irrational ideas of fairness and adherence to procedures and rules as well as the commitment to truth. It may also require measures that lead to a decrease in the number of convictions. Confidence cannot be restored to the institutions and personnel who are responsible for preparing and deliberating on evidence on which verdicts are based, if one starts from the premise that no opportunity to obtain evidence should be lost, and no person genuinely believed to be guilty should be acquitted. To search for legal truth without agreed standards on the conduct of that search (due process) is like trying to generate scientific truth without agreed standards for tests. Standards inspire confidence in the data generated, and reduce the need to consider subjective factors like the actor's good faith or honesty. The existence of standards and procedures of proof can also work to reduce the cost of criminal justice. An unrestricted process of free proof leaves no room for the concept of a *fair trial*. As such, it places no limits, other than the mere fact of cost, on the criminal justice process. By contrast, a rights-based process may legitimize outcomes at less cost than one fully committed to truth. And as we argued earlier in our analysis of Hill's proposals,[90] free proof is not only far more expensive than due process, but without the latter, no legal system can exist. Traditional practices, particularly when understood in terms of rights and due process, can provide a far more practical method for achieving legitimate convictions than a total commitment to truth. Consider, for example, the right to ask for a solicitor when arrested. If confessions in a police station are inherently suspect, a mere right to ask for a solicitor is less likely to protect the weak and vulnerable than a prohibition on asking questions in the solicitor's absence. Indeed, if one accepts that police stations are inherently oppressive and the service provided by solicitors hopelessly inadequate, then one might wish to abolish as admissible evidence confessions made in custody, even on videotape. A right to a solicitor, particularly one that is routinely not enjoyed, provides a relatively inexpensive mechanism for legitimizing confession evidence.

Whilst reforms will be unable to remove all due process and rights (even those which have a tenuous link to the accuracy of verdicts), the dominant media understanding of miscarriage in terms of truth places reforms that have no persuasive link to accuracy at a severe disadvantage. The technical nature of legal rights places further difficulties in the way of making any appeal to *public* support. Again, consider the right to silence, as discussed in the Royal Commission's Report. While the Commission recommended

---

[89] See section C of Ch. 5.   [90] See p. 250 above.

no change in the restrictions on comment at trial about a suspect's failure to volunteer information when questioned, it first undertook a detailed examination of the existing opportunities for adverse comment that showed the lack of any need for change.[91] The right to silence was a right already riddled with exceptions. As such, while some publicity was likely to follow the Government's decision to ignore the Commission's recommendation, and some commentators treated the changes as an important infringement on the right to silence, the difficulties of seeking to educate *the public* into the exact significance of the changes were considerable.

At this point one needs to ask what, at the end of the twentieth century, should be the leading guide to reform? What are the 'basic values which criminal justice should seek to uphold', and is it possible to present 'a consistent, comprehensive account of the workings of that system'?[92] The Royal Commission has been severely criticized for failing to formulate an answer to the first two of these questions or to achieve the account required by the third. 'Our evaluation of the Runciman Commission is that it fails on . . . these counts, fudging and compromising on issues of principle and providing a strangely piecemeal and incoherent analysis of the system and a seemingly contradictory set of proposals for change.'[93] As well as being criticized for failing in these tasks, the Commission was also widely criticized for adopting a spurious and *ad hoc* notion of 'balance',[94] in order to trade off justice against cost,[95] and for adopting an optimistic approach,[96] which denied that rights and truth needed to be traded off at all. But the many and varied responses that the Commission's Report generated serve to illustrate the difficulties in providing a straightforward and consistent explanation of the values that inform, or should inform, the practices of criminal justice. Reactions to the Royal Commission's Report would seem to suggest that, beyond truth, commitment to other values such as due process, fairness, and rights did not provide clear and consistent choices for reform in a uniform way to many commentators. In other words (and as our arguments in Chapter 2 and *Tragic Choices* analysis both suggest) there is no stable trade off between the values that different systems' communications and the legal system's communications about criminal justice

[91] The *Runciman Report*, n. 19 above, ch. 4.
[92] L. Bridges and M. McConville, 'Keeping Faith with Their Own Convictions: The Royal Commission on Criminal Justice', *Modern Law Review*, 57 (1994), 76.
[93] Ibid.
[94] See A. Sanders, 'Thinking about Criminal Justice', in M. McConville and L. Bridges (eds.), n. 19 above, ch. 12, 144–8, and see n. 72 above.
[95] 'The 1993 Royal Commission report appeared to have no overall philosophy whatsoever. Its terms of reference exhorted the commissioners to "have regard" ' to cost, and its hotch-potch of recommendations appeared to be determined less by justice than by economics' (D. Rose, *In the Name of the Law: The Collapse of Criminal Justice* (London, 1996), 323).
[96] See R. Nobles and D. Schiff, 'Optimism Writ Large: A Critique of the Runciman Commission on Criminal Justice', in M. McConville and L. Bridges (eds.), n. 19 above, ch. 4.

rhetorically regard as fundamental. Criminal justice practices (including the praxis of reform) enjoy more support through having rhetorical values that *cannot* be reduced to each other, or embodied in those practices. Limiting criminal procedures to a set of practices that have a close relationship to a single and consistent set of basic values would be extremely rational, but it would not create criminal *justice*.

F. CONCLUSION

> The other reason why the authorities seem so intractable in these matters is, I think, that they are only too aware that, once one case has been remedied, then energies will merely switch to another. The injustices in this country stack up relentlessly. The longer the public's attentions are concentrated on a few cases, the less likely they are to grasp the full enormity of the problem.[97]

Unlike the members of the Runciman Royal Commission and many of its critics, and many who write in the media, we are sceptics about the ability of the legal system to produce true verdicts or those that accord with the rhetoric of due process and rights. The miracle of conviction is that, despite scepticism, it continues to appear to offer objective truth and justice. But the more successful the acceptance of the objectivity and legitimacy of conviction the more difficult the task of the Court of Appeal. In particular we do not believe that the Court of Appeal can ever deal adequately with the disjunction between the fundamental values that it espouses in its rhetoric, and current or reformed practices. We have illustrated the challenge of scepticism in Chapter 2. The press, which generally operates in a non-sceptical manner in order to utilize convictions for routine reporting, will periodically adopt a more sceptical approach and subject the Court of Appeal to strong criticism. To carry this paradox to a higher philosophical level, the rationality that arose from the period known as the Enlightenment, with its strong commitment to a scientific paradigm, offers both legitimacy and threat to the legal system. On the one hand, it has encouraged the legal system to present its traditional practices as likely to produce accurate verdicts. On the other, the scientific paradigm offers a serious challenge to the legal system. Not only does it expose processes that do not contribute to accuracy to criticism for their irrationality, but it also provides a standard for truth that law cannot hope to live up to. Law both gains, and loses, from being misread as science.

Different communities have different conceptions of miscarriage of justice. Even though, as we have suggested, there may be no clear meaning of justice in modern society, miscarriage of justice carries widespread abhorrence. However, that abhorrence cannot be simply translated into

---

[97] B. Woffinden, *Hanratty: The Final Verdict* (London, 1997), 452.

legal activity or legal reform. *Tragic Choices* analysis helps us to understand the underlying problematic. Fact scepticism and value scepticism cannot be eliminated by rational reforms. For a whole range of reasons the sacrifice of fundamental values is a precondition of the allocation of resources at the first-order level in criminal justice. The first-order level gives priority to a particular process of investigation of criminal offences and a particular process of trial. The responsibility of the second-order level, both in the tasks of investigation (whether in the hands of the Criminal Cases Review Commission, the police, an independent inquiry, or the Court of Appeal) and in appeal, is to remedy and manage miscarriage. We have tried to show throughout this book why the latter task of managing miscarriage is likely to take priority over the former and why other communities, particularly the media, will inevitably find that neither task has been achieved adequately or to their satisfaction.

Where does this analysis leave those committed to reforming criminal justice so as to narrow the gap between its practices and the values of truth or due process? With, we hope, a greater awareness of the difficulties that they face? Our analysis may reduce the optimism felt by reformers who expect the media's episodic construction of miscarriages as evidence of a crisis of confidence in criminal justice to lead to the introduction of increased rights for suspects. They should also be wary of reforms to the appeal process. High profile miscarriages that concentrate attention on the inability of the legal system to correct its mistakes can lead, as in 1995 and before, to changes in the appeal process. But if an appeal process has an unavoidable relationship of deference to the body that it reviews, it is unlikely to operate in a manner leading to radical changes in the procedures for investigation and trial. Those who seek improvements in the accuracy or fairness of first-order procedures would do well to concentrate on direct reforms. Although an appeal body has some ability to produce change in the institutions it reviews, it is unlikely to demand or procure major change. High profile miscarriages of justice generate hostility and impatience towards bodies with official responsibility for remedying mistakes. Reformers should not confuse the focus of this hostility with the appropriate site for reform: the first-order institutions that generate mistakes. But even when reformers concentrate on the procedures that produce miscarriages, rather than the bodies with formal responsibility for correcting them, using miscarriages of justice as a platform for change is made problematic by considerations of tragic choice. Imagine a sympathetic civil servant reading a list of radical reform proposals (which might include anything from the abandonment of confession evidence to the replacement of the adversarial process with an inquisitorial one). He might respond as follows:

If I make these changes, then, *ceteris paribus*, you claim that we will move closer to justice. You have not (and probably cannot) cost these changes in terms of the number of factually guilty persons who will not be convicted (even if you can cost them in terms of the schools and hospitals that we will not be able to afford). You tell me that, when these reforms have been introduced, criminal justice will continue to produce high profile miscarriages and perceptions of crisis, as these are a systematic consequence of the relationship between law and the media. Even if we change criminal justice to an inquisitorial process, we would be importing procedures whose outcomes we cannot really predict, from countries whose practitioners also recognize a gap between their procedures and the rhetoric of justice. And then, of course, *ceteris paribus* never applies. So a change that closes the gap between justice and practice in isolation may actually increase it over time, and throughout criminal justice (for example, stricter due process rules may increase the willingness of the police to engage in corruption). Well, in view of the current crisis, I shall of course institute some reforms, probably in the Court of Appeal.

This book reflects our commitment as academics to the better understanding of criminal justice. We describe what we see, not what we would like so see. And what we see is neither particularly optimistic nor, in an objective sense, ethical. We do not wish our work to be read as a celebration of its conclusions, nor as a denigration of the work of those who commit themselves to the improvement of criminal justice. Our answer to the problems set out in the previous paragraph would have very little to do with rational problem-solving. Imprisoning the factually innocent is wrong. Denying suspects fair procedures is wrong. This is an ethical view that we share with reformers. But we cannot escape the tragic choice of trading off truth and due process (including rights) or the wider trade off between criminal justice and values such as education, health, and personal security.[98]

We wish to end this book with an apocryphal story, which highlights how a search for knowledge and the results of that search do not and should not be conclusive in determining one's own actions or one's assessment of the actions of others. The story is of the rabbis of Auschwitz. The rabbis meet to discuss, in the light of their current experiences, evidence for the existence of God. In assessing their current experiences they are forced to agree that the evidence points clearly to the conclusion that there is no God. It is the Sabbath. Having ended their discussion, they go to pray.

---

[98] Or the even more tragic trade off between all of these values and the mundane aspects of private consumption, such as underarm deodorant, G-Plan kitchens, and personalized car number plates.

Bibliography

ADAM, H. L., *The Penge Mystery, the Story of the Stauntons* (London: Pearson, 1913).

AITKEN, C. G. C., *Statistics and the Evaluation of Evidence from Forensic Science* (Chichester: John Wiley, 1995).

APPIGNANESI, L. and MAITLAND, S. (eds.), *The Rushdie File* (London: Fourth Estate, 1989).

ARCHBOLD, J. F., *Criminal Pleading Evidence and Practice*, 20th edn. (London: Sweet & Maxwell, 1918).

—— *Criminal Pleading Evidence and Practice*, 25th edn. (London: Sweet & Maxwell, 1931).

—— *Criminal Pleading Evidence and Practice*, 35th edn. (London: Sweet & Maxwell, 1962).

ASHWORTH, A., 'Plea, Venue and Discontinuance', *Criminal Law Review* [1993], 830–40.

—— *The Criminal Process: An Evaluative Study*, 2nd edn. (New York: Oxford University Press, 1998).

BALDWIN, J. and MCCONVILLE, M., *Negotiated Justice: Pressures to Plead Guilty* (London: Martin Robertson, 1977).

—— *Courts, Prosecution and Conviction* (Oxford: Clarendon Press, 1981).

BARRY, B., The Liberal Theory of Justice: A Critical Examination of the Principal Doctrines of A Theory of Justice by John Rawls (Oxford: Clarendon Press, 1973).

Beck Inquiry, Report of the Committee of Inquiry into the Case of Mr. Adolf Beck, Cd. 2315 (London: HMSO, 1904).

BECK, A., 'Is Law an Autopoietic System?', *Oxford Journal of Legal Studies*, 14 (1994), 401–18.

BENNETT, W. L. and FELDMAN, M., *Reconstructing Reality in the Courtroom: Justice and Judgment in American Culture* (New Brunswick: Rutgers University Press, 1981).

BENTHAM, J., *The Book of Fallacies* (London: John and H. L. Hunt, 1824).

—— *Rationale of Judicial Evidence, specially Applied to English Practice*, v, ed. J. S. Mill (London: Hunt & Clarke, 1827).

—— 'On the Declaration of the Rights of Man and the Citizen Decreed by the French Constituent Assembly in 1791', in B. Parekh (ed.), *Bentham's Political Thought* (London: Croom Helm, 1973), 257–90.

BENTLEY, D., *English Criminal Justice in the Nineteenth Century* (London: Hambledon, 1998).

BLACKSTONE, W., *Commentaries on the Laws of England (1765–69)*, iv: *Of Public Wrongs* (1769), Facsimile edition (Chicago: University of Chicago Press, 1979).

BLOM-COOPER, L., *The Birmingham Six and Other Cases: Victims of Circumstance* (London: Duckworth, 1997).

BRANDON, R. and DAVIES, C., *Wrongful Imprisonment: Mistaken Convictions and their Consequences* (London: Allen & Unwin, 1973).

BRIDGES, L. and MCCONVILLE, M., 'Keeping Faith with Their Own Convictions: The

Royal Commission on Criminal Justice', *Modern Law Review*, 57 (1994), 75–90.

CAHN, E., *The Sense of Injustice* (Bloomington: Indiana University Press, 1949).

CALABRESI, G. and BOBBITT, P., *Tragic Choices* (New York: W. W. Norton, 1978).

CALLAGHAN, HUGH (with Sally Mulready), *Cruel Fate: One Man's Triumph over Injustice* (Dublin: Poolbeg, 1994).

CHIBNALL, S., *Law-and-Order News: An Analysis of Crime Reporting in the British Press* (London: Tavistock, 1977).

CHOWDHURY, S. R., *Rule of Law in a State of Emergency: The Paris Minimum Standards of Human Rights Norms in a State of Emergency* (London: Pinter, 1989).

COHEN, H. J., *The Criminal Appeal Act, 1907* (London: Jordan, 1908).

COHEN, L. J., 'Freedom of Proof', in W. Twining (ed.), *Facts in Law* (Wiesbaden: Franz Steiner Verlag, 1983), 1–21.

COHEN, S. and YOUNG, J., (eds.), *The Manufacture of News: Social Problems, Deviance and the Mass Media* (London: Constable, 1973).

COLEMAN, J. L. and HOLOHAN, W. L., 'Review of Tragic Choices', *California Law Review*, 67 (1979), 1379–93.

COLEMAN, R. F. and WALLS, H. J., 'The Evaluation of Scientific Evidence', *Criminal Law Review* [1974], 276–87.

COMMISSIONERS ON CRIMINAL LAW, *Eighth Report*, 1845, Parl. Pap. (1845), vol. xiv, 161.

CONAN DOYLE, A., *The Case of George Edalji, Special investigation* . . . Reprinted from the Daily Telegraph, etc. (London: Blake, 1907).

CORNISH, W. R., *The Jury* (London: Allen Lane, 1968).

Criminal Cases Review Commission, Introducing the Commission.

Criminal Cases Review Commission, *Annual Report 1997–98* (18 June 1998).

DEAN, M., 'Criminal Appeal Act 1966', *Criminal Law Review* [1966], 534–48.

DEGEORGE, B., *Interpreting Crisis: A Retrospective Analysis* (Sweden: Almqvist & Wiksell, 1987).

DERSHOWITZ, A. M., *Reasonable Doubts: The O.J. Simpson Case and the Criminal Justice System* (New York: Simon & Schuster, 1996).

Devlin and Burns, Inquiry into certain matters arising subsequent to the conviction at Liverpool Assizes on 27 February, 1952, of Edward Francis Devlin and Alfred Burns of the murder of Beatrice Alice Rimmer (the Gerrard Report), Cd. 8522 (London: HMSO, 1952).

The *Devlin Report*, Departmental Committee on Evidence of Identification in Criminal Cases, HC 338 (London: HMSO, 1976).

DEVLIN, P., *Trial by Jury* (London: Stevens & Sons, 1956).

—— *The Judge* (Oxford: Oxford University Press, 1979).

DICKSON, B., 'The Prevention of Terrorism Acts', in C. Walker and K. Starmer (eds.), *Justice in Error* (London: Blackstone Press, 1993), 178–95.

Donovan Committee Report, Interdepartmental Committee on the Court of Criminal Appeal, Cmnd. 2755 (London: HMSO, 1965).

DWORKIN, R., *Taking Rights Seriously* (London: Duckworth, 1977).

—— *Law's Empire* (London: Fontana, 1986).

EASTON, S. M., *The Case for the Right to Silence*, 2nd edn. (Aldershot: Ashgate, 1998).

ELLIOTT, M., 'The Frontiersmen', *Modern Law Review*, 44 (1981), 345–52.

ENRIGHT, S., and MORTON, J., *Taking Liberties: The Criminal Jury in the 1990's* (London: Weidenfeld and Nicolson, 1990).

ERICSON, R. V., 'Mass Media, Crime, Law and Justice', *British Journal of Criminology*, 31/3 (1991), 219–49.

—— 'Why Law is Like News', in D. Nelken (ed.), 1996, 195–230.

ERICSON, R. V., BARANEK, P. M., and CHAN, J. B. L., *Representing Order: Crime, Law, and Justice in the News Media* (Toronto: University of Toronto Press, 1991).

FERNANDEZ-ARMESTO, F., *Truth. A History and a Guide for the Perplexed* (London: Black Swan, 1997).

FIELD, S. and THOMAS, P., (eds.), *Justice and Efficiency? The Royal Commission on Criminal Justice* (Oxford: Blackwell, 1994).

FINKELSTEIN, M. O. and FAIRLEY, W. B., 'A Bayesian Approach to Identification Evidence', *Harvard Law Review*, 83 (1970), 489–517.

FISHMAN, M., *Manufacturing the News* (Austin: University of Texas Press, 1980).

FOOT, P., *Murder at the Farm: Who Killed Carl Bridgewater?* (London: Sidgwick and Jackson, 1986); revised edition, *The Final Story* (London: Review, 1998).

FRIEDLAND, M. L., *The Trials of Israel Lipski* (London: Macmillan, 1984).

GALLIGAN, D. J., *Due Process and Fair Procedures: A Study of Administrative Procedures* (Oxford: Clarendon Press, 1996).

GARAPON, A., 'Justice out of Court: The Dangers of Trial by Media', in D. Nelken (ed.), 1996, 231–45.

GIERE, R., 'Justifying Scientific Theories', in E. D. Klemke, R. Hollinger, and A. D. Kline (eds.), 1988, ch. 19.

GLASGOW UNIVERSITY MEDIA GROUP, *Bad News, Vol. 1* (London: Routledge and Kegan Paul, 1976).

GLASSER, T. L. and ETTEMA, J. S., 'Investigative Journalism and the Moral Order', in R. K. Avery and D. Eason (eds.), *Critical Perspectives on Media and Society* (New York: The Guildhall Press, 1991), 203–25.

GRABOSKY, P. and WILSON, P., *Journalism and Justice: How Crime is Reported* (Sydney: Pluto Press, 1989).

GREER, D. S., 'Anything but the Truth? The Reliability of Testimony in Criminal Trials', *British Journal of Criminology*, 11 (1971), 131–54.

GREER, S., 'Miscarriages of Justice Reconsidered', *Modern Law Review*, 57 (1994), 58–74.

GUDJONSSON, G., *The Psychology of Interrogation, Confessions and Testimony* (Chichester: John Wiley, 1992).

—— 'Psychological Vulnerability: Suspects at Risk' in D. Morgan and G. Stephensen (eds.), 1994, 91–106.

GUEST, S., *Ronald Dworkin* (Edinburgh: Edinburgh University Press, 1992).

HABERMAS, J., *The Theory of Communicative Action, Vol.2, Lifeworld and System; A Critique of Functionalist Reason*, trans. T. McCarthy (Cambridge: Polity, 1987).

HALL, S., CRITCHER, C., JEFFERSON, T., CLARKE, J., and ROBERTS, B., *Policing The Crisis: Mugging, the State, and Law and Order* (London: Macmillan, 1978).

HARRIS, D. J., O'BOYLE, M., and WARBRICK, C., *Law of the European Convention on Human Rights* (London: Butterworths, 1995).

HART, H. L. A., *Punishment and Responsibility* (Oxford: Clarendon Press, 1968).

HART, P. 't, 'Symbols, Rituals and Power: The Lost Dimensions of Crisis Management', *Journal of Contingencies and Crisis Management*, 1/1 (1993), 36–50.

HAY, C., 'Narrating Crisis: The Discursive Construction of the "Winter of Discontent" ', *Sociology*, 30/2 (1996), 253–77.

Heilbron Report, Advisory Group on the Law of Rape, Cmnd. 6352 (London: HMSO, 1975).

HENHAM, R., 'Human Rights, Due Process and Sentencing', *British Journal of Criminology*, 38/4 (1998), 592–610.

HEYDON, J. D. and OCKELTON, M., *Evidence: Cases and Materials*, 4th edn. (London: Butterworths, 1996).

HILL, PAUL (with R. Bennett), *Stolen Years: Before and after Guildford* (London: Corgi, 1991).

HILL, P., 'Finding Finality', *New Law Journal*, 146 (1996), 1552–4.

—— 'The Role of the Journalist', in C. Walker and K. Starmer (eds.), 1999, 271–84.

HILL, P. and YOUNG, M. with Sargant, T., *More Rough Justice* (Harmondsworth: Penguin, 1985).

HILLYARD, P., *Suspect Community: People's Experience of the Prevention of Terrorism Acts in Britain* (London: Pluto Press, 1993).

HODGKINSON, T., *Expert Evidence: Law and Practice* (London: Sweet & Maxwell, 1990).

HOLMES, O. W., *The Common Law* (Boston: Little, Brown and Co, 1881).

HOME AFFAIRS COMMITTEE 6TH REPORT SESSION 1981–82, *Miscarriages of Justice*, HC 421 (London: HMSO, 1982).

HOME AFFAIRS COMMITTEE 1ST REPORT SESSION 1998–99, *The Work of the Criminal Cases Review Commission*, HC 106 (London: HMSO, 1999).

Home Office, Government Reply to the Sixth Report from the Home Affairs Committee Session 1981–82, HC 421, Cd. 8856 (London: HMSO, 1983).

Home Office Memorandum to the Royal Commission on Criminal Justice, *Forensic Science Memorandum* (London: Home Office, 1991).

Home Office Discussion Paper, *Criminal Appeals and the Establishment of a Criminal Cases Review Authority* (London: Home Office, 1994).

House of Lords Session 1992–93, 5th Report, Select Committee on Science and Technology, *Forensic Science*, HL Paper 24 (London: HMSO, 1993).

HOWARD, M. N., 'The Neutral Expert: A Plausible Threat to Justice', *Criminal Law Review* [1991], 98–110.

HOWETT, D., *Crime, the Media and the Law* (Chichester: John Wiley, 1998).

HOWSON, C. and URBACH, P., *Scientific Reasoning: the Bayesian Approach*, 2nd edn. (Chicago: Open Court, 1993).

INMAN, M., 'The Admissibility of Confessions', *Criminal Law Review* [1981], 469–82.

JACKSON, J. D., 'The Ultimate Issue Rule: One Rule too Many', *Criminal Law Review* [1984], 75–86.

—— 'Two Methods of Proof in Criminal Procedure', *Modern Law Review*, 51 (1988), 549–68.

—— 'Law's Truth, Lay Truth and Lawyer's Truth: The Representation of Evidence in Adversary Trials', *Law and Critique*, 3/1 [1992], 29–49.

JESSEL, D., *Trial and Error* (London: Headline, 1994).

JONES, C., *Expert Witnesses: Science, Medicine, and the Practice of Law* (Oxford: Clarendon Press, 1994).

Judicial Statistics for England and Wales 1997, Cm 3980 (Lord Chancellor's Department, 1998).

JUSTICE, *Criminal Appeals* (London: Stevens, 1964).

—— *Home Office Reviews of Criminal Convictions* (London: Stevens, 1968).

—— *Miscarriages of Justice* (London: Justice, 1989).

—— *Remedying Miscarriages of Justice* (London: Justice, 1994).

JUSTICE AND THE COUNCIL FOR SCIENCE AND SOCIETY, *Science and the Administration of Justice* (London: Justice, 1991).

KAYE, T., *Unsafe and Unsatisfactory: Report of the Independent Inquiry into the Working Practices of the West Midlands Police Serious Crime Squad* (London: Civil Liberties Trust, 1991).

KAFKA, FRANZ, *The Trial*, first published in 1925, translated by W. and E. Muir (London: Secker & Warburg, 1956).

KEE, R., *Trial and Error: The Maguires, the Guildford Pub Bombings and British Justice* (London: Hamish Hamilton, 1986; Harmondsworth: Penguin, 1989).

KEMPSTER, J., *The Perversion of Justice by the Criminal Departments of the State* (London: Police Review, 1905).

KENNEALY, P., 'Talking about Autopoiesis—Order from Noise?', in G. Teubner (ed.), 1988, 349–68.

KENNEDY, L., *Ten Rillington Place* (London: Victor Gollancz, 1961).

—— (ed.), *Wicked beyond Belief: The Luton Murder Case* (St Albans: Granada, 1980).

—— 'Reforming the English Criminal Justice System', in *Truth To Tell: The Collected Writings of Ludovic Kennedy* (London: Transworld Publishers, 1991).

KEPPLINGER, H. M. and ROTH, H., 'Creating a Crisis: German Mass Media and Oil Supply in 1973–74', *Public Opinion Quarterly*, (1979), 285–96.

KING, M., 'The Truth about Autopoiesis', *Journal of Law and Society*, 20/2 (1993), 218–36.

KING, M. and SCHUTZ, A., 'The Ambitious Modesty of Niklas Luhmann', *Journal of Law and Society*, 21/3 (1994), 261–87.

KLAWANS, H. L., *The Trials of an Expert Witness: Tales of Clinical Neurology and the Law* (London: Bodley Head, 1991).

KLEMKE, E. D., HOLLINGER, R., and KLINE, A. D., (eds.), *Introductory Readings in the Philosophy of Science*, revised edn. (New York: Prometheus Books, 1988).

KNIGHT, M., *Criminal Appeals: A Study of the Powers of the Court of Appeal Criminal Division on Appeals against Conviction* (London: Stevens, 1970) and *Supplement 1969–73* (London: Stevens, 1975).

LACEY, N., *State Punishment: Political Principles and Community Values* (London: Routledge, 1988).

LANGBEIN, J. H., *Torture and the Law of Proof* (Chicago: University of Chicago Press, 1977).

LAUDAN, L., *Science and Relativism: Some Key Controversies in the Philosophy of Science* (Chicago: University of Chicago Press, 1990).

LAWTON, L. J., 'The Limitations of Expert Scientific Evidence', *Journal of the Forensic Science Society*, 20 (1980), 237–42.

LEVY, J. H., (ed.), *The Necessity for Criminal Appeal as Illustrated by the Maybrick Case and the Jurisprudence of Various Countries* (London: P. S. King, 1899).

LEWIS, D. and HUGHMAN, P., *Most Unnatural: An Inquiry into the Stafford Case* (Harmondsworth: Penguin, 1971).

LLEWELLYN, K. and HOEBEL, E. A., *The Cheyenne Way: Conflict and Case Law in Primitive Jurisprudence* (Norman: University of Oklahoma Press, 1941).

LLOYD-BOSTOCK, S., *Law in Practice* (London: Routledge, 1988).

LUHMANN, N., 'The Representation of Society within Society', *Current Sociology*, 35/2 (1987), 101–8.

—— 'The Unity of the Legal System', in G. Teubner (ed.), 1988, 12–35.

—— 'Closure and Openness: On Reality in the World of Law', in G. Teubner (ed.), 1988, 335–48.

—— 'Law as a Social System', *Northwestern University Law Review*, 83 (1989), 136–50.

—— 'The Coding of the Legal System', in G. Teubner and A. Febbrajo (eds.), 1992, 145–185.

—— 'Operational Closure and Structural Coupling: The Differentiation of the Legal System', *Cardozo Law Review*, 13 (1992), 1419–41.

MCBARNET, D. J., *Conviction: Law, the State and the Construction of Justice* (London: Macmillan, 1981).

MCCONVILLE, M., *Corroboration and Confessions: The Impact of a Rule Requiring that no Conviction can be Sustained on the Basis of Confession Evidence Alone*, Royal Commission on Criminal Justice Research Study No. 13 (London: HMSO, 1993).

MCCONVILLE, M. and BRIDGES, L. (eds.), *Criminal Justice in Crisis* (Aldershot: Edward Elgar, 1994).

MCCONVILLE, M., SANDERS, A., and LENG, R., *The Case for the Prosecution* (London: Routledge, 1991).

MACDOUGALL, A., *The Maybrick Case* (London: Balliere, 1891).

MCEWAN, J., *Evidence and the Adversarial Process: The Modern Law*, 2nd edn. (Oxford: Hart Publishing, 1998).

MCGURK, T., 'When Television is "a Court of Last Resort"', *The Listener*, 25 February 1988, 9–10.

MCKEE, G. and FRANEY, R., *Time Bomb: Irish Bombers, English Justice and the Guildford Four* (London: Bloomsbury, 1988)

MCKENZIE, M., 'A Guide to Proceedings in the Court of Appeal Criminal Division', [1997] 2 *Criminal Appeal Reports* 459–91.

MAGUIRE, M. and NORRIS, C., 'Police Investigations: Practice and Malpractice' in S. Field and P. Thomas (eds.), 1994, 72–84.

MAHER, G., 'Balancing Rights and Interests in the Criminal Process', in A. Duff and N. Simmonds (eds.), *Philosophy and the Criminal Law* (Wiesbaden: Franz Steiner Verlag, 1984), 99–108.

—— 'Reforming the Criminal Process: A Scottish Perspective', in M. McConville and L. Bridges (eds.), 1994, 59–68.

MALLESON, K., 'Miscarriages of Justice and the Accessibility of the Court of Appeal', *Criminal Law Review* [1991], 323–32.

—— *Review of the Appeal Process*, Royal Commission on Criminal Justice Research Study No. 17 (London: HMSO, 1993).

—— 'Appeals against Conviction and the Principle of Finality', in S. Field and P. Thomas (eds.), 1994, 151–64.

MANCHESTER, A. H., *Sources of English Legal History 1750–1950* (London: Butterworths, 1984).

MANSFIELD, M. and WARDLE, T., *Presumed Guilty: The British Legal System Exposed* (London: Heinemann, 1993).

MARK, R., *In the Office of Constable* (London: Collins, 1978).

MASON, J. K., 'Expert Evidence in the Adversarial System of Criminal Justice', *Medicine, Science and the Law*, 26/1 (1986), 8–12.

MATTHEWS, R., 'Tipping the Scales of Justice', *New Scientist*, 13 Dec. 1997, 18–19.

MAY, SIR JOHN, *Report of the Inquiry into the circumstances surrounding the convictions arising out of the bomb attacks in Guildford and Woolwich in 1974: Interim Report on the Maguire Case*, HC 556 (London: HMSO, 1990); *Second Report on the Maguire Case*, HC 296 (London: HMSO, 1992); *Final Report about the cases of Patrick Armstrong, Gerard Conlan, Paul Hill & Carole Richardson (the "Guildford Four")*, HC 449 (London: HMSO, 1994).

MILLER, H., *Traces of Guilt: Forensic Science and the Fight against Crime* (London: BBC, 1995).

MILSOM, S. F. C., *Historical Foundations of the Common Law*, 2nd edn. (London: Butterworths, 1981).

MIRFIELD, P., *Silence, Confessions and Improperly Obtained Evidence* (Oxford: Oxford University Press, 1997).

MOENSSENS, A. E., INBAU, F. E., and STARRS, J. E., *Scientific Evidence in Criminal Cases*, 3rd edn. (New York: Foundation Press, 1986).

MORGAN, D. and STEPHENSEN, G., (eds.), *Suspicion and Silence: The Right to Silence in Criminal Investigations* (London: Blackstone Press, 1994).

MULLIN, C., *Error of Judgement: The Truth about the Birmingham Bombings* (London: Chatto and Windus, 1986; final edn., Dublin: Poolbeg, 1997).

—— 'D. N. Pritt Memorial Lecture', *Socialist Lawyer*, Spring 1992, 14–17.

MURPHY, W. T., 'Systems of Systems: Some Issues in the Relationship between Law and Autopoiesis', *Law and Critique*, 5/2 [1994], 241–64.

NAPLEY, D., *The Technique of Persuasion* (London: Sweet & Maxwell, 1970).

NELKEN, D., (ed.), *Law as Communication* (Aldershot: Dartmouth Publishing, 1996).

NOBLES, R., SCHIFF, D., and SHALDON, N., 'The Inevitability of Crisis in Criminal Appeals', *International Journal of the Sociology of Law*, 21 (1993), 1–21.

NOBLES, R. and SCHIFF, D., 'Optimism Writ Large: A Critique of the Runciman Commission on Criminal Justice', in M. McConville and L. Bridges (eds.), 1994, ch. 4.

—— 'Miscarriages of Justice: A Systems Approach', *Modern Law Review*, 58 (1995), 299–320.

—— 'The Never Ending Story: Disguising Tragic Choices in Criminal Justice', *Modern Law Review*, 60 (1997), 293–304.

NORRIE, A., *Crime, Reason and History* (London: Weidenfeld and Nicolson, 1993).

O'CONNOR, P., 'The Court of Appeal: Re-Trials and Tribulations', *Criminal Law Review* [1990], 615–28.

O'CONNOR, P. and ASHMAN, P., 'Moot Point . . . A Court of Last Resort?', *Solicitors Journal*, 134/45 (1990), 1292–3.

ORMROD, R., 'Scientific Evidence in Court', *Criminal Law Review* [1968], 240–7.

PAGET, R. T., and SILVERMAN, S. S., *Hanged—and Innocent* (London: Gollancz, 1953).

Papers relating to the Case of George Edalji, Cd.3503 (London: HMSO, 1907).

PAREKH, B. (ed.), *Bentham's Political Thought* (London: Croom Helm, 1973).

PATTENDEN, R., *English Criminal Appeals 1844–1994* (Oxford: Oxford University Press, 1996).

PELLEW, J., *The Home Office 1848–1914* (London: Heinemann, 1982).

PHILLIPS, J. H. and BOWEN, J. K., *Forensic Science and the Expert Witness* (London: Sweet & Maxwell, 1985).

PLOTNIKOFF, J. and WOOLFSON, R., *Information and Advice for Prisoners about Grounds for Appeal and the Appeals Process*, Royal Commission on Criminal Justice Research Study No. 18 (London: HMSO, 1993).

POLLAND, H. B., 'Introduction' to H. J. Cohen, *The Criminal Appeal Act, 1907* (London: Jordan, 1908).

RADZINOWICZ, L., *A History of English Criminal Law*, i (London: Stevens, 1948).

RAWLS, J., *A Theory of Justice* (Oxford: Oxford University Press, 1972).

REINER, R., 'Investigative Powers and Safeguards for Suspects', *Criminal Law Review* [1993], 808–16.

Report of the Judges in 1892 on the Court of Criminal Appeal (London: HMSO, 1894), Parl. Pap. 1894, vol. LXXI, 173.

Return of Criminal Appeal Bills (1906), H.L. Pap. 201.

RICHARDS, S., *Philosophy and Sociology of Science: An Introduction*, 2nd edn. (Oxford: Blackwell, 1987).

ROBERTS, P., 'Forensic Science Evidence after Runciman', *Criminal Law Review* [1994], 780–92.

—— 'Science in the Criminal Process', *Oxford Journal of Legal Studies*, 14 (1994), 469–506.

ROBERTS, P. and WILLMORE, C., *The Role of Forensic Science Evidence in Criminal Proceedings*, Royal Commission on Criminal Justice Research Study No. 11 (London: HMSO, 1993).

ROBERTSON, B. and VIGNAUX, G. A., *Interpreting Evidence: Evaluating Forensic Science in the Courtroom* (Chichester: John Wiley, 1995).

—— 'Explaining Evidence Logically', *New Law Journal* (Expert Witness Supplement), 6 February 1998, 159–62.

ROCK, P., 'News as Eternal Recurrence', in S. Cohen and J. Young (eds.), 1973, 73–80.

—— *The Social World of an English Crown Court: Witness and Professionals in the Crown Court Centre at Wood Green* (Oxford: Clarendon Press, 1993).

ROLPH, C. H., *The Queen's Pardon* (London: Cassell, 1978).

ROSE, D., *In the Name of the Law: The Collapse of Criminal Justice* (London: Vintage, 1996).

ROSE, J. with PANTER, S. and WILKINSON, T., *Innocents: How justice failed Stefan Kiszko and Lesley Molseed* (London: Fourth Estate, 1997).

ROSHIER, B., 'The Selection of Crime News by the Press', in S. Cohen and J. Young (eds.), 1973, 28–39.

Roskill Committee Report, Departmental Committee on Fraud Trials (London: HMSO, 1986).

Rowland, Inquiry into the confession evidence made by David John Ware of the murder of Olive Bachin in respect of which murder Walter Graham Rowland was convicted (the Jolly Report), Cd. 7049 (London: HMSO, 1947).

Royal Commission on The Law Relating to Indictable Offences, C. 2345 (1879), Parl. Pap. 1878–9, vol. XX, 169.

Royal Commission on Criminal Procedure, the *Philips Report*, Cmnd 8092 (London: HMSO, 1981).

Royal Commission on Criminal Justice, *Runciman Report*, Cm 2263 (London: HMSO, 1993).

ROZENBERG, J., 'Miscarriages of Justice', in E. Stockdale and S. Casale (eds.), 1992, ch. 4.

SAMUELS, A., 'The New Court of Criminal Appeal', *Solicitors Journal*, 110 (1966), 714–16.

—— 'Appeal against Conviction: Reform', *Criminal Law Review* [1984], 337–46.

SANDERS, A., 'Thinking about Criminal Justice', in M. McConville and L. Bridges (eds.), 1994, ch. 12.

SANDERS, A. and YOUNG, R., *Criminal Justice* (London: Butterworths, 1994).

SANDMAN, P., 'Mass Media and Environmental Risk: Seven Principles', *Risk: Health, Safety and Environment*, Summer (1994), 251–60.

SCHIFF, D. and NOBLES, R., 'Review of *Justice in Error*', *British Journal of Criminology*, 34/3 (1994), 383–7.

—— 'Criminal Appeal Act 1995: The Semantics of Jurisdiction', *Modern Law Review*, 59 (1996), 573–81.

SCHLESINGER, P. and TUMBER, H., *Reporting Crime: The Media Politics of Criminal Justice* (Oxford: Clarendon Press, 1994).

SHAW, S., 'The Law and the Expert Witness', *Proceedings of the Royal Society of Medicine*, 69 (1976), 83–7.

SHUTE, S., GARDNER, J., and HOLDER, J. (eds.), *Action and Value in Criminal Law* (Oxford: Clarendon Press, 1993).

SIBLEY, N. W., *Criminal Appeal and Evidence* (London: Fisher Unwin, 1908).

SMART, J. J. C. and WILLIAMS, B., *Utilitarianism: For and Against* (Cambridge: Cambridge University Press, 1973).

SMITH, A. T. H., 'The Prerogative of Mercy, the Power of Pardon and Criminal Justice', *Public Law* (1983), 398–439.

SMITH, J. C., 'Criminal Appeals and the Criminal Cases Review Commission', *New Law Journal*, 145 (1995), 533–5 and 572–4.

SMITH, R., 'Forensic Pathology, Scientific Expertise, and the Criminal Law' in R. Smith and B. Wynne (eds.), 1989, 56–92.

SMITH, R. and WYNNE, B. (eds.), *Expert Evidence: Interpreting Science in the Law* (London: Routledge, 1989).

SPENCER, J. R., 'Criminal Law and Criminal Appeals—The Tail that Wags the Dog', *Criminal Law Review* [1982], 260–82.

—— 'The Neutral Expert: an implausible bogey', *Criminal Law Review* [1991], 106–10.

STEPHEN, J. F., *A History of the Criminal Law of England*, i (London: Macmillan, 1883).

STEPHENS, M. and HILL, P., 'The Role and Impact of Journalism', in C. Walker and K. Starmer (eds.), 1999, ch. 13.

STEVENTON, B., *The Ability to Challenge DNA Evidence*, Royal Commission on Criminal Justice Research Study No. 9 (London: HMSO, 1993).

STOCKDALE, E. and CASALE, S. (eds.), *Criminal Justice under Stress* (London: Blackstone Press, 1992).

STONE, M., *Cross-Examination in Criminal Trials*, 2nd edn. (London: Butterworths, 1995).

SWARD, E. E., 'Values, Ideology, and the Evolution of the Adversary System', *Indiana Law Journal*, 64 (1989), 301–55.

TAPPER, C. F. H., 'The Meaning of Section 1(f)(i) of the Criminal Evidence Act 1898', in *Crime, Proof and Punishment: Essays in Memory of Sir Rupert Cross* (London: Butterworths, 1981), 296–322.

—— *Cross & Tapper on Evidence*, 8th edn. (London: Butterworths, 1995).

TAVUCHIS, N., *Mea Culpa: A Sociology of Apology* (Stanford: Stanford University Press, 1991).

TEUBNER, G., 'Introduction to Autopoietic Law', in id. (ed.), 1988, 1–11.

—— (ed.), *Autopoietic Law: A New Approach to Law and Society* (Berlin: de Gruyter, 1988).

—— 'How the Law Thinks: Towards a Constructivist Epistemology of Law', *Law and Society Review*, 23 (1989), 727–57.

—— 'Social Order from Legislative Noise? Autopoietic Closure as a Problem for Legal Regulation', in G. Teubner and A. Febbrajo (eds.), 1992, 609–649.

—— *Law as an Autopoietic System*, trans. A. Bankowska and R. Adler, ed. Z. Bankowski (Oxford: Blackwell, 1993).

TEUBNER, G. and FEBBRAJO, A. (eds.), *State, Law, and Economy as Autopoietic Systems: Regulation and Autonomy in a New Perspective*, European Yearbook in the Sociology of Law (Milan: Giuffre, 1992).

THOMAS, D. A., 'The Criminal Appeal Act 1966', *Modern Law Review*, 30 (1967), 64–7.

THORNTON, P., 'Miscarriages of Justice: A Lost Opportunity', *Criminal Law Review* [1993], 926–35.

THORNTON, P., MALLALIEU, A., and SCRIVENER, A., *Justice on Trial: Report of the Independent Civil Liberty Panel on Criminal Justice* (London: Civil Liberties Trust, 1992).

TREGILGAS-DAVEY, M., 'Miscarriages of Justice within the English Legal System', *New Law Journal*, 141 (1991), 668–70 and 715–17.

TUCHMAN, G., 'Objectivity as Strategic Ritual: An Examination of Newsmen's Notions of Objectivity', *American Journal of Sociology*, 77/4 (1972), 660–79.

Tucker Committee Report, Departmental Committee on New Trials in Criminal Cases, Cd. 9150 (London: HMSO, 1954).

TULLOCK, G., 'Avoiding Difficult Decisions', *New York University Law Review*, 54 (1979), 267–79.

TWIBELL, J. D., HOME, J. M., SMALLDON, K. W., and HIGGS, D. G., 'Transfer of Nitroglycerine to Hands during Contact with Commercial Explosives', *Journal of Forensic Sciences*, 27 (1982), 783–91.

UGLOW, S., *Criminal Justice* (London: Sweet & Maxwell, 1995).

UNGAR, S., 'Hot Crises and Media Reassurance: A Comparison of Emerging Diseases and Ebola Zaire', *British Journal of Sociology*, 49/1 (1998), 36–56.

WALKER, C., 'Introduction', in C. Walker and K. Starmer (eds.), 1993, 1–16.
—— 'Miscarriages of Justice in Principle and Practice', in C. Walker and K. Starmer (eds.), 1999, 31–62.
WALKER, C. and STARMER, K. (eds.), *Justice in Error* (London: Blackstone Press, 1993).
—— (eds.), *Miscarriages of Justice: A Review of Justice in Error* (London, Blackstone Press, 1999).
WALKER, R. J., 'The Criminal Appeal Act', *New Law Journal*, 116 (1966), 1205–7.
WARD, J., *Ambushed: My Story* (London: Vermilion, 1993).
WEAVER, P., 'TV News and Newspaper News', in R. P. Adler (ed.), *Understanding Television: Essays on Television as a Social and Cultural Force* (New York: Praeger, 1981), 277–93.
WILLIAMS, G., *Proof of Guilt: A Study of the English Criminal Trial*, 3rd edn. (London: Stevens, 1963).
WINDLESHAM/RAMPTON REPORT, *Death on the Rock* (London: Faber, 1989).
WOFFINDEN, B., *Miscarriages of Justice* (London: Hodder & Stoughton, 1987).
—— 'The Independent Review Tribunal', *New Law Journal*, 139 (1989), 1108–9.
—— *Hanratty: The Final Verdict* (London: Macmillan, 1997).
YANT, M., *Presumed Guilty: When Innocent People are wrongly Convicted* (New York: Prometheus Books, 1991).
YOUNG, M. and HILL, P., *Rough Justice* (London: BBC, 1983).
YOUROW, H. C., *The Margin of Appreciation Doctrine in the Dynamics of European Human Rights Jurisprudence* (Dordrecht: Martinus Nijhoff, 1996).
ZANDER, M., 'Legal Advice and Criminal Appeals: A Survey of Prisoners, Prisons and Lawyers', *Criminal Law Review* [1972], 132–73.
—— 'What is Going On?', *New Law Journal*, 143 (1993), 1507–8.
ZANDER, M. and HENDERSON, P., *The Crown Court Study*, Royal Commission on Criminal Justice Research Study No. 19 (London: HMSO, 1993).
ZUCKERMAN, A. A. S., *The Principles of Criminal Evidence* (Oxford: Clarendon Press, 1989).
—— 'Miscarriage of Justice and Judicial Responsibility', *Criminal Law Review*, [1991], 492–500.
—— 'Bias and Suggestibility: Is There an Alternative to the Right to Silence?', in D. Morgan and G. Stephenson (eds.), 1994, 117–40.

Index